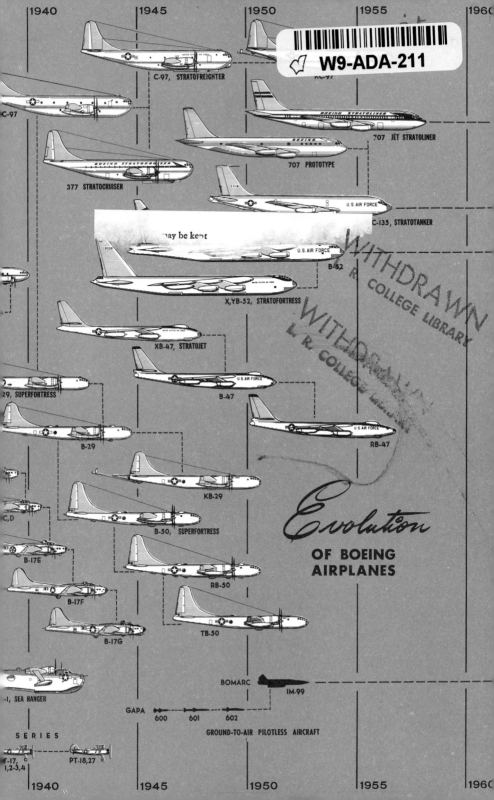

Evolution
OF BOEING AIRPLANES

1940   1945   1950   1955   1960

C-97, STRATOFREIGHTER

RC-97

C-97

377 STRATOCRUISER

707 PROTOTYPE

707 JET STRATOLINER

C-135, STRATOTANKER

B-52

X,YB-52, STRATOFORTRESS

XB-47, STRATOJET

B-47

RB-47

29, SUPERFORTRESS

B-29

KB-29

C,D

B-50, SUPERFORTRESS

B-17E

RB-50

B-17F

B-17G

TB-50

-I, SEA RANGER

BOMARC
IM-99

GAPA
600   601   602

GROUND-TO-AIR PILOTLESS AIRCRAFT

SERIES

-17,
1,2-3,4

PT-18,27

1940   1945   1950   1955   1960

VISION

A Saga of the Sky

VISION

A Saga of the Sky

HAROLD MANSFIELD

DUELL, SLOAN AND PEARCE
New York

629.109
M310

34398
October 1956

Contents

Illustrations

Following page 54

Illustrations in the text

Foreword

As any book is a reflection of its author, the development of the theme of this book is my own and is not intended to represent the view of the Boeing Airplane Company, which provides the subject matter of the story. I am grateful to the management of the company for giving me the freedom to take a searching look at the successes and failures of the past and give my own interpretation of the steps of progress that have been made and their relation to the national and international problem.

This book is not a company history in the accepted sense, though it is factual throughout, and as accurate a portrayal of happenings as humanly possible, based on scores of interviews, search of records, and diligent rechecking of finished copy with the dozens of individuals involved in the story. But it is not primarily a factual presentation. It is the story that I see in a forty-year period of astonishing progress in the air. Episode by episode, this book seeks out the reasons for that progress and infers from them a hopeful outlook for the future, if the principles found so successful in technical progress are applied with equal open-mindedness to problems in the human realm.

In order to tell the story in an interesting and readable way it has been necessary to center attention on certain individuals, somewhat to the embarrassment of those most prominent in the story, such as Claire Egtvedt and Bill Allen, who are of modest nature. Concern has also been expressed that this centering of attention omits due mention of many others both in the company and in the armed services. While this is true, it is hoped that the reader will recognize the author's necessity of drawing a sharper focus. The selection of the individuals brought into the story has been entirely by the author and not by the Boeing Company, and has been for the purpose of developing the theme.

It was likewise the author's decision to concentrate more on the engineering than the manufacturing and other phases of the business.

Special credit is due Reynolds Phillips, managing editor of *Boeing Magazine*, for his capable assistance in the research that has made this book possible.

H. M.

BOOK ONE

THE CHALLENGE

1. *Just Forty Years?*

"Listen, John . . . the 707."

The heavy sky-filling sound of jet engines was arresting, even to those who had heard it often. John Haberlin joined his wife at the window. Generally speaking, the sound pulled all Seattle to the window or to the front porch, because the jet transport was still a novelty. But Haberlin looked with the eye of one who had spent his life working on airplanes. When the giant jet swept out into view, Johnny glowed.

"Coming by kinda low," he said, as if hiding from his wife a rival affection. It wasn't really that. It was something in him too deep to express. Haberlin, a thirty-year man in the engineering department of Boeing Airplane Company, had had little to do with the new 707 transport, but he felt pride and satisfaction in it. The plane represented the bigness of man's achievement in the air. He believed that all America must share his feeling. The airplane belonged to America.

Yet Haberlin knew that the jet transport was by no means the end of a line of progress. Recently he had been transferred to the military pilotless aircraft division. "You'll find yourself giving up your old ways of thinking," Dick Nelson, the project engineer, had said when introducing him to the division. "You'll begin to think in terms of ramjet and rocket speeds." The ramjet engine ate the air's oxygen as it went along, but its huge appetite required a speed of at least seven hundred miles an hour before it would even get started. The rocket, disdainful of air and atmosphere, carried its own oxygen along. It went faster. And the "crew" to manage the craft at these speeds had to be built along with the ship.

3

"Let me show you..." Nelson walked over to a bench containing a maze of circuits and electronic tubes. In a test frame, sparkles of light were chasing each other like a tiny merry-go-round. "This is the sort of thing we're working with. You might call this the captain. It's a word machine. Gives commands, a word at a time."

"I see." But Haberlin knew now that he hadn't seen at all then. You couldn't see till you got into it. The things that were being done in the air these days, and the new things under way on paper, were stirring to the imagination. "Where are we headed?" he wondered.

Brenda Haberlin brought him abruptly back to earth. "What about that speech you have to write?"

"Can't get started." The assignment Haberlin had been given, to respond in behalf of the thirty-year men tomorrow night at the company's annual thirty-year award banquet, wasn't coming easily. Seeking inspiration, he settled into a chair and looked out across Puget Sound at the Olympic Mountains. The throaty thrust of jet engines was still in his ears.

"It would be trite to say how far we've come from fabric covered jobs to this," he thought. "Still..." His memory turned back to the time, forty years ago, when he joined the Royal Flying Corps in Canada. It was about then that Mr. Boeing was starting his plant. Seventy miles an hour made those early machines almost shake apart. Now, at six hundred, the jets seemed to be coasting. That got him thinking. Had all this really happened in just forty years?

It took six thousand years or so for men to learn how to travel seventy, maybe eighty, miles an hour. Then in forty years they had pushed it up to six hundred. "How about that?" The inevitable slide rule came out of his pocket.

"Six thousand years. Three hundred generations of fathers and sons. An increase of about 2.7 miles per hour for each generation. Except my generation. We go to six hundred, all in one jump."

He squirmed in his chair. How come? What was at the foot

of such an extraordinary spurt of progress? What was happening? What did it mean for the future? The questions weren't easy to answer.

Thinking of his speech, John Haberlin looked northward in the direction of Vancouver, British Columbia, where he had learned to fly. He felt again that beckoning challenge of the sky, as he had felt it when a noisy engine and a flimsy wing first lifted him off the ground. Bill Boeing must have felt it, too. It was a challenge that had shaken the shackles off men's minds....

2. *Meant to Fly*

The rainy sky had cleared and it was California-warm. At old Dominguez Ranch, a few miles south of Los Angeles, the atmosphere was charged with anticipation and mystery. Twenty-five thousand people packed the grandstand to the top rails, while other thousands swarmed the edges of the field to see America's first international aeronautical tournament.

It was January 1910. Like all America, but with a lusty boom spirit of its own, the California public was responding to the new allure of machines and inventions of all sorts. "The motor car, the wireless, the flying machine! What will we have next?" Every man and boy took a second cousin's pride in America's Henry Ford and Thomas A. Edison.

Today this new-century public was on the broad Dominguez acreage that had been turned into a flying field. Milling crowds were eyeing in wonderment the latest Curtiss, Bleriot, and Farman flying machines, which stole attention from the balloons and dirigibles in the background.

William E. Boeing of Seattle was there. Tall, mustached, with intent eyes behind thin-rimmed glasses, he had the air of a distinguished college professor. He was moving toward the landing area where a Farman biplane was approaching low. It was a machine larger than the others, with four wheels instead of three, two vertical tail planes in back, and a wide cloth-covered surface well out in front of the wings—a horizontal stabilizer. As it jounced to a stop, its peppery motor idled down. The motor was a rotary type; fastened behind the lower wing, it spun around with the propeller, cylinders and all. The aviator stepped down from his perch on the wing and walked toward the crowd. Boeing was out in front. "Monsieur Paulhan, my name is Boeing. I like your machine and the way you fly it."

"*Merci*, Monsieur Boeing." The Frenchman clicked his heels militarily and did a quick bow. Boeing asked him more about the Farman. Would it be possible for him to take a ride in it? "*Oui, Monsieur*," said Paulhan, but added that it couldn't be done until tomorrow after the endurance competition.

Boeing walked over to his motorcar and drove off. Next afternoon he was back, joining in the crowd's roaring applause as Paulhan completed forty-seven laps around the 1.6 mile course. Glenn Curtiss had dropped out at ten and Charles Hamilton at twelve times around. At the first opportunity Boeing asked again about the flight. "*Oui*, Monsieur Boeing." Paulhan would be glad to take him. A little later. Boeing waited and watched while various dignitaries went up in the machine with Paulhan.

Another day was much the same. Every time he thought he was about to get a flight, someone with special priority would arrive. The flashing-eyed Frenchman was a great favorite. Thinking to make a more definite arrangement, Boeing visited the aviator at his hotel, but learned that the $10,000 cross-country event was on the next day's program.

The course was to Lucky Baldwin's ranch, twenty-three miles away, and back. When it came time for the birdmen to start, a breeze had come up. This was a dangerous thing; a gust from the side might throw them. All balked but Paulhan. He twirled a scarf about his neck and climbed onto his place on the wing. The Farman lifted, lurched, then steadied into the wind. The crowd shouted. Some pursued along the country road on horses, motorcycles and automobiles. In one of the racing motor cars Madame Paulhan was praying aloud and crying. Paulhan winged along at a height of 1,000 to 2,000 feet, turned successfully over the Baldwin Ranch, and made his way back to the field in an hour and two minutes. When he arrived, the yelling crowd burst out of the grandstand and onto the field. Two men hoisted the birdman to their shoulders and the pressing, shouting thousands bore him happily off the field.

After Paulhan's triumph, Boeing didn't see him again. The wide spreading wings of the Farman, on which the visitor from Seattle had pictured himself aloft, were crated and hauled away. Cleanup crews swept the litter from Dominguez Field. "Well, how do you like that!" Bill Boeing didn't mention his disappointment to anyone, but it left a mark. He returned to Seattle, not knowing that Paulhan, too, had departed in a seething mood. The French aviator had been summoned to defend himself in court against the Wright brothers.

Aviation in 1910 was still a frail venture into the art of flying. When the Wright brothers had first taken up the challenge, they had found one of the keys to the art in the bicycles they built for a living. If they turned a corner on a bicycle without leaning into the turn, they would spill. It was the same with the flying machine. They found that by pulling down on the trailing edge of the outside wing in a turn, they could make the machine bank properly, and this became their basic patent. The court decided that the aileron devices which Paulhan and Glenn Curtiss had hinged to the trailing edges of their wings were a violation of the Wright patent. The Frenchman returned to Paris to build a plane without ailerons, with a wing that was limber at the back like trailing feathers on a bird.

There was many a trick to be learned about flying. In Europe and in America, the zeal of competition was fanning an adventurous faith. The flying machine would yet be important. To the inspired few, the newborn publication *Aircraft* summed it up:

You cannot tether time nor sky.
The time approaches, Sam must fly.

When the noisy excitement of the Los Angeles air meet was re-created nine months later at Belmont Park, New York, Paulhan was not there, but Glenn Curtiss was on hand to defend the Gordon Bennett trophy he had won at Reims, France, the year before.

Among Curtiss' fans was a Navy lieutenant named Conrad Westervelt. A couple of years earlier he had watched all day while Curtiss tested the wind with his finger and finally, in the still air at dusk, hopped two hundred feet. Westervelt, an engineer, was serving as junior officer in the Navy Construction Corps at New York; he obtained permission to represent the Navy Department at the Belmont Park meet. Enthralled, he watched LeBlanc of France take ten speed events with a Bleriot monoplane. With other spectators he gasped at the flying skill of the French aviator Latham in a 100-horsepower Antoinette racer. Claude Graham White of England won the Gordon Bennett trophy. Ralph Johnstone, who flew to 9,714 feet in a 30-horsepower Wright flier, was the only American to set a world's record. Lieutenant Westervelt reported that aviation's progress was astounding. The Navy should watch closely the developments in Europe as well as in this country.

Advanced to Assistant Naval Constructor, U.S.N., Westervelt was sent to Puget Sound Navy Yard and then to the Moran Shipyard in Seattle. At Seattle's University Club, a host introduced him to Bill Boeing. "I expect you could give me a few pointers," said Boeing. "I have a boat under construction that isn't doing so well right now."

Westervelt and Boeing, both bachelors, found many interests in common. Boeing also had studied engineering, in Sheffield Scientific School at Yale. Weekends they played bridge, cruised up the Sound in Boeing's yacht, talked about things mechanical. Westervelt came to know and appreciate some of the thoughts that were going on in Boeing's active, even restless mind. If others thought him aloof, it was because they didn't understand his background, Westervelt decided. Boeing had been a lone operator since boyhood. His German-born father died when Bill was eight. His Viennese mother continued to bring him up in strict fashion. But with a spirit of independence and a supply of funds, he was on his own at an early age. The family had large holdings of timber and of iron ore in Minnesota's fabulous Mesabi Range. As part of his upbringing, young Bill went to school away from home, partly in America and partly in Switzerland.

When his mother remarried, Bill didn't hit it off well with his stepfather. In 1903, a year before he was to graduate from Yale, he decided the time was ripe to move west and acquire timber on his own. He was twenty-two then. His hunch proved a good one. It was this desire to do things, Westervelt thought, that explained Boeing's outfitting of expeditions to Alaska, his purchase of the Heath shipyard on the Duwamish in order to finish building a yacht, and his interest when a flier named Terah Maroney brought a Curtiss type hydroplane to Seattle. He and Boeing talked about airplanes and discovered a bond of interest in memories of the two great aviation meets of 1910. "Let's go out and take a flight with Maroney," Boeing proposed.

It was July 4, 1914. "I've been wanting to do this a long time," Westervelt admitted on the way out. "Isn't this a day for it?" The sky was blue. The Olympic Range behind them and the long Cascade skyline ahead were the rim on a bowl of beauty. In the center of the bowl lay Lake Washington.

At the edge of the lake, Maroney was ready to take them up. The plane was nosed into a board ramp, its pusher propeller idly flailing the air. The two straight wings were covered with muslin on the lower as well as the upper side. The machine was supported on rods that extended up from a sledlike float in the middle. The engine was hung between the two wings, its tall radiator almost making a back to the pilot's seat.

"Would you like to go first?" Westervelt asked.

"All right." Boeing climbed up beside Maroney on the front edge of the lower wing and steadied his feet on the open foot rest that reminded him a little of a shoeshine stand. A mechanic in coveralls, agile as a log-boom jockey, was pushing the machine to head out into the water. Maroney gunned the engine in short spurts. Boeing adjusted the goggles he had been given, then used both hands to hold on.

The taxiing out was jiggly, vibrant with noise. The race down-lake was a prolonged drive for take-off speed, wind in the face, water rushing at them. Boeing tightened his grip. The water began to get less bumpy. He felt a shake and a boost. There was a surge of power against the small of his back. The din of the motor filled his ears as the water dropped away.

In another minute the whole landscape was tilting up beside him like a flat picture plate being raised on edge and he realized they were banking and turning away from the lake. Boeing looked down upon Westervelt and the tiny group on the shore. They seemed something detached, a detail in the picture plate. Maroney was winging straight over trees and housetops, still climbing. They were perhaps a thousand feet in the air. Boeing settled more comfortably in his seat. He felt a certain mastery he had been seeking. It all seemed right. The hour-glass shape of Seattle below with Puget Sound and the Olympics in the distance, unrolled before him. Man was meant to fly.

When they got back Westervelt was eager for his turn, and he, too, was filled with enthusiasm after the flight. "Wonderful. We've got to do this more."

Boeing, short of words, found Westy a screen on which his own feelings were displayed. "Let's," he said.

More flights with Maroney cultivated the seed that was growing in Boeing's mind. One day the idea broke through. "There isn't much to that machine of Maroney's," he told Westervelt. "I think we could build a better one."

Westervelt hid his surprise. "Of course we could," he said. "Would you like me to make some inquiries?"

Westervelt wrote to Jerome Hunsaker, who had established a wind tunnel and the country's principal store of aviation technical information at Massachusetts Institute of Technology, and to others. What could they tell him about the theory of stability and control? About the Wright patents, now available for use, about weights, stresses, motors?

With the aid of his naval engineering tables, he studied strength requirements. He took a tape out to Maroney's ramp and measured the supporting members of his plane, then took the figures home to check the stresses. "My gosh," he told Boeing. "There isn't any reason this thing should hold together. The strength of the parts is just about equal to the load they have to carry."

Herb Munter, the local exhibition flier, was getting a new plane ready for flights, down on Seattle's Harbor Island. Westervelt suggested they talk to him. Munter's headquarters were a fifty-foot shiplap hangar on the dredged-up sand flat. They found Munter inside working on his craft.

"What type machine are you building?" Boeing asked.

"It's a Munter."

Boeing looked up and then fixed his eye on a wing rib. "You design this yourself?"

Munter's pride was evident. He brushed back a shock of red hair. "This is my fourth."

"Where are the others?"

"Washed out."

"You built them all here?"

"No, the first two I built at home in the kitchen. Mother helped me. We went by a picture of the Curtiss in *Aerial Age*. The last two have been my own. Main thing is to make them so they're easy to take apart for crating. We're on the move a lot. See how this comes apart? It's going to be a honey."

"Did you study engineering?" Boeing asked.

"No, I went to high school nights."

Westervelt turned to look out the hangar door, the top half

of which went up with pulleys, the bottom half lying down to form a ramp to a plank runway about three hundred feet long, twelve feet wide. "You take off from here?" he asked.

"Sure," said Munter. "Works fine. So long as the wind is blowing in the right direction."

"Do you think the public is interested in flying?" Boeing asked.

"Mostly they come out to see if you're going to crash," Munter grinned. "I've built my show around that. End up by diving straight at the ground. Then I pull up just high enough so the tail doesn't hit."

"Isn't that terrifying?"

"Not bad. The thing won't go any faster straight down than it will on the level. About forty or forty-five. But I let 'em think it's tough."

Was that all there was to aviation, risking your neck like a trapeze performer? The possibility of building a pleasure airplane for his own use intrigued Boeing. But he felt restless about other things developing in 1915. True, business was good around Seattle. Elliott Bay was being dredged and its silt poured out on mud flats to make more plant sites. But across the world the Triple Alliance had swept all Europe into a mortal struggle. The great liner *Lusitania* had been sunk by a German U-boat, taking the lives of 114 Americans among the 1,153 who perished.

Boeing was disturbed when he read the newspapers. The unnatural contrast between peace at home and war across the Atlantic was distressing. Perhaps because of his schooling and frequent trips abroad, Europe seemed nearer to him. Wasn't it likely that America would be drawn in? What were we doing to prepare? He thought of the urgent effort that must be going into airplane development in the countries at war, and then of the plane in which they had been flying. Wasn't America falling behind?

One day, plans in mind, Boeing asked Herb Munter to join him and Westervelt for lunch. "We're going to get a group

together to build some airplanes," he said. "Will you join us?"
"Sure."
"You'll have to quit this exhibition flying."
"But I'm under contract. I'll have to finish the season."
"Then come down and see us when you've finished it."

They planned to start on two airplanes, to be called B & W's for Boeing and Westervelt. They would get motors from the Hall-Scott plant in San Francisco. They'd put Ed Heath, down at the shipyard, to work on the pontoons. Westervelt would have Jim Foley, a marine architect in his office at the Moran Shipyard, lay out the wings and body. Foley had a good notion of strength requirements and things like that.

Boeing wrote to Glenn Martin in Los Angeles.

"I'm going down there to learn to fly," Boeing told Westervelt a few days later.

At Griffith Park in Los Angeles, Bill Boeing was an earnest pupil. He went out with Floyd Smith, the instructor, at dawn each day, while the air was quiet. Again about dusk it would be still enough for more instruction.

Before he returned to Seattle, Boeing bought a $10,000 seaplane from Martin. It looked huge when Floyd Smith uncrated it on Lake Washington in October 1915. "I'd like you to show Herb Munter how to operate it," Boeing told Smith. "He's going to be our pilot."

After Munter was briefly checked out, he and Boeing cruised the plane over Seattle. In behalf of an Aero Club that Boeing and Westervelt had formed, they tossed overboard a load of missile-shaped cards calling attention to America's need for preparedness. Munter was concerned with his flying. "Machine feels heavy," he said. "It's sure different from mine."

The following Sunday Boeing watched while Munter made a flight with John Hull, one of the Aero Club members, as a passenger. Munter seemed to be banking unusually steeply over the lake. The plane slipped, dived straight for the water. Boeing gasped. He saw it hit, then come up again to float motionless, wings on the water, tail in the air. A motorboat brought the two men ashore. Munter was dazed and apologetic.

"Forget the airplane," said Boeing. "You and Hull are all right. That's the main thing."

The Martin was repaired in a new hangar Boeing had erected on Lake Union. Munter took it up again, anxious to prove he could manage it. Again he stalled on a turn, dove to the water, crushed the pontoons. Again he escaped unhurt.

"We won't fly that any more," Boeing decided. "Fix it up as a land plane and we'll sell it. Wheels will make it lighter."

At the Heath shipyard, the pontoons for the first B & W were progressing. Boeing examined the wood that had been selected, the fitting and glueing of the two plys that would form the pontoon structure.

"Keep it light," he cautioned.

The old shipbuilder seemed affronted. "Mr. Boeing, they're so light now, I'm afraid to open the door or they'll blow out."

The war in Europe was growing in intensity. The German embassy had warned American shipping against the submarine peril. The French, British and Germans were sending up aviators with machine guns. Airplanes diving on each other with raking gunfire, wings and fuel tanks bursting into flame, aviators turning into fiery torches as they plummeted to earth; these were the blazing new images of warfare in the air.

Boeing and Westervelt knew the implications were grave. They talked of forming a permanent company to manufacture airplanes, but the Navy had other plans for Westervelt and he was ordered to report for duty in the East. An appeal to Secretary Josephus Daniels only confirmed the Navy's need. The international situation was growing more ominous. "Go ahead on your own," Westervelt told Boeing regretfully.

Boeing asked Hunsaker at M.I.T. for advice and, on his recommendation, hired a brilliant Chinese engineer named T. Wong, a recent M.I.T. graduate.

In June 1916, the first B & W was finished and ready for flight.

It was a crisp-looking airplane there on the ramp at Lake Union; wings straight and pert, spruce struts gleaming with new varnish. Its 125 horsepower and its span of fifty-two feet were identical with those of the Martin, which had been a great aid in determining dimensions, but it was lighter and its wing section was different.

Inside the hangar, Boeing kept looking at his watch. "Where is that Munter?"

Jim Foley said he would be along soon.

"I'll take it out myself," said Boeing.

He got in, taxied out to the middle of the lake, swung around to head north and gunned the Hall-Scott full out. The plane gathered speed. It skipped along for a time, throwing a good deal of spray. Then Boeing lifted it into a quarter-mile straight-away flight and set it down again. When he got back to the ramp Munter had arrived. "Taxi it around and try out the controls," Boeing said. "But don't fly it."

Munter taxied for several days, wondering if Boeing was afraid to let him fly. One day when he was practicing small hops off the water he concluded it was time for action. He hauled back on the stick, roared into the air and winged across the city to Lake Washington. Boeing rushed over. "Don't ever do that again unless I authorize it," he said. Then he looked at the airplane with pride. "How was it?"

"Good."

 *B & W*

3. *Learning Things*

The twenty-one men working for Bill Boeing gained zeal from the sight of their B & W in the air, and from Engineer Wong's promises of something better. Boeing's view of the future developed sharper outlines, less confused with the question of war or peace. One day the airplane would be accepted as a means of transportation. It was time to incorporate a company. Boeing asked his attorneys to draft the broadest possible articles. Their charter would allow them to manufacture airplanes or other products, operate a flying school, and "act as a common carrier of passengers and freight by aerial navigation." On July 15, 1916, the articles of the Pacific Aero Products Company were approved by the three incorporating trustees: William E. Boeing, president; E. N. Gott, Boeing's cousin, vice president; J. C. Foley, secretary.

The remaining shipbuilding work at the Heath yard was closed out. Carpenters took up the ways, put in a new floor and laid out a clean shop.

The two B & W's had followed closely the lines of the Curtiss and the Martin. Engineer T. Wong had other ideas for the next plane, which he identified as Type C. Wong had a passion for study. At M.I.T. he was fascinated by the work of Gustave Eiffel, builder of the Paris tower, whose writings Jerome Hunsaker had translated. Eiffel had measured wind forces to learn their effects on his tower structure. With a flat plate tilted in various ways, he'd learned about the loads on a plane surface with air rushing by it, and that was what an airplane was. It was a delicate balance of forces in four directions, the pull of the propeller against the drag of the machine through the air; the lift of the wing against the downward pull of gravity. The wind lifted the wing as it would lift your hand when you'd hold it out of a moving car and tilt it upward, or as it pushed against Gustave Eiffel's flat plate. Wong wanted to apply some of Eiffel's calculations in designing the new Model C for Mr. Boeing.

"We've learned some things that the Wright brothers didn't know," Wong told General Manager Foley. "Now we know how to make a plane inherently stable, so it will return to normal if it is forced off balance in any direction."

"That's the way it should be," said Foley.

"We don't need a vertical fin on the tail to stabilize it, because if we tilt the wings up—that's called dihedral—you can tip the plane one way or the other and it will come back level. We can also do away with the horizontal stabilizer by staggering the top wing ahead of the lower one to give a broad surface. Then we'll balance the elevator, put part of it ahead of the hinge line, so it will be easier to move. The part in front of the hinge will catch the wind on the opposite side and help the pilot." Foley couldn't see any flaws in Wong's concepts. Model C went from theory to form.

The plight of the Allies was growing more desperate. America couldn't stay on the sidelines if its friends were losing. Commander Westervelt wrote that the Navy would surely be buying some school machines. The chance for a contract would be good if the Model C could meet Navy requirements. Bill Boeing told the men to finish it as fast as they could, but to make it right.

Everyone was at the hangar for the first flight of the "C," November 23, 1916. The day was bright and cool, and there was a low wind from the southwest. All was in readiness, but not Herb Munter. For the past week, following Boeing's instructions, he had been taxiing the plane and taking short jumps off the water. He was unhappy about the controls. "You can't fly a plane with that tiny rudder and no stabilizers on the tail," Herb insisted.

Wong was polite but firm. "The controls have been thoroughly proved out." He turned to Boeing with reassurance. "The model has been in the wind tunnel for six hours. Mr. Munter will feel differently about it when he gets it in the air."

Foley looked at Munter. "You're not the engineer, you're the driver," he said.

"I know something about airplanes and it doesn't look right to me," said Munter.

"It's just something new that you've got to get used to," Boeing interposed. "Let's get started."

Munter lifted the airplane off Lake Union without trouble. He climbed to about two hundred feet. He knew he'd have to turn promptly to the right to stay over water while trying things out. He pushed the rudder pedal cautiously. Better not try the aileron yet; one thing at a time. If he got into too steep a bank, it would be hard to right it again without a stabilizing fin.

The plane banked itself, without aileron. "Wong's dihedral did that—the uptilt of the wings," Munter thought. He shoved the stick to the left to decrease the bank with opposite aileron. Instead, it went into a steeper bank. Muscles and mind straining, he jammed his foot hard on the rudder pedal to straighten it out. The turn tightened instead. He had a sinking feeling. "Why did I give in?"

He could see he was running out of lake; Queen Anne Hill ahead. If the plane banked any steeper he would spiral into a spin and he wouldn't have enough altitude to pull it out. He thought of the hole he had made in the lake twice before.

Munter was pushing now with all the strength of his arms and legs. His body against the machine. He was leaning and pressing and urging, almost out of the narrow cockpit. He thought he felt a favorable response. The plane was slowly beginning to straighten. He pressed harder. It was straightening out. He headed down and slapped the unruly craft onto Lake Union with a solid smack.

Herb Munter taxied back to the ramp and climbed out, wrenched off his helmet and stomped over to the waiting group. "Put on some more rudder and some fin."

"It has enough," said Wong.

Munter just looked at him.

"You'd better take it out again and get used to it," Ed Gott suggested.

"I'll take it out again when you've made the changes," Herb said. He was shaking.

"But there is no reason to change it," said Wong. "You have not given it a full trial."

"She's going to stay right here till you do," Munter said, and walked off.

Model C

It was in January 1917 when Munter again cranked up the Hall-Scott to taxi the "C," now sporting a large rudder and a vertical stabilizer in front of it, but still without horizontal stabilizers. Alternating with Ed Hubbard, a new pilot, he taxied it for several weeks, just up to flying speed.

"Keep taxiing it and getting the feel of it," Boeing told them. "Hop off a little, but don't fly it." It was clear he wasn't taking any chances. Munter made the most of the limitation. For weeks he practiced take-offs and landings, sharpening his skill. Gradually the airplane took on a friendly feel. He found he could land it on the forward step of the pontoons, skating along in perfect balance like a ski jumper converting from air to snow. In bad weather he liked the solid footing of the twin pontoons. He was thankful that Boeing and Westervelt were boat men who appreciated stability on the water.

He began to feel the stability, too, of the plane's wing stagger and dihedral angle when he hopped off the water. It felt comfortable. With the tail fixed, Wong's other ideas seemed to have worked out all right. "Why shouldn't an airplane be stable?" Munter thought. "It ought to fly itself, and I can just go along for the ride."

But the importance of a complete flight test was growing. Two more planes were coming along and they needed to know more about the airplane's control system, its performance. The war situation was growing worse and Boeing was talking about adding floor space so a hundred more men could be employed.

The Kaiser had announced that Germany would no longer be bound by the Sussex Pledge protecting neutral shipping. In a short period, eight American ships were sent to the bottom of the Atlantic by U-boats. On April 8, 1917, President Wilson requested and Congress quickly agreed to a declaration of war.

Next day, Boeing's permission in hand, Herb Munter lifted the "C" off Lake Union and churned straight on into the sky. The new controls seemed to work well. "It's O.K.," he announced on landing. Boeing moved at once. Now they could demonstrate the plane to the Navy and go after an order. He called a meeting of the three trustees, changed the company name to Boeing Airplane Company, headed for Washington to talk about war business.

Boeing hadn't been long in the East when a wire came from Foley that Wong was resigning. Boeing tried locating engineers in the East, then returned to see if there weren't some seniors at the University of Washington he could use. He had offered to make the University a gift of a wind tunnel like the ones at M.I.T. and in Washington, D. C., if they'd establish a course in aeronautics.

Professor C. C. Moore, head of mechanics and masonry at the school of civil engineering, walked over to one of the seniors. "You're wanted in the Dean's office."

Claire Egtvedt, slight, neatly groomed, a serious student, went promptly.

"How would you like a job working on airplanes?" asked Dean Fuller.

"*Airplanes?* I don't know."

"William E. Boeing needs two or three engineers. You have a good record. If you're interested, go to his office tomorrow morning at nine."

"You mean ... before graduation?"

"Mr. Boeing is quite anxious. The war."

Claire Egtvedt glanced out the window across the green campus, into some strangeness beyond. The war. He had failed to pass the physical exam for military service. Perhaps this was his job. "Thank you," he said. "I'll be there."

At William E. Boeing's office, Egtvedt found Phil Johnson, a mechanical engineering student, also waiting. Boeing was courteous. He introduced them to Jim Foley. "Mr. Foley will take you down to see our plant."

There wasn't much said on the way out. Egtvedt turned to Phil, a cheerful youth and a good friend. "What do you think?"

Phil Johnson was serious. "Not exactly what I'd expected to do, but ... the war's on."

After four miles through the industrial fill south of Seattle, they came to a narrow plankway leading a mile and a half over the mud flats to the Duwamish River. Across the bridge the planks led to a two-story frame building with the old lettering, E. W. HEATH still showing, and a new sign, BOEING AIRPLANE COMPANY. They entered the door marked OFFICE. Jim Foley showed them to the drafting room upstairs. It was a loftlike room, with heavy beams, a board floor, and unadorned board walls. In front of the multipaned windows there were five or six drafting tables on horses, with stools.

They met Joe Hartson, chief draftsman, and Louis Marsh, whom they had known at the university. Louis' pleasant drawl dissolved the strangeness. "Guess we're going to get some airplanes designed."

Hartson showed them to their tables, gave Johnson some drafting work.

"Your job will be to figure stresses," he told Egtvedt. Claire Egtvedt thought he was going to like this all right. Stress analysis, at least, was a subject he felt he knew something about. He was glad Phil Johnson was here. Phil was bent over his drafting table, digging in as though he'd belonged here all the time. Claire took a walk out in the plant, where carpenters were sawing out spruce wing ribs. Airplanes. He was in the airplane business.

While Herb Munter was putting the first Model C through speed, climb and altitude tests on Lake Washington for local Navy officers, the next two Model C airplanes were being completed in the shops for official tests at the Naval Air Station in

Pensacola, Florida, and the drafting room was at work on revisions for a production model.

Word came that the Navy had immediate need for fifty trainers. They'd buy the ones that came closest to meeting their performance requirements. Boeing should get its machine to Pensacola right away. The two new Model C's were dismantled and crated with care. Munter and Claude Berlin, Foley's factory superintendent, would go with them. Bill Boeing and Vice President Ed Gott coached the pair thoroughly. "Pensacola can make or break us," said Boeing. "If the tests succeed we are a going concern."

4. *Out of the Storm Cellar*

Pensacola was hot and steaming. Herb Munter had expected that July would be warm in Florida, but the humidity was something he'd never experienced. He and plant superintendent Berlin had arrived a day ahead of the airplanes and at the Centralis Hotel they met Floyd Smith, from the Martin Company. "You've got a rough deal ahead of you, Herb," said Smith. "These guys are tough."

Out at the naval station Munter watched a Curtiss Jenny settling to the water's surface. It had a couple of extra wing sections in the middle and a big pontoon, plus wing-tip floats. The station was said to be entirely equipped with these Curtiss N-9s. Glenn Curtiss was the experienced producer in the business, the Navy's standby.

At headquarters Munter and Berlin met naval constructor H. C. Richardson and Lieutenant G. B. Strickland, the inspector. These men, with Lieutenant R. W. Cabaniss, head of the flying school, and Lieutenant Pat Bellinger, would constitute the trial board.

Lieutenant Strickland showed them around the base. "You can set up here in the storm cellar," he said. It was a low brick building, not really a cellar.

The sky was heavy, as though a squall were approaching, when Herb Munter was ready to taxi the Model C onto the bay and check it out. Strickland was on hand. "Pretty choppy," he said.

"It's all right," said Herb. He would show them some flying. The wind was up to twenty miles an hour when he was ready. The motor sounded good. He raced it and ripped off the water in four hundred feet. Berlin saw Strickland watching closely. The lieutenant said nothing.

The speed trials were set for Saturday. Munter went out to practice, to get used to the atmospheric conditions. He tried jumpoffs at high angles, steep banks, spiral dives, and a seven-hundred-foot vertical dive. The plane felt good. No tendency to side-slip or tailspin. On shore, Strickland's interest appeared to be growing. "How much of a plant do you have out there in Seattle?" he asked Berlin.

"About 50,000 square feet. We can add whatever may be needed."

On Saturday Munter exceeded the seventy-mile-an-hour high-speed requirement without trouble, but he knew he was going to have trouble with the forty-mile low speed. They hadn't quite done it in Seattle. Now there was a nine-mile crosswind. He was required to hold twenty-five feet off the water for the measured course. Munter put the nose high and offset it with power, mushing through the air, the tail squishing along above the water's surface. The best he could do was to hold it down to 40.8. He came back to face the board. Strickland seemed eager to see him. "My God, Munter, how do you keep the air-plane in the air at that speed? It isn't even supposed to fly."

Munter shrugged, submerging his relief. "Good airplane." His high-angle technique must have done the trick. Cabaniss confided that no one could meet the forty-mile requirement, but they had set it because they would like to achieve a low speed for school safety.

Munter's timed attempt to reach 2,500 feet altitude was disappointing. He tried various angles of climb, but at 1,800 feet the wings wouldn't lift another inch. "I don't understand it. We made 2,500 easy in Seattle," he said afterward.

"It's the atmosphere here," said Strickland.

Herb was beginning to like it in Pensacola. These people knew about airplanes. They were tolerant. He felt like the horseman who reaches open field and wants to gallop. He took the "C" up, cavorted and spiraled, and then brought it in on the step with the clean perfection he had learned in his weeks of practice on Lake Union. It was a landing with style and grace, like a champion skater gliding past the boxes. The instructors on the Curtiss planes gathered about afterward and wanted to know how it was done.

In a day or so the weather turned so squally that it stopped all flying at the base. There was a rough-water test to be done. The wind was thirty miles and the waves at least three feet high, maybe four. Strickland asked Munter if he thought the Boeing could handle the sea. Herb pulled on his flying cap. "This is the day," he said. He asked Berlin if he'd like to go along. While the trial board watched they taxied boldly out into the wind.

They heaved and fell with the swells but she rode well. Herb kept a ready hold on the throttle and his feet solid on the rudder as they swung across the wind. They had never confronted anything like this on Lake Washington or Lake Union. Berlin was watching a high crest bearing down on them from the side. He looked nervously around at Munter. The plane rocked. The wave went under, wings dry. Munter grinned. They did some more turns. She was a seaworthy boat. Munter cut off the motor and the plane weathercocked neatly into the wind.

Strickland was impressed. "Didn't think you could do that," he said when they got back.

"Twin pontoons," said Munter.

Berlin wired the plant that things looked good. The Navy

seemed to like the plane, its performance and stability. They were a little concerned, though, that it was stiff on control. A plane that was stable was naturally heavier on control, because it wanted to stay put. It was clear now that Wong had designed a plane that was inherently stable.

When the news was received that the Seattle plant was to build fifty of the Model C's for the Navy, Bill Boeing was all business. New organization charts were drawn up. Professor J. W. Miller of the University of Washington faculty, the new chief engineer, was rushing drawings to the shops. Boeing Airplane Company began to look like a factory.

Enthusiasm was dampened some when two landplane versions of the Model C purchased by the Army met with disfavor at McCook Field in Dayton. Herb Munter, after finishing his demonstration there, saw them being dismantled and asked, "How come?"

"We're sending them to the mechanics' school in Minneapolis to show how an airplane shouldn't be built," he was told.

But everyone at the Seattle plant was too busy to be more than temporarily annoyed over this. The pressure of production was on, with things running a little behind. Ed Gott had moved in as general manager. Young Phil Johnson, whose ready, capable way had impressed Bill Boeing, went into the production office.

It was May 1918 when Bill Boeing went with Herb Munter to San Diego to see that the first plane was received satisfactorily. The Naval Air Station was being run on a strictly war basis. They felt an air of unfriendly commotion about the place. "Your planes are so late we are having to bring others in to take their place," they were told. Boeing wired Gott to put on three shifts. Gott was general manager now; Foley had left.

Munter rushed flight preparations and got the airplane into the air, with the San Diego officers watching. He made a rough landing. The commanding officer didn't think twin floats would be safe for students and he didn't like the Hall-Scott engine, said it was an oil-eater. Could they change to a single float like the Curtiss and put in a different engine?

Gott wired back in anguish when Boeing wrote him of this possibility. "The effect would be catastrophic. We'd have to lay off everybody for six months while the changes were engineered." Boeing sensed that at least they'd better get started on something new. He asked Gott to modify one of the "C's" to a single float and to start design of a pusher-type flying boat they had been talking about.

Boeing had left San Diego when Munter finished his demonstration and the Navy instructors began flying the plane. "My pilots tell me your airplane is stiff," the commanding officer said. "Its control isn't good."

"Commander, we have given it more stability so it will hold straight and level flight. We thought that was desirable." Herb couldn't get it. The plane was all right in Pensacola. Why not here? "If you want it to handle more like the Curtiss"—when he hit the "C" in Curtiss there was a sharpness in his voice that didn't much disguise his feeling—"I can take out some dihedral."

"I suggest you do that."

Munter readjusted the wing angle and got into trouble at home for taking the liberty. The plane had been approved by Pensacola. It wasn't his place, or San Diego's, to be trying out new theories. The official report from San Diego to Washington was that the Boeing had many peculiar features of controllability and should be tested more exhaustively. "The plane is a radical departure. The large stagger of the wings, large dihedral, shortness of tail, and absence of horizontal stabilizing surfaces have never before been employed to such a degree in Navy seaplanes." San Diego wasn't going to be the guinea pig.

Boeing was in Washington when he heard the news. The Navy said the chances of additional trainer sales were poor, but that Boeing could bid on some Curtiss HS-2L flying boats they planned to buy. They also agreed to give the Model C trainer another trial at Hampton Roads, Virginia.

Boeing summoned Herb Munter to Washington. They met at the Hotel Washington. Boeing was stern. "Now we are in trouble," he said. "Go down to Hampton Roads and see if you can get us out of it."

At Hampton Roads with two Model Cs, Munter was met by Commander Pat Bellinger, who had been on the trial board in Pensacola. They hit it off well from the start. Boeing arrived later, as one of the planes was being prepared for flight. "We've tried to give you a good, quality job of workmanship," he told the officers. Boeing watched the group examine the trainer. An inspection officer came to an aileron cable that was frayed at the terminal until it was almost parted. It was too short; the wrapped end of the cable had been forced into a small sleeve which could not contain it. The inspector jerked on the cable and it came off in his hand.

"This would have been embarrassing if we'd been flying," he said.

Boeing felt his footing in the airplane business slipping away and grasped for words to pull himself back. "Gentlemen, I don't know how this could have got by. Whoever is responsible will be discharged immediately."

He scrawled a note to Gott, at once. "A fine state of affairs. What is the matter with our inspection? If I were judging the machine, I would condemn it for all time. I want a complete report made. For the good of the company the person responsible has to go. Any such laxity is unpardonable and I for one will close up shop rather than send out work of this kind."

Gott defended inspection and Miller shouldered responsibility. The cable had been made short purposely to keep the aileron from hitting a wing spar, he said.

"Replace them in all machines with longer cables," Boeing ordered. "We're lucky we've had no fatalities."

Munter got the tests off well. The trial board said that despite San Diego they'd like to have the planes.

But no more of the "C's" were to be ordered beyond the fifty. The Navy decided it didn't need any more trainers of any type.

Instead of its own Model C, Boeing was given fifty Curtiss HS-2L boats to build.

Producing the Curtiss planes, large flying boats, required a further enlargement of the plant. But the order was viewed as a dubious blessing by Professor Miller and his small engineering staff. Were they losing out on Boeing airplanes just when they were beginning to make progress? The Boeing wind tunnel was completed at the university. The two young engineers, Claire Egtvedt and Louis Marsh, now Miller's eager assistants, had been flying in the "C" airplanes at every opportunity, to gain more knowledge. Claire Egtvedt was happy Miller had put him on design work. It was a bigger challenge than figuring stresses. In the air, he'd strap a clipboard to one leg and make careful notes to take back to the drafting room. The clean rush of wind against his face seemed to clear thought for action. The din and vibration were an incessant urging to new and better ideas.

The Curtiss flying boats were just getting well under way in the shops and concern about Boeing's own design was just reaching major proportions when a crescendo of whistles, horns and yells pierced the walls of the plant, driving airplanes out of mind.

It was November 11, 1918. The rumors of an armistice had turned real. The great war was over. A floodtide of laughing, back-slapping men burst out the gate and joined the grandest parade of the century to the center of town.

5. *Production Needed*

The plant whistle sounded new and strange on the morning of November 12, 1918. It had an exhilarating note of freedom, no longer the strident note of military need. Somehow it seemed less businesslike, though, less certain of its purpose.

To Claire Egtvedt, spreading out the partial drawings of a new Navy flying boat that would probably never be, the morning whistle was a question and a hope. Would there be work after the HS-2L flying boats? Egtvedt was now deep in aerodynamic theory. Perhaps the postwar problem would give him a chance at original design. To Phil Johnson, checking over material orders and the routing of parts through the shop, the whistle was a call to action. Johnson was now manager of the production office. He needed to know what to do about a stack of papers ready to go to the superintendent. Would contracts be changed because of the armistice?

The questions of both men pulled them magnetlike to Ed Gott's office, where they found a group already gathered. Gott was bouncing and talking loud into the telephone, nervously adjusting his thick-rimmed glasses. He was trying to get Mr. Boeing in Chicago. When he got him, the conversation was short. Gott put down the phone and announced: "We keep going as we are, until we hear further from Mr. Boeing." The gathering broke up. Claire Egtvedt stopped in at Phil's office. "What do you think Mr. Boeing has in mind?"

"You can't expect him to have all the answers in a day." Phil wouldn't say, "I wish I knew, too." There was an essential difference between the two young airplane men. Claire's mind was sensitive and searching. Phil was quick-seeing, but he wore a casual air. There was a twinkle in his gray-blue eyes. Claire dreamed and then did. Phil did and then dreamed.

Yet there was also an essential likeness between the two. Both were soft spoken, both had been brought up in the discipline and parental encouragement of religious Scandinavian homes. The university, perhaps the war, had instilled in both a desire to achieve. That desire was finding its own channel. In Egtvedt, it came through when he gazed beyond the three dimensions of space and the fourth dimension of time to an engineering idea taking form in his mind. In Johnson, it flowed swiftly when he saw an idea take form in metal, and helped men give it form. While waiting for Boeing's word and thinking of the future, Claire Egtvedt and Phil Johnson had a feeling the future didn't depend entirely on Boeing, but also on them. Here was a new challenge. Wasn't challenge, in reality, an opportunity?

Boeing's word came as fast as a mail train leaving Chicago November 12 could huff and whistle across plains and mountains to Seattle. During the days and nights this required, the world was rapidly changing hue. On the Western Front in Europe, after four long years, all was quiet. America rejoiced that the world had been made safe for democracy. The talk was all of disarmament, of the return to normal, of building a better world.

Boeing's letter narrowed the change to a simple business proposition. The Navy would probably not cancel the HS-2L contract, but might cut it in half, salvaging the work already done. No new production contracts could be expected either from Army or Navy. The Post Office had spoken encouragingly of the development of an air-mail service, but this would not come fast. They should look for their own market. It seemed to him that the flying boat offered the best possibility for commercial sale. Landing fields were scarce but water was plentiful in the Puget Sound country. They should start right away developing two sizes, one of them about 100 horsepower, the other perhaps 200.

"I look for a splendid future in peacetime," Boeing continued, "but there is going to be a gap of six months to two years when it will be a hard struggle. In the meantime we should keep our shop occupied with other work. Comb the field and see what we might go into. I can suggest showcase work and interior woodwork."

Boeing's letter was sufficient. Miller assigned Egtvedt to look into engines and begin sketching the first flying boat, the larger of the two proposed sizes. It would be called the B-1, "B" for Boeing, their first commercial design. Louis Marsh worked on the hull lines. The rest searched for other work. They lined up a job building the fixtures for a glove store. Other furniture work developed. Joe Hartson had the idea of building sea sleds, "automobiles of the sea." They would be wingless second cousins to the seaplane. A license agreement was arranged with the Hickman Company in Boston, which had such a design.

Word came from the Navy canceling twenty-five of the fifty HS-2Ls. Then Miller announced his plan to return to the university. Engineering was split in two. Claire Egtvedt became head of Experimental while Phil Johnson handled the production end. With the B-1 it was decided they'd get clear away from the Model C's problems of too much stability. They'd pattern the wings and tail surfaces after the more conventional HS-2L boats. Very little wing stagger. Dihedral upsweep in the lower wing only. A regular horizontal stabilizer. No balance on the elevators. The boat hull would be built of two plys of light mahogany with a layer of fabric glued between. The airplane would be a pusher, with a 200-horsepower motor mounted high under the fifty-foot upper wing, propeller behind. When the plan was complete enough, it was presented to Boeing.

"Go ahead and build it," he said. With space for mail bags or two passengers behind the pilot, the B-1 flying boat would be an ideal commercial airplane to fly the northwest skies, Boeing thought. He could see air transportation becoming a reality, bringing people and nations closer together.

The idea was timely. President Wilson was now in Europe with a plan for a League of Nations. His Fourteen Points were a new hope to millions. There would be peace and commerce between nations. The year 1919 would start a new era.

When a businessman in Vancouver, British Columbia, E. S. Knowlton, asked the postmaster there if he would permit mail to be taken by air from Canada to the United States as the feature of an exposition, the postmaster readily assented. Knowlton called W. E. Boeing. "Can you bring a plane to Vancouver and fly a bag of mail back around the third of March?" Boeing said he'd like to. He asked Eddie Hubbard to pilot the plane. Hubbard was now doing the test flying for the plant. Munter had left to go into a new flying business for himself.

Vancouver Postmaster R. G. MacPherson sent a message for the occasion. "When we mount upon the wings of eagles, no line of demarcation then shows between Canada and the United States. May the first airplane mail be the harbinger of thousands more to follow...."

The Boeing "C" was fifty minutes on the way to Vancouver when Hubbard tapped Boeing on the shoulder and pointed silently at blackening clouds ahead. In a moment, a change of wind hit them with a wild gallop. The sky closed about them, filling with snow. Wiping his goggles with his sleeve, Boeing looked back at Hubbard. No use trying to outshout the engine. Hubbard pointed down and pushed the stick forward, starting down. Boeing nodded. No ground outline appeared; no bottom. Groping downward, Hubbard finally saw black water and leveled off above it. For twenty minutes, with blinding snow in their faces, they bucked along, watching a blurred shoreline to the right. Hubbard identified Anacortes and set the plane down in the bay. Boeing was pale when they climbed ashore. "Good job, Eddie," he said.

They stayed there overnight. Next morning with weather improved, they made it on in to the Royal Vancouver Yacht Club. On March 3 they headed back with the sixty letters that constituted the first international air mail. The 125 miles to Seattle was a little too much for the fuel capacity of the "C" against a headwind and they put down at Edmonds, just north of the city, to take on gas. Three hours after leaving Vancouver they nosed the pontoons up to the ramp of the Lake Washington hangar. Eddie Hubbard jumped lithely out of the plane and helped Boeing down with the mail bag. There was a dream in Eddie's eyes.

"Mr. Boeing, if we can do this in the 'C,' it would be a cinch in the B-1 flying boat. I'd sure like to fly up there and back on a regular basis."

The B-1 was out of engineering and into the shops now, except for some detail drawings. Egtvedt and Gott went east to display one of the "Cs" at the National Aeronautical Exposition—their first real opportunity for public recognition. But in the New York Armory it was one airplane among many.

"Nice workmanship," said a sightseer who paused to look at the "C."

"Sort of a Curtiss," said another who came by.

"More like the Aeromarine," his companion argued.

A Curtiss man told of their plans to build a network of air fields and establish flying schools throughout the East. "Does Boeing plan anything like that?"

"No," said Egtvedt, "we'll just manufacture airplanes." Waiting around, he had his first chance in some time to have a good talk with Gott about the business.

"We're getting badly in debt," Gott told him. "We have a good-size plant now—eight buildings. We need production. A few experimental planes won't bring anything in."

An Italian lieutenant named Cantoni came by. He had the S.V.A. airplane on display down the corridor. It was one of the best: fast and well designed. Cantoni proposed that Boeing be licensed to build and sell it as a sport plane. "You're going to have trouble catching up with Curtiss," said the Italian. "Curtiss has the reputation. You still have to prove yours. You need a plane that's already popular."

This made sense. If they didn't license the S.V.A. someone else would, and they'd be that much further behind. They told the lieutenant they'd see what Mr. Boeing thought of the idea. Boeing turned it down.

When the show was over Egtvedt went to McCook Field in Dayton. Major Reuben Fleet, in charge of contracts for the Air Service, arranged for a lieutenant from the engineering division to show him around. "We have a hundred different planes here," said the lieutenant. "Ninety-seven of them aren't worth a darn."

They walked through a long hangar. The lieutenant pointed out the Thomas Morse pursuit plane and the Martin bomber, which he said were O.K. There was a bewildering array of experimental models, many of them unconventional. One was shaped like a halibut. "The Army paid $75,000 for this design," said the lieutenant. "The only way you can get it off the ground is with a chain and block. You can see why we'd rather design them ourselves."

Egtvedt moved on to Cleveland, where there was a good deal of flying activity. He asked about new equipment for local passenger flights. "We can get war surplus de Havillands for a song," they said. He returned to Seattle, the bright colors in his sunrise well faded. The HS-2L work was all but finished. The growing starkness of the outlook was reflected on people's faces. The plant crew was down to eighty from the wartime four hundred. Boeing decided the divided engineering department was an unnecessary luxury and Johnson was put in the shop as assistant superintendent to organize the furniture and sea-sled work. That left Egtvedt in charge of all engineering. The raised eyebrows of some of the older officials would have bothered him if it weren't for Boeing's seeming confidence.

When the B-1 was completed and sent to Lake Union for test, there were bets, half in jest, that it wouldn't fly. Boeing refused to join. "I think the boys have done a good job," he said. The engineers were anxious to see if the water would break cleanly along the sides of the hull. Egtvedt and March got in the back seat to watch while Eddie Hubbard taxied. "It's coming clean," Egtvedt noticed as Hubbard gathered speed. The big Hall-Scott was deafening now. Marsh was gesturing wildly.

They were taking off. They hadn't expected to fly but the boat had popped right out of the water. Hubbard looked around with a grin. He was continuing to climb. They reached about three hundred feet when the engine coughed, then sputtered.

"The pump! The pump!" Marsh shouted. The fuel pump driven by the engine had slipped out of gear and the engine wasn't getting any gas. The two passengers strained in a futile effort to assist Eddie, who was reaching for the hand pump with one hand. They could see he was battling to hold the stick forward. The strength of one arm wasn't enough. The horizon was dropping, the nose coming up. Hubbard couldn't handle the sudden load on the elevator. With the heavy fuel tanks down in the hull and propeller up high behind the wings, the airplane wanted to nose up when the power was cut off.

Pushing hard with both hands, Eddie was able to lower the elevators enough to bring the nose back down. Momentarily he released one hand for the pump. They heard the engine catching hold. But instantly the surge of power reversed the forces and sent the airplane rocketing downward. When Eddie got the nose back up, the engine again began to die. Again they humped and roared downward. Three or four times they rocketed and dived. Finally Eddie put it down on the lake. Wet with perspiration, he just sat there for a while. "We can fix the fuel feed, but that elevator . . ."

"We went too much by the HS boat, I guess," Claire said. "This is a different airplane."

Back out at the plant they studied the problem, realizing they didn't really know very much about control surfaces. You had to make an elevator longer to make it more effective, but the longer you made it, the more force the pilot had to overcome. Wong's balanced elevator was one solution, but it was too tricky, too touchy. There must be some other way. Claire Egtvedt stared at the dozen elevator doodles his pencil had been making. He started to toss them all in the waste basket, then looked back. One of the sketches, upside down, suddenly looked different. Why not make the elevators wider instead of longer? That would give them the same area for the lift they needed, but it wouldn't be half as hard for the pilot to pull. Odd, no one thought of that. Elevators had always been long and narrow.

B-1

Revisions and testing of the B-1 continued, along with work on two smaller planes, one of them a land plane. But Ed Gott announced unhappily that all work under construction, including the sea-sleds, if sold, wouldn't pay the overhead. The furniture business was making some contribution, but it wasn't very profitable. "We can't stay in the aircraft business unless we can get production orders from the government," he wrote to Joe Hartson, who had established an office in Washington.

"Get busy and design something that we can sell," Hartson replied.

"We couldn't develop anything in time to do any good," said Gott. "Get hold of an established design that they're planning to buy, and we'll bid on it. We can sell something they want quicker than something we have developed."

"I don't agree with you," said Hartson. He had been in to see the Army and Navy again and again. He had shown the Navy the B-1 drawings. "A small-size Curtiss boat," they had commented. He sought an Army experimental contract. "What claim have you to one?" Colonel Hall in the supply office asked. "What have you developed except the C-type trainer? What successful land machines have you designed? Who is your designer? What experience has he had with military requirements? What original ideas has he developed?" Hartson found himself out of answers.

As fall turned to winter of 1919, spirits in the front office were as downwashed as the steady rain that drained into the Duwamish. Boeing was advancing money from his personal account almost weekly to meet the payroll. One day Gott could stand it no longer. He took the books in to Boeing. "Do you think we should close up shop?" he asked. "We're going to finish the year $90,000 in the red."

Boeing was a man fighting with himself. He had lain awake nights thinking about this. He didn't like to start something and not finish it. But he had to face the facts. Possibly they could close down the airplane part of the business and keep on with other work until conditions were better. But that would be losing the start they'd gotten. The thing that concerned him most was the men at the plant. Young fellows like Johnson and Egtvedt and Marsh, trying to make a go of it.

"I'd hate to break up the organization," he said. "But we can't keep on like this indefinitely. If we can't get some business with an assured income . . ." he paused a long while, ". . . we'll have to close."

Hartson wired there was a chance to get a contract remodeling fifty wartime de Havillands.

"We'll take it only if it's certain there's a profit in it," Gott wired back. "Not just for the sake of staying in the aircraft business. We've decided to go out of business unless there is an assured opportunity."

Hartson negotiated zealously and a contract to rebuild the DH's was drawn. It would give them work to last until May 1920. Phil Johnson, who had taken Berlin's place as superintendent, organized the shop force to hit the job hard.

6. *Airplanes, Not Cement Sidewalks*

To make the de Havilland remodeling a financial success, the emphasis had to be on manufacturing. Overhead was slashed. The sole survivors in Engineering were Claire Egtvedt and his assistant Marsh. No staff. But from what they had seen at Dayton they knew they could design better airplanes than the Army was getting, if only they had a chance.

"Looks like our chance is running out," said Marsh. His voice was flat, not the genial Marsh.

What had become of their hopes and dreams? The question followed Claire home at night. Alone, he could search for an answer. "Isn't progress a right thing? If I have ability that can help bring it about, is there any power that can keep me from using it?" He went to see Gott and found Boeing with him in his office. This was the time; he was going to say what was on his mind, no matter what the consequences.

"We are building airplanes, not cement sidewalks," Claire began. The ring in his voice gave him new confidence. "If you want to build cement sidewalks and just do work requiring a minimum of engineering, then you can do away with engineering. Do away with it. Just mix the materials, pour them into a form and collect your money. But if you want to build and sell airplanes, you first have to create them. That takes research and development and testing and engineering. The airplane isn't half what it ought to be. We have a foothold again now. Can't we hire a few engineers and try to build a future?"

Gott seemed about to answer when Boeing rose to his feet. "Claire is right," said Boeing. That put a spring back in Egtvedt's step. He organized plans for new engineering work. Meanwhile a sports landplane they were building was nearing completion, in time for the Aero Show in San Francisco in April 1920. There was a hope of sales to men who had learned to fly in the war.

A finishing crew worked overtime to get the plane ready by the time the freight boat left for San Francisco. They polished the varnished surfaces and began crating the machine while mechanics completed the cockpit installations and adjusted the controls. They worked all through the last night. At five o'clock in the morning, carpenters putting the last board in place on the crate heard a cry, "Wait! Wait! I'm still in here!" The last mechanic, flashlight in hand, scrambled out.

Egtvedt and a newly hired salesman, H. C. Berg, who had won a national prize selling automobiles, went to the San Francisco show. But the experience was cheerless. They listened long to complaints about the post-war slump and came back with empty order book. The services of Berg weren't required much longer.

Eddie Hubbard bought the B-1 to start a mail service from Seattle to Victoria, B. C., carrying out the plan he'd mentioned to Boeing after their Vancouver flight. The smaller flying boat was completed and sold in Canada, but further sales looked unlikely. Joe Hartson resigned to go to work for the Hickman Sea Sled Company, a business with more promise. In May 1920, Ed Gott packed his bag to see what he could do for the company in Washington.

A new force had emerged in the nation's capital to counter the downtrend in the airplane business. General Billy Mitchell, assistant chief of the Air Service, had a vision of air power that was challenging all the old concepts of warfare. The design group at McCook Field had caught fire from Mitchell and had begun to work on bigger, more powerful planes. One of these was called GAX, for Ground Attack, EXperimental. It had three wings, two Liberty engines, a 20-mm. cannon and eight machine guns. Lieutenant C. N. Monteith, military head of the design office, told civilian designer Mac Laddon not to spare the horses, that Mitchell wanted it rough and tough. Laddon employed shoulder-high bathtubs of armor plate to protect the crew and engines, and devised rotating slots in the armor for viewing the ground. When it was ready for flight, Army test pilot Harold Harris regarded the creation uncertainly, especially the ribbon-type radiators which had been placed above the engines so they wouldn't be vulnerable.

"The engines should cool all right in the air," said an engineer from the equipment section, "but don't get them too hot on the ground."

"Take it easy when you land," said the designer who had contributed the landing gear. It looked tiny now under the big frame of the airplane.

Another admonished him, "Don't try a turn till you get to 5,000 feet. It may be unstable spinwise."

Harris invited engineer Monteith to go along. Monty was a cheerful and able young officer, highly regarded at McCook. When Harris got the triplane to the end of the runway, he waited to cool the radiators, then took off. He got off easily and climbed to three hundred feet, when the ribbon radiators burst. No power. His instructions made it clear he couldn't turn back sharply to the field. He was headed for the river and a corner of the city. He knew of a cornfield across the river that he might make with a slight turn, but he couldn't see the ground over the high armor sides, and it was difficult to survey terrain through the slots. Monteith rode the front gunner's turret in helpless isolation. Harris got enough coughs of power out of the engine for a wide turn and made it back to the field at fence-top level.

Monteith got out, thoroughly shaken. "This is ridiculous. If we can't design safer airplanes we shouldn't design them."

But when General Mitchell arrived for a demonstration of the GAX, the plane was in flying shape with new-type radiator and they were ordered to fly by with guns firing. Harris and crew passed in review, everything wide open. The roar of the motors, the beat of the big propellers, the cannon booming, the machine guns spitting fire, all were the thunder of Thor. "That's what we need! That's what we need!" Mitchell shouted.

Back in Washington Mitchell was optimistic about the future of the Air Service. "We've scraped up $5 million to buy some Martin bombers and some new types," he told Ed Gott, "including twenty armored attack triplanes—the GAX type. Go on out to Dayton and see Bane."

Colonel Thurman H. Bane was head of the engineering division at McCook Field, and Major Reuben Fleet was the contracting officer. Gott called Fleet and left promptly for Dayton. A bid for the building of twenty GAX attack planes was entered in competition with other manufacturers. Boeing's bid turned out to be low. On June 7 the contract was awarded and Phil Johnson began looking for additional help and armor plate.

There was also a bidding competition on an advanced experimental version of the GAX, built around a new engine that McCook Field was interested in. There would be three of these. When plans were submitted, it looked as if Boeing might win this order too. Heartened, Egtvedt talked with Major Fleet in Dayton about original Boeing designs.

"Why don't you go to Europe and brush up on the latest there?" Fleet asked. "Then come back and we'll see what ideas you have."

Boeing thought such a trip would be a good idea. During the next two months, French and British factories and unfinished wartime developments of Germany, including a giant monoplane, gave Egtvedt a fresh outlook. He was particularly interested in the work being done in Germany with light steel tubing, welded together, for the airplane structure in place of wood. He returned in November 1920, to find that Boeing had won the contract to build the three experimental armored planes designed as an improvement on the GAX, to be called the GA-2s, but that the GAX contract had been reduced from twenty to ten planes and had already lost its savor.

"This is a helluva way to build airplanes," said a foreman watching his crew struggling with a piece of the heavy armor plate.

"Aw, cheer up," said Phil Johnson. "At least we don't have to worry about scratching it." Phil sauntered off, but turned to look back. He was biting his lower lip. This wasn't the way things should be.

The sea-sled business was now acknowledged to be a fiasco. Even the furniture business was being carried at a loss. Foreman

Walter Way, realizing the bedroom sets weren't selling well, asked Johnson about getting a set at cost. "Cost?" said Phil. "Why pay the cost? Buy it at retail and save money."

The three GA-2s didn't interest Ed Gott. "We need quantities of at least fifty or a hundred," he said. When an invitation came to enter the Navy competition for design of a new shipboard fighter, Gott was annoyed. He insisted that the military system of experimental work and procurement was completely unsound for Boeing or for any other airplane manufacturer. "You get the design work, then somebody else can still outbid you to produce them," he said. "Our business, first and foremost, is to construct airplanes. What we need is production orders." A $300,000 deficit as of December 1920 underscored his argument.

7. *The Pursuit*

The cold word from Dayton in January was that there wasn't enough money to keep even a small part of the airplane industry alive. It was going to be a case of survival of the fittest. The L.W.F. Company was in the hands of receivers already. Billy Mitchell's campaign wasn't doing well. The only new planes the Army could buy were two-hundred MB-3 type pursuits designed by the Thomas Morse Company, Egtvedt learned on a Dayton visit.

"Everybody is going to be scrapping for that order," said Major Fleet.

"Will you give all two hundred to one company?" asked Egtvedt.

"We're getting bids on quantities of fifty to two hundred."

In Seattle the challenge was taken up. They'd have to bid low, or there was no use bidding. Phil Johnson unrolled the drawings and called in the shop foremen, one by one, to get their ideas as to the amount of work on the various parts. Then they met in Gott's office. When the estimates were added, the price came to $10,175 per plane for fifty; $6,617 for two hundred.

Ed Gott went to Dayton for the bid opening. Major Fleet began reading the bids: "Aero Marine, $1,832,000; Boeing, $1,448,000; Curtiss, $1,982,000; Dayton-Wright, $2,201,000." Gott was concerned. "We must be off," he thought.

"L.W.F., $2,133,000; Thomas Morse, $1,926,000." Gott was now thoroughly alarmed. Thomas Morse had built the airplane. Morse's figure was $478,000 higher than Boeing's. A $400,000 loss would mean disaster.

"Boeing is low at $1,448,000."

A silence followed. Gott looked around. Some of the men were glaring at him. When the meeting broke up, none of them came over to congratulate him. They gathered in small groups. "He'll lose his shirt," someone was saying. A Curtiss man came up with a friendly air. "You can withdraw," he counseled. Gott went to the Miami Hotel and called Phil Johnson. "Everyone says we'll go broke at these figures. Think we should withdraw?"

"We're in business," boomed Phil. "Let's stick to our guns. We can build 'em for that, easy."

Boeing backed Phil up. But there was still a question about the bid being accepted. The whole thing was now in the hands of Washington. The pressure was on General Menoher, chief of the Air Service, to split the business. There were reports that it was up to Secretary of War Weeks, that it was up to President Harding, that the whole project might be dropped for another year while the Secretary of War and Secretary of Navy re-surveyed the arms program.

Five weeks had elapsed when Ed Gott, beetled and drawn, went to Secretary Weeks.

"I will have made my decision by next Saturday," the Secretary said. "The question is whether it is worth an extra $800,000 for us to split the business up. I don't think it is. I don't think the President will favor it. But I must look into it thoroughly."

The following Saturday there was celebration on the Duwamish. Boeing had been awarded the government's biggest plane order since the war: two hundred Thomas Morse type MB-3A pursuits. The news spread to the shops, and the day soon gathered the full proportions of a Roman holiday.

Work got under way fast. The remaining stocks of furniture were sold out. Old employees were rehired. Tools and materials were ordered in quantities that seemed astronomical. But the breeze of production enthusiasm didn't bring cheer to the engineering loft. It wasn't because of lack of things to do. The engineers were hopping busy getting drawings to the shops. Yet Claire Egtvedt felt swept with the tide, no mainsail, no rudder. He threw listless looks at the paper they were pushing out.

Airplanes, but not one of them a Boeing design.

They did have some research studies coming along. These kept the spirit alive. Two new engineers, Fred Laudan and Herman Haase, were experimenting with joints between metal and wood. If they put too many small holes through the wood, it chawed the wood to pieces, they found. If they used a couple of big ones, the bolts would pull out of the wood. "There is no good answer. You need metal to fasten to metal." Claire recalled the welded steel structures used in Germany. But torch welding was difficult work. Louis Marsh helped him run some strength tests on different kinds of welds. The results went to Ed Gott.

"We can get nearly twice the strength if we use an electric arc welder," they told Gott. "It takes only half as long as with a torch. But we'd have to build a special machine to do it."

Gott thumbed the report, then nodded. "Make a drawing of what you want, and I'll okay it."

The GAX triplane was ready to fly, down at Fort Lewis, Washington, where it had been trucked piece by piece and assembled in a big tent hangar the Army had erected. Everyone went down to see the maiden flight.

It was a cool gray day in May 1921. The 125-foot canvas front of the hangar was rolled up and out came the behemoth, wing upon wing upon wing, with rows of struts like fenceposts.

Harold Harris had come from Dayton to fly it. Ready as a Canadian Mountie, he stuffed cotton in his ears, scrambled up the high armored side, and started the Libertys. When he revved them up, the engines bellowed out of their iron closets and the sides of the ship brayed back the clamor. The multi-wings buzzed with vibration. Lieutenant Harris taxied for a while, then clattered down the runway and lifted the black monster over the fence. He swung about overhead for fifteen minutes and returned. When he had turned off the din, they asked, "How does she fly?"

Harris pulled out his ear plugs and pounded his head. "Don't hear." The question was repeated in his ear.

The lieutenant just stared for a minute, lips tight. Then he slapped down his flying helmet. "What is this airplane supposed to be for?"

"Ground attack."

"How can you attack the ground with an airplane you can't see out of, and that's too unwieldy to maneuver close to the ground? If you ever design anything for military use, think first what it's going to be used for, and then design it."

The GAXs were delivered to Kelly Field where the officers found a new way to enforce discipline. "Watch your step," they'd say, "or you'll be ordered to fly the GAX."

Next time he was in Dayton, Claire Egtvedt discussed philosophy of design with Lieutenant Monteith in the engineering division. "The trouble here," said Monteith, "is that there are too many cooks. The equipment branch has the last word on equipment, the power plant branch has the last word on power plants, and so on. They all have their own goals. They don't have a common goal, like a company that has to meet competition."

"Does the Army intend to stay in the design business?"

"It's falling apart. All our best engineers are leaving to go to work for industry."

Egtvedt talked with the people in the flight section. "How do you like the Thomas Moore MB-3?" he asked.

"Oh, it's O.K.," they said at first.

"What don't you like about it?"

"Too touchy. She'll spin at the drop of a hat."

"That so? How does it fly otherwise?"

"Not bad, but too slow."

At Selfridge Field, Egtvedt watched while the young pilots went through mock combat in the pursuits, one winging over and diving with motors, props and wires screaming, the other whipping down onto his tail and dog-fighting across the sky. Hangar talk was vivid. Egtvedt heard the men blame their airplane when they came out on the short end of a duel.

"If you were designing a pursuit, what things would you consider most important?" he asked them.

"Think about what we have to do," one man answered. "We have to pursue the other fellow, outdodge him, turn inside. Speed and maneuverability are everything. The boys at McCook hang on a lot of equipment that doesn't mean a thing. Just loads the airplane down. We want 'em stripped for action."

Think first what it's going to be used for, and then design it. ...Pursuit.... We have to pursue the other fellow.... Stripped for action. Claire Egtvedt sat in a Pullman car, watching landscape go by.

What interfered with speed on the pursuit? The wires between the wings. Their shrill whistle showed how badly they wanted to be out of the way. How about a thicker wing? Fokker was using one. Strong enough to cantilever—hold itself up, partly at least. Get rid of the wires. Make the lower wing short and just use it to brace the upper wings at the middle.

Maneuverability they wanted. How fast could an airplane turn? As fast as the pilot dared turn it. How fast did he dare? It would pull apart. Look how Laudan's bolts pulled out of the wood, all sizes, if you pulled hard enough. Metal tubing was the answer. Electric arc welding, with the welding machine they'd

worked out. They could build a real pursuit. If they only had
the chance.

Claire's pencil made eye-satisfying, free-hand ellipses, wings,
bodies as he moved with his thoughts across Iowa, Nebraska,
Wyoming, homeward. The rocking of the rails only nudged at
a consciousness that was being directed along a higher course.

"We've got to design our own pursuit," Claire told Marsh
when he got home. "I have some ideas." They got started with
them, just between times, just between themselves, calculating
loads, arrangements, structures. There was no new design competition. Besides, Gott didn't favor these contracts. They were
doing better just bidding on existing designs. Was there no
break-through?

Something told Egtvedt to look at the other fellow's point of
view. Gott had backed him lots of times when he needed it.
Gott was pitching hard all the time. Look what he'd done to
land the MB-3A contract in Washington. "Maybe it's myself
that's been standing in my way," he thought. Just this seemed
to make him feel less constricted. There must be a way to move
ahead. Was designing to the specifications of government engineers the only way to build a military airplane? Why not
design and build it your own way, then take it to the Army?
Mr. Boeing would go for that. But would the Army?

The plane would simply have to be good enough to sell itself.
That was the challenge. The more he thought about it, the more
right it seemed. How could the Army refuse it if it were best?

A meeting with Boeing was set for January 3, 1922. It was a
new year; new outlook. Conditions were improving. Financial
writers said business courage was replacing business depression,
that the two couldn't exist together. Boeing's timber was beginning to sell. The zest and teamwork of the men at the plant,
given a big job to do, were an inspiration.

With hope in his heart, Egtvedt went with Ed Gott to
Boeing's uptown office in the Hoge Building to make his proposal. "We are in the pursuit plane business now. The pursuit

is different from anything we've built before. When you see the young fellows in the Air Service up there, rolling and diving and dog-fighting, you realize that they have to have a superb airplane. The MB-3A is far from being what they need. It's based on the old French Spad. We know how to build a much better airplane than that." Boeing's eyes were kindling. Gott was thoughtful. "When the MBs are finished," Claire continued, "we should have a better plane to offer."

No disagreement there.

"Gott has often pointed out that the rules governing military design competitions are unsound. You bid for the design, make an experimental model and someone else may build it. Even if it's a successful design, you can't look forward to anything." Gott was nodding. "You don't get out the best design because you don't have the incentive and you can't stray very far from the specifications.

"What I'd like to do is go out on our own to build the best pursuit we can. The Boeing pursuit. The design will belong to us—at least till we sell it to the Army. It will be entirely up to us to make it the last word in performance, efficiency and general utility for the purpose—a pursuit airplane."

Boeing was on his feet now, looking out over Elliott Bay. The Olympic skyline, spectacular in winter, was in full view but his eyes narrowed as though focusing on a point out beyond, seeing what he had planned and wanted and expected to see all the time.

"We would go to all the sources available," said Claire, "here and abroad, to get information and data. We wouldn't have to put in all the contrivances and devices that the Air Service thinks up. It would be designed for one purpose only—combat work."

Boeing didn't even ask how much the project would cost. He turned about. "That's exactly what we should do," he said. "Do it on our own. Keep it a secret. Develop the best pursuit that can be built. Then, we'll take it back to Dayton and enter it in competition with the others."

Egtvedt didn't remember getting back to the plant. Somehow he was back there. Working, delving in details, sighting past details at a fix, delving in details again. In the days and weeks that followed, he'd often work through the dinner hour, go out for a bite, then come back to light up the drafting room again. So did Marsh. So did Laudan and Herman Haase, and Bob Minshall, an energetic youth doing part-time work while finishing aeronautical engineering at the university. All of them were enjoying it, but Egtvedt was embarrassed over the extra time the men were putting in without pay. "Better go on home. I'll see you in the morning," he kept telling them, late at night.

"Claire, we're having the time of our life down here," said Marsh.

Boeing came down often. He'd stop in at the drafting room and ask to see "The Pursuit." It had no name or number. "Keep after the improvements," he said. "Be sure they're right and go ahead." Egtvedt kept after the facts to work with. From the National Advisory Committee for Aeronautics he got data on thicker wing sections, new control and stability studies, but he felt these were still inadequate.

A plan was worked out for a tapered wing, different from the Fokker. They decided to tuck the radiator under the engine. It would get the full sweep of the wind in a climb, but with minimum resistance in level flight. With a short bottom wing, they got rid of much of the drag of the wires between wings. Ways were sought to minimize the drag of other parts sticking out in the wind. Parasite drag, engineers had come to call it. Everything besides the wing was parasite drag; it stole the gains you made by putting more power in the engines.

With the pursuit design progressing and MB-3A production coming into full flow, Boeing expanded the company's management structure. He went from president to chairman of the board. Ed Gott was elected president, Johnson vice president and general manager, Egtvedt secretary and chief engineer.

Plant activity reached concert pitch. Planing mills were whining high C on the wing ribs. Metal hammers beat a rhythmless discord. The first MB-3A was delivered in July 1922, and behind it the assembly floor was filled to the doorways. Some of the planes were in skeleton form, others in various states of half dress, their unbleached linen still hanging on the wall.

One day Boeing walked with Egtvedt out through the plant to view the progress. He was wistful. "When we started this business it was kind of an adventure," Boeing said. "Look what it's become." He was silent for a long while. Egtvedt saw him reach up behind his glasses and dry the corners of his eyes.

Everyone had a warm feeling for the two hundred MB-3As. They had lifted the company off shaky legs and given it vigor and strength. When Bill Boeing looked at the cost sheets just before Christmas 1922, he knew that their bid had not been too low. They would end the job with a real profit. The three hundred Boeing employees got a bonus that Christmas.

Now the whole company felt like venturing into new designs. They had sought to get the Army interested in a transport airplane, but failed, then they talked with the Navy and found there was an opportunity in the trainer field. Boeing promptly authorized the start on a new trainer design. "We can build one new experimental plane each year on our own," he said. "We have the pursuit under way. This can be next."

The pursuit design was complete and ready for construction except for one hitch. They needed a Curtiss D-12 motor. Ed Gott arranged to borrow one from the Army, provided they could complete the machine and get it to Dayton for test by July 1923. The engine arrived in January, simultaneously with word that the new Curtiss pursuit was already in the air and had made a speed of 169 miles an hour. That was a shade faster than the Boeing was expected to go.

Johnson put the best shop crews to work on the pursuit. It went together fast. On April 29, 1923, Frank Tyndall flew it at Camp Lewis and liked the way it handled. "Only thing I can suggest," he said, "is a little better longitudinal stability." This stability thing still seemed to be the principal uncertainty in designing airplanes. The plane went back to the plant for tail surface revision, then performance tests were run at Sand Point.

On June 6 Gott notified McCook Field the plane was ready to send east for trials. Next day, Tyndall ground-looped it in the soft ground at the end of Sand Point Field. Johnson surveyed the damage to wing tips and propeller. It would take two or three weeks to make repairs. There wouldn't be time to get a new propeller; they'd have to cut off the tips of the damaged one and reshape it. With time running so short, they decided to ship the plane to Dayton after repair without further test.

 *PW-9*

8. *Trials*

It was late June when the airplane crates arrived in Dayton, Claire Egtvedt watching over them. At McCook, while a crew of Army mechanics was assembling the plane, someone brought word that Egtvedt was wanted in the Engineering office.

"Where's your design data?" demanded an engineer named Niles.

"Didn't you get the specifications we sent in?"

"These don't tell me anything. I can't release the ship for flight unless I know more than this."

Egtvedt went over the data with him.

"Well, I'll release it for performance tests," Niles finally agreed, "but I'll have to see your stress analysis and the dimensions of all the members before we'll stunt it or try it for combat work."

"You mean all our figures?"

"How do I know you haven't slipped up on areas or moments of inertia?"

Egtvedt thought of saying that they'd built airplanes before, but didn't. "I'll wire the plant," he said.

They had trouble getting the engine to work properly and there was discussion about the fuel system. It was July 20 before the plane was cleared for performance tests. Harold Harris took it up.

"What speed did you clock?" Egtvedt asked when he got back.

"She'll do at least 165," said Lieutenant Harris.

A couple of engineers standing by perked their ears. One of the pilots came over to Egtvedt. "You've got a fine little airplane here," he said. "I like its looks."

Harris drew Egtvedt aside. "The climb is good, but longitudinal stability is bad," he said. "You couldn't possibly hold a gun steady on a target. It hunts up and down all the time." This, from Harris, hurt.

"We knew the plane was a bit tail-heavy, but didn't think it was serious. It shouldn't be too hard to fix."

"The plane is controllable, all right, but this will be a mark against you," said Harris.

Egtvedt worked nights on the mathematics of the stability problem. He took it personally, because of the difficulty they had had on the first hop of the B-1 flying boat. At the field, the maintenance men were still having trouble with the engine and this kept him running days. He wrote Marsh that they'd have to enlarge the stabilizers and move the engine forward to get better balance, but they couldn't do that while the tests were going on.

Harris was encouraging, though. He said six different pilots had now flown the Boeing and they all thought it was more maneuverable than the Curtiss. Lieutenant Alec Pearson, considered one of McCook's headiest pilots, was emphatic about it. "It closed my lower eyelids on the turns," he said. "If it turned any faster, it would put me out." Other sections of the McCook staff were taking increasing interest. "This armament installation is the best I've ever seen," said the head of the armament section.

General opinion was that the Boeing and the Curtiss were close together on speed, the Curtiss better perhaps on stability, the Boeing better for maintenance. The Curtiss wing-skin radiator had to be fixed after almost every flight. Official high speed and climb tests were yet to be run when Egtvedt was told August 1 that the supply officer had been authorized to buy twenty-five Curtiss pursuits.

"Can't we get it held up at least till you have comparative performance?" he asked Major L. W. MacIntosh, new head of the engineering division. MacIntosh wired General Patrick, recommending equal consideration be given Boeing. But George Tidmarsh, the Boeing representative in Washington, had learned that the Army had decided to go ahead with the Curtiss order without awaiting results of the Boeing tests.

On August 6 they ran the high-speed test and could get only 159.5 miles an hour. But the McCookites were becoming attached to the little Boeing. "Let's try the Curtiss high-speed propeller on it," someone suggested, recognizing that the propeller rebuilt in Seattle after the ground loop might be handicapping the plane. They installed the new propeller and got 167.6 miles per hour, a shade better than the Curtiss. They climbed to 20,600 feet—two hundred feet higher than the Curtiss on the first try. On the second they made 21,700 feet but the Curtiss made 22,000. They got the landing speed down to sixty-five miles per hour; two miles lower than the Curtiss.

Egtvedt went to Washington to talk to General Patrick. The General hadn't yet received the report on the tests. "Boeing does not have the facilities aerodynamically to work out anything of any significance," Mason Patrick said.

"But we . . ."

"You are a small outfit. Curtiss has research facilities, a big engineering department. You cannot expect to compete with them on a matter of this kind."

Egtvedt felt a hot flush blurring his planned argument, then it flooded out discretion and took command. It conjured up words ready to leap back. He looked about the room. The mahogany orderliness of the place restored a semicalm. He remembered where he was and to whom he was talking. "General," he said, "I hope the results of the tests out at McCook will convince you we have the ability to provide something that you would want to purchase." Egtvedt departed as through an escape hatch. The corridors of the Munitions Building offered no solace.

The procurement of the Curtiss was too far along to be stopped, but Dayton would give Boeing an experimental order for the pursuit being tested and for two others under way at Seattle. The planes would be called the PW-9s: pursuit, water-cooled, type number nine. There was no money for any more.

In Washington, disconsolate, Egtvedt completed the deal. When he got an invitation to watch a battleship bombing exercise off the Virginia Capes, he grabbed it. It would be a holiday from worry.

The transport *St. Mihiel* turned out to be something less than a pleasure cruiser. The bunk room was steamy hot through the night of September 4. Egtvedt was glad when the sounding of reveille intruded upon the heavy breathing about him at 5:30 A.M.

The trial about to take place was the first since Billy Mitchell's bombers attacked a group of captured German ships in 1921. The Navy had turned out full force for that exercise, expecting to see the dreadnoughts ride serenely through Mitchell's fireworks. Two years later the smoke still hadn't cleared from the furore that following their sinking. This time the exercise was being played down—simply a means of disposing of the battleships *Virginia* and *New Jersey* in accordance with the Covenant on Naval Armaments of February 1922. But it was a deadly serious game. These two ships had cost U. S. taxpayers $12 million in 1904. If they could be wiped out by a few Martin bombers, Mitchell would hold trump cards in his campaign.

When Egtvedt and George Tidmarsh got out on deck after

With Model C and first international air
mail: Eddie Hubbard (left) and Boeing.

PW-9 inspection, Claire Egtvedt at right.

A Model 40 mail plane crosses Ruby Mountains.

William E. Boeing, Phil Johnson, with Navy fighter.

Passengers await "80" Trimotor departure.

Monomail over Lake Washington.

P-26 pursuit, B-9 bomber.

The 247, first of the twin-engine transports.

Over-the-weather Stratoliner.

Atlantic Clipper takes off.

Original B-17
Flying Fortress.

Flying Fortress assault on Fortress Europe,
vapor trails behind.

The B-29 Superfortress.

Bill Allen takes a B-47 flight.

At right, Stratojet leap-off from Boeing Field, JATO-assisted.

Pan American Stratocruiser arrives at New York.

The intercontinental B-52, flaps extended for take-off.

Renton rolls out the jet 707.

mess, the sea and sky were obscured in heavy fog. "What's our position?" Tidmarsh asked an officer.

"Off Cape Hatteras. A hundred eighty miles from Langley Field."

By 8:30 the fog had thinned enough to reveal the battleships on the horizon. In a few minutes more the sun burned hot on the deck. There was a buzz of excitement.

"Great day for Mitchell," someone was saying. The General was to lead the attack personally. Eyes were watching the sky for him. General Pershing, General Patrick and other high officers were on the bridge. Two blimps carrying photographers approached at low altitude and circled pompously.

At nine o'clock the drone of engines signaled the first attack. Six Martin bombers, big biplanes, were headed for the *New Jersey* at an altitude of about 10,000 feet. They were flying single file, spaced a considerable distance apart. The announcer said they carried six-hundred-pound bombs.

Eighteen bombs dropped. Four of them hit the deck with an eruption of smoke. One or two dropped into the water close to the *New Jersey*'s hull. This was considered the most destructive point of aim because of the effect of the water pressure on the hull. A boat went over to check the damage, which was minor. Then seven more Martins approached at 6,000 feet altitude, each carrying a 2,000-pound bomb. All sent up fountains of water two hundred yards astern.

"They'd have to do better than that in war," said Egtvedt. The *New Jersey* was a sitting duck, yet they'd missed her.

An artillery major said he could easily have shot the bombers down with anti-aircraft.

"Look, though," said Tidmarsh. "She's beginning to list." Now they could see a hole torn in the side amidships, flooding some of the *New Jersey*'s thirty-three watertight compartments. The bombers went back to refuel and reload.

Egtvedt was thoughtful. "Major McDill told me in Dayton that they've cancelled all experimental bomber contracts due to lack of efficient design," he said. "They want to be able to carry

4,000 pounds, and to have speed enough to offer some protection."

"Think we should get into that field?" Tidmarsh asked.

"Guess we'd better pull out the irons we already have in the fire," said Egtvedt. He was thinking of General Patrick and the pursuit, and the new trainer they were building to demonstrate to the Navy. "But I certainly think we should get into it eventually."

Just before noon the third attack by the string of seven Martins, this time with two 1,100-pound bombs each, approached at 3,000 feet. They passed up the *New Jersey* and centered on the *Virginia*, sitting proudly with her massive stacks and bulwarks. Before the spectators were well set for the new inning, the bombs dropped and a tremendous belch of black smoke enveloped the battleship, pluming upward in a column 1,500 feet high. The thunderous report was echoed by a chorus of exclamations from the *St. Mihiel*'s decks. When the smoke cleared, the *Virginia* looked like a toy ship that had been kicked by a heavy boot. The precise handiwork of its superstructure was swept away. All three stacks and both masts were gone. A lone crane and a turret stood watch over a deckload of junk. In the *Virginia*'s distress another bomb plunged deep alongside, shaking her to the heart. She heeled over, bathing her wounded side, then kept on rolling. In a rush of foam her keel came out of the water. Yard by yard the Atlantic claimed her. The spectators watched her go. No one liked to see a ship sink, even an empty one. Egtvedt felt as never before the deadly possibilities of the airplane.

In the afternoon another flight finished off the *New Jersey* and sent her hunting the depths for her companion. A Navy Department representative said it was an impressive demonstration of coast defense. "Obviously they wouldn't have the range to touch a fleet at sea," he added.

Phil Johnson wrote that the new Navy trainer they were building had been flown. "Everyone is tickled pink with it.

Eddie Hubbard says it's the best ship he has ever handled." They had equipped the trainer with the new Lawrence radial engine, in which the Navy had taken quite an interest. The engine was air-cooled and had the advantage of eliminating the radiator. Anxious to give it a demonstration, Egtvedt went to Pensacola to meet Hubbard with the new plane.

The Boeing was in competition not only with a Huff-Daland but also with planes submitted by Martin and the Naval Aircraft Factory at Philadelphia. "Yours looks about the best," one of the instructors confided to Hubbard. "The Martin is too big. The Philadelphia plane is too dangerous—falls into a spin from almost any position. The Huff is your closest competition." After several days of flying, Lieutenant G. L. Compo, the engineering officer on the trial board, came to Hubbard. "We can't get your plane into a tailspin," he said. "It's too stable."

"Isn't that good?" asked Eddie Hubbard.

"As long as other planes spin, we can't buy a trainer that you can't learn to spin in."

Egtvedt and Hubbard decided they could make the ship spin by adjusting the stabilizer to its maximum up angle. The technique of getting into a tailspin was to stall a plane by slowing it to less than flying speed, then kick the rudder over which should put it into a spiral dive. The stabilizer adjustment would cause it to stall, or lose flying speed, at a steeper nose-up angle, and should ensure that it would go into a spin when it suddenly nosed down.

Hubbard took Compo along to try it. They went up to 2,600 feet. Hubbard stalled and kicked the rudder hard over. They went into a spin quite normally but after about four turns Hubbard noticed the spin was turning faster and getting flatter. The nose wouldn't stay down. He kicked the opposite rudder and pushed over the stick. The controls had no effect. The earth was twisting below like a great wheel. He gunned the motor to put a slipstream on the tail and improve his control. It only spun more rapidly. "Must be turning so fast that the slipstream misses the tail," he reasoned.

It occurred to him to readjust the stabilizer, but the spinning had him whipped back in the corner. Drawing up all his strength against the invisible force, he got hold of the handle, but the load on the stabilizer was too great. He couldn't move it.

Pensacola Bay, gyrating wildly, was coming up fast. All he could do was pull back on the elevators to make the plane flatter, and check the drop as much as possible. They kept whirling flatly, then hit. The pontoon twisted off under them and they sat there on the water. Hubbard and Compo looked at each other blankly for a moment, then climbed up on top of the upper wing. They were there talking it over when Egtvedt arrived full speed across the bay in a flying boat.

"What did it look like?" Hubbard asked Egtvedt.

"Like a falling maple seed. A flat spin."

"Who ever heard of a flat spin?" said Hubbard. "There is no such thing."

Compo began to laugh. "But we did it. Safest way I ever saw to wreck an airplane. You come down so easy."

Egtvedt wasn't so sure he was being funny.

"It's nothing," said Compo. "I want to be the first to go up again when you get it fixed."

They hashed and rehashed the accident. While they were having a Curtiss pontoon installed, they lengthened the rudder, moved the engine forward two inches, and put the stabilizer back to zero. "You'd better wait till we try it," Egtvedt told Compo. In the new condition, they found they could successfully tailspin it and bring it out without going into the uncontrollable flat spin. But there was concern now about rust in the steel tube body, around salt water. The Huff-Daland had only a steel engine mount and a stick-and-wire body. That would be easier to maintain, some argued. The conclusion of the competition was delayed.

9. *Much to Be Discovered*

There'd have to be some more business landed soon. Egtvedt stayed east to see what could be done. Principal production work in the plant now was on an Army order for the rebuilding of two hundred de Havillands with welded-steel frames, cloth covered—a job that wouldn't take long. Three of the DH's were being further remodeled into observation planes, but these had developed the same longitudinal instability—nose hunting up and down—as the first PW-9 pursuit had. "We'll have to experiment with the center of gravity and add more stabilizer," Marsh wrote. Egtvedt wondered if there weren't some better way than trial and error to solve these problems.

Seeking new leads for some orders, he visited Army fields and Navy bases to talk to pilots and engineering officers. Christmas of 1923 caught him at Randolph Field, San Antonio. Major Ralph Royce, the commanding officer, said he'd better come out to the house to spend the holiday.

"What new planes does the Air Service want for Christmas?" Egtvedt asked Royce.

"First we need to find a Santa Claus," said the major. "There are no appropriations for new planes. I'll have to keep nursing my Jennies." They were planes left from the war.

To most congressmen, disarmament and aircraft appropriations didn't seem to go together. Billy Mitchell was getting into trouble.

Barnstorming pilots who were overhauling their Jennies, getting ready in the spring to sideslip over barbed-wire fences into cow pastures from town to town, gave Egtvedt the facts of their business. "When I crack this plane up I can get another Army Jenny for $700," said one. "A new plane would cost me $4,000. The season is short. You figure out how many rides I'd have to sell at five dollars a hop to buy a plane from you. Don't bother to figure my gas and lodging."

Egtvedt mounted the long steps of the Post Office Building in Washington to talk about mail planes. "I agree we should be developing some new ones," said Colonel Paul Henderson, second assistant postmaster general in charge of the air mail. "But so far I haven't been able to sell the idea."

At the Post Office overhaul base at Maywood, Illinois, Egtvedt was told politely, "The DH's we've rebuilt are serving very well. The plywood sides polish up nice, and there's no fabric for the mail bags to punch through."

With the spring thaw of '24, however, new hopes sprouted. The Navy declared Boeing the winner of its competition and ordered forty-nine of the new trainers, to be called NB-1s and NB-2s, "N" being the symbol for Navy trainer, "B" for Boeing. Colonel Henderson announced the Post Office could buy one experimental mail plane from each company that wanted to go ahead and build one and could meet the specifications. Mr. Boeing authorized a Boeing entry. It would be partly based on the NB trainer, but would have a plywood body and would use the Liberty motor which the Post Office required because the government had a big stock of them from the war.

The Air Service said it was going to put the Boeing PW-9 pursuit through a mock-combat competition with the Curtiss to decide which plane would be purchased with the new year's appropriation. Engineer Bob Minshall went to observe the trials at Selfridge Field where Major Tooey Spaatz was in command. Spaatz ordered all his squadron pilots to take turns fighting each other, one in the Boeing, one in the Curtiss, then to trade planes and do it again. Young Minshall watched wide-eyed as the rival planes burned tighter and tighter circles. The PW-9 would usually end up on the inside. To Minshall's joy, the pilots came down afterward and pinned bouquets all over the Boeing.

"Nothing mean about it," they said. "Just like driving an automobile."

The results of the combat trials upset Washington, George Tidmarsh, the company representative there, reported. "The Army was all set to buy the Curtiss again. General Patrick still doesn't want to buy from us, but he can't ignore the tests." In September 1924, the Army decided to order both types, giving Boeing a contract for twelve. "We're beginning to get somewhere," Egtvedt thought.

The NB trainers were coming out. The mail plane was under way. The plant was busy. It all looked good again.

On January 16, 1925, Boeing discontinued the office of chairman and resumed the presidency, Johnson was elected first vice president and general manager, and Egtvedt vice president and chief engineer. Gott had resigned after a disagreement with Boeing.

The new vice president and chief engineer received no warning to batten down the hatches for an approaching storm. On February 5, Lieutenant Al Williams got an NB-1 trainer in a flat spin and crashed, unhurt, at Anacostia, Virginia. While other Navy pilots were laughing at the famous flier's slip, Lieutenant H. J. Brow rode another NB like a whirling dervish into San Diego Bay. Someone counted thirty revolutions per minute. Thoroughly alarmed, the Navy ordered all further flying stopped while the Bureau of Aeronautic Engineers ran wind-tunnel tests. No one was hurt yet.

March arrived. The Navy design section looked at the test results and proposed larger tail surfaces as a cure for the trouble. Anacostia pilots said no, the body would have to be lengthened to give the tail more wind. George Tidmarsh wired that the time element was critical. "They'll soon be planning next year's procurement. We have an enormous sales resistance to meet."

Lieutenant Ralph Ofstie arrived in Seattle to make flight tests with enlarged tail surfaces. For some days he couldn't get the plane into its unusual spin—into auto-rotation, as they had come to call it. Then he took one of the men from the plant along as a passenger and the precocious craft did her trick. The rudder was useless. But he got out of it with maximum down elevator.

Ofstie and Eddie Hubbard kept trying different tail modifications. Theory upon theory was checked. Evidence was conflicting. Fin and stabilizer changes seemed to have little effect.

The clock struck April. "Everyone's laughing at us," wrote Tidmarsh from Washington. "They say we've been hauling in the money and this serves us right." Work was under way on a new wing, forced draft. Another plane was being constructed with a lengthened body. "We're clogged with unshipped planes," said Phil Johnson. "We'll have to lick this or shut the place down."

It turned May. Ofstie went to Anacostia with a new set of the tail surfaces, to try to get the ship cleared. He felt that with proper flying procedure, it was O.K. "You'll have to prove it to me personally," said Lieutenant Commander Marc Mitscher, head of the Bureau of Aeronautics plans division. "I'll ride with you." Ofstie took Mitscher to 4,000 feet, dumped the plane into a normal spin entry, then tried to straighten out. The spin flattened and the tail was whipping around faster. The desolate whine of the wind through the whirling wing wires increased its pitch. Ofstie tried everything. They flattened onto the ground with a twisting crunch. The lieutenant pulled a sprained ankle out of the wreckage and turned, done dog, to Mitscher. "I'm terribly sorry, Commander."

After this, the Navy washed its hands. "There's been divided responsibility between you and us," Rear Admiral W. A. Moffett told Boeing. "We want it distinctly understood now that it's all on your shoulders."

There was a mighty hope that the new wing would be the solution. "If the wing doesn't cure it, I'll be greatly astonished," Egtvedt wrote Tidmarsh, "and more chagrined than I've ever been in my life."

It was June when Hubbard took the plane up. He entered a spin that looked normal for a while. Then—was it happening?

Hope fought what eyes were seeing. "No, it can't be. Straighten it out, Ed. Straighten it out!" Egtvedt's spirits whirled in torment with Eddie all the way to the ground and flattened like the limp linen fabric that lay in a heap, Hubbard climbing out of it. Hubbard's ankle was injured and they sent him to the hospital.

Phil Johnson tried to reassure Washington, "We're doing all we can. There is no scientific solution. We've got all they have at NACA, Europe, anywhere. We just have to keep experimenting."

The plane with a lengthened body was ready for flight. Les Tower, a lanky blond who had come from a Montana farm to study engineering and learn to fly, put down his drafting tools and walked over to Egtvedt one morning. "I'd be glad to fly it for you if you want me to," he said. He got the job.

Tower found he could hold the new plane in a spin for two turns and then it would straighten itself out nicely. That didn't pacify the naval inspector at the plant. "Hell, we want a free-spinning airplane," he said. "One you can spin all you want and get it out any time you want to."

Tower went back at it like an engineer. He started by varying the amount of throw on the elevators, plotting and calculating the effect. Egtvedt for the first time began to feel a sense of orderliness. "Les Tower is a find," he told Phil. "In these things, we don't need a pilot so much as an engineer in the plane."

July. Tower found that by limiting the up-throw of the elevators to twenty degrees, it was impossible to get into any kind of spin, flat or regular. Grasping at this, Phil Johnson reminded the Navy that when the NB-1 was first demonstrated at Pensacola it was unspinnable. "We changed it, to make it spin, at your request. If you want to eliminate the hazard, let's return the plane to its original condition, a nonspinnable airplane."

The Navy said they'd consider the suggestion. In September, they decided to accept the planes, limiting the up-throw of the elevators to twenty degrees as Les Tower proposed.

January 7, 1926, the Navy released the planes for training

flights, but no stunting would be allowed. Egtvedt sighed, a sigh of relief, not of success.

Work went on. Man is made of springy metal. Bent under pressure, he bounces back to form through a power not his own —as long as he has something better to think about. At the plant on the Duwamish they had plenty to think about. Getting the rest of the NB trainers out of the shops. There was trouble with vibration in the new radial engine. Fred Laudan, the project engineer, said they'd have to weld a fitting for a brace-wire on the engine mount to steady it. He went with Phil Johnson to the shops to see about the change.

"Can't do it without tearing down the engines," the welding foreman objected. "We'll burn up all your engines."

"If we have to disassemble them it's going to cost an awful lot of money," said Walter Way, the assembly foreman. "You better weld them in place."

"Won't work."

Fred Laudan looked to Johnson, many years the junior of these factory-wise supervisors. "Well, now," asked Phil, disarmingly, "if you *did* have a case where you had to weld it in place, how would you go about it?"

"I'd probably fit a little piece of asbestos over it like this, and come in at it this way."

"That's the way we'll do it," said Phil Johnson. He was out the door fast, the two foremen gazing after him, Laudan suppressing a smile.

Alongside the trainers on the assembly floor, the PW-9 pursuits were coming well. A Navy carrier-fighter version of the PW-9 had been worked out; the Navy wasn't too enthusiastic, partly, no doubt, because of the NB-1 trouble. But that mischievous child had its virtues. The five hundred tests of the NB-1 had proved the advantages of light-weight, air-cooled engines, and a Navy fighter was being designed around the air-cooled Wright.

These were the regular projects. Then there was the special

project, the air-size Kirsten model. In a padlocked shed back of the woodshop was a thing of wonderment that carried Egtvedt outside the board walls, outside the plant and right into the blue. Frederick Kirsten, a thin-faced professor with a squint of genius in his eye, had sold Boeing on trying out a whole new principle of propulsion in flight. "Let the wings be the propeller," said Kirsten. "We can make a wing in strips that will rotate like the blades of a lawnmower. Change the angle of the blades and you can fly up, down, forward or backward." Egtvedt was skeptical about its mechanical complexity, but intrigued. Its novelty washed away the flat spins, the exasperating rigidity of airplane design rules.

Viewed through the doorway of the Kirsten shed, the brood of planes in the plant looked much like the original Wright brothers machine. Was the whole of the art circumscribed in the Wright papers and the deductions from them?

Knowledge is gained by accurate observation, but wasn't observation a tricky thing? It seemed to depend on the point of view. Didn't people see mostly what they expected to see? Didn't they often fail to see the answer because they were looking the wrong place? Ptolemy thought he observed the sun circling the earth and his deductions straitjacketed astronomy for centuries. Was there a higher principle of flight still to be discovered?

Egtvedt thought of the long-ranging sea gull, using the tiniest package of energy; the quick converting perch and push of the hummingbird; the hornet's bullet drive. Knowing only nature's law, they had no stability problems, no enigmas of autorotation. Wasn't there much to be discovered? Edison's fact-packed mind had concluded that we know only the millionth part of 1 per cent about anything. "We've been putting most of our time on structure and strength," Egtvedt thought. "We've been taking aerodynamics and propulsion for granted." A nagging picture came into view: General Patrick saying that they didn't have any research.

Egtvedt went back to the NB trainer. There was no longer

the frantic compulsion to solve the problem, but he wanted to see order and law in it. "Sometimes we'd get autorotation and sometimes we wouldn't, with the ship in the same condition," he recalled. "That's odd. There has to be some variable."

Where to find it? When did the normal spin become the flat, uncontrollable one? Like a top, when it got spinning. How did you spin a top? By giving it a good start. It was the rudder that started all the turning in the first place. If you threw the rudder over too far, it would get the spinning turn going faster and faster, tighter and tighter. If you put in a stop to limit the throw of the rudder.... That was it, he was sure. Les Tower did some tests that seemed to confirm it. Egtvedt put the whole thing out of mind. Well, almost out of mind. He could see better now how great was the need for aerodynamic research.

Word came that the Post Office would buy the experimental Boeing Model 40 mail plane, recently completed. It was loaded on a freight car for delivery to the air-mail base at Concord, over the hills from Oakland, California.

10. *Flying the Mail*

The engine-driven twentieth century was rolling well by 1926. If the Boeing Company had emerged from under a cloud, so had America. The war by now was a nightmare forgotten. The post-war slump was a thing of the past. Peace and prosperity, which had before unlocked the young century's inventive treasures, had returned now to put them to work. The country breathed deeply, stretched its arms and felt good. "The business of America is business," said President Coolidge.

But the aviation business was one that had not yet grown robust. Coolidge appointed the Morrow Board to study its needs and problems. Billy Mitchell, recently demoted from general to colonel, told the board that America was asleep. Aircraft men paraded the images of risk, uncertainty, and small reward that had discouraged healthy planning and research. Fliers remembered the dream of Tennyson's "argosies of magic sails dropping down with costly bales." "Give air commerce some support and the dream can come true," they said.

Awakened by the Morrow Board's report, Congress passed the Aviation Five-Year Program, changing the Air Service to the Army Air Corps, setting up a plan for five years of Army and Navy procurement, and giving industry proprietary rights to its designs. If a company came up with a good plane, the services could negotiate directly with it. This new program was what the aircraft people had been hoping for.

The Air Commerce Act was passed to encourage civil aeronautics. It established federal rather than state regulation of the airways and appropriated more funds for beacon lights along the air-mail routes. The Post Office Department, which had successfully recreated the old Pony Express in the modern image, now laid plans to turn the air mail over to private operators.

Phil Johnson and Claire Egtvedt moved to the driver's seat of the Boeing Airplane Company. Bill Boeing had begun to think of retirement. "I want to retire at fifty if I can manage it," he said. He would be fifty in 1931. He gave Johnson the presidency and stepped again to the position of chairman of the board. Egtvedt became first vice president.

Phil took stock. The assembly shop was well occupied with PW-9 pursuits and their Navy counterpart, the FB fighter. The experimental air-cooled Navy fighter was being finished. There were five hundred employees now, fifty men in Engineering. Monty Monteith, who had finally left the engineering division at McCook, was a new addition to the department. Although not large, Boeing was still just about as big as anything in the airplane business. That was all on the plus side of the ledger.

On the liability side, in spite of the market's rosier hue, they had few new orders on the books.

Eddie Hubbard had strayed. "My heart isn't in this test flying," he had said. "I want to operate commercial airplanes. It's time to start using the airplane to serve the public." Eddie's mail route to Victoria seemed to him only a beginning. When he had gone east the year before to talk to the Post Office he had met Ed Gott, now vice president in charge of sales for Fokker Aircraft. "We're going to get clear out of the military field," Gott had said. "Nothing but commercial ships. Why don't you work with us? We can form an operating company and bid for the Pasco, Washington, to Elko, Nevada, air-mail route." This had been the call of the open road to Hubbard. He had ended up, however, not flying the Elko route but operating Fokkers in Los Angeles and serving as western representative for Gott's company.

Other competitors were active. Keyes of Curtiss was organizing an operating group with the hope it could become the American Express of the air. Henry Ford was getting into the airplane business. Detroit could build the air age overnight. Ford would produce the big Stout trimotor, possibly he'd form a company to operate it.

Phil Johnson felt a responsibility. "Claire," he said, "I'd like to talk with you about our engineering." Egtvedt saw Johnson, the executive, wrinkle over his eye, but casual in the old manner. "We've sold the Post Office one mail plane," said Phil. "You can bet a lead nickel they aren't going to buy any more. What do we have coming along in new designs for commercial operators?"

"I've been thinking about a passenger version of the 40, and a flying boat," said Claire.

"We're going to have to organize our engineering to meet the future. It's been a little loose, Claire. You are gone a lot of the time. That's necessary, but you should have more responsibility delegated and keep these projects coming along."

"I've wanted to do this," said Claire. "We need more research and development work. Now that we have Monteith here, he could take charge of all experimental work and Louis Marsh can handle production engineering." Johnson approved. Monteith was a good organizer, he felt.

They now put renewed emphasis on the pursuit project. The PW-9C was about to be put through a combat competition with the latest Curtiss. One thing was causing serious difficulty. In maneuvers, the flying wires would run against the landing wires where they crossed between the wings. If fastened together, there was no give and one would pull out. If not fastened, they chafed and broke.

"I have a man who's pretty good at coming up with ideas," said Fred Laudan, the project engineer. "I'll put Johnny Haberlin on it."

Haberlin had been working on cockpit arrangements. He was the sort who was happy working on a small part or a big one. To him, the weakest link might hold the very key to success; each job was a challenge, an interesting problem to be solved. Haberlin considered the crossed-wires problem.

"No use looking at the can'ts," he thought. "What is it we want them to do?" He wanted them to seesaw freely without touching each other. He held two crossed pencils in his left hand and moved them with his other hand, as though they were wires in tension. He noticed that with only one hand free, he could move but one pencil at a time. "That's it," said Haberlin. "Hold one rigid and let the other slip." He quickly sketched a bullet-shaped finger to separate the crossed wires with one end screwed tight, the other loose.

"Well," said Fred Laudan, "that was simple."

Laudan came into the drafting room jubilantly waving a telegram a few weeks later. "The good Lord gave us the right answer on that one," he said. "Our flying wires held in the dog fight. That Handy Andy gets us an order for forty planes."

The Boeing was winning elsewhere, too. In October the new Navy FB-3 set a world speed record for pursuits at the National Air Races in Philadelphia. Meanwhile, Experimental Design 69,

a Navy fighter equipped with the new Pratt & Whitney air-
cooled Wasp engine, got in the air for its first tests. Les Tower
was all smiles. "This is it," he said. "The Wasp makes us an
airplane."

Early in 1926 Phil Johnson had been mulling over the possibility of starting a company to carry passengers between
Seattle, Vancouver and Victoria. "It would give us a chance to
demonstrate a commercial product," he said. Egtvedt liked the
idea; he only wished that Hubbard were still around. Boeing
agreed to back the plan. Design projects were set up for a flying
boat and a passenger land plane, and Phil sought Eddie Hubbard's return to manage the operation. Organization and operating plans were well along, but no word from Eddie. It was the
sort of thing he had wanted to do all along; surely he'd be
interested.

It was late fall when Eddie returned to Seattle, but he didn't
want to talk about a Puget Sound airline. He was hopping with
enthusiasm over a bigger challenge. The Post Office was going
to put its Chicago to San Francisco route up for bids November
15. "This is the opportunity of a century, Claire," he said.

Egtvedt was taken aback. "You're talking about a huge undertaking."

"I've got all the figures on mileage and pounds of mail carried.
If you can produce some mail planes I know we can operate
them successfully."

Egtvedt's pulse quickened. "That's a lot of country. The
distances are big. You'll have winter blizzards to contend with."

"We could do it."

"Night flights? Are the beacons in all the way?"

"Every twenty-five miles."

"We have the experimental 40 mail plane." Egtvedt was
tumbling fast. "We could modify that. Probably could make
room for a couple of passengers and still have space for mail.
How much capacity would you need?"

"The DH's will carry five hundred pounds. The Douglas

that Western Express is using will carry 1,000 pounds. We ought to beat those, and have some allowance for growth."

"The 40 might do it, if we had a little more power."

"Let's get away from the Liberty motor. It's a dodo."

The new Pratt & Whitney Wasp should be just right, Egtvedt felt. It was two hundred pounds lighter than the Liberty. "How would you like an air-cooled motor? We could allow two hundred pounds more for mail."

"Good." Eddie was eager. "I think we can get our costs way under the amount the Post Office allows."

The thought of the bid stopped Claire short. "We'll have to talk to Bill. Have you ever discussed anything like this with him?"

"No, just local flying, but Mr. Boeing's pretty game, you know."

"Let me work on the design end," said Egtvedt. "You work out the personnel and maintenance costs and I'll figure the operating cost of the plane. We can put our figures together and we'll have something to show Bill."

A few days later the newspapers carried a story on Post Office plans. The New York to San Francisco route would be turned over to private operators in two pieces: New York to Chicago, and Chicago to San Francisco. Bill Boeing took *The New York Times* at home. His wife Bertha got a look at it first. She noticed the story dealing with the air mail. She had often talked flying with Eddie Hubbard and this looked interesting. She folded the paper with the story on top and watched her husband read it. He didn't say anything. Neither did she.

Within a day or two Hubbard and Egtvedt went up to Boeing's office armed with a fat file and an idea that was fairly walking under its own power. They laid it all out. Boeing was silent quite a while. "This is something foreign to our experience," he said.

"I've logged 150,000 miles on the Victoria route without any trouble," said Hubbard. "And made money."

"But this is over the whole western half of the country.

You've got mountain ranges and winter storms to contend with. It would be a mighty large venture. Risky."

They went over it all again. When there was nothing left to say, Egtvedt and Hubbard departed. "It was a good try," said Egtvedt.

There were things in Bill Boeing that didn't show. Strong roots, in rocky soil, but growing tenaciously. He didn't reach back for the phrase in their original articles of incorporation, "to act as a common carrier of passengers and freight," or to the hope Eddie Hubbard had voiced when they brought that first mail bag back from Vancouver, B. C. But they were there. Boeing liked to finish what he had started. For years they had talked the utility of the airplane. The public wasn't listening. Here, at last, was the opportunity to offer the airplane as a public service.

Boeing had the resources. His company had the reputation. If anybody could, they could go at it with success and safety as the goal. He found it hard to avoid admitting these facts, just to himself. He tossed through the night. The idea had gained command by morning. Boeing was up for an early breakfast. Bertha knew something was astir. "What's on your mind, Bill?" she asked.

"Maybe we'll bid for the Chicago to San Francisco route." Boeing looked at his wife. "What would you think of that?"

"Why not? It will develop a market for planes," she said.

"It will be a hazardous thing. Big."

Egtvedt got to the plant at 7:30 A.M., bringing back the stack of paper that had seemed so alive the day before. The telephone operator hailed him. "Call Mr. Boeing right away. He's been trying to get you for half an hour."

Egtvedt hurried to the telephone. "Get Hubbard and come on up here," said Boeing. "I want to talk some more about that proposition. It kept me awake all night." When they got to the Hoge Building, Boeing wanted to go over the figures again, wanted to know about the bond that would be required, compared Hubbard's cost with the Post Office figures. Egtvedt and Hubbard had planned to base the bid on a bigger load than the Post Office carried. Air-mail poundage had been increasing and they thought some publicity would increase it more. Besides, there was the opportunity for passengers and express, which Post Office planes couldn't carry. The plan would require the building of a fleet of twenty-five planes, to be ready on the line by July 1, 1927.

The Post Office would allow up to $3.00 per pound for the first one thousand miles and thirty cents for each additional one hundred miles. The figure they came up with was $1.50 per pound for the first thousand and fifteen cents for each additional one hundred miles. A vast difference, but that was the way they came out.

"Those figures look all right to me," said Boeing, finally. "Let's send them in."

On January 28, word came that they were low bidders. Way low. The nearest bid was $2.24. Harry S. New, the postmaster general, doubted that theirs was a reliable bid. Rival companies assured him it couldn't be done and he didn't want a bankrupt carrier on his hands at the start of this most important transcontinental air-mail contract. The bid had been entered in the name of Edward Hubbard and Boeing Airplane Company. The Post Office required a $500,000 bond to insure performance of the contract. Bill Boeing underwrote the bond and the contract was signed.

The spruce wing ribs, the arc-welded steel-tube bodies, the stretched linen covering for the 40-A mail-transports were the finest, fastest workmanship that had yet gone through the shops. Through eleven years of trial and triumph, the men of Boeing had gained a confidence. They had built five hundred military airplanes of miscellaneous types. Yet deep down, every one of them had longed to see their airplanes out one day serving the public. Now that dream was within reach. They dug in. Phil

asked Oliver West, the production chief, whose memory for
part numbers was a marvel to the staff, to shepherd the work
through the factory. West didn't lose a sheep.

Boeing Air Transport was organized as a separate company,
with Phil Johnson as president, Ed Hubbard as vice president
in charge of operations, Boeing as chairman of the board.
Egtvedt became general manager of the airplane company.

While the 40-A's were building, Charles A. Lindbergh headed
out over the Atlantic for Paris in his little Ryan monoplane.
The suspense that built up in the thirty-three and a half hours of
his silent crossing was cracked open when the sight of silver
wings appeared in the Paris twilight. The floodlights and the
acclaiming thousands at LeBourget Field May 21, 1927, awakened
the world to flight. The airline plan was timely.

In Seattle the race to build the 40-A's finished with a sprint.
On June 30, all twenty-five planes were gassed up and waiting
along the line, ready for the official start, the midnight transfer
of the mail at Omaha from Post Office de Havilland to Boeing
Air Transport.

Next day a plucky Chicago newspaper woman, Jane Eads, of
the *Herald and Examiner*, was to be the first Boeing Air Transport passenger. She was the center of attention. In high heels,
knee-length business suit, feather boa and felt cloche, she was
headed for the clouds. At 9:30 P.M., in the harsh white of arc
lights, Pilot Ira Biffle helped Jane up on the step pad of the
lower wing and through the low door to the tiny cabin between
the two wings. Biffle jazzed the motor twice and pushed out
into the black.

Model 40

Jane Eads' heart palpitated as she began her role of trail blazer
in a new form of transcontinental travel. The pilot, out of sight
and out of hearing in the open cockpit behind, seemed far
away. Alone with the night, behind the constant vibrant drone
of the motor, cutting the darkness at ninety-five miles an hour,

Jane found companionship for a time with a thin crescent moon beyond the left wing. Now and then a sparkle of light drifted by in the black below. She wasn't sleepy. She turned the switch on the glazed dome light in the ceiling. Cozy. The sea green of the little walls was broken by a sliding window on either side. She let in the cool air. This was fun.

Later the crescent disappeared and Jane began to feel rocky. The plane tilted and tipped, then dropped as in a hole. Was it supposed to act this way? "I'm scared," she admitted to herself. Then with a hard jolt she realized they were landing. Iowa City.

They passed over Des Moines without coming down. A city without buildings, just strings of jewels. The flight over western Iowa was under a canopy of stars. It seemed strange that the sky should be lighter and more real than the earth below. The Boeing flew straight and steady into the western night. The changeless roar of the engine was strong, sweet music. How odd, and how wonderful, to be settling for the night up here! She found the leather-cushioned seats just large enough to curl up on, kitten fashion. It was peace.

The landing jolts of Omaha awakened her. Reporters were there to interview *her.* "I could fly forever," said Jane. "I love it." She transferred to a new plane, piloted by Jack Knight. Shoving off at 1:45 A.M., Knight wished Jane "a merry trip." "Same to you—and a *safe* one," she called back.

Before morning the air grew choppy. Great flashes of lightning lit up the sky. The crackling streaks seemed to be breaking all about them. The plane was being lifted and thrown about. Jane put her head on her knees and tried not to think about falling. Then it ended as suddenly as it had begun. There was a yellow fringe on the horizon behind, which grew and flooded the earth with a golden glow. She remembered how a pilot had told her he never knew why the birds sang so sweetly until he saw his first dawn from the sky. They came down at North Platte, then lifted again for Cheyenne, with the sun setting fire to the edge of the clouds on the horizon ahead.

Out of Cheyenne, past the bald, rippling foothills, she saw

what she first thought a mirage, the snow-crested magnificence of the Medicine Bow range. Hugh Barker, the new pilot, pushed the Boeing higher and higher. Jane grew drowsy and her legs were heavy with the altitude and the bumping. The road seemed as rocky here as it was below. They skinned past Elk Mountain and into Rock Springs.

A veteran now of the ups and downs and the vast, changing topography of the states, Jane flew on past the impossible white flats of the Great Salt Lake country, the forbidding waterless gulches of Nevada, the ultramarine blue of Lake Tahoe. Suddenly the yellow, razor-topped hills below her opened into San Francisco Bay. Twenty-three flying hours after leaving Chicago, Jane Eads put her foot on California soil, like an explorer who had discovered a new world. Air transportation.

Boeing Air Transport made money in its first month, and in the second and third. The public interest, aroused by the Lindbergh flight and now by a sky trail to California, was ringing the cash register. By the end of the year the line had carried 525 passengers and 230,000 pounds of mail. No serious trouble. But winter was harder going. Snow piled deep at Cheyenne, Salt Lake City, and Rock Springs. Blizzards tried to sweep the plains free of commercial airplane intrusion. Clouds hung low over the Sierra Nevada hump.

The Boeing pilots got the weather by telegram. But storm centers could pull in front of them on the way, and behind them. All they could do was get under, follow railroad tracks, watch intently for known valleys and passes through the mountains. What was up ahead? Look for a place to sit down or go on through? That was the decision that pressed on the pilot, alone with the mail, a $25,000 airplane, perhaps a passenger, and his own hide. Bill Boeing and Phil Johnson came to dread the ringing of the phone in the night. They had had no tragedy yet. Would this be one?

"I'm sure you could give your pilots the weather by short-wave radio," said Thorp Hiscock, Boeing's brother-in-law, at dinner with Johnson and Boeing one night. "With a two-way telephone they could get it from each other." Hiscock had a ranch in Yakima, Washington, but most of his waking hours he tinkered with radio.

"Could you build it?" asked Phil.

"Just put me to work."

Johnson could see that Boeing was reticent. He had said he didn't like to have relatives in the organization. "But Thorp may have just what we need," Phil counseled. When Boeing consented, Hiscock went to work in a shed at the plant and erected a tall pole for an experimental aerial. The Bell Laboratories were consulted. They were getting started on the problem, too. They weren't too hopeful of two-way communication because of the noise and interference of the airplane's engine.

"We'll work at it," said Hiscock. He put a short-wave receiver on a truck to cruise away from the plant while he broadcast records of the Two Black Crows, because they offered voice dialogue instead of music. Bill Lawrenz, his helper, drove the truck farther and farther away as Thorp tinkered. Lawrenz listened all the laughs out of the two somber comedians. Late at night, maybe up in the Cascades or down near Portland, he'd hear Hiscock sign off: "I'm going home now, Bill." Lawrenz, who couldn't talk back, would wheel around to spend the rest of the night getting home. "It's for science," he'd console himself.

Later they installed a short-wave set in a 40 and Eddie Allen, a Boeing Air Transport pilot, took Lawrenz's role as guinea pig. They moved from Seattle to Oakland where equipment was available. They tried every kind of shielding for the engine's interference. One day Allen didn't show up at the hangar. The hangar crew thought he was sick, but when they didn't locate him at home, they sent out a missing-persons alarm. He was found next day sunning himself on a beach. "I've run out of ideas," said Allen. "It's quieter here to listen for a new one."

By perseverance, the two-way radio was perfected, and with the help of Western Electric, was installed on the line.

Finding that the route was not paved with gravestones, more and more passengers sought tickets. The crawl-in box cabin of the 40 was admittedly inadequate. Monty Monteith, now chief engineer, went to work designing the Model 80, a big tri-motored biplane powered by Wasps. It would carry eighteen passengers, with window curtains and leather chairs. Steve Stimpson, San Francisco manager for the line, thought of adding a girl to the crew to serve box lunches and show the passengers the sights.

First the 40's, then the 80's gained a certain romantic fame. They were reliable, but to Claire Egtvedt they already appeared old and slow. Egtvedt no longer went to the shed where the Kirsten machine had pointed awkwardly to a new day in aeronautics. The Kirsten project had been written off as impractical. But the open hope it had stirred was in Egtvedt's consciousness. Boeing was established in the pursuit plane line —hauling passengers across the country—a major company in the airplane business. Had they arrived at their goal, or was this just a beginning? He had a feeling they had only touched the challenge of the sky.

BOOK TWO

THE INSPIRATION

What was the source of the kind of vision that made for aviation's burgeoning progress? When John Haberlin thought of those early years, how they had stepped into the unknown and found a footing, he felt there was a guiding hand toward progress that helped those who reached for it.

He remembered how often he had reached for it at night, alone with a problem assigned to him. He'd think and think till his mind was going in circles, then he'd put the puzzle away, knowing perfectly well that there was a right answer, and he'd go on to bed. What was it that would wake him up at four or five in the morning with the answer? It wanted to put itself on paper faster than he could sketch it. Then he'd gulp breakfast and get down to the plant to see if it would work, and it would.

Some explained it with a word they couldn't explain, inspiration. Others saw in it a law of science that was always there, waiting to be discovered or put to work. Haberlin thought of the phrase his minister had read from the Bible: *"Every good gift and every perfect gift is from above, and cometh down from the Father of lights. . . ."*

There were gifts in the late twenties and the thirties that would help men out of a world emergency.

1. *The All-Metal Idea*

The breeze that makes San Diego delightful was rustling the pepper trees and the palms along the bay shore. It was spring of 1928. Claire Egtvedt paused on the walkway to enjoy it for a moment before going to see Admiral Reeves aboard the aircraft carrier *Langley*. There was a familiar music in the air: the singing of Wasp motors in the F2-Bs and F3-Bs that were Boeing's contribution to the fleet. In the distance he could see several of the tiny fighters cutting scallops in the sky.

Commander Gene Wilson, the Admiral's senior aide, had told him the pilots liked the F2-B (the *F* meant fighter; *B*, Boeing), which weighed in at less than 2,000 pounds empty, and made 160 miles per hour. They weren't so enthusiastic, he said, about the next model, the F3-B, which had more wing span and was 900 pounds heavier, five miles an hour slower. "The kids really put up a howl when I told them we were going to make it still heavier, for a five-hundred-pound bomb. You've got to do the impossible and design one that'll carry a five-hundred-pound bomb, and still be as light as the F2-B."

Egtvedt had answered that they'd learned not to call anything impossible or they'd find someone else doing it. He was glad now he had said it because the new plane, the F4-B, was turning out to be a beauty. By changing from steel to duralumin, they had trimmed it down to 1,660 pounds and still it could carry the five-hundred-pound bomb. If the Admiral approved the new ship, they'd be in line for a big order from Washington.

The *Langley* was tied up to dock opposite the Administration building. Gene Wilson went with Egtvedt to the Admiral's cabin. Joseph Mason "Bull" Reeves, commander of aircraft squadrons,

Battle Fleet, met him with a hearty handshake. "Wilson tells
me the F4 is looking good," the Admiral said. They sat at a long,
green baize-covered table. Beyond it the metal bulkhead was
covered with sea charts.

"We were happy the way the ship turned out," said Egtvedt.
"A fleet of them would make a real striking force, wouldn't it,
Admiral? A lot more versatile than torpedo planes." Up to now
carrier fighters had been used only to protect the fleet. If they
could be used as an attacking force they'd become much more
important. Egtvedt remembered what aerial bombs had done to
the *Virginia* and *New Jersey* back in 1923.

"Striking force? Do you know what striking force is? Let me
tell you about it." "Bull" Reeves was speaking quietly now. He
was a scholar of naval science. "Your five-hundred-pound bomb
won't penetrate deck armor. A sixteen-inch projectile from a
battleship's turret delivers 60,000 foot-tons of striking force at
a single point. A flight of thirty-six F4's can deliver eight tons of
bombs, if they can get past enemy fighters. A battleship delivers
eight tons of projectiles every time it fires a round from all its
turrets, and it can keep on firing. A hundred rounds each from
four two-gun turrets is eight hundred tons of steel; two hundred
rounds, 1,600 tons. Multiply that by the force of the projectiles
striking at 2,000 feet per second and you get nearly 100,000,000
foot-tons of destructive force. One battleship."

Egtvedt reeled a little under the weight of the figures. Here
was a man who played a big game and knew how to play it for
keeps. "I'm not belittling your product," "Bull" Reeves continued.
"We love it. But I want you to see its place. The battleship is
called the capital ship because it carries the big punch. The
cruiser comes next. It's our patroller. Then we have the de-
stroyer, which can get around fast with torpedoes. A torpedo
plane can carry only 1,750 pounds. It's relatively ineffective, but
we take it along just as a football quarterback has his sneak play.
Sometime, under certain weather conditions, we may need the
torpedo plane to sneak in.

"The fighter plane is primarily to keep our ships from being bothered by enemy planes. It has an important job. If it can carry a five-hundred-pound bomb, so much the better, but there is nothing in the aircraft line that can pack the punch of a dreadnought. The airplane has its place, but it just isn't as effective a weapon as those we already have in the fleet. The airplane isn't a dreadnought."

With that the furrow in the Admiral's forehead melted. "Now back to the F4-B. If it turns out to be what Wilson says, we're going to want plenty of them. It'll be a more effective weapon than what we have. Any time you can make an airplane more effective, there's a use for it."

Egtvedt was glad for that last. He took it as a compliment to the men who had worked hard on the F4-B. But he left the carrier rudely awakened. *The airplane isn't a dreadnought. It just isn't as effective a weapon as those we already have.* He had never thought of it that way before.

"Bull" Reeves' words were a grain of sharp sand that he knew would remain an irritant until the truth of the Admiral's claim was dissolved. They hadn't yet built what Billy Mitchell called "air power." An irritant could be a stimulant. It brought a flood of ideas, like tears that wash a sandspeck from the eye. The airplane wasn't what it ought to be. It couldn't range out and defend our shores as the battleship could. Once again there came the dream that made the Model 40 mail plane, the trimotored 80, even the Navy fighters look awkward and out of date. A dream of something better. Each morning Egtvedt reminded himself that he was the general manager now and that a company does not exceed the vision of its leader.

In September 1928, a group from Boeing went to the Los Angeles air races. They watched the F4-B climb to altitude and back to set a record, then saw the F2-Bs take a sizzling first, second and third place in the fifty-mile Navy pursuit race. For Egtvedt, the hotel room was a haven of peace after the din of the races. It was the same with Eddie Hubbard. The two had come to be close friends. In earlier days, they had roomed together. The holiday at the air races offered a chance to discuss hopes and views.

"I have an idea, Claire," Eddie said one afternoon. "Why shouldn't we go entirely to metal when we build our next transport? We have to line the mail compartment with metal anyway, so the mailbag locks won't tear the fabric. We have to put metal plates up front for accessibility to the engine controls. Why not go the whole way, nose to tail?"

Eddie was the stimulus Claire Egtvedt needed. "We could do that," he said. He laid a piece of stationery on the dresser, drew the front view of a wing, long and slender. "Here's what we could do. If the body's going to be metal, easiest way to make it is perfectly round. Set it here on the wing." He drew a circle for the body, on top of the single wing. That was all there was to it, a low-wing monoplane. "Here is an airplane with minimum drag."

"Can you do that?" asked Eddie. It looked too simple. "Where's your landing gear?"

"You could pull the gear up into the wing after you get off the ground. Dragging that thing through the air costs more than all the mail you carry."

"You think we could do it?"

"It's just a question of whether we could afford the cost of working it out. There'd be a lot of new engineering." The corrugated-metal "flying washboard" surface on the Ford and Junkers trimotors wouldn't do. It would have to be a smooth metal skin. But without the corrugations there would have to be more stiffening on the inside. They would probably have to use thicker metal for the skin and make it carry part of the load. Then they could use a lighter frame. This was what was called *monocoque* structure, but no one had much experience with it yet. "It will depend a lot on how big an airplane we build," Claire said. "If it gets too costly we could never do it."

"The 80 is too big," said Eddie. "In bad weather we leave it in the barn and take out the 40s. I'd rather have smaller planes and more of them. More frequent flights. More flexibility. The 80 is a lot of airplane to herd around."

"I'd certainly like to try our hand at an all-metal monoplane," said Claire. "Make it just as clean as we could make it. We've got to do it sooner or later, that's a cinch."

Bill Boeing was highly interested when he saw the monoplane sketch. Its cleanness was appealing to the eye. He wondered if they couldn't get to work on it as a secret project, bring it out as a surprise. Egtvedt said he'd have the engineering department investigate.

Chief engineer Monty Monteith, a man of stature both physically and professionally, could tackle a big problem with ease. Author of the textbook on aerodynamics used at West Point and many universities, the man who had shepherded scores of experimental designs through McCook Field before he came to Boeing, he was regarded as one of the most surefooted engineers in the business. But Egtvedt's proposal was a new one to Monty. "I don't think so. I don't think it'll have the strength," he said.

Almost everyone knew of his concern over internally braced, or cantilever, monoplanes, where the wing was supported entirely by structure inside. He had watched his friend Lieutenant F. W. Neidermeyer fall to his death when the center section support gave way on an experimental monoplane. He had seen the wing of another monoplane develop flutter and fail the time Harold Harris made the first parachute escape at McCook, in 1922. Flutter was the term for a flapping that might start in the wing and get worse and worse until the thing came apart.

"We just don't know enough about flutter," said Monty. "Maybe on a slow ship cantilever is O.K., but when we get into faster ships, it's an unknown."

Monty wanted to lead the race as much as anyone. New ideas were fine, but the chief engineer was the guy responsible if they didn't work.

"Keep it simple," Monty had written in his textbook. "Then there's less chance for something to go wrong."

Things like retractable landing gear would add to the speed but they were an invitation to trouble. Suppose something went wrong? Wasn't it better to know you had a landing gear out there to come down on? But he knew also that the airplane business lived on advancement. That was his conflict, inside.

Monty agreed that a smaller transport was the thing. The 80 and the Ford trimotor were too big and slow. So were the Fokker F-10 and the new Keystone. "But the all-metal idea will take time to develop," he said. "We should get under way with a six-passenger cabin transport not quite so advanced. Make it a monoplane, but a high wing, that we can brace externally from the body." Everyone thought this sounded reasonable and he was authorized to go ahead with the design.

The new idea for a fast, low-wing monoplane was growing, nonetheless. Egtvedt's talk with Bill Boeing had been well timed. The Kelly Act had put the five-cent air-mail stamp into use. Air transportation was taking on a big look. In a year when bigness was the measure of success, businesses everywhere were expanding and combining for strength. Bill Boeing could see this and had talked with Seattle banker Dietrich Schmitz and then with Joe Ripley of the National City Bank of New York about a public offering of Boeing stock. On November 1, 1928, Boeing Airplane & Transport Corporation stock went on the market and sold quickly. Shortly after, United Aircraft & Transport Corporation was formed, largest organization of its kind in the country. It took in Boeing Airplane Company, Pratt & Whitney, maker of the Wasp motors, Chance Vought, the Hamilton Propeller Company, Boeing Air Transport and Pacific Air Transport. Negotiations began also for purchase of National Air Transport, which operated from Chicago to New York. Boeing became chairman of the new corporation; Fred Rentschler of Pratt & Whitney, president.

"Now is the time to build up our engineering and research," said Boeing. A brick administration building was erected at the

Seattle plant with a big area allotted to Engineering. Preliminary design work was begun on the all-metal low-wing proposal. Its simple, smooth lines were rapidly winning favor over the more conventional high-wing design that was under way.

But two shocks hit in quick succession. In Salt Lake City Eddie Hubbard was rushed to the hospital with an internal disorder and died December 18, 1928. Eddie Hubbard, who had built an airline. Seven days later Claire Egtvedt was taken to the hospital critically ill.

There were weeks when everything hung in the balance, weeks of a new kind of struggle for Claire, and of prayerful anxiety for his wife. Then he began to recover. The Board gave him the new title of vice president and consulting engineer. "When you're strong enough, get away from the plant, go wherever you want to go," Bill Boeing told him. "Take your time about coming back."

Phil Johnson's broad shoulders carried both the airline and the plant management at Seattle. In Johnson's absence from the plant he left Gardner Carr, his assistant, in charge. Faces changed, but work continued.

Steadily the new airplane called "Monomail" came into trim being, first on the drawing boards, then in metal. The high-wing project was dropped. The new idea was in its place. There was something irrepressible about an idea that was right. Disbelieved, pushed aside perhaps, it had unseen armor protecting it. It would keep coming. "We must not dismiss any novel idea with the cocksure statement that it can't be done," said Bill Boeing in an interview. "We are pioneers in a new science and a new industry. Our job is to keep everlastingly at research and experiment, and let no new improvement pass us by. We have already proved that science and hard work can lick what appear to be insurmountable difficulties."

Monteith supervised the Monomail's break with tradition. It was an experimental ship. Why not make the most of it? Monty had made young Bob Minshall design engineer because he was quick at devising things. The rotund Bob whipped out ideas for the Monomail. Jack Kylstra was made project engineer to organize the product of a teeming drafting room. Lysle Wood was given the job of designing the *monocoque* body structure. "Make it rugged," Kylstra told him. What they couldn't learn from past experience, they made up for with beef.

A bridge-type structure of square dural tubing for the inside of the wing was worked out with the help of an Army-circulated paper on internally braced wings, by an engineer named E. C. Friel. A retracting landing gear was designed. The clean, simple lines of the airplane were inspiring.

 *Monomail*

It was decided not to carry passengers at all in the first Monomail. The five-cent air-mail stamp had worked wonders and the ability to carry a big mail load was the main thing now. This impetus to the mail had already prompted Boeing to build twenty-five all-mail planes called the Model 95s. They were fabric-covered biplanes much like the 40 but faster, with Pratt & Whitney Hornet engine.

Monty Monteith was proud of the 95. When Captain Ira Eaker of the Air Corps asked him if one of them would be suitable for an endurance flight with aerial refueling, Monty said, "Sure," and showed how they could move the instrument panel, put a passageway to the mail compartment ahead and fill it with extra gas tanks.

There was national interest in endurance flights in 1929. Ira Eaker and Major Carl "Tooey" Spaatz had started it when they circled for 150 hours over southern California in the trimotor Fokker *Question Mark*, in January. Since then there had been a lot of record attempts. "Why not an endurance flight over a regular airline route to show the reliability of the mail plane and the Hornet engine?" asked Eaker. "Just shuttle back and forth from coast to coast as long as we can stay in the air. It'll be a good test, too, of the military possibilities of cross-country refueling."

A 95 mail plane named *Hornet Shuttle* was fixed up for the refueling experiment. On August 27, 1929, with Lieutenant Bernard Thompson, Captain Eaker pointed it to the east out of Oakland. The day was fair. The mountains passed under. At Elko, Nevada, Clair Vance lowered fifty feet of hose from a Boeing 40. Thompson reached up and caught it, held the nozzle to the fuel tank till it was full. Eaker pushed on into rain and thunder east of Salt Lake City. In the darkness over Cheyenne, he sighted the lights of Slim Lewis with more fuel. They closed, the storm tossing them about. Lewis settled over them, kept coming down. "You're sitting on us," Thompson shouted. Eaker dived and Lewis pulled away. They found quieter air at a lower altitude and Thompson got his fuel.

They refueled again at Omaha, then at Cleveland—after eight attempts to get the hose connected, then at New York, where they made their U turn. The second evening they were back over Cleveland. Lieutenant Newton Longfellow lowered two five-gallon cans of oil on a rope. While his helper was tying on a third, another can fell free and hit the 95 with a crash that shook their teeth. Eaker was blinded with an oil bath. When he got off his goggles, Thompson had crawled back, black with oil. "Let's get out of this thing. The front spar is broken," he yelled. Both were wearing parachutes.

Eaker tried the throttle and found the engine and propeller undamaged. He rocked the wings and found them steady. "We're going to land," he said. They groped into Cleveland.

After repairs a new start was made September 1 from New York. Thirty-three hours later the *Shuttle* reached Oakland and began the long return eastward, into doubtful weather. In Immigration Canyon, west of Salt Lake, the engine wasn't getting gas. It sputtered and quit at 7,500 feet with precipitous mountains some 2,000 feet above them on the right and only slightly lower on the left. A switch to another tank didn't help. The only possibility of a forced landing was to the left, where the slope was less vertical. Eaker stalled the 95 against the slope at 7,000 feet. They rolled fifty feet, caught in a hole, spun around and stopped. A plugged fuel line had ended the experiment. The two men climbed down the mountain to a stream and a road.

"Looks like we failed," Thompson said.

"Don't you ever think it," said Eaker.

Major General James Fechet, chief of the Air Corps, got a report from Eaker. "This shows what could be done with refueling."

2. *Bomber Experiment*

Claire Egtvedt felt the refueling attempts were a clumsy way to go after more range. He had just been touring the airplane plants of Europe. In Germany, he had climbed through Dr. Claude Dornier's fabulous twelve-engine 169-passenger Do-X flying boat, a more imaginative approach to the problem, he felt. The big ship could carry enough fuel for a flight across the Atlantic. "It's an amazing accomplishment," he told the doctor. But as he looked back, the Do-X was in some ways quite fantastic. The structure was remarkable, but the multiplicity of engines, all racked up on struts above the wing, made it cumbersome and hugely complex.

Would the airplane ever be a rival to the surface ship? He thought of Admiral Reeves. *The airplane just isn't as effective.* Wasn't there some other approach? He thought of putting a row of engines inside, gearing them to a driveshaft that would turn a big propeller out front. No, that would be too complicated. Better go back to the Monomail and take it a step at a time. Maybe someday there'd be engines big enough so it wouldn't take twelve of them to fly a ship like Dornier's.

Egtvedt had been interested in the bombers under development in Europe, especially in England, where they were using long slender bodies. He suggested that design work be started on a Boeing bomber. They hadn't yet done anything in this field. Now Admiral Reeves' remarks stood as a challenge.

The bomber was the military weight-lifter. The bigger bomb load it could carry, and the more gas for range, the better. And the larger the wing area at a given power and speed, the more weight it could lift. That was axiomatic. But if you got too big a wing, the structural weight became impossible. That explained why all bombers were biplanes, if not triplanes. By adding one wing on top of another, you got more area. When Egtvedt suggested enlarging the Monomail idea into a twin-engine monoplane bomber, therefore, it didn't sound right.

Monty said they could make a study of the monoplane, but meanwhile would get started on a biplane design. Both the Keystone and the Curtiss Condor were twin-engine biplanes.

Designer engineer Bob Minshall went with Egtvedt to talk with the Army about bomber prospects. General Fechet said he'd like to see Boeing compete in the field. "If there were more competition the Air Corps might get some better bombers. Go talk to Foulois at Wright Field."

"Let's try the monoplane idea on them," said Minshall on the way to Dayton. "Maybe it won't carry as big a bomb load, but it would make a sizzling good bomber."

Brigadier General Benjamin Foulois, chief of the materiel division at Wright Field, formerly McCook Field, and Major Jan Howard, his engineering chief, gave them the bomber picture. Major Hugh Knerr, operating bombers at Langley Field, came in during the talk. "The Keystone is too slow for a day bomber," said General Foulois. "A hundred miles an hour isn't enough in daylight. We're having Fokker and Douglas bring out a faster plane that can be used either for bombing or observation. If you want to get into bombers, we'd rather have you compete with the Keystone for a night bomber. We haven't any funds for an experimental contract, but if you want to get into it on speculation, we'd like to have you do it."

"How important is speed in the night bomber?" Egtvedt asked.

"Not so important as with the day bomber," said Foulois. "How about it, Knerr?"

"That's right. We count on the darkness for protection," said Major Knerr. "Of course, speed helps a bit if you get caught in searchlights." Knerr sounded like one of the Billy Mitchell school, an action man. Bob Minshall was making motions at Egtvedt that this was the strategic moment.

Egtvedt approached his subject casually. "What would you think of a type somewhat different from the Keystone and the Condor?" He laid a three-view drawing of the Monomail on the General's desk. "We've been giving some thought to enlarging this plane, putting on two engines and external bomb racks."

Knerr and Howard were on their feet looking over the General's shoulder. "Say now, that looks interesting," said Major Knerr. Jan Howard's eyes brightened.

"What will it do?" Foulois asked.

"We haven't completed our study on it yet," said Egtvedt. "We'll get it to you as soon as we can."

"Do that," said Jan Howard, now taking the lead.

Egtvedt wired the plant: "Cease all work on bombers until further advised re new opportunity." When they got back to Seattle there were long discussions. Phil Johnson favored going ahead with the new design. He thought Boeing would approve building an experimental model on speculation. Monteith cautioned against haste: "Let's not bet on the wrong horse. We shouldn't write off the biplane until we're sure."

The difference of opinion didn't stump Phil. "Let's design it both ways, then," he proposed. "We'll find out which is better."

That was fair enough. John Sanders went to work on the monoplane and Al Soderquist on the biplane. The intramural

rivalry was intense for a few weeks. Both Sanders and Soderquist designed around new 600-horsepower Hornet engines,
with an alternate design using the 600-horsepower Curtiss Con-
queror. But the further they went, the plainer it became that the
monoplane was going to show the best performance. The reduction in drag offset the lack of wing area. Speed made more
difference in the lift of the wing than the number of square feet.
Soderquist finally came around to Sanders' drafting table. "I
can't make my clunk do what a low-wing monoplane can do,"
he said.

Minshall wondered if Monty's real concern about the airplane wasn't still the question of the monoplane's strength and
the possibility of wing flutter. The Monomail hadn't been flown
yet and this one would be bigger, faster. But he thought they
could beef it up enough to meet Monty's standards. They did.
When Phil Johnson took the drawings east in January 1930,
both Dayton and Washington urged him to go ahead on a
speculative basis. If the experimental model met specifications,
it would surely merit an order for several service-test models.
"It's the only forward thinking in bombers we've seen," said
General Fechet. Bill Boeing and the United Aircraft & Transport Corporation board in Hartford, which now controlled
expenditures, authorized the project.

The Monomail had been a well-kept secret until the wings
and body were taken to be assembled on the recently completed
Boeing Field, a mile down the highway. Then Seattle was astir
with interest. Fans crowded the fenced-off area. This plane
didn't look like other airplanes. But somehow it looked as an
airplane should. Something meant to fly. Body slender, smooth,
round, resting neatly on a silver wing. A wing turned slightly
up, slightly back, outstretched for flight.

Employees brought their families to look. Now it was something real. Painted there on its side was the name *Monomail*,
once mysteriously murmured through the plant. Bold on its

tail, the Department of Commerce letters X (for experimental) 725-W, meant that it was ready to become airborne.

Seeking the best pilot to fly the plane, Minshall and Monteith had chosen Eddie Allen. Eddie had studied the Monomail. When he climbed into the cockpit, he was in key with his airplane. In his gentle, high voice Eddie called down to a mechanic: "I'm going to try a couple of runs at this setting, then I'll be back." The blades of the metal propeller could be adjusted on the ground, and he was trying to determine the best pitch. He taxied down the runway, then back. "Set them two degrees flatter." Eddie seemed more concerned about the propeller setting than anything else.

Eventually he was ready for a take-off run. Everybody watched as he revved up the engine. He started to roll, picked up speed, and raced for the end of the field. Then there was a screeching of tires and a cloud of dust as he stopped short. "I couldn't get airborne with the propeller set for cruising," said Eddie. "I think we'd better run some static thrust tests." They tied the airplane to an anchor and used a spring scale to measure the strength of its pull. The dilemma was painfully clear. The whistle-clean airplane was capable of great speed in the air, but to get this speed the propeller blades would have to take a big bite of air with each turn. They'd have to set the pitch of the blade steep. But when they did that on the ground, the propeller would just blow the air sideways. To get enough power at low speed required a flat pitch. That wasn't good for flying.

Eddie agreed on a compromise setting. On May 22, 1930, with the Hornet roaring her loudest, the Monomail sailed into the air, a beautiful sight. Down from the flight, Eddie climbed out nodding and smiling. "It's as smooth as it looks," he said. Later he drew Egtvedt aside. "It's a shame, though. This airplane wants to get up and go, but you can't get the power out of the propellers."

Testing went on. After some weeks Slim Lewis, chief pilot of Boeing Air Transport, came up to try the plane. Monty and

Gardner "Dick" Carr and some others were watching him from a rooftop at Plant One when he tried some steep banks, pouring it on. They saw him pull up sharp.

"No, he wouldn't dare," Monty gasped. Up, up and over on his back went Slim Lewis, in a loop. "It won't stand that," cried Monty, his long legs covering in seconds the stairs and the distance to his car. Commercial airplanes weren't meant for stunting. He raced to the field, skidded to a stop in the gravel by the hangar and jumped out, waving his fists at the sky.

"How're we going to get him down?" he demanded of John Wilson, the chief inspector. Lewis pulled up into another loop. Monty came down with two powerful arms on top of John Wilson's slight shoulders. "We've got to get him down," he shouted. Helplessly they watched Lewis do a third loop. Then he came down, grinning until he caught the looks of his audience. "Well," said big Slim Lewis, "my boys have to fly all kinds of contraptions that you guys put together up here. I want to be sure they're good and sound before I let 'em fly 'em."

Inspection showed a few popped rivets on the metal fairings at the wing root, but no real damage. A few weeks later Lewis took the plane on down to Cheyenne, enthusiastic. But he hadn't reckoned seriously enough with Eddie Allen's findings concerning propeller limitations. When he took off in Cheyenne's rarefied air 6,000 feet above sea level, he barely got over the tree tops at the end of the field. The Hamilton Standard people, now part of the United Aircraft & Transport group, advised bringing the plane to Pittsburgh for tests with different propellers. They had started to develop a controllable propeller that could take off at one pitch and be shifted to another in flight. Monty didn't think that was the answer. It would add weight—and something else to go wrong. He thought they should increase the supercharging, the air supply to the engines, so they could get more power at altitude.

After the Pittsburgh tests a more expedient solution was found, a smaller propeller, without gearing, turning at a faster speed. Then the pitch didn't make so much difference. But Egtvedt didn't feel they'd solved the problem. Neither did Gene Wilson, Admiral Reeves' former aide who was now the president of Hamilton Standard. Wilson wanted a controllable propeller device, a geared-down engine that would turn a big propeller with a big bite, and enough supercharging to give power at high altitude. "We need all three," he said, "if we are going to have any progress."

Sometimes progress was a disturbing thing. If it solved an old problem, it might uncover a new one. It was always the hard path to take. The old way, the familiar way, was so easy. Why not settle back in it? Why disturb things?

It had been disturbing to the pilots on the line when the big 80 trimotor had put them inside a closed cockpit. Fliers of the purple twilight, they liked the breath of the night on their faces. They wanted to be able to look out, to lean over the edge and follow the railroad or the fence row. This attitude was so strong that it was decided to build one of the 80s with an open cockpit. A place was made for the two pilots atop the square nose.

It was a sun-baked day in July 1930 when pilot Clair Vance ferried the new plane to Oakland with Fred Collins, assistant sales manager, as co-pilot. Collins flew over the Siskiyous, then Vance said he'd take over. Collins, sun-drowsy and well fed at Medford, leaned on his arm for a nap. His peace was shared by the half dozen Boeing people relaxing in the armchairs of the eighteen-passenger cabin. Harold Crary, publicity manager, went forward and climbed up the ladder to the sky-roof cockpit to see what was doing. He found both Collins and Vance bowed and limp, the sun blazing down on the backs of their necks, the big airplane droning on. Crary shook Fred Collins vigorously by the shoulders. Fred waved a sleepy arm to the left. "He's flying it."

"Nobody's flying it," cried Crary, beating Vance on the back. The stable 80 hadn't noticed the neglect. It bore well the fruits of earlier lessons in stability. But pilots soon decided the closed cockpit was better, after all.

The rocking-chair comfort and the accident-free record of the 80 gave the trimotor a growing popularity. On other lines the trimotored Fords and Fokkers were equally popular. Passenger traffic was growing. The government was encouraging this under the Watres Act with air-mail rates that allowed a premium for passenger planes. To take advantage of the Act, the second of the two Monomails, partly built, was redesigned to carry six passengers, but its cabin was tiny compared to the walk-around cabin in the 80.

Since the Monomail appeared to be too small, some of the younger engineers thought a twin-motored transport could be designed along the lines of the new bomber, but Monty didn't favor this. The bomber was an experiment. It was still unbuilt. A plane for airline use had to be tested, reliable.

Nor was the bomber development coming easy. The plan to put engines in the wing was new. They had always been above or below the wing. When the NACA ran wind-tunnel tests at Langley Field to help solve the problem, the word was surprising. The best results came from putting the two engines out in front of the wing. As if the structural problem weren't bad enough already. But the figures were unmistakably clear and a housing, or nacelle, was devised to hold the engines out there. A ring of metal was put over the rough cylinder heads to smooth up the air flow.

This hurdle past, the bomber design began to look more promising. The plane was going to be much faster than the Monomail. The propeller on the Monomail was less effective because it had to send the air back over a big body and thick wing root. The bomber, with its engines out in front of the wing, would avoid that. Its expected speed went up to 175 miles per hour.

The chance of winning the next bomber competition seemed excellent. As far as could be learned, no one else was working on such an advanced plane. The project was kept a close secret.

There was a lively pace in the shops, with work also under way on contracts for 177 F-4B Navy fighters and their Army counterparts, the P-12 pursuits. To keep the pursuit line going, design work had just been started on a low-wing monoplane pursuit. One thousand men were employed now, all on military planes. That didn't seem right, after all that had been done on mail planes and trimotored transports. There was a great desire to get a new transport going.

"The question is," said Monteith, "whether it should be a single or a trimotored airplane. Is it more economical to operate a small fleet of large transports or a large fleet of small ones? If we go ahead with the Monomail it will have to have a larger cabin. We've got to provide better facilities. We're up against real competition for passenger comfort."

The trimotor looked like the best bet. Just so long as it didn't get too big for the hangars on the airlines. Designs were started on a new twelve-passenger trimotor.

3. *Why Not a Twin-engine Transport?*

When 1931 rolled around, Phil Johnson asked department heads for reports and recommendations for the new year. One of these requests fell on the desk of ruddy, forthright, young Fred Collins. Erik Nelson, the sales manager, was away and Fred was in charge. He had just returned from five months of flying the 80 trimotors and felt a little rusty on things at the plant. But he was filled with ideas about flying equipment and more than a little impatient with the slow trimotors.

"Why aren't we building a twin-engine monoplane transport like the twin-engine bomber?" The idea hit him with gale force. "Must be some reason or it would have been thought of already." Collins wasn't an engineer. His job was to sell airplanes. But Fokker had just brought out a twin-engine monoplane, an observation plane for the Army that was attracting attention. Why not a transport? The more he tried to set up reasons against it, the greater the force that tore them away.

Safety? Certainly two engines would be better than one, as in the Monomail. Performance? He'd seen the bomber figures in Engineering. Neither a trimotor nor a single-engine plane could equal them. Operating cost? He scoured the trade magazines and Army correspondence files for data. He found some Air Corps figures showing that the cost of operating a tri-motored Ford was $229 an hour, that of a two-motored biplane Keystone bomber only $175. He expected the cost of construction would be greater for the new plane, but the increased revenue would offset that.

When Collins got his sixteen-page presentation ready, he took it straight to Phil Johnson's office and handed it to W. A. Patterson, Phil's new assistant. When Pat Patterson had read the paper he walked into Fred's office: "I think you got something. But you'd better have Engineering go over it."

Collins sent copies down to Engineering and also discussed the proposal with Claire Egtvedt. "It's certainly worth looking into," said Egtvedt. Two weeks later Monteith made his report. "The plane can be built," said Monty, "but Collins has overlooked one thing. Its service ceiling with one engine out of commission will be only 4,000 feet." Monty didn't bother to add that the Medicine Bow range, where Boeing Air Transport crossed it, reached 10,000 feet. Work went ahead on the *trimotor* transport design in two versions, a monoplane and a biplane.

All hands were busy now getting the secret experimental bomber ready for flight. On April 29, Les Tower took it up.

It was a surprise, a falcon in the air over Seattle—long black body, barrel-nosed; long low wing carrying two powerful engines. Perhaps not so graceful as the Monomail, but unmistakably sinewy. Its burning speed was evident.

By June the new plane was tested and trimmed for its flight to Wright Field. Slim Lewis and Erik Nelson were the pilots, with John Sanders, project engineer, as passenger in the rear gunner's seat. This was zero hour for Sanders, his months of planning and effort now going to the big test. He noticed a heavy tingle of vibration from the engines, but it was swallowed in the tingle of his own excitement. They sailed east over the Cascade Mountains, Sanders thoroughly pleased with his racing perch until a sudden air shock nearly catapulted him overboard. He decided this craft called for safety belts all the way.

They averaged 158 miles an hour on the long trip to Dayton, stopping at Cheyenne and Chicago. Sanders thought of the one-hundred-mile-an-hour Keystones the Air Corps had just bought. Relics now, he felt. No official welcome awaited them at Wright Field. They had trouble, in fact, finding a place to park their new offering. But when the Army test crews got it in the air, they knew they had hold of something.

B-9 Bomber

There was concern about the vibration of the 575-horsepower Hornets, but the bomber's top speed of 185 miles an hour seemed to answer all arguments. That was five miles faster than most pursuits. The ship would be invulnerable until faster pursuits could be built. It wasn't long before a contract was drawn for seven of the planes, to be called B-9s—Air Corps Bomber Number Nine. The bomber's success spurred interest, too, in Boeing's new monoplane pursuit, though the Wright Field engineers decided they'd prefer to have the pursuit wings braced with wires instead of internally braced. Given the name P-26, the new pursuit held the promise of a large order.

Salesman Fred Collins kept seeing in the B-9 bomber a future twin-engine transport. He carried the picture in the front of his mind when he visited bases along the Boeing Air Transport line. Flying in the slow-droning 80 did nothing to erase it. Slim Lewis, who'd liked the Monomail, was in agreement with Collins. "Why not?" said Slim. "It's the sort of thing we need." Slim Lewis talked with Thorp Hiscock. Hiscock, who had his own enthusiasm for advancement, talked with D. B. Colyer, operations vice president of Boeing Air Transport. Colyer sent a note to Phil Johnson: "I think the idea is worth a good study by the engineers in Seattle."

The engineering department undertook the study, on top of the one under way on new trimotored transports, a biplane improvement of the Model 80 and a monoplane more like the Ford and the Fokker. The trimotor plans were completed in July 1931. Phil Johnson sent them to the operating heads of the four lines making up the United System. Reactions were varied but unenthusiastic. One thought biplanes more comfortable than monoplanes, though the latter were faster. One thought too much importance was being given to speed. Another thought the opposite. One thought passenger and cargo space should be interchangeable.

When the twin-engine monoplane was roughed up—a ten-passenger low-wing plane—Johnson sent the plans to the same four. Two of them thought the trimotored monoplane would be better. One suggested a single engine with twice the power. One thought the twin-engine plane would have a quieter cabin, but would have to be able to fly well on one engine.

While the transport plans were making the rounds in July, Phil Johnson was opening offices in Chicago for a consolidation of the four airlines in the United Aircraft & Transport group:

Boeing Air Transport, National Air Transport, Pacific Air Transport, and Varney Air Lines. Combined under the name United Air Lines, they became the largest air transport organization in the country, operating 120 planes, 32,000 miles a day, with Phil the president. Newspapers called the youthful executive "King of the Air at thirty-seven." Phil retained the presidency of Boeing Airplane Company but designated Claire Egtvedt, now well recovered from his physical setback, vice president in charge of the plant.

Once again, Egtvedt gazed from the driver's seat at the question, "Where are we going?" He thought especially about the new transport. Two things he had learned. Airplane development was coming fast, uncomfortably fast, and would pass by the company that hesitated. But to be successful, the new idea had to be right; the one that met a need. Vision was seeing what was right. Was the answer all in the engineering figures? The figures that showed the twin-engine plane wouldn't have enough single-engine ceiling for passenger safety? They couldn't be ignored, but figures could rule you if you didn't rule them. Was it to be found in conflicting opinions and advice? Advice served best when it stimulated thought; it wasn't authority. Wasn't the right idea the one that looked right to the eye, measured right to the mind, felt right to the heart?

Claire Egtvedt thought of the Monomail. It was a beautiful thing. It held more promise than anybody knew, if it weren't for the propeller problem. He thought of the twin-engine B-9 bomber. It had followed logically out of the Monomail. Now it was shattering all the old concepts of bomber design. The twin-engine low-wing transport flowed from these as inevitably as a river flows from its source. "Let's work to get the ceiling up," he told Monteith. "Let's see, too, if we can get an airplane that's better from the passenger viewpoint."

Monty was in good mood. Wright Field had just load-tested a wing of the B-9 and found it the most rigid wing they'd seen. His doubt about monoplane structure was fading. "O.K.," he said. "One thing I'd like to do is give the passenger wider seats and more space between them. I shudder to think how we cram them into the seats we've been using."

In Chicago, Phil Johnson looked out at the new sign, UNITED AIR LINES, to him a symbol of leadership. Phil had been brought up with planes and engineering. It was natural for him to want to lead in equipment. He pictured United bringing out the ideal transport, jumping way out ahead of the others.

When Johnson and Egtvedt got together, obstacles flew out the window and thoughts soon centered on the monoplane they would call Model 247—twin-engined, all-metal, low-winged, streamlined at every corner, with retracting landing gear. Johnson wasn't satisfied with the speed and climb performance of the design so far. "Clean it up some more. Cut down the weight," he urged.

Monty asked Bob Minshall to spearhead the new effort, with Frank Canney as his project engineer. Egtvedt suggested they hold it to eight passengers and use only one pilot, to keep the plane small and light as possible, but Phil balked at the single pilot. Meetings were called at the Cheyenne maintenance headquarters and the operating people contributed their ideas. After the sessions, Erik Nelson reported, "We've got to get in ten passengers and still keep the weight from going up."

When the design looked right and the cruising speed came up to the 150 miles an hour the operating people had set as a minimum, Phil Johnson's enthusiasm grew. He sold Fred Rentschler, United Aircraft president, on replacing the whole United fleet with the new planes, in a bold bid for supremacy. The Board agreed. A $3 million order was placed for sixty of the 247s, to be constructed in secret. The first plane would go in service by the end of 1932.

Details of design were completed, and production got started. There was a schedule to meet; no time to lose. Employment went up to 1,200. The work came on top of Army and Navy orders for 110 P-12E pursuits and ninety two F-4B4 fighters. Through-

out the generally bad business year of 1932, the plant on the
Duwamish was bustle and hum.

In October 1932, the B-9 bombers were being considered for
a quantity production order. Glenn Martin had now built a
somewhat similar plane, but it didn't seem to be much competition. There were reports it was full of bugs. The only complaints about the B-9 were the engine vibration and a twisting
of the long slender body. The body could be fixed and the
equipment laboratory at Wright Field was working on a new
rubber engine mount that would help the vibration.

In December, with everything set for news of the contract
award, a big Martin delegation marched into the procurement
office at Dayton. The verdict came soon. "The Martin B-10 has
won the competition. You can stop work on the B-9."

"How come?" Bob Minshall asked Jake Harman, the bomber
project engineer.

"You'd be amazed what Martin did in two months," said
Lieutenant Harman. "Practically rebuilt the whole airplane. Put
on an enclosed cockpit, a larger wing, new engines. Yours shake
like the devil. They put the bomb racks inside and got their top
speed twenty-two miles above yours."

Then too, Martin had gotten his bid down a few dollars under
the Boeing bid. This, thought Minshall, must have been the main
reason Martin won. It couldn't have been that Boeing was slow
on its feet at the end of the race and let Martin improve on
Boeing's design.

The shock of the B-9's defeat was snubbed short by excitement over work on the Model 247 transport. Dick Carr was
running the plant twenty-four hours a day to make Phil Johnson's deadline. The 247 would put United Air Lines way out in
the lead. Erik Nelson on a visit to the Douglas plant had seen
a full-scale wooden model of a twin-engine monoplane built
along lines similar to the 247, but it would take them months to
get it in production. No one seemed concerned about the

Douglas threat. The 247 was going to be a superb ship. At noon, February 8, 1933, the new transport, silver-bright, lifted off Boeing Field and winged out over Puget Sound. "They'll never build 'em any bigger," said Monteith.

247 Transport

Monty probably would have thought twice before he'd have put that remark in writing. It hadn't come from pondering the airplane of the future. It came out of the exuberance of the occasion, his way of saying that the great new transport, revolutionary in form, was the last word.

But his remark was revealing. Not only did the 247 seem the ideal size, but there was a law of "diminishing returns" which said the bigger you made the airplane, the more difficult the problem of structural strength. Good airplanes couldn't get much larger. There was another rule of thumb that said the lift of an airplane would increase as the square of the speed, and the speed would go up as the cube of the power. To double the speed of a given plane, you'd need eight times the power, because of the increased drag at the higher speed. Obviously speeds weren't likely to go much higher.

But he who writes the text must take heed lest he fall into its pages; lest the rule that applies under given circumstances be taken as a limit to progress. Real law, universal, eternal law, is what makes good things possible, not impossible.

Where now was the limited view that the biplane was superior to the monoplane because of greater wing area? That the twin-engine monoplane transport would be impractical?

The 247 brought a revolution in airline schedules, in comfort and revenue, especially when an improved new Wasp engine was installed. The new Wasp was supercharged to deliver its 550 horsepower at 8,000 feet altitude instead of 5,000. It was geared down to put more power in the propeller. And Hamilton Standard had come through with a controllable propeller that could be shifted to steep pitch in flight, to put the power to work. The ceiling of the plane went up to 27,000 feet; it could fly at 11,500 feet on one engine. Top speed went to two hundred miles an hour, and United advertised three mile a minute schedules. William E. Boeing was selected as winner of the Guggenheim Medal for "successful pioneering and achievement in aircraft manufacture and air transportation."

This was Bill Boeing's hour of triumph. He had promised himself retirement at fifty. He was fifty-one now. With his goal in mind, he had been gradually selling his stock in United Aircraft & Transport. In August 1933, Boeing withdrew from active participation. Fred Rentschler became vice chairman and Phil Johnson moved to New York as president of the sprawling organization. Claire Egtvedt walked with thoughtful step to a new desk as president of Boeing Airplane Company.

The sixty-plane series of 247 transports coming through the plant was stimulating but now the production job was half done. What was to follow it? Transcontinental and Western Air had wanted to buy the airplane and begin taking delivery after the twentieth ship had been delivered to United. But TWA was a competitor of United. "We're going to buy somewhere else if you won't sell," Jack Frye, the TWA president, had said. Egtvedt put the proposal to the United Aircraft board in New York. The answer was No. They would have to finish the sixty before taking new orders.

Now Douglas was building a similar plane for delivery to TWA next spring. The Douglas would have a bigger cabin—sixteen passengers instead of ten—and wing flaps to slow down the landing speed. Other airlines, forced by competition, were falling in line behind TWA for the new Douglas. As Martin had done with the bomber, Douglas was doing with the transport. Where did that leave Boeing? Back with pursuits?

Egtvedt was thoroughly disturbed. He'd decided there was more employment, more dollar value, more engineering opportunity in the bigger planes. Besides, the P-26 monoplane pursuit, now in full production, was hampered in speed by its external wire bracing. A new internally braced experimental model was under way for submittal to both the Army and the Navy, but it was being tortured by design changes, and other pursuit builders were making a strong bid for the market.

Competition was a fierce thing. It wasn't just a matter of getting ahead, but staying ahead. "We've got to start on a larger transport and a new bomber," Egtvedt said. He proposed that the United Aircraft board allocate funds for these. But United Aircraft & Transport was in deep trouble in the winter of 1933-34. The new Democratic administration was clawing through the files of the Post Office Department. Former Postmaster General Walter F. Brown had sought to build a systematic air transportation pattern through the air-mail routes. A special Senate investigating committee now charged that many of his routes had been granted without competitive bidding.

At the hearings, United protested that it had only one such route, a branch line from Omaha to Watertown, South Dakota, which they had been asked by the Post Office to operate. Other lines protested the charges. The hearing-room temperature grew torrid. Bill Boeing fumed as he sat in the witness chair answering Hugo Black's questions about the value of Boeing stock, which had mirrored the booming growth of the company. What did that have to do with air-mail contracts, Boeing asked himself. Hadn't they taken their contracts under straight competitive bidding? Hadn't the Post Office been afraid to take their bid at first because it was so low? Weren't they entitled to reward for pioneering and success?

On February 9, 1934, President Roosevelt cancelled all airmail contracts and ordered the Army to take over the mail. Twelve Army pilots lost their lives in two months of operation that followed. Then the job was given back to the airlines but Postmaster General Farley decreed that for five years no airline executive who attended former Postmaster General Brown's route-planning meetings could contract to carry the mail. Phil Johnson had to resign to permit United to regain its contract.

Then a law was passed prohibiting air-mail contractors from being associated with any aviation manufacturing companies. That meant the United Aircraft & Transport Corporation would have to be split up. Bitterly, Bill Boeing sold out the rest of his stock and left the airplane business.

A committee in Hartford decided to form three new companies from the fragments of United Aircraft & Transport. One was United Air Lines. Another took in Pratt & Whitney and the other Eastern manufacturing companies. The third, in the West, weakest in capital funds and lowest in backlog of business, comprised Boeing Airplane in Seattle, Stearman Aircraft in Wichita, Kansas, which had been acquired by United in 1929, and a small subsidiary in Vancouver, British Columbia. Claire Egtvedt, presiding over the western remnant, recalled the grim days of the flat spin. This one seemed bigger and flatter.

4. *Project A*

That spring of 1934 everything seemed to be going backward. Everything. Profits from the 247 transport had been squeezed down almost to the red line and the P-26A pursuits were coming out at a loss, with costs increased under NRA and a succession of design changes. Both these contracts would soon be finished, then there'd be nothing. Good men were being laid off by the scores.

The attempt to build a successor to the P-26 pursuit was failing. The new experimental Navy fighter and Army pursuit didn't sell. "The big planes take so much effort we can't give the attention to pursuits," said Monteith. "We just can't spread our design people that thin."

There was no chance of getting back in the bomber business without a new model. Egtvedt wanted to build an experimental prototype of a new twin-engine bomber along with a prototype of an advanced twin-engine transport—one incorporating wing flaps and having a larger capacity than the 247. By building the two types out of the same basic design, it would be possible to offer both the Army and the airlines lower prices. But getting money for experimental work was the problem. When the legal and financial separation of the United Aircraft companies was completed and United's capital was reallocated, the Boeing Airplane Company would have $582,000 cash. The money needed to meet payroll and obligations for the remainder of the year totaled $743,000. There was some more money due for P-26s but the contract was in controversy and might be several years in the Court of Claims.

Egtvedt was completely wrung out. The whole organization had been working from the heart; surely effort like that couldn't lead to failure. "Man's extremity is God's opportunity," he reflected. Things might look black, but this couldn't be the end of the line. It took a certain faith to know that what looked like a setback might be the setting for a greater gain.

Down in Engineering and out in the shops were the men who had brought about a marvelous advance in the airplane, the people who were the Boeing Company. There wasn't any thought of defeat in them. They came in from the shops and suggested a plan of alternating work, one group on for two weeks, then off while the other group worked the next two, to preserve the staff. Then, when the plan was put in effect, a lot of them came down on their time off and worked without pay.

That was how things stood when Claire Egtvedt got a call from Brigadier General Conger Pratt, chief of the Air Corps Materiel Division at Wright Field: "Can you be here personally for an important meeting May 14? It's a secret matter and I'd rather not say more on the phone."

There were stair steps leading to progress in Dayton, in Washington, elsewhere, paralleling the steps that had been taken in Seattle. To those who climbed them, there was a new view.

Some were too busy to climb them; others, content, stayed below. Some thought them too dangerous. But there were those who had a high goal in their hearts, as had George Leigh Mallory, the British mountaineer, who explained why he wanted to climb Mount Everest: "Because it is there."

The Army Air Corps was made of men like Mallory. They chose to fly. Fast, high, into the challenge of the sky. The uniform of a second lieutenant was awkward on the lean figure of Jake Harman when he left the University of Idaho to attend Army flying school. There was an eager gleam in Jake's eye. "I want to fly bombers," he said, when everyone knew that pursuits were the thing for a young fellow to get into.

"Why?"

"Because they are air power." Jake had been reading Billy Mitchell. But when he got to flying Keystone bombers at Langley Field in 1929 he felt cheated. One day when Harman was pushing along over the landscape a pilot in a Ford trimotor passed him by with a pleasant wave. This was absurd, Jake thought. He couldn't even keep up with a passenger plane.

When the squadron commander sought Harman's help brushing up on mathematics to enter Air Corps engineering school, and then suggested that Harman apply also, there flashed before him the hope that he might some day help get better bombers. "Would they take me, a lousy second lieutenant?" he asked.

"Put down a good reason and I'll see you get in."

Jake Harman gave as his reason: "To see to it that the Air Corps gets some fast, long-range bombers." Major Hugh Knerr, who had been writing up the needs of bombardment aviation, encouraged Harman.

When three years later Jake found himself the bombardment project officer at Wright Field, at the time the Boeing B-9s and the first Martin B-10s were coming in, he thought he'd better try to make good that goal. "We're getting the speed, now let's go after the range."

Range was synonymous with size. To carry a bigger gas load, you had to have a bigger wing, a bigger airplane. How big could you go? The subject became a favorite one at the field in 1933. Jan Howard, the chief engineer; his assistant, Al Lyon; Jimmie Taylor, chief of the aircraft branch; Hugh Knerr, who'd been sent to Dayton "to do something about his squawks" and was now heading the field service section, would kick the subject around. Harman got in on the discussions.

Did the long-standing notion still apply that you couldn't make a plane much bigger because you'd have to put so much weight into the structure that you'd end up with a white elephant? Now there were all-metal structures to work with; more strength.

What about control? Could a pilot handle the control surfaces on a big plane? How big? What about power? The power plants were always the limiting thing. You took what range you could get, after you found how big a structure the engineers would permit, and how big a power plant was available. And you didn't get any range.

"Why not go at it the other way around?" Harman asked. "If we want to get a long-range bomber, why not lay down a plan of what we need instead of what we think we can get? Start from there." Brash, perhaps, but Harman was hankering to try it. So were the others. They prepared a list of future bomber categories: (1) Wing span, 75 feet; gross weight, 15,000 pounds; that took in the present B-9 and B-10; (2) 100-foot span, 40,000 pounds gross; (3) 150-foot span, 60,000 pounds gross; (4) 200 feet, 150,000 pounds; (5) 250 feet, 200,000 pounds; (6) 275 feet, 250,000 pounds; (7) 325 feet, 300,000 pounds, and so on up the ladder. Fantastic? Who could say? How could they ever know without setting up some projects to find out?

In the fall of 1933, Major Jimmie Taylor budgeted a project for a 5,000-mile bomber in category Number Three, skipping Number Two, reaching into the future as far as he dared. "Here's your chance," he told Harman, "if the budget goes through." Jake Harman's pencil flew as he worked up the requirements: an airplane that would carry 2,000 pounds of bombs 5,000 miles, five times the range of the B-9 and B-10. A thirty-ton airplane, four times as heavy as the latest bombers. Labeled "Project A," it challenged all the limitations on airplane design.

The budget request was O.K.'d by General Pratt and sent on to Washington. It asked only for money for the engineering, but $600,000 would be required for the building of such a plane. One airplane.

When Brigadier General Conger Pratt endorsed the proposal, he knew something of the Washington situation. He had spent some stormy years there as chief of operations just after Billy Mitchell was court-martialed. For a time he worked for Benny Foulois, now chief of the Air Corps. Two of Pratt's assistants had been Tooey Spaatz and Harold George. Spaatz was now in California in command of the First Bombardment Wing. Out there, he had spent many a night talking air power with Colonel Hap Arnold, CO at the field, Hap Arnold who had gotten in trouble when he upheld Billy Mitchell too vigorously.

Captain Hal George was now head of tactics and strategy at the Air Corps tactical school in Montgomery, Alabama, where Billy Mitchell's writings were the center of discussion. "In future warfare," General Mitchell had said, "aircraft will project the spearpoint of the nation's offensive and defensive power against the vital centers of the opposing country. Woe be to the nation that is weak in the air." Said Hal George to the young air officers, "Future wars will begin with air action. The enemy's industrial fabric will be a more vital target than his armed forces."

This kind of talk was having its effect. Not that Washington was in agreement on the strategic role of the airplane. Far from it. But there had been some steps in this direction.

In 1931, General Douglas MacArthur, the Army Chief of Staff, had put the fire extinguisher to a long-smoldering dispute between Army and Navy by obtaining from Admiral William V. Pratt, Chief of Naval Operations, an agreement that Army air forces would defend the coasts of the U. S. and its overseas possessions. It was MacArthur's thought that a GHQ Air

Force, directed out of Army headquarters, would perform this role, adding to the Army's capability and ending the feud over a separate air force. "We'll buy that," said Air Chief Benny Foulois when the General Staff put the plan on paper the following year. "But we'll need funds for long-range observation planes. We should keep enemy aircraft carriers at least 250 miles from our shores."

Of course there was no enemy. Japanese troops had burst in on Mukden to wrest Manchuria from China, but that was in the Orient where anything might happen. The League of Nations had censured the aggressors. There were also weird goings-on in Germany. A party leader named Adolf Hitler, who had written a book about his "battle" while imprisoned in Munich for insurrection, had battled his way to the chancellorship. He was saying something about the Third Reich, about rebuilding the empire of Frederick the Great. The new chancellor had dissolved parliament. But that was the Germans' scrap. America was safe on its own continent.

As an exercise, Benny Foulois in 1933 asked his assistant, Brigadier General Oscar Westover, to fly a trial mission in defense of the Pacific Coast. After the maneuvers were over, Westover assessed the results. Observation and pursuit planes used in the tests appeared "woefully obsolete," he reported to the General Staff. Modern bombers, with their speed and defensive fire, could go it alone. If flown in formation, with silencers and camouflage, "no known agency could frustrate" their mission.

It was soon after this that the double-sealed secret envelope containing General Pratt's proposal for a long-range experimental bomber crossed the desks of Foulois, Westover, Spaatz. General Pratt proposed that Boeing and Martin be invited to submit proposals. These two companies, Pratt thought, were probably the most capable of handling such a project. If the proposals looked good, they'd be given design contracts. Then the better design would be chosen and a contract awarded for

building the plane. Wright Field was willing to put all its experimental money into this one project, Pratt said.

Foulois presented the proposal to the General Staff. The
project would further the plan for a mobile GHQ air force,
he pointed out. A range of 5,000 miles would protect Alaska
and Hawaii. The General Staff agreed.

Claire Egtvedt stepped into Conger Pratt's carpeted office in
Dayton on May 14, 1934, as onto a ship for a foreign land. Nine
or ten chairs flanked the General's desk. Various officers were
arriving and sitting down. Captain Al Lyon said he was acting
for Major Howard who was away. C. A. Van Dusen of the
Martin Company was there.

"The purpose of this meeting," General Pratt began formally,
"is to discuss a procedure under which the Air Corps will consider proposals for construction of a long-range airplane suitable
for military purposes. An airplane weighing about thirty tons
that will carry 2,000 pounds of bombs a distance of 5,000 miles."

Egtvedt caught his breath at the audacity of the plan. He
looked over at Van Dusen who was blinking his eyes; at Captain
Lyon, who was smiling over their surprise. The General continued: "Before I go further, may I ask if you gentlemen are
interested in discussing such a project?" Egtvedt nodded. So did
Van Dusen.

"Good," said General Pratt, and he outlined the data, especially cost estimates, that he'd like to have submitted by June 15
in order to determine upon the award of a design contract.

June 15. One month away. Egtvedt shut his eyes to fix a swirl
of thoughts. Out of hazy outlines he could see a great thing
taking form in the plant, a thing that no one would believe, a
super-airplane. Boeing should build it. Hadn't they been heading
toward it all along? He told General Pratt that the Boeing Company proposal would be on his desk on June 15.

Back in Seattle, a secret area was set off in Engineering and a
preliminary design was drawn for a 150-foot-wing span, four-

engine giant monoplane labeled XBLR-1: *EX*perimental *B*omber, *Long R*ange, Number 1, Air Corps Project A.

The use of four of the new 1,000-horsepower Allison engines would make the airplane possible, though they would provide a bare minimum of power for the weight. The plane would be so different from anything yet built that there could be no leaning on old engineering. Everything would have to start from scratch. Samples of all the critical parts would have to be built and tested. The entire staff of design engineers and aerodynamicists went to work on it. "Strange," said Monteith, shaking his head, "a year or two ago I would have said this was ridiculous." The plans went together like something in a dream, to make the mid-June deadline.

On June 28 a design contract proved that it was no dream and the Project A plane was given the new name XB-15. Jack Kylstra was made project engineer. A place was set aside to build a full-scale wooden "mock-up" model of the control cabin and other parts as required by the contract. If the mock-up and the design data looked good enough, there'd be a chance to build the plane. Representatives from Wright Field came out to consult. There were things in the design to tax the imagination: a wing with a passageway big enough to get out to the four engines in flight; six machine-gun turrets; a flight deck instead of a cockpit, with places for flight engineer, navigator, radio operator and two pilots; sleeping quarters for the crew; kitchenette with hot plates and coffee percolator; a 3,800-pound landing gear.

"There won't be any power left to fly the airplane when we get through driving all this equipment," said Jack Kylstra.

"Put a gasoline engine in the back end to generate 110-volt electricity," Lieutenant Bill Irvine suggested. "That oughta run your percolator." His idea went into the plans.

While the designing of the "improbable" XB-15 was getting started, United Air Lines was looking seriously at the Boeing proposal for a new twin-engined transport, to compete with the Douglas DC-2. By now the proposed plane had grown to twenty passengers, from the ten in the 247. But its performance wasn't good enough. Not a big enough step forward. Thorp Hiscock, now in charge of technical development for United, gave the plans some study. Since the day he proved the two-way radio to be possible, Hiscock had been busy ten to fifteen hours a day in his laboratory proving other things possible, such as automatic pilot equipment and de-icers.

"Why not go to four engines?" Thorp Hiscock asked. Then he added, "I've been talking with General Electric about superchargers. We've been supercharging the air for the engines for a long time. I think it's time we scaled up our cabins and supercharged the air for our passengers, so we can take them above 15,000 feet."

On June 30, 1934, the Boeing twin-engine transport design work was put aside and plans for a four-engine transport were started, with a side study on cabin supercharging. To Claire Egtvedt, things were now coming clearer. "Our business is manufacturing big airplanes," he thought. "We opened up this field; we should stay with it." The idea of a transport and a bomber of parallel design still appealed to him, and when the design of a twenty-four-passenger four-engine transport was started, he suggested that the engineers keep in mind a bomber of equivalent size. It would be about halfway between the twin-engine B-9 and the giant experimental Project A.

Engineering ticketed the potential bomber Model Number 299 and the transport Model 300. They started design work first on Model 300, but Egtvedt's thought went more and more to the four-engine bomber—the still empty file labeled "Model 299."

Everyone understood that Project A, the XB-15, was an experiment. Its purpose was to learn how to build a maximum-size airplane, and it might be years before planes like that could be built in quantity for Air Corps use. The present contract was for design only. They wouldn't know for a year whether they would get a contract to build even one airplane. Yet Project A had been so arousing, so agitating to the imagination, that it was hard to think any more of a twin-engined bomber like the B-9, or the successor to the B-9 they had been planning to offer the Air Corps for production. Egtvedt thought of "Bull" Reeves: *The airplane isn't a dreadnought.* Now those ringing words took on new meaning. *The airplane can be a dreadnought.* Aluminum replaced the grey steel walls of "Bull" Reeves' cabin. The sound Egtvedt heard was no longer the throbbing of the ship's motors on the third deck below, but the roar of Wasp engines on long wings. The fleet was a new kind of fleet. The dreadnoughts were in the sky. Not water-bound. Powerful. Eagles of America's freedom. Egtvedt shook himself. Was he dreaming?

5. *Flying Fortress*

A circular came in the mail from Wright Field August 8, 1934. Specifications for the next production bomber: bomb load, 2,000 pounds; *required* top speed, two hundred miles per hour; range, 1,020 miles; *desired* top speed, 250 miles per hour; desired range, 2,200 miles; a crew of four to six. Interested companies should submit bids for construction of up to 220 airplanes.

Claire Egtvedt read it through. To be eligible for the competition, a flying airplane would have to be submitted by August 1935. One year. Preliminary design of the Model 300 four-engine transport was well along and a few ideas had been set down for the similar-size Model 299 bomber. Egtvedt thought of the estimated performance of the 300, and looked out the window. Again the picture of a fleet of flying dreadnoughts. He read the circular again. "Multi-engined," it said. That was the term the Air Corps had always used to describe the twin-engined category, because occasionally someone would submit a tri-motor. Would a four-engine bomber be considered? Could they afford to build such a plane on speculation?

The stakes would be big. He knew the decision before him would have to be right, or there might be no Boeing Airplane Company. He flew to Dayton to talk to Major Jan Howard, the engineering chief. "Would a four-engine plane qualify?"

Major Howard looked up quickly, squinted, then smiled. "Say, now." He looked at the circular. "The word is 'multi-engined,' isn't it?"

Egtvedt flew back to Seattle and preliminary design work was started in earnest on the four-engine bomber. The plant situation was critical. Total employment was down to six hundred from 1,700 at the first of the year. United Air Lines were uncertain now about a new transport. To build a big four-engine bomber for the Army competition would take all the company's manpower and most of its capital. The plant was operating in the red. The prospect of building twenty-five to 225 bombers loomed like a golden harvest. But the prospect of risking everything on one costly experiment was a terrifying thunderhead over that harvest.

Egtvedt asked Bill Allen, the company lawyer, to come down for a talk. "Bill," said Egtvedt, "I don't want to jeopardize the future of this company. You know what little we have left here. If we undertake this four-engine bomber there'll be lots of unknowns. The design studies for the XB-15 make that clear enough."

"Do you think you can build a successful four-engine airplane in a year?" Bill Allen, like Phil Johnson, had a way of heading right for the point.

Egtvedt looked over the roof of Engineering to the buildings of the plant. "Yes. I know we can."

The board of directors of the newly independent Boeing Airplane Company held its first meeting September 26, 1934, when United Aircraft & Transport was finally dissolved. The sum of $275,000 was voted to design and construct four-engine bomber Model 299, to be delivered to Wright Field for trials by next August. The plant was reorganized on a one-job, maximum-effort basis. Dick Carr stepped down to superintendent and gave Fred Laudan the job of supervising the 299 construction, to start just as soon as Engineering could get the drawings out.

Monteith and Minshall had observed that the younger engineers were coming up with some of the best ideas. The job of project engineer went to Giff Emery, a wiry bundle of energy, and quiet, studious Ed Wells became assistant project engineer. Egtvedt went over NACA airfoils and body designs to select the streamlined shapes nearest to the requirement.

Three-view plans were drawn: a beautiful monoplane measuring 103 feet in span and sixty-eight feet in length, using four 700-horsepower Hornet engines. It was neither a low nor a high wing; more of a mid-wing, a structure with strength and integrity. The results of one hundred hours of wind-tunnel testing were a tonic. The top speed would be at least 235 miles per hour; range, 3,000 miles. That news spurred the seventy-three engineers through their six- and seven-day-a-week, long-hour schedule. There were engineering controversies. "Let's don't stretch our luck," said Monteith, looking over Ed Wells' drawings of landing flaps on the wing. They did seem huge. "Leave the flaps off. We'll have good brakes."

"We can leave them off," Wells said, "but I wonder if we can afford to lose the performance." He laid out the comparative data showing the plane could land and take off with 2,000 pounds greater load by using the device. The flaps went in.

By December a good share of the drawings were in the shops and the men were pouring in the rivets. Treasurer Bowman tallied a net loss of $226,000 for the four months since Boeing had been an independent corporation. Dick Carr surveyed the plant and said it was inadequate for any quantity production of four-engine bombers. Work went on. The Board dug for another $150,000 needed to finish the ship.

By the first of July, 1935, the 299 body and wings were ready to go to Boeing Field, draped over with canvas because of military security regulations. Newspapers spread rumors about a great "mystery ship." Almost simultaneously, in a secret double envelope, a contract came from Wright Field for construction of the even larger "mystery ship," XB-15. Project A would become a reality.

The month of July in the Boeing Field hangar, getting the 299 ready for flight, was rugged. Fred Laudan checked in with the day shift, out with the night. The final week there were no shifts. All worked as long as they could. Flight date was set for Monday morning, July 28. From Saturday morning, everyone stayed to see the job through.

The ship came out in the light for taxi trials, a gleaming giant bristling with five machine-gun turrets. Newspaper reporters called it an aerial battle cruiser, *a veritable flying fortress*. Test pilot Les Tower sat in the instrument-filled control cabin, rehearsing his role. So did Louis Wait, his assistant, and Henry Igo of Pratt & Whitney, who would be the flight engineer.

Before sunup on July 28, a cluster of men stood on the edge of Boeing Field, shivering a little in the morning mist, their hearts and soles of their feet catching the rumble of four idling engines at the far end of the field. The rumble grew to a burning, firing roar and the big form was moving toward them down the runway, racing past them. Les Tower lifted her slowly, surely, over the end of the field. As though timed by a stage crew, the sun popped over the ridge of the Cascades, its brightness glistening on the polished wings that streaked to meet it, and the 299 was a receding speck in the sky.

Claire Egtvedt shut his eyes and smiled. Minshall turned to Ed Wells, who had been promoted to project engineer. "Nice work, Ed. Great work."

299 Flying Fortress

August 20 at 3:45 A.M., Tower, Wait, Igo and little Bud Benton, the head mechanic, were cutting the darkness toward the Cascade Mountains with a nonstop flight plan for Dayton.

There hadn't been time to run many flight tests. Most of the time had been spent getting new engine parts out from Hartford and putting things in working order. Henry Igo had been up all night with his power plants and was pretty groggy. So were Wait and Benton, though none of them would admit it.

Les Tower, who'd had his sleep, rode the controls over the mountains like a cowboy. Once in a while he'd turn around with a grin and ask Igo how the fans were turning. Two hours out, Henry Igo came up from his study of the temperatures and manifold pressures. "Let's give her the works," he said. Tower put the propellers in manual high pitch and let the Hornets go to work.

"Our ground speed is 235 miles an hour," yelled Louis Wait, who was navigating. It was exhilarating. Bud Benton served fried-egg sandwiches. The automatic pilot flew the airplane.

Exactly nine hours after leaving Seattle they were coming down at Wright Field. Two thousand miles nonstop at 233 miles an hour. Bud Benton was dancing. "It's impossible. Unheard of."

Claire Egtvedt and Ed Wells, awaiting them at Wright, were under the cockpit door when they got out, to shake their hands heartily and pat them on the back. Bud Benton wondered why there were so few people around.

"You're not supposed to be here," said Wells. "Claire and I estimated you'd be due an hour from now. The field expects you in two or three."

The days that followed were in high key. A twin-engine Martin B-12 and a twin-engine Douglas B-18 were the competition, but all eyes were on the "Flying Fortress" as the newspapers now had it named. Pete Hill, head of Dayton flight test, was plainly impressed, even awed by the big fellow. He assigned Lieutenant Don Putt, a spirited young pilot who was enthusiastic about the plane, as project test pilot. The competitive evaluation began, according to the rules: speed, endurance, time to climb, service ceiling, structure and design, power plant, armament and equipment installation, maintenance, landing characteristics, utility as a type.

Preliminary flight test results looked excellent. Egtvedt and Wells were buoyant. Oliver Echols, who had taken Jan Howard's place as chief of engineering, followed the plane's tests like a Yankee fan the world series. Jake Harman wore a big grin. Brigadier General A. W. Robins, the new CO succeeding General Pratt, was cordial. The 299 would win the competition for sure.

One morning in October the tower crew at Wright Field watched the Flying Fortress warm up for take-off. The four engines gave their battle roar, the ship rolled down the runway, first slow, then slithering-fast, then lifted. The duty officer whistled. It was an impressive sight, watching the big ship clear the ground. The airplane was climbing steeply. Too steeply. "Hey, what?" It was heading straight up, falling off on a wing. The officer hit the emergency button. The plane was coming down, straightening out again now, almost but not quite enough. Going to hit.

There was a belch of flame and smoke from the wing tanks as the 299 hit ground. Fire trucks streaked toward it.

Jake Harman, bombardment project engineer, in conference with General Echols, heard the sirens, heard someone say "299," raced out and hailed a field car, teeth set. Fire trucks were pouring foam on the burning plane and a crowd was standing transfixed when Harman arrived. He scrambled, with Lieutenant Giovanelli, onto a flatbed truck.

"Back it in there!" he shouted at the driver. Pulling coats over their heads, with arms shielding their faces, Jake and Giovanelli dove from the truckbed into the furnace and dragged out Pete Hill, the pilot, and Les Tower. Don Putt, face gashed and burned, had jumped from the front end shouting, "Look at the control stand." Two other crew members scrambled out the back end. All were rushed to the hospital.

It was discovered that the ship had been taken off with the control surfaces locked. This was a new thing, having tail surfaces so big they had to be locked from the cockpit against the whipping of the wind on the ground.

Major Hill died that afternoon. A bitter blow. Les Tower, who had been on the flight as an observer, was badly burned but expected to live. Putt and the others would be all right. General Robins telephoned Egtvedt in Chicago where he'd been trying to sell the four-engine transport to United.

"Oh no. No," Egtvedt whispered. It was word the body couldn't bear. He headed desolately back for Dayton.

There was no airplane now for the final judging. The last item on the evaluation sheet—utility as a type—was all that was left, but that called for flights by operating commanders. The 299 was ineligible under the rules.

"There must be some justice in the world," wrote Treasurer Bowman. "Maybe we can sell the design to England." He added, "Our bank account is overdrawn."

Les Tower rallied but he was taking the failure personally, blaming himself for not having discovered the oversight about the control lock. It took the heart out of his recovery. Egtvedt assured him it wasn't his fault. Then word came that Les Tower was worse, Les Tower was gone.

Les Tower. Losing an airplane was nothing like losing a man.

The flotsam and jetsam of the wreck began to wash in. There were statements in Washington that this was more airplane than a human being could handle, and the rumor grew that the twin-engine Douglas B-18 would get the production contract.

Egtvedt clung to Dayton and Washington to see what could be done. He found the Air Corps was full of friends. Men like Tooey Spaatz and Hap Arnold insisted the Flying Fortress must be carried on. Arnold was a brigadier general now, in command of the first wing of the new GHQ Air Force, under the Army General Staff. Commanding General of the GHQ force was Frank M. Andrews, and Colonel Hugh Knerr was his chief of staff. Knerr and Andrews took up the campaign for the four-engine plane. At Dayton, Jake Harman wouldn't let go of the rope he was pulling. The new engineering head, Oliver Echols,

who had been down at the Air Corps Tactical School listening to
Hal George's strategic bombing concepts, grabbed the rope to
give the others a hand. There would be a way.

The six hundred people left on the Boeing payroll in Seattle
were doing their Christmas shopping with a prudent peek at the
bottom of the purse when news came through that the Air Corps
had ordered the Douglas B-18 for production but would place a
service test order for thirteen of the four-engine Boeings, plus a
fourteenth to be built for structural tests. The airplane would be
known as the B-17.

6. *The Transoceanic Step*

Douglas won the production order; still, the building of thirteen Flying Fortresses and the experimental XB-15 would be a
sizeable undertaking. Claire Egtvedt's thoughts were pulled far
from engineering and design as he considered the program ahead
in 1936. There was a business to manage; there were contracts to
be kept; stockholders expecting the business to operate at a
profit, not at a $334,000 loss like last year's.

Then there was the problem, always most evasive, most trying,
of work for the future. Egtvedt wanted mightily to capitalize on
the new bomber design with a plane that would put them back in
commercial business. It had looked for a while in the fall of 1935
as if United and American Air Lines would both buy the Model
300 four-engine transport. Then their interest cooled and they
ended up putting some money in a pool, which TWA, Pan
American and Eastern joined, to help Douglas build an experimental four-engine landplane called the DC-4. This seemed to
kill the chances of selling a domestic airliner.

Pan American Airways had just bought three Martin flying

boats for their overseas routes. Their future requirements weren't clear, but their plans were big. Pan American dealt with oceans. Already they were pioneering the transpacific route and beginning to think about the Atlantic. That would take big airplanes of long-range, large-passenger capacity. Egtvedt considered the possibility of doing something with a commercial adaptation of the XB-15, but Pan American needed flying boats. He wondered if the Boeing plant facility was suited for building and launching huge flying boats. He wondered, too, if they could finance such a project.

The present plant wasn't even adequate for four-engine bomber production, and that had to be taken care of first. Even if they had to borrow the money for it, it was imperative that they get a site next to Boeing Field, the King County Airport, for future expansion of land plane production.

Egtvedt called Bill Allen down to talk about this and about reorganizing the staff for the new days ahead. With the aid of Elmer Sill, the realtor, they got the plant-site program under way, then turned to the organization question.

"You're loaded down," said Allen. "You should have an executive vice president to take the administrative load."

Monty Monteith, a good administrator, was the logical choice. Monty had already given Bob Minshall most of the engineering responsibility, and Bob could now be made chief engineer. Erik Nelson, vice president in charge of sales, was going to leave the company. To fill his position Fred Collins was promoted. They had another go-getter in the sales department, Wellwood Beall, a new man who'd been over in the Orient seeking pursuit-plane business, but who might be more useful in Engineering. A graduate of the Guggenheim School of Aeronautics in New York University, Beall had been in charge of engineering instruction at the Boeing School of Aeronautics in Oakland for a short time before he joined the Seattle organization. He'd be a good man to start a service department to handle engineering contacts with the customer.

The changes were made effective February 19, 1936. They

brought other promotions along the line. Work to do. New jobs. Raises. Smiles. Wellwood Beall swung into Fred Collins' office.

"Congratulations, Mr. Sales Manager."

"Congratulations yourself," said Collins. The two young men had become close friends.

"Anything you'd like out of Engineering?"

"Yes, let's have some commercial airplanes around this place."

Wellwood Beall went back to his corner of Engineering, fiddled with his T-square and doodled on a yellow pad while he thought over the whirlwind events of the past year and a half.

It had started when the company's sales prospects were dragging bottom and Beall got the sudden order in August 1934, to go to China and sell some pursuits. He'd called his fiancée, Jean Cory, in Oakland; four days later they were married and sailing on the *President Jackson* for Shanghai. In China, Beall sold ten P-26 type pursuits to the Cantonese provincial government. Caught in the great Yangtse flood while at the inland town of Kiukiang, he spent three days watching swirling water from a second-floor window. At Hangchow, he met T. Wong, head of the Central Aviation Manufacturing Company, who recalled his days as chief engineer of the old Pacific Aero Products Company.

Back in Shanghai, Beall and Jeannie were at the Cathay Hotel at a cocktail party, where Americans were making each other at home in the Orient. Out on the Wang Po River they could see one of the President boats at anchor. Chinese coolies were trotting up the Bund with the ship's cargo, singing their minor, mystic rhythm. The sound coming in through the open windows was in strange contrast to the excited comment over a bit of unusual news at the party. Captain Ed Musick had just flown a Pan American Sikorsky-type clipper to Midway Island. The rumor was that China and the U. S. would be linked by a regular air service before the end of the year.

"That's a lot of poppycock," said Beall. He was flashy with bow tie, trim mustache. "It's a beautiful stunt. You can do lots of things with airplanes as a stunt, but it'll be ten or fifteen years before that sort of thing is commercially practical. Don't let anybody kid you." The guests were glad to be put straight on this, though a little disappointed. Beall didn't much notice the frown on Jeannie's forehead.

Not long after, the Bealls headed back for the States. After a whirling year, all was suddenly quiet, slow. Jeannie twitted Beall: "Isn't this boat kind of slow for an airplane man?"

"Well, peaceful anyway."

"Did you think over that statement you made about air travel to China being ten or fifteen years off?"

"I don't think they can do it. I don't think they can get equipment that will do it."

"I'll bet you'll have to eat those words," said Jeannie.

That rebuke of Jeannie's haunted Beall as he sat now, fiddling with his T-square and doodling. Collins was right, they should be building some commercial airplanes. Beall thought back to that afternoon in the Cathay. "A lot of poppycock." Since his return Pan American had put the first of its three new Martins in service on the Pacific. Why hadn't he kept his big mouth shut?

Beall walked out into the shops, possessed of an idea. "Maybe I can do something to correct that mistake." He walked past the receiving storeroom, where they were piling up stocks of structural aluminum tubing, some of it three inches across; past the machine shop, where a machinist was shaping a big hunk of steel into a wing terminal; through the welding shop, idle now; through the empty body shop; in and out the doors of the smelly anodizing and paint shops, and into the big wooden assembly building on the Duwamish backwater. That was where the parts for Project A were going together.

The wing shop had taken over the whole floor, to stretch the 149-foot span of the XB-15 between the balconies of the high, barnlike building. The structure of the main wing was going together. It would mount four 850-horsepower twin Wasps. The Allisons originally contemplated hadn't panned out. Another half wing that would soon be tested to destruction under a load of lead was almost completed. Beall looked into it from the large end, through the inside structure toward the tapered tip. He shook his head. You had to see it to believe it. The "M's" and "W's" of the structural members were repeated dozen upon dozen like some low attic braced for a phenomenal snow. Under the bracing there was a heavy inner skin of corrugated aluminum, to which was attached the smooth outer metal skin. A wing big enough to crawl through.

The people who said it wouldn't hold together with its thirty-five-ton load should see those two wing spars that constituted the main lengthwise structure. They were built like a bridge truss, out of pieces of that big square tubing. Ernie Orthel, the wing-shop foreman, spotted Beall. "You like it?" he asked.

"It's weird and wonderful," said Beall.

"Every morning when I come to work," said Orthel, "I tell myself, 'It's the wing of an airplane.' "

Beall went on back by the outside road, walking slowly, eyes squinting at a sky full of thoughts, hands in his pockets. There *was* a way he could correct this Cathay folly. Action would out-speak words. Pan American needed big airplanes, long-range air-planes. It was Boeing that was building big airplanes, building the XB-15, long-range bomber Number One. He could see those great wings flying to China, carrying not bombs but fifty, maybe seventy passengers.

In the days that followed, Beall spent his spare time looking at data on the XB-15 and adding things up. He went to Bob Min-shall, now the chief engineer. "Why shouldn't we get into the flying boat business—submit a Clipper design to Pan American?"

"We've already discussed that," said Minshall. "Claire and I both talked with Pan American about it last year. We just got a letter from Frank Gledhill a couple of weeks ago." He showed Beall a letter dated February 28, 1936, from Gledhill, the Pan American vice president and purchasing agent, asking if Boeing would be interested in submitting plans for "a long-range four-engine marine aircraft" built around engines of 1,000 to 1,250 horsepower.

"That would be right in the XB-15 class," said Beall.

"That's right," said Minshall. "But we can't do it."

"Why not?"

"Money. Facilities. Manpower. Look at the date when they want the drawings. We're up to our neck now in drawings for the B-17s and the XB-15." Minshall looked tired. Responsibility was putting furrows in his round, full face.

"I'd like to work on it, if that would help," said Beall.

"We've already written Gledhill that we won't be able to enter a proposition by that date."

Beall went home disturbed. The thought of a transoceanic flying boat based on the B-15 seemed important, powerful. It wasn't an idea original with him, he'd found, but he was inspired with it. He tried to shrug it off; it was none of his business, he was supposed to be the service engineer. But the idea wouldn't be put off. It was there. When he said No to it, the word fell short of its mark. Something bigger than himself kept saying, "Yes, yes."

"What's bothering you?" asked Jeannie.

"Remember what I said about a commercially practical trans-ocean airplane being ten years off?"

"Yes." Jeannie was matter-of-fact.

"I think we could build one now, based on the B-15."

"You could?" Jeannie left Beall with his thoughts.

Beall got out some paper and began making layouts on the dining-room table. Even if the project wasn't authorized, there was nothing to stop him working on it at home. He started with the B-15 wings and tail. The bottom of the body would have to be a boat hull, with a step at the back so you could get the nose up for take-off. The sides might as well come straight up from the outer edge of the hull bottom. That would provide good, straight-sided passenger compartments, like a ship.

Night after night he worked there on the dining-room table. A control cabin like the one in the XB-15 would give room for desks for flight engineer and navigator and radio operator behind the pilots. That would take all the space in front of the wings. They'd need a full deck below for the passengers. A two-deck airplane. Beall thought the sponsons, or short sea wings, that Martin used on its flying boats would be safer than wing tip floats to stabilize it on the water. They would be big enough to contain the fuel tanks, too.

After some throwaways, the sketch was beginning to take a positive form. Occasionally Jeannie would glance over Beall's busy shoulders. "It looks a little like a whale," she said. Jeannie had pictured it more round and sleek like the Flying Fortress.

"What's that? What did you say?" Beall was preoccupied.

"I said it looks like it really should sail."

"Yeah, yeah."

Beall took the sketches to Bob Minshall.

"Say," said big Bob. "I'd like to talk to Claire about this." Egtvedt was in Dayton. Minshall called him, suggested they try to get an extension of the Pan American deadline. Egtvedt said go ahead and try. Minshall wrote Gledhill right away, March 31. Gledhill agreed.

Minshall promptly got up steam. He relieved Beall of the service engineering assignment and gave him eleven men to complete the layout and performance calculations. With sleeves rolled high, they got into the details. The giant craft would be 109 feet long, with a wing span of 152 feet, much too large to be assembled in the plant, but the hull and wings could be built inside and assembled afterward on the ramp. There'd be space in the hull for seventy-four passengers and a crew of six. With gross weight of 82,500 pounds—six tons more, even, than the XB-15—they could get a range of 3,500 miles. Ralph Cram, head of aerodynamics, went to the NACA for data on hull lines. The XB-15 wing was adopted unchanged for the proposed boat.

In April, out in the assembly building, the XB-15 test wing was piled high with bags of lead shot for its destruction test. Lanky John Ball, head of the stress unit, watched cold-eyed as his men added a bag here, a bag there. Jack Kylstra, project engineer on the XB, was watching intently. Others gathered for the spectacle.

The wing was crackling as its design load was being approached. "Put on another increment," John Ball ordered. The men cautiously added bags. The spectators took a safe distance. Stark silence, except for an ominous snap. "Next increment." This was 94 per cent of design load. Monteith stood solid on both legs, watching; Bob Minshall was rubbing his chin.

"Another increment," said Ball. The bottom skin was wrinkled.

"One hundred per cent load." The wing held. Cheers broke out.

"Add another increment," called Ball, his eyes brightening. More bags of lead went on. The air was tight. "One hundred six per cent."

A cannon went off. In one instant the explosive report filled the building, bit their ears, rivets peppered the wall, people ducked for cover, and the proud wing lay crumpled on the timbers built to catch it. It had done the job it was supposed to. The giant XB-15 would fly, and so would the big Clipper ship that was on Wellwood Beall's mind.

The general layouts and performance estimates for the proposed flying boat, labeled the Model 314, were complete by the time Egtvedt returned to Seattle in late April. Egtvedt was enthusiastic when Minshall showed them to him. On May 9 he left with Beall and aerodynamicist Ralph Cram for New York to show the plans to Pan American Airways. Beall sat beside Egtvedt on the flight east. He had a portfolio of watercolor drawings his artist wife had made of the passenger compartments and central dining salon. It was impressive. "They ought to be able to sell tickets to London on this," he said.

Egtvedt agreed. "But it's the B-15 wing that should give us the advantage," he said. The bouncing little DC-3, making one of its frequent descents for fuel, seemed incongruously small. Egtvedt was opening his mouth and trying to yawn, his ears obviously hurting with the pressure change. "Some day we've got to have a plane that doesn't murder a man with sinus trouble," said Egtvedt.

In New York, Frank Gledhill was tremendously interested in the 314, and André Priester, the little Dutch dreamer who was

Pan American's chief engineer, smiled from ear to listening ear. Egtvedt called lawyer Bill Allen to join them for contract negotiations. In Pan American's high tower in the Chrysler building, and nights at the Barclay hotel, they compromised on problems of cost and performance guarantees, and on June 21, 1936, a $3 million contract for six Boeing 314 Clippers was signed, with an option for six more.

7. Over the Weather

While the meetings with Pan American were going on in the Chrysler building's high spire, a meeting of a different sort was taking place in the Munitions building in Washington. The officers of the Army General Staff were assembled: G-1, the general for Personnel; G-2, Intelligence; G-3, Operations; G-4, Supply. The Chief of the Air Corps was there, Major General Oscar Westover. His assistant, Hap Arnold, was sitting on the sidelines with General Frank Andrews, head of the GHQ Air Force. Oliver Echols, the Air Corps engineering chief from Dayton, was there and with him Jake Harman. The meeting was for the purpose of discussing bombardment airplane procurement policy.

General Westover explained the bomber program. The Air Corps had a quantity of twin-engine B-18s on order and thirteen four-engine B-17s were under construction for service test. This year they'd like to allocate funds for more B-17s.

"Isn't that the Boeing airplane that crashed in Dayton?" asked one of the generals.

"Yes, unfortunately we lost the experimental plane."

"And the bigger one—Project A—is that project still going on?"

Oscar Westover squared himself in his chair. "Yes, it's under construction."

"Why do we need airplanes that big?"

Westover looked at Colonel Echols and Echols nodded to Lieutenant Harman, who unwrapped the charts he had prepared and stuck them along the walls with pieces of masking tape. The charts compared the capabilities of bombers according to performance and size. The Martin B-10 was shown as a starting point, then the twin-engine Douglas B-18, the Boeing B-17 Flying Fortress, the XB-15, in Category Three of the developmental list made up in 1933, and finally the still bigger XB-19, an experimental project in Category Four which they had just asked the Douglas Company to design. Westover explained the added power of the bigger ships, their greater range, how increased speed enabled them to perform more missions per day, and how larger wing area enabled them to carry a larger load. No one interrupted, but there was a restlessness among the listeners.

One chart showed the big airplanes as troop carriers; the bigger the shell of the plane, the more troops it could carry. When the Air Chief came to this chart, G-3 broke the tension. He jumped up and waved an arm at the chart. "Why haul people around in the air?" he demanded.

Westover faltered, as a man struck by a weapon he couldn't see, couldn't understand. Before he had recovered, G-4 was concurring. "I guess that's a good question. Now I have a question I'd like to ask. Isn't it a fact that airplanes are getting too big for their metals?"

Westover turned to Echols. "Will you answer that, Colonel?"

Oliver Echols, a solid engineer, slow of speech but penetrating, rose to his feet. "I don't see that they are getting too big for their metals. At one time we built bridges out of wood. When we had to have bigger ones, we built them out of a low-grade iron. Finally we needed to get them still bigger, and we used high-grade materials, high-test cables. You decide what you need—what you want to do—and you can find the technical means of doing it."

"I still think they're getting too big for their metals," said G-4.

Another general took issue with the 5,000-mile range of the

XB-15. "That's absurd," he said. "The Navy will protect our shores. The Air Force should be confined to three hundred miles off shore."

General Frank Andrews came forward. "Gentlemen, I suggest we have a war game on paper so we can all see just what the big bombers can do." There was banter and confusion. The meeting was adjourned, off key.

G-4 prepared the report to Chief of Staff Malin Craig. Concentration on the big bombers was inconsistent with national policy and threatened unnecessary duplication of function with the Navy. No country had or was soon likely to have aircraft capable of attacking the United States. The twin-engine B-18 was equal to any mission assigned to the Air Corps and was much less expensive than the proposed four-engine ships.

True, there was no threat of war. The disturbing sounds from Europe and Africa were dim and inarticulate. The ear hears nothing without first listening. There were a few things it was nicer not to hear. Like the news about Ethiopia surrendering to Il Duce, and der Fuehrer sending his troops into the Rhineland.

Back in Dayton, a few months later, Jake Harman was still simmering over the Washington rebuff when Oliver Echols called him in. "Look, Jake," said the Colonel. "I have an idea. We aren't going to get any more than the thirteen B-17s for a while. We could make it fourteen if we made a flying airplane out of the one that is supposed to be used for static tests. I doubt if we need those tests, after the successful XB-15 wing test in Seattle, and all. What would you think of taking that plane and making a new model out of it? Go all out. Put turbo-superchargers on the engines. Whatever you can think of."

"Sounds like a good idea."

"What would turbo-superchargers do for the speed of the 17?" The turbo-supercharger was a device which General Electric was perfecting to take power from the engine's exhaust to run a turbine that would feed pressurized air back into the engine. It would make flight possible at much higher altitudes.

Harman got out his slipstick and worked the numbers back and forth. He got it quickly. "Two hundred ninety miles an hour at 25,000 feet." Maybe he was a little high.

"Get hold of Boeing and see if they'll do it," said Echols. "I'll see if I can dig up some money."

In one corner of the engineering department at Seattle, a few drafting tables were separated from the rest by a glass partition and a door on which were stenciled the words RESTRICTED AREA. PRELIMINARY DESIGN. There was no general traffic through this enclosure. The place had an aura of mystery. It had been used by Ed Wells and Giff Emery and the team that laid out the first lines of the original 299 Flying Fortress. Thereafter it had been set aside as a permanent place for free thought on things new.

The men in Engineering nodded assent when quiet Ed Wells was chosen to head the group of designers who would work in there, apart from the rest. They'd see Ed slip in and out of the place. Wells the person would disappear in the Wells of silent, orderly thought. They had a feeling he was in his right place there; a tap on the shoulder and he'd come out of that thought with a smile, not a frown.

Every so often Claire Egtvedt would come down and lean over Ed Wells' table. This time he had a new question. "Do you have enough information on turbo-superchargers to put them on the B-17?"

"I'm not sure," said Ed. "But we can get it."

"Wright Field wants to equip the static test ship for high altitude."

"How high?"

"Twenty-five or thirty thousand feet."

"Not cabin supercharging?"

"No, just engines," said Egtvedt. "But if we get the airplane up there, we'll have to do something about the air in the cabin sooner or later. Oxygen masks won't be so good for long flights."

Wells shuffled through some drawings and brought up the three-view outlines of the Model 307 four-engine transport they'd been working on, an improvement on the 300, which didn't sell. Egtvedt scrutinized it with one eyebrow lowered, one gathered high, and nodded. He had seen it before in a slightly different form. Now the body cross-section was a perfect circle, and from the side it had the symmetry of a slenderized dirigible. It was this way because provision was being made for a cabin that could be supercharged, or pressurized within, maintaining low-altitude atmospheric pressure at high altitudes, as Thorp Hiscock had suggested back in 1934. A circular structure was best because air pressure wants to expand equally in all directions.

"The interesting thing," said Ed, "is that when you supercharge the cabin you're forced into a better-looking design."

"That shows it's the right thing to do," said Egtvedt, pleased.

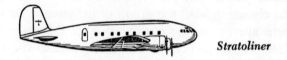

Stratoliner

The new transport design called the Stratoliner, utilizing the wings and tail surfaces of the B-17 Flying Fortress, was timely. With all the opposition in Washington to further B-17 purchases, the transport market took on new importance. And it seemed to be opening up. Some of the airlines were unhappy about the joint project for the Douglas DC-4 four-engine transport. When sales manager Fred Collins unveiled the Model 307 drawings and explained that the plane could be put in the air quickly because of Boeing's four-engine bomber experience, Pan American and TWA saw a possibility of jumping ahead while the other lines were waiting for the DC-4.

The financing of such a project would be a problem, but the Board was already planning an issue of new stock to give the company needed substance for the work ahead. "We'll see if we can get the airlines to help with the cost of the supercharged cabin development," Egtvedt told Wells. "If we can't, we'll do it ourselves. This is a development that must come. We might as well get it behind us." Pan American said they'd underwrite part of the cost. To them, it was a chance to get up over the weather. TWA said they were interested in supercharging, but they wouldn't want it installed right away.

Things went together fast as 1936 drew to a close and 1937 opened into spring. Cigar-champing Stanley Umstead from Wright Field flew the first B-17 and liked it. On the third flight the brakes locked and the plane skidded eighty yards to a stop on its nose with the tail pointing at the sky, but Superintendent Fred Laudan's men pulled the tail back down and repaired the nose damage.

TWA signed for six of the thirty-three-passenger four-engine Stratoliners, and Pan American signed for three. The Air Corps contracted to have turbo-superchargers installed in the B-17 static test ship. With 173,000 shares of new stock sold, plans were made to double the size of the new building on the Boeing Field site up the Duwamish, to be called Plant Two.

The old assembly building at Plant One was crammed to the balconies with the first two 314 hulls, trussed up in the three and a half carloads of lumber that formed the work platforms. The hulls looked impossibly huge, with riveters attacking them at four different levels on a half mile of plankways. More like houses than airplanes. "They'll never fly," was the universal comment of visitors.

At Plant Two, more B-17s were completed for delivery to General Frank Andrews' GHQ Air Force. When Andrews and his command pilots, Bob Olds, Barney Giles, V. J. Meloy, Caleb Haynes, and others, got their hands on the control columns, they celebrated by breaking cross-country speed records, flying majestic formations, drilling on bombing technique with the mysterious new "Blue Ox" bombsight. The 17 proved a stable, steady platform from which to set the sight. "We can drop 'em in a pickle barrel," Andrews boasted to the General Staff.

There was still opposition, both in the General Staff and Congress. "In big ships of that character we have too many eggs in one basket," said one Congressman debating appropriations.

"I am happy to say that we carry no money in this bill for anything bigger than two-engine planes." But General Andrews told the General Staff flatly that he didn't want any more two-engine bombers. And Oliver Echols promised the next models of the Fortress would be made still more effective, with turbo-superchargers pushing the speed to more than 270 miles per hour and the operating altitude to 25,000 feet, making them almost invulnerable to attack. By August 1937, the appropriation bill had been changed and the Air Corps ordered thirteen of the supercharged airplanes, to be called the B-17Bs.

The first thirteen B-17s were completed. Materials were coming in for the four-engine Stratoliners. At Plant One the Model 314 Clippers were pressing the walls. Boeing Airplane Company had suddenly become a hatchery full of big chicks. The one that was first in the incubator—the one labeled Project A—was getting so large and full-feathered that it would have to fly soon.

XB-15

8. *Running to Keep Ahead*

The XB-15 was a 5,000 mile bomber, capable of spanning a continent, a deadly weapon in the hands of someone who wanted it to be one. But also an airplane; a big, beautiful airplane, with red and white tail stripes bright in the morning sun. Powerful and strong, it had a paternal look. Why?

Ed Wells, twenty-seven, *summa cum laude* at Stanford, engineer, American, stood under the great wing. The XB was out on the concrete apron now, in front of Plant Two, just across the Pacific Highway from Boeing Field. To Ed, the new plane was a symbol of what they were trying to do: stretch, strain, work to make the airplane something superior. This wasn't a business you could walk in. You had to run to keep ahead. Still, you had to know what you were doing every step, or you'd be in real trouble. As Jake Harman once put it, "You've got to be just as conservative as you can allow yourself to be while you're running ahead real fast." Because you were always trying to make the airplane do something that an airplane had never done before. Here was an example. Project A. Trying to see how big you could make a plane; how far you could make it go. Why?

Ed thought of the preamble to the Constitution. "We the people of the United States, in order to ... provide for the common defense ...and secure the blessings of liberty to ourselves and our posterity..." *To secure the blessings of liberty.* There was virtue in strength if that strength was virtue. America wanted to preserve, not to disturb. The government even hesitated to buy this sort of plane lest someone think they had aggressive intent. "Be sure to explain that its purpose is to defend our coasts," Washington had cautioned when the new bomber first emerged into public view.

The XB-15 and the B-17 Flying Fortresses, bought with coins that said "In God We Trust," were power for defense. The motive of the user was what would give the airplane its power for good or for evil. Wasn't motive, really, a litmus test of vision, to prove whether or not it was a source of lasting power?

Standing under the wing, Ed Wells sensed that the source of America's power was born of the liberty and integrity under God of the country's founding fathers. But there seemed also to be another power, through history, threatening people's liberty. At a distance just about equal to the XB-15's range from Seattle, on an almost straight path along the 50th parallel, daylight was fading into night at the height of Seattle's morning. Adolf Hitler, fifty-eight, reader of the "bible" of his own writing, der Fuehrer, stood before a painting of Frederick the Great, noting that when the light struck it right it became a mirror. Hitler was pondering the source of power, too. It was possible, by means of shrewd and unremitting propaganda, "to make people believe that heaven is hell—and hell, heaven." Conquest was "not only a right but also a duty," his own text said. Humaneness was "a mixture of stupidity and cowardice." Der Fuehrer saw not only the Third Reich, but one day the German race as "master of the world."

Ed Wells wasn't thinking of Hitler, but of the work to be done to make good America's trust. He had no illusions about the XB-15, now nearly ready for flight. It was notable as a proof of what could be done with size, and how range could be stretched, but he knew it was far underpowered. The B-17 could fly circles around it. If they could get the 17 up to high altitude with turbo-superchargers, it would be a tremendously effective airplane, much less vulnerable to attack than the 15, impressive as the Project A giant might be.

Wells went into the high-roofed assembly building to see how the turbos were coming on the B-17A. Charlie Morris, who had been assigned to head this special project, was there. "I'm worried about what these things are going to do to the air flow," said Charlie. "Ralph Cram and the aerodynamics boys think it'll be O.K., but I don't know."

The turbo-supercharger, developed by Dr. Sanford Moss of General Electric with the aid of Wright Field, was a turbine wheel with many little paddles like a steam- or water-driven turbine, except that this one was to be turned by flaming exhaust gases. A supercharger was to be mounted on top of each engine nacelle, and the exhaust gas would be routed to take a torrid whirl through its blades, emerging on the surface of the nacelle before fanning away in the slipstream. It was this air disturbance on the wing that concerned Morris.

But they had already concluded this was the only place the turbos could go. The turbine wheels couldn't go on the bottoms of the nacelles because the landing gear retracted there, and besides, if there were ever a fuel leak it would come right down into the turbo. The exhaust stacks were always put on top to avoid this danger.

"Clean it up the best you can," said Wells. "We're running some more wind-tunnel tests." Wells went on to the superintendent's office to ask about preparations for the XB-15 flight.

On October 15, 1937, Eddie Allen wheeled the giant XB to the far end of the Boeing Field runway. Gentle, thoroughgoing Eddie Allen was now a consulting engineer and test pilot for various companies and was rated best in the business. Major Johnny Corkille, the Air Corps representative at the plant, was with him at the controls. Top mechanic Mike Pavone was at the flight engineer's station. They had rehearsed their roles well and taxied for several days, testing brakes and getting the feel of the control surfaces.

Satisfied, Eddie cut loose, rolled ponderously down the runway and took off. The big ship came off the ground like an airplane. The two auxiliary gas engines that Bill Irvine from Wright Field had proposed were working away in the back end, charging the ship's seven miles of electric wiring. Eddie found the bomber stable and airworthy, though sluggish in speed. Tests continued through November, until the big plane was ready for delivery.

While Colonel Bob Olds and the GHQ Air Force were gaining headlines with a good will flight of six B17s to Buenos Aires, made in two 2,500-mile jumps, the XB-15 slid down to Hamilton Field, California, to widen the eyes of field crews there. Private R. F. Fowler of the 31st Bombardment Squadron sent the *Air Corps Newsletter* his impressions: "Because of the distance between motors, the most practical means of communication is the radio. The weather report is all important. The crew on one engine may be enjoying perfect weather while the crew on the neighboring engine is engulfed in a blizzard. Each man is equipped with a compass, because at the last landing one person got aboard unnoticed and wasn't found for days."

The XB-15 was remarkable. But it wasn't ordered for production.

Adolf Hitler and Benito Mussolini proclaimed the Rome-Berlin axis. In March 1938, Nazi storm troops marched into Austria. Der Fuehrer looked again on the face of old Frederick the Great and nodded.

The B-17A was ready for a trial flight with its GE turbo-superchargers. Johnny Corkille would be the test pilot. Corkille, a steady officer, had tested all the B-17s and had come to love them. When he'd set one of them down on the runway from a flight, usually he'd be whistling a little tuneless tune. He had some apprehension, however, about this flight.

To see just how much the whirling turbo would disturb the air flow over the top of the wing, Charlie Morris and Ralph Cram had stuck tufts of yarn all over the wing surface. Bill Irvine was out from Dayton for the test. Corkille took off with the turbos disconnected. Irvine was riding behind him, watching the yarn tufts as the plane climbed to 10,000 feet, where the superchargers were to be turned on.

Corkille cut them in. There was a rumble throughout the ship and things began to shake. Irvine noticed the yarn tufts flapping idly over a ten-foot area behind each engine, not streaming with the wind as they should. Corkille turned the turbos off to reconnoiter. "Watch the instruments," he said. Then he pushed the turbos on again. The engine instruments surged to 25 per cent more power, but the air speed indicator was dropping. The plane was shaking again. Suddenly it grew violent, heaving and throwing them with a clapping of metal. Corkille snapped the turbos off a second time, drops of perspiration on his brow, and got the ship steadied. He looked around quickly. "See about the tail."

A mechanic ran aft. The disturbed air flow had whipped it mightily but it was still intact. Corkille got back on the field as fast as he could. He was shaking when he climbed out and told Ed Wells, "We'll not try that again. Not me."

The blow came at a critical time. They had been planning to put the turbos on the B-17Bs under the contract for these planes that had recently been increased from thirteen to thirty-nine planes.

"We can't jeopardize our delivery schedule on the B," Egtvedt said. "If the turbo won't work we'd better give it up."

Captain Bill Irvine, not the type to let go, drew on a cigar and blew the smoke at the ceiling. "I think we can make it work," he said.

"The contract allowed $75,000; we've already spent $100,000 on it. How much farther can we go?" Egtvedt was beginning to weary of the battle against the costs of big-plane unknowns. It looked now as if the Clippers, too, would come out at a loss.

Irvine reported to Wright Field that things didn't look good for the turbos. But Oliver Echols, who had started the project, was far enough away to miss seeing the obstacles. "I want it done," said Echols.

Bill Irvine went to Wells and Charlie Morris.

"They won't work on top of the nacelles," said Morris. "I guess that's proved. And we can't put them on the bottom."

"Can't we?" asked Wells. "We haven't proved that yet." He was studying the NACA wind-tunnel results.

"What about the landing gear and the fire hazard?" Morris asked.

Irvine took a calloused view. "The fuel isn't going to leak down there. If we have the wing vented, any fuel that leaks will go out the trailing edge."

Morris brightened. "Well, I guess we could get the pipes around the landing gear. It's mostly a structural problem."

In a few weeks, Morris came up with a design; Oliver Echols dug up some more money and another start was made on the B-17A.

If supercharging the engines was a problem to Wells, now assistant chief engineer in charge of military projects, so was supercharging the cabin of the Stratoliner transport to Wellwood

Beall, assistant chief engineer in charge of commercial projects.

Cabin pressurization up to now was only an idea, not a reality. The Air Corps had experimented with it in the Lockheed XC-35, sealing the pilot's compartment and ramming in air, but there was no provision for constant ventilation and pressure regulation. A transport would have to be comfortable for passengers. It would require a combination of pressurization and air conditioning. Altitude conditioning.

Beall gave the job to Nate Price, who'd been working out the heating system for the Model 314 flying boats. There were months of experimenting, with a fifty-gallon oil drum for a "pressure cabin" and a motor-driven blower to supercharge it. Jim Cooper and other engineers helped. The result was a device that would automatically maintain the proper differential between outside and inside air pressure.

Beall took it to the patent attorney. "In a few years this ought to be in every airplane in the country," he said.

Beall's other commercial project, the Pan American Clipper, was approaching the zero hour for the first launching in late May 1938. Most of the 50,000 parts were now in it. Factory Manager Fred Laudan, quick-stepping, quick-talking, was all over the plant and in and out of project engineer Ed Duff's office to see about final changes. Laudan, meticulous but pleasant about it, had lost his last spare hair about the same time as the last piece of scaffolding came off the hull. Now carpenters were cutting away the whole back side of the assembly building so the hull could be dollied out to a newly built dock, where high derricks could attach its wings. Out there it looked for the first time like an airplane, a tremendous flying boat. *Atlantic Clipper*, Pan American Airways had named it.

314 Clipper

A national radio network had its microphone set up on the dock when the day came for the launching, May 31. Tide tables set an insistent deadline of 5 P.M. for the ship to hit the water so there would be ample depth to get out through the shallows and link up to a barge for the trip down the river, under the Spokane Street drawbridge and into the bay. Lowering it into the water would be a delicate operation. When the hour struck, the ship began to move and the radio men were on the air:

"This mighty triumph of American enterprise, this great Flying Clipper ship that will span the Atlantic and the Pacific carrying the flag of the United States to world supremacy in the air, is being lowered majestically into the water here at the plant of Boeing Airplane Company in Seattle." The announcer spotted Laudan coming by. "The vice president and factory manager of this plant, Mr. Fred P. Laudan, is directing the operation. We are going to ask him to say a few words to our nation-wide radio audience." An assistant grabbed Laudan's arm and coaxed him to the microphone. "Mr. Laudan, what does this occasion mean to you?"

The harried Laudan spared one glance from his ship. "Me? It means just one great big headache."

Newspapermen from the East arrived for the flight. Jim Piersol, *The New York Times* reporter and something of an aeronautical engineer, wore a skeptic's scowl. "The tail is too small for all that airplane," he said.

"Quit worrying," said Wellwood Beall. "It's been tested. It's based on the B-15 and that's doing all right."

Wednesday afternoon, June 1, the ship was towed to a buoy off Duwamish Head. She rode regally past Port of Seattle piers. A Pan American tender launch and three Coast Guard picket boats followed, carrying press and officials. The engines would be run up first, with the ship tied to the buoy, then they'd do some taxiing. Eddie Allen revved up the four 1,200 horsepower Wright Cyclones with a roar that roused the hillside and sent up great tails of spray. After a time the fourteen-foot propellers were stilled and Eddie leaned out the high window of the control cabin. His small shoulders and intent, sensitive face looked tiny above the big hull.

"Going to taxi?" someone asked from the press boat. Eddie shook his head. They had to change the fifty-six spark plugs.

Thursday Eddie taxied easily about the bay. Cars lined the hillside streets. Afterward the press wanted to know when he'd fly. "Just possibly tomorrow," said Eddie. "We have a thousand controls and each of them has to be adjusted two or three times before we go up."

It was 3:30 Friday when the *Atlantic Clipper* struck out for the open water of Puget Sound. The picket boats were trailing hawklike. The Clipper was way ahead now, pushing out past Alki Point, where the first white settlers of Seattle climbed wooded shores eighty-seven years ago.

There was a fresh wind sweeping down from the Straits of Juan de Fuca and the water was choppy. Eddie seemed to be having difficulty. The ship rocked when he slowed it down, as though in delicate balance. "Keep as close to him as you can," Beall coached his Coast Guard skipper. They had to allow a good deal of open water between them for safety's sake. Eddie swung around into the lee of Magnolia Bluff. He slacked speed and felt his way back toward the city before a following wind. The right wing was low. "Guess they aren't quite used to it," Beall said to André Priester of Pan American.

"Seas are tricky," said Priester. Eddie started a turn to starboard, toward the mooring. Beall saw the right wing coming down. He stiffened. It was still coming down. "Do something, Eddie!" The wing tip hit the water, started sinking, the left wing pointing high to the sky.

"Get over there. Come in behind," Beall shouted to the picket boat pilot. The wing tip seemed to be digging in and taking the ship with it. The right outboard engine was nearly down to the water. Eddie was gunning the right engines full out and had the tail hard over. They couldn't bring the picket boat very close. Then, slowly, the wing began to come up. Now it was in the clear; the ship swinging around the other way. "It's going on over," Beall shouted. The roll didn't stop at center; the left wing was going low.

Eddie cut the engines dead. A man crawled out the navigator's turret on top, with life jacket. Then another, and another. They were crawling up the high wing, out toward the tip. Their weight brought it down into balance against the wind. It stayed level.

Beall heaved a great sigh and got over to the Clipper. The crew threw a sea anchor out to hold it until they could get a tow. Beall turned to Priester. "I'm glad we put watertight flotation compartments in the wing tips. They may have saved her."

By dark they got the ship back to the barge.

"Not seaworthy?" asked reporter Piersol.

9. *Extremity*

The *Atlantic Clipper* had been lightly loaded and the fuel was in the wing tanks instead of in the sea wings, so the center of gravity was high. That may have made her unstable. Next test they'd ballast. Saturday, June 4, they put 2,600 gallons of gas in the sea wing tanks, and a ton of lead shot in the passenger compartments. Tomorrow she'd fly: 6 A.M. was cast-off time.

The bay was still as a mill pond. The newsmen were aboard the picket boats with questioning gaze as the boats cut the water again on the trail of the 314. Things went better on the water, but there were no indications of flight. All day the ship taxied back and forth. Occasionally it stopped while mechanics came out to work on the engines. It grew late. Eddie headed back. Then, turning into Elliott Bay, the wing tip went in the water again. Again they got it out.

The newsmen demanded to see Claire Egtvedt. "What *is* the trouble?" they asked.

"Remember," Egtvedt said, "no one has operated a boat like

this before. The co-pilot gunned the engines on the wrong side by mistake. We may decide to lower the tips of the sea wings some to make it steadier."

André Priester stepped in. "Those troubles are trivial," he told the reporters. "The real news is in the high-speed runs. The spray curls back clean, under the sea wings. This is a real airplane—not one that covers itself with spray so it can't get off well."

Tuesday the plane was loaded to 77,500 pounds, just 5,000 pounds under its maximum, and was set for flight, but there was a strong wind up. At five o'clock a message came from up-Sound that the wind was slackening. It was a good omen. Eddie headed the Clipper west. With throttles open, he skipped off the water past Duwamish Head and Alki Point, then taxied downwind. At the end of a long run he put about and prepared for a take-off to the north while Beall in the lead picket boat got the other craft into position.

At 6:17 P.M. the great roar of the Cyclones sounded across the water and Eddie was moving toward the picket boats. They raced full speed ahead to stay parallel. Salt spray in the face and high excitement aboard, they bounced through the waves as the big-hulled flying boat roared past them, sailing high on the step. Everything was rushing: water, wind, airplane. Ahead, the great hull skimmed the surface, lifted up, straight on up, steady into the air, up and up into the northern sky. Yells of applause broke into the wonderful freshness of the wind. They watched the flying Clipper sail out of sight.

After a thirty-eight-minute flight, Eddie Allen landed on Lake Washington, where further testing was to be based. Beall caught up with him at Matthews Beach later in the evening. "We had power to spare," said Allen. "But when I got off the water I couldn't turn. Just not enough rudder for that big body. When we got to 2,000 feet I used the ailerons and power on one side for a wide ten-mile turn."

Beall looked at Allen, painfully. "I was wrong," he said. "I guess we don't know as much about control surfaces as we thought we did."

The Clipper model went back in the wind tunnel with a double instead of a single tail. When the change was engineered and installed in the ship, Eddie Allen came back to fly it again. The twin rudders turned it all right, but now the plane had a peculiar, weaving course of flight, not straight and stable. There were some things you just couldn't learn in the wind tunnel. You got approximate results and then you had to try them out in flight. A central fin was added between the two tails, giving the ship a triple tail. This worked, both for control and stability. The angle of the sea wings was also lowered for better stability on the water.

These were expensive changes, with six of the big planes under construction. From the cost figures, Claire Egtvedt could see plainly that the Clipper contract was going to come out with a loss. The Stratoliners would too, unless they could sell some more of them, to take advantage of the engineering and tooling that they'd already paid for. The cost of research and engineering for big airplanes, though Egtvedt thought of it as an investment for the future, was tremendous. He looked at the charts. The original 299 Flying Fortress had taken 153,000 man-hours of engineering. They had thought that was a lot. But 280,000 hours were going into the B-17B. The Clippers were taking 380,000.

Egtvedt wondered if anyone quite realized what this meant. You wanted to build something new that would be an advance to aviation, something that was needed. You had to guarantee what your new thing was going to do before you had ever built one of them. You couldn't sell enough to make it a good production job—and yet you had to put a price on it that wouldn't scare the customer clear away.

You knew it would take you three or four years to finish the job. The cost of labor and materials might go up in the meantime. You had a plant full of new people who had to learn how to do the job. Then there were changes that you hadn't figured on and other changes the customer wanted. They all cost money.

You had $14 million worth of orders to fill and only $4 million working capital. Your capital was already spent for plant and equipment, for materials and work in process, so you had to borrow from the banks to make your payroll. You could get more capital to work with if you could make a profit. But not if you were operating at a loss. And you were the man responsible. Everybody looked to you. Employees, stockholders, customers. Wearied and worried, Egtvedt sat at his desk and pulled out his slide rule, wishing desperately that the little white stick in the friendly brown case could solve this as it would an engineering problem, but it could not.

Fred Laudan came in to say that union negotiations were deadlocked. Last year the union got an increase and now it was back for more. "Ten cents an hour or strike."

"We can't do it," said Egtvedt. "Our wages are already 20 per cent above the rest of the industry average."

"We've told them that again and again," said Laudan. "We're at the end of our rope."

Egtvedt had the union spokesmen in his office and told them the facts.

"All right," was their reply. "We strike tomorrow." One of the men got up and stalked the floor, shouting angrily about cooperation.

Egtvedt's face was white. "You just want to break the company and put your own men out of a job. I tell you"—Egtvedt's fist came down on his desk—"you walk out and there won't be any jobs to come back to."

That brought a furious rebuttal. In the middle of it, burning with frustration and unaccustomed rage, Egtvedt walked out of the room. For minutes he stood at the window of his outer office, searching for calm. Finally he turned. "I guess I can go back in now." Then he gave it to them again, straight and cool. Every week's payroll required a new bank loan and this would be the last straw, they probably wouldn't be able to get any more loans. The union backed down.

Jake Harman was out from Dayton to see about the B-17A which was getting its turbo-superchargers installed underneath the engine nacelles.

"It's going to work," said Ed Wells. "We have the structure licked and the wind-tunnel data looks good." Behind the 17A on the assembly floor were the bullet-round bodies of the first three Stratoliner transports. Lysle Wood, project engineer, and N. D. Showalter, who supervised the Stratoliner body design, were optimistic. Wells showed Jake Harman through the transport with pride. This was a good chance to give the proposed pressurized version of the B-17 a plug.

"We can get you better than three hundred miles per hour at 25,000 feet, and a bomb load of 9,900 pounds," he told Harman.

Jake didn't spark. "Got some bad news for you on that," he said finally. "The War Department turned down Oliver Echols' request for a pressurized bomber project." Then he added, "This won't make you happy either: they've asked us to put no four-engine bombers in our estimates for fiscal 1940 and '41."

Ed Wells went back to his engineering.

Hitler was shouting at Nürnberg about rebuilding an empire strong enough to last a thousand years. "The German Reich has slumbered long. The German people is now awakened and has offered itself as wearer of its own millennial crown." Hitler's shrill voice drilled sharp into the ears of Franklin D. Roosevelt at the White House. The President wanted to know how much the airplane industry could expand its production if need should come.

Then he called in his military men. If it was going to be war, it would be in the air, he told them. Hap Arnold, made chief of the Air Corps when Oscar Westover was killed in an accident, listened soberly, glad that the White House realized this. Oscar Westover had said that the future of aviation, both military and civil, was "indelibly linked with the success of the big airplane," and he'd called the Flying Fortress "the most successful type of plane, everything considered," ever developed for the Air Corps. But Arnold was concerned about Boeing's ability to produce. None of the B-17Bs was delivered yet, not even the B-17A; only the first thirteen B-17s. He asked Boeing to work out a license agreement with the Consolidated Aircraft Company in San Diego, so they could produce the 17 if need be. Consolidated engineers were quick with an alternate plan. "The Fortress design is four years old," they said. "Let us design something new that's faster, longer range. We could get it out in a hurry." Arnold couldn't deny that that made sense. Consolidated got started on the B-24. A replacement for the B-17?

Strange, that at the hour the warning bell was ringing in Europe and in Washington, the future of the Flying Fortress should be in doubt. Still, new things were happening. On December 31, 1938, Eddie Allen and a crew of four took the first Stratoliner up. The flight went well. The B-17A with its turbos was also finally proved out and made ready for delivery in January. Finally the *Atlantic Clipper* was tested and approved by the Civil Aeronautics Authority. It, too, would be delivered in January.

The year finished with a $500,000 loss and Claire Egtvedt felt the horns of a dilemma. The only hope of recovering the loss was to keep the B-17 in production. But the 17 might be losing out. Egtvedt had memories of what had happened to the B-9 and the 247. The only way they could prevent that would be to come up with a new bomber design. But that would take time and money. They didn't have the money to do it without Army support, and passage of time simply meant more loss. The commercial ships were dragging them more and more in the red.

To gain a little more freedom to grapple with the problem, Egtvedt put Bob Minshall in the job of assistant general manager, a position Monteith had resigned because of ill health. Jack Kylstra became chief engineer. Egtvedt set out with Ed Wells to talk to the Army about the pressurized bomber design based on the B-17 and the Stratoliner. The new plane would at least use the wings and tail surfaces they were already making.

Oliver Echols was unenthusiastic. "The only official requirement I have is for 3,000 miles range and three hundred miles per hour," he said. "That's the specification Consolidated is designing to. It's only a shade better than the B-17B. Your improved model could do that easily. But that isn't what we *need*. What we need we've known for a long time. We need at least 4,000, better 5,000, miles. And we don't want to sacrifice speed and altitude to get it. We need better armament. Nothing less than fifty-caliber. Tail guns especially."

"We can put in a lot of armament and cut down the performance, or we can keep the performance up and stay out of the fighters' way," said Wells. "Which is better?"

"Both," said Echols. "We ought to have both."

At Langley Field, Bob Olds was equally earnest. "Our job," he said, "is to defend these coasts. If there's an aircraft carrier approaching our shores, we have to be able to go out and bomb it before it gets close. Thank God, we have the B-17. It's the only thing that can do it. But we're skating on thin ice. We have to bomb them by daylight, and we only have enough radius to reach the carrier on its last day. We want radius enough to work them over the second day out. But we haven't been able to get any money for that kind of airplane."

The operating people always talked about radius rather than range. The radius was the distance to the target, plus the return trip, plus allowance for spare fuel, military load, head winds, and contingencies. The B-17 had a range of 3,000 miles but the Air Corps called its radius 1,000 miles. To do what Bob Olds was talking about would require a range of 5,000 miles.

Egtvedt and Wells took stock on the way back. "It's obvious the airplane they're buying and the airplane they need are two different things," said Wells. Egtvedt knew it, too, but the idea came hard. More new development. More research. More expense. High speed and long range both, Echols wanted. You couldn't do it with any conventional design. They were going to have to head out again into the unknown.

"On everything we've done so far," Claire said, "we've started out with a purpose—an honest purpose. That's what we've got to keep doing. We've got to build the airplane that we think best meets the need."

Back in Seattle, Wells got Giff Emery, now heading the preliminary design group, started on a superbomber study. "See if you can find some way to get the drag down," he said. "Way down." That was their only hope of accomplishing what Oliver Echols asked.

They started on the engine nacelles. These were the big drag items on the wings. "Let's try putting water-cooled engines inside the wings. Do away with the nacelles; just have a propeller shaft coming out." It was at least a new approach. It didn't look too promising at first. Then the engine manufacturers said they could build a flat type engine that would fit better in the wings. That brought a new ray of hope. Ralph Cram and his staff worked on the aerodynamics side. Things were beginning to go together.

The day arrived for delivery of the *Atlantic Clipper* to Pan American Airways. It was January 29, 1939. Under a lead-gray sky, pilot Earl Ferguson lifted the big flying boat from Lake Washington on its delivery flight to Astoria, Oregon, where the ship would change hands. Frank Gledhill and other Pan American people were along to complete the transaction. Wellwood Beall, as seller, co-pilot and radio operator, was having his day.

The course was set to the mouth of the Columbia River. The plan was to fly visual contact with the ground; there was no commercial airway radio beam over this route. They stayed low because of the covering clouds. It seemed odd droning along in a huge boat over hills and treetops. They were more than halfway across when the clouds darkened, and in an instant they were blind in a sky full of snow.

"The forecast didn't give us anything like this," said Beall. Ten minutes passed. Instead of coming out of the storm, they were getting in deeper. Pilot Ferguson veered west to be sure he was clear of some hills. The big ship was being buffeted heavily. Another five minutes passed. Beall wanted the worst way to know where they were. What were the wind drift and the new compass heading doing to them? His heart pounded.

"Shall I call Grays Harbor Coast Guard to give us a bearing?" he asked Ferguson. The call might be regarded as an emergency procedure.

Ferguson nodded. "Go ahead." His forehead was wrinkled. Beall requested the radio bearing from Grays Harbor. A voice blared in his earphones. "You're right over us. We can see you." Relieved, they headed out to sea until they emerged from the snow cloud, then swung around under it up the huge mouth of the Columbia River. They sat down nicely opposite Astoria and anchored.

A rowboat came out and took them to shore. They had to scramble up the muddy slope from the river's edge.

An Astoria banker led them to his office, where the sale was to take place by means of an elaborate telephone conference with Pan American's New York office, a New York trust company, and the Civil Aeronautics Authority in Washington. It was approaching the 2 P.M. deadline for the call.

The lawyers had mimeographed a fifty-four step routine. "Is the airplane at Astoria in fit and sound condition?" asked New York. Beall affirmed that it was.

"Is Mr. Gledhill there to receive it?" Gledhill said "Yes."

"Mr. Beall, have you the certificate of title?" An electric shock struck Beall. He'd forgotten the certificate. It flashed before his eyes, there in its metal frame on the wall of the stairway to the control cabin, out there in the middle of the river. He had no voice. Quickly, Frank Gledhill fished out a blank piece of paper and nodded vigorously to Beall. Beall stammered, "Yes, yes, I've got it here."

"Will you sign it and pass it to Mr. Gledhill?" Beall signed the blank paper.

"Civil Aeronautics Authority, will you record the transaction?" It was recorded in Washington. The $100,000 final payment check was handed to Beall. Phones clicked. Beall looked around at worried faces.

"What the hell have we done here?" asked the Astoria banker.

"It's all right," said Gledhill. Then he turned sternly to Beall. "Beall, you happen to be the most valuable guy in the world at this moment." He grabbed Beall by the back of his coat collar. "Let's go get that damn piece of paper."

Beall's feet sank ankle deep in the mud bank. What if the certificate wasn't there? What if the rowboat overturned in the choppy water? What if ... They got out to the ship. The certificate was there. The screwdriver shook in Beall's hand as he got it off the wall. He gave it to Gledhill and sat down. Limp, happy.

"You need a vacation," said Gledhill. "Better come along on the maiden flight to Hong Kong."

Pan American was planning to start operation first on the Pacific, then the Atlantic. On February 22, the Clipper Ship— Number Two—soared out over San Francisco's Golden Gate Bridge. Aboard, Wellwood Beall thought of the time he had headed out this way before, five and a half years ago. He wished Jeannie could be with him now. Hawaii, Midway, Wake, westward in the sky. Beall thought of the people at the Cathay, his words of wisdom: "Just a stunt. . . ." Those people would know better now. They'd know that he knew better.

Over the blue expanse between Honolulu and Wake Island they passed above the sailing clipper *Trade Wind*. Captain W. A. Cluthe circled a salute.

With stops en route, the trip lasted three weeks. On March 14 Beall stepped onto the Pan American dock at San Francisco. The newsboys on the dock were shouting something. News of their flight? He could hear a little better now: "Nazi troops in Czechoslovakia."

In Washington, an apprehensive Congress was considering Roosevelt's proposal for a half billion dollar defense program,

$170 million of it for airplane procurement. Claire Egtvedt, with Jim Murray, the company's vice president and eastern representative, was holding close to Washington and Dayton. They found the Air Corps people brutally frank about Boeing's chances. "You are good at design, but poor on production. You haven't delivered a single B-17B." Egtvedt felt no one realized the struggle they had with turbo-superchargers and other modifications. There had been no opportunity to work on a production basis. But the record didn't look good.

They learned that the B-17 would be in the defense program, all right, but maybe its production would go to one of the California plants. The schedule now called for delivery of the first two "Bs" in May. Fred Laudan said it was going to be tough to make that. "We've got to," said Egtvedt. Laudan hired more men, though he knew that new hands couldn't get them finished.

Sales manager Fred Collins and his new assistant, Ben Pearson, were working hard to get more orders for the Stratoliner transport. Eddie Allen had finished his part of the initial testing of the Stratoliner. The pressure cabin hadn't been tried in the air yet, though it had been pumped full of air in the plant and given a ten-man rubdown with soapsuds to see if the air would bubble out at the seams. It didn't.

On the weekend of Beall's return from the Clipper flight there were two representatives of the Dutch airline, KLM, in Seattle to fly in the Stratoliner. The visitors weren't so interested in the supercharging as in the control problems of a four-engine plane. "What happens," asked Albert vonBaumhauer, the engineer of the two, "if you have two engines out on one side and the rudder clear over for a maximum angle of yaw"—that would have the airplane crabbing sideways—"and then you put it in a stall?"

Bob Minshall looked at Ralph Cram. "You have no reason to do that with a big ship like this," said Cram. Still, vonBaumhauer wanted to know. He had made a study of this. It was agreed that they would try out various angles of yaw at low speeds, not stalling speed, and would get some measurements of forces with a spring scale attached to the control column. They would also do sideslips, stall tests, and other stability tests.

It was a gloriously bright Saturday afternoon in March 1939. Mount Rainier was out bold. Phones rang. The sheriff's office had a report that a giant plane had crashed in the Mount Rainier foothills near Alder, Washington. Radios went on. An eyewitness said it had fallen out of the sky in pieces. It was a four-engine plane. Hope against hope. The Stratoliner was flying in that vicinity.

The sight in the mountain woods was heartrending. Sheriffs' deputies had taken Boeing test pilot Julius Barr out from the pilot's seat; vonBaumhauer, the Hollander, from the co-pilot's seat; chief engineer Jack Kylstra, Ralph Cram, Earl Ferguson, Ben Pearson, Peter Guilonard, the other KLM man, Harlan Hull, the chief pilot of TWA, Bill Doyle and Harry West, Boeing men.

The stark story was pieced together. They had been near stalling speed, at the point of starting the stability tests or possibly the sideslip tests. The cabin supercharging had not been in operation, was not a factor. They had gone into a spinning dive. At an altitude of 3,000 to 5,000 feet, still with plenty of room but with hills looming black and imposing below, they had pulled out of the dive so suddenly that the wings and tail surfaces broke from the excessive loads.

That bleak night, Bob Minshall who was in charge in Egtvedt's absence, asked, "What am I going to do? What am I going to do?"

Claire Egtvedt came home. The President's rearmament program was authorized and the first $50 million for airplane procurement appropriated. An initial order for Consolidated B-24s was placed, before the experimental model was built. No Boeing planes were included among the orders. Neither was the first B-17B going to be out in May. In spite of everything that had been done, that schedule just couldn't be met. The plant was still operating at a loss.

Ed Wells came to Egtvedt about the new superbomber design. "We've got 4,500 miles range and 390 miles an hour. It looks wonderful. But, as you said, we've started out with an honest purpose and I've got to be honest about this. It isn't a good airplane. With the engine in the wings there's no good way to retract the landing gear, and the structure isn't good around the engines. We can't make the wing any thicker. It's awfully wide already to keep the chord in proportion." The chord was the width of the wing measured from the leading edge to the trailing edge.

Claire Egtvedt listened. One more blow. "Man's extremity . . ."

10. *Lightning Strikes*

"We have an opportunity here," said Eddie Allen, "that exists nowhere else. We've come to the point where we need exhaustive research. Not just on the ground. In the air. Flight research. Flight and aerodynamic research."

Eddie Allen was in Bob Minshall's office. His brown eyes were earnest. He sat on the front edge of his chair, his heels hooked over the rungs, and leaned toward Minshall.

"You're right about that," murmured Minshall.

"Now," Eddie's finger shot up. "You can't do that sort of thing in small airplanes. You have to carry all kinds of instruments and equipment. The Boeing Company is the only company in the world that has a stable full of big airplanes. You have the background in big airplanes. You have the need. You have the future in big airplanes. You're the ones to do it."

"Just what do you have in mind, Eddie?"

"The day when you build an airplane and call in a pilot like me to test it, is over. There should be a full-time, fully staffed department constantly carrying on this flight research, and the same department should carry on a constant program of wind-tunnel research. The two go hand in hand. And they should both be part of the process of designing the plane, not just testing it."

"Would you be willing to head up a department like that?"

"I'd like nothing better," said Eddie. "On one condition. We should be free to do our own work. We should report directly to you, not to Engineering. We may want to explore some ideas they wouldn't approve. But of course we'll work very closely with Engineering."

Minshall talked to Egtvedt about it. Egtvedt okayed the plan, and they made Eddie Allen director of aerodynamics and flight research. Wellwood Beall took Jack Kylstra's empty chair as chief engineer, with Ed Wells as assistant chief. Lysle Wood had Beall's old job as chief commercial projects engineer and N. D. Showalter was chief of military projects.

There was a spirit to go ahead. Showalter was a pilot, too. Eddie Allen asked him if he'd go along to test the Number Two Stratoliner. Quick-stepping little Arthur Price, the pre-flight inspector who had given the final O.K. on every plane since 1930, looked up from his checklists like a bookkeeper and nodded, "She's ready." Eddie and Showalter repeated the stall tests and found the ship came out nice and straight. They tried the cabin superchargers at high altitude. It felt wonderful. Over-the-weather flying was here to stay.

Eddie said he wanted to work on the extreme angles of yaw but he'd start in the wind tunnel. They should fix the plane so it couldn't get into those extreme angles even in test flights, if that was what the pilots were doing up there the day of the crash. A new $16,000 ten-foot wind-tunnel model of the airplane was built, with propellers powered by little electric motors and with remote control on its tail surfaces—something they hadn't had before.

Eddie didn't recruit a team. The men he needed gathered around him. George Schairer, an aerodynamicist who had left

Consolidated, asked Eddie for a job. Eddie took him on, told him to spend most of his time with the new model in the University of Washington wind tunnel. He did and they came up with a new stabilizing dorsal fin not only for the Stratoliner but for the B-17s as well. "What should be more stable than a plane you have to aim bombs from?" asked Eddie.

George Schairer at twenty-five was proving a brilliant analyst. He looked the part, with a high forehead, thin-rimmed glasses. Schairer talked with Beall and Wells about the pressurized superbomber studies. The problem was how to get the drag of the airplane low enough. When they had tried putting the flat engines inside the wing they had cut out the usual nacelle drag and slicked up the body, but still hadn't reached the performance goal. "Had you thought of going at it the other way around?" asked Schairer. "The wing itself is your biggest item of drag. Instead of enlarging the wing and putting the engines in it to get rid of the nacelles, why not make the wing just as small as we can and then go to work to clean up the nacelles?"

Beall looked at the ceiling. Wells studied the tabletop.

"That's what we did at Consolidated on the B-24. Used a high aspect ratio"—aspect ratio was the ratio of the wing length to its chord—"long and narrow, just the opposite of what you have here." Consolidated's B-24 bomber, Schairer explained, was going to employ an airfoil section, or wing cross-section, developed by David R. Davis, a consulting engineer. It had what they called laminar flow—made the air lie down flat over almost all of its surface. Davis called it a "wonder wing." "I thought it was just a lot of fast talk," said Schairer, "until I went in the wind tunnel with it against the best one of ours. Davis beat us hands down."

"Can we buy it from Davis?" asked Beall.

"I'll ask him."

Eddie Allen and Schairer made studies of what the new wing would do for the superbomber. They got 390 miles an hour and pushed the range up to 5,333 miles, with 2,000 pounds of bombs. They'd have to make the wing carry forty-seven pounds of load per square foot to do it. That was stretching it pretty far com-

pared to the thirty-two pounds per square foot in the Fortress
and thirty-four in the internal engine plan. But it would give
them the performance they were looking for. The problems of
untried flat engines, structure around the engines, place to retract
the landing gear, were swept neatly away. The internal engine
plans went into a bottom drawer. But negotiations with Davis
were slow. Finally Beall said, "Let's develop our own wing. We
don't need the Davis patents. We can work out something
better."

Schairer and Eddie Allen got at the job.

The old enthusiasm was returning. That could work out any
problem. They were on the right track now for a superbomber.
The new design was given the designation of Model 341. Meanwhile, Pan American opened transatlantic air travel with the big
314 Clippers and the B-17B Flying Fortresses were being
delivered.

In Washington, the GHQ Air Force was put with the rest of
the Air Corps under General Hap Arnold. In August the Air
Corps staged a big air show at Wright Field, at which Bill Irvine
was named project officer to recapture some world records for
the U. S. Jake Harman and Stanley Umstead flew the B-17B from
Los Angeles to New York in a record nine hours, fourteen
minutes. Bill Irvine took the B-17A to 33,400 feet altitude and
259 miles per hour with load. Major Caleb Haynes entered the
B-15 in the heavyweight carrying brackets. When the four-day
celebration was over, six new world records had been set, five
of them with the big Boeings, one with a Grumman amphibian.

The President's rearmament program was going ahead, and it
seemed inconceivable that the Flying Fortress would not be
ordered in greater numbers. Lawyer Bill Allen went to talk
things over with Egtvedt. "Why don't you try to get Phil Johnson back in the company?" Allen suggested. "The need now is
production. That's Phil's long suit."

The proposal rocked Egtvedt at first. But then, what Bill Allen
was saying was true. Production was Phil's long suit. He had

what the company needed now, maybe what the country needed. Egtvedt had to admit that his own heart had never quite left Engineering. If he were relieved of the management burden he could better counsel the young engineers, better help in creating and selling the new superbomber. That was the company's need too. That might even be the country's greatest need.

Egtvedt talked to Phil, who had been in Canada for two years getting Trans-Canada Air Lines started. Phil was not eager. He was all set for retirement. This was late August, 1939. Then...

September 1, out of false stillness, *Blitzkrieg*. Lightning struck Poland. Foot soldiers ran without direction from under Hitler's screaming dive bombers. Europe, all the world, went into shock. Communist Russia attacked Poland's rear. Nazi tanks raced on. *Blitzkrieg*.

September 8, President Roosevelt declared a state of national emergency. On September 9, Phil Johnson became president of Boeing Airplane Company with Claire Egtvedt as chairman.

BOOK THREE

THE TEST

The days of World War II were a desperate dream. Engineers and pilots had done things with the airplane in those days that they otherwise never would have dared. Days of test, those were. Test of the ability to produce. Test, bitter test, of the product in skies full of fire. Test of freedom's ability to survive, and then of its ability to win. They were days that called out for courage. Out of courage and out of the fire had come new strength.

1. *Mounting Pressure*

Phil Johnson greeted tension with a friendly air. Phil was heavy now, impressive of figure, yet with that casualness he couldn't lose. "This is a slightly different proposition that we had here in the '20's," he said, settling into the executive chair to survey the situation of Boeing.

He used to know what an airplane was. Now the planes were so enormous and complicated that no one man could know them. There were a dozen different kinds of engineering involved: mechanical, structural, hydraulic, electrical, aerodynamic, radio, acoustical, sanitary—he didn't remember what all. Scores of different skills and semi-skills were now used in the plant.

The financial situation. They were over their heads. Treasurer Bowman showed a loss of $2,600,000 for the first nine months of 1939. They had used up all the bank credit. They'd have to get some money somewhere quickly to buy materials for the planes on order.

The backlog of orders amounted to $28 million on September 30. There were still thirty-two of the B-17Bs to be delivered, and a new appropriation under the 6,000-plane program had brought orders for thirty-eight B-17Cs, with an option for forty-two more. That wasn't many, compared to 6,000. Was Washington just looking at numbers, ordering mostly small planes so the money would go farther? Still, thirty-eight more Fortresses was no small job. They were getting a contract, too, for 255 primary trainers to be built at the Stearman division in Wichita, Kansas. This would amount to $2,800,000, a big job for Wichita. Stear-

man had built 179 of the primary trainers for the Army and
Navy in the past five years.

There were nine Stratoliners to be delivered and Pan American
was about to order six more 314 Clippers. All of the first six flying boats had been delivered now and Pan American had made
good its plan for an airway to Europe. Europe. No one knew
what was going to happen there. Did the quick knockout of
Poland mean general war? The question left Phil with a feeling of
insecurity. He supposed that this, more than anything else, was
what had led him to say he'd come back. A sixth sense kept telling
him that was the thing he had to do.

England and France were crying for airplanes. Some kinds of
airplanes, that is. Not Flying Fortresses. "Flying targets," the
British called them. Phil believed thoroughly in the Fortress, but
that didn't change the fact that Douglas and Lockheed both had
big orders on their books from the Allies because they were building twin-engine bombers; Curtiss and some others had big orders
for pursuits. Boeing had none.

The signs weren't clear, except one that said there was much
to be done. Phil Johnson grabbed the control column and took
off. He talked the financing problem over. In October he went
east with Bill Allen and two Seattle bankers to see about getting
a loan from the Reconstruction Finance Corporation. He asked
Allen to start work on a plan to sell new stock. "We've got to
get rid of the deficit, get some capital to work with," Phil said.

He called in Beall and Eddie Allen to talk about new designs.
The superbomber—Design 341—was coming along well. Wright
Field was highly interested, but they had no requirement for it
yet. Congress was still turning down appropriations for long-
range bombers because they were "aggressive," might get us
embroiled in Europe's troubles.

"Superbomber" was a word that variously struck pride, security, and dread in the minds of Americans in 1939. A great prayer
went up from America that its people might be preserved from
involvement in war. It was hard to admit that the prayer was not

of completely honest conscience, that there were other humans crying out for help and support. The fear of war overrode this. Would the building of superbombers increase this risk? Isolationists said it would. Our job was to fortify ourselves, that was all. This, generally, was the view that prevailed. This, too, was the prime concern of the military establishment.

No one feels the digging, marrow-piercing threat of war like the responsible heads of the military establishment. M-day, to them, meant responsibility for lives and country on their shoulders, and planning for M-day had to be their incessant preoccupation. Chief of Staff Malin Craig, though no air man, had appointed an Air Board to make a study of hemisphere defense, before his term of office expired September 1, 1939. The day that Hitler invaded Poland, the Air Board's report hit the desk of George C. Marshall, beginning his six-year term as Chief of Staff. No longer were naval forces and coastal defense batteries sufficient to protect the U. S., the report said. Airplanes could hop from Europe to South or North America. A threat to the western hemisphere was a threat to the United States. The distances and the speed of air action spelled only one answer—a flexible, long-range air fleet.

General Marshall was impressed. "This establishes, for the first time, a special mission for the Air Corps," he said. Military airplanes at last had a job of their own. Marshall appointed General Frank Andrews as G-3, Chief of Operations, on his staff, and Flying Fortress-loving Frank Andrews became the first air officer ever to sit with the generals who governed the Air Corps.

The impact quickly hit Wright Field. When Ed Wells visited Dayton late in 1939, he found the place astir. "Keep working on that big bomber," said Oliver Echols. "We're going to have a new requirement soon. It'll take all you've got to meet it." Jake Harman was on the Requirements Board; also Don Putt, now experimental bombardment project officer. Jake himself was production bombardment chief under Major K. B. Wolfe, in charge of the production division. A piece of paper that came from Major

Putt's desk was the seal on a plan long in making. The official notice reached Seattle February 5, 1940.

"R-40-B," it was labeled. The circular asked that all interested companies submit proposals, within one month of receipt, for a 5,333-mile, high-altitude, high-speed bombardment airplane, with detailed data and drawings. *Urgent.* A full scale mock-up to be built by August 5, 1940. The first airplane to be delivered by July 1, 1941, and any additional planes one a month thereafter.

The bell rang that put Engineering on an all-out basis. Beall took command, organized the forces. He put Don Euler in charge of Preliminary Design; Lyle Pierce would be project engineer. Eddie Allen was called upon for wing, tail, and performance data. John Ball, with his assistant George Martin, would oversee the structures. Detail design groups were assigned. Ed Wells would supervise the over-all effort, with N. D. Showalter as his chief assistant.

"Let's get the speed up over four hundred," Beall had been urging all along. With the wing Allen and Schairer were developing, this appeared within reason. High altitude would help get this speed. Ed Wells proposed putting two turbo-superchargers on each of the four 2,000-horsepower Wasps they were planning to use. But to carry the fuel for 5,333 miles with a ton of bombs would require an airplane of at least 85,000 pounds gross weight. That was a plane twice the weight of the B-17 Flying Fortress. The only way they could get that speed and range was to cut down drag. With twice the weight, they couldn't allow any more drag than the B-17 had. That raised immense problems.

The small low-drag wing would have to carry sixty-four pounds per square foot. For years everyone had agreed thirty to thirty-five pounds was the limit.

"How far do we dare go?" asked project engineer Pierce.

Eddie Allen was reassuring. "You can get away with it if you have a big enough flap," he said. Eddie was the man who had to fly it and his confidence gave them courage. A huge flap was planned that would add one-third to the lift of the wing; then it could be rolled downward and the curvature would have the effect of adding another one-third. The landing speed would still be fairly high, but Eddie said it would be within bounds.

The new wing was the big gain in the war against drag, but that wasn't enough. All rivets would have to be flush, all metal joints on the outside of the airplane would have to be butt-joints, not overlaps. The turbo-superchargers would have to be completely covered over. Gun turrets could not protrude.

War on drag. The nacelles would have to be skin tight. There'd be no room to tuck the landing gear up into them. Instead, the gear would have to fold up flat in the wing. The wing structure was a new problem: less weight but more strength; smaller dimensions but more room for fuel tanks.

"Obviously we can't use the bridge-type truss structure," said George Martin. All Boeing planes since the Monomail had used this type structure. It was sturdy, Monteith's pride. Martin felt that spars made of flat plates of sheet metal, with flanges bent up for rigidity, were the answer. The flanges could be formed on the hydraulic press and the gas tanks could fit up close to the flat plates. Web construction, this was called. It wasn't new. It was used, in a little different form, in the Northrop monoplane, in 1930. Monteith had been afraid of it then, and so had almost everyone in the Army. They called it a "tin can structure" until Jack Northrop proved its strength by driving a steam roller over one. "The California plants are going over to web structure," said Maynard Pennell, a stress engineer who had just come from Douglas. "We might as well get in the parade."

Beall okayed it. "You'll make Fred Laudan happy. He never did like riveting those tubular spars."

How to pressurize the body when you had to open up huge doors to drop the bombs, was a problem. It was decided to pressurize the control room up front and the gunner's compartment in the back, then connect the two with a long tube over the bomb bays that you could crawl through. Designers measured the chunky Beall for size and built a sample tube for the mock-up.

When it was finished, Beall tried it out. Twenty feet down-tube his voice came back hornlike, "I can see light," and a moment later he wriggled out the other end with a puff. "It's O.K., boys, I made it."

Phil Johnson's refinancing program was carried out. A special stockholders' meeting was called to authorize 450,000 shares of new stock. Part of the proceeds would be used to wipe out a $3,471,686 deficit. A $5,500,000 RFC loan was obtained for new working capital in the meantime. Phil moved then to the problem of production. "We've got to start earning this back," he said. In December he had brought in Oliver West as a special assistant. West, since the days when he was production office chief for Phil in the '20's, had been in charge of maintenance and mechanical phases of United Air Lines, and then had gone with Johnson to Canada to organize TCA's ground operations. West told Phil that Boeing would have to have a new plant with modern equipment to operate successfully.

"Yeah, sure," said Johnson. "Just what we need." He knew something of what plants cost and could see the company going right back in the red, though they had all realized that old Plant One was far from ideal, built as it was piece by piece around an old shipyard and separated by the river from railroad tracks and flying field. West did some planning for an "ideal plant," working with the Austin Company, builders, using the existing unit of Plant Two and the earlier plans for its expansion as a starting point.

Claire Egtvedt felt that quantity orders were the real need. The big reason for past financial losses was the small lots of planes put through the shops: ten Stratoliners, six Clippers, then another six. Quantity orders would put production on a paying basis, help in the war emergency, perhaps get the new plant West was talking about. If the U. S. government wasn't buying enough Fortresses, Boeing should land some orders from the British and French, who were buying planes now by the thousands. But they

wanted smaller planes. Egtvedt negotiated for orders to build a
Douglas attack bomber.

French troops were standing watch in the Maginot Line. Nazi
troops were massed behind the Siegfried Line. Colonels George
Kenney and Tooey Spaatz were in Europe observing for Hap
Arnold. "Germany put more planes in the air in one raid over
Poland than we have in our whole air force," they reported.
Fred Collins was in Washington to see if the Air Corps would
exercise its option to buy forty-two more B-17s. Ed Wells and
preliminary design chief Don Euler were in Dayton awaiting
decision on the superbomber design competition when the
pent-up needs of the day began to pop into the open with demands for action.

First, Collins learned the forty-two B-17s would be purchased
under the option. The 17 and the new B-24 had been tested
together. The B-24 was better armed, but the B-17's turbos took
it to better altitude and gave it higher speed at high altitude.
Escaping the pursuits was better than fighting it out with them.
The four-engine bomber appropriation, still limited, would go
to Boeing instead of Consolidated.

But Washington wanted Boeing's price reduced.

"We can't reduce the price below the figure in the option,"
Phil Johnson said. "We'll lose money."

"We won't buy," said the War Department.

Tooey Spaatz and Bob Olds got in touch with Beall and Jim
Murray in the Washington office. "We've got to do something
to save the heavy-bomber program." They got together in a
room and thrashed it out. Finally they knocked off the electrically operated cowl flaps, external bomb racks, and another item
to bring the price down. The War Department approved. The
contract for forty-two B-17Ds was signed.

They were still waiting for word on the superbomber. With
Don Euler, Beall went in to see Oliver Echols, who wanted to
talk about the B-17. "Figure out how to get some more guns in

those Forts," said Echols. "Tail guns especially. And some armor plate to protect the crew."

Minshall parried from Seattle. "A tail turret will upset our whole balance in the airplane. We'll lose all our performance advantage if we load it down." Unenthusiastically, they got some studies started.

Still no decision on Model 341 in the superbomber competition. Beall hung on. He learned the 341 was the only entry over four hundred miles an hour. Then Echols called him in. The Colonel was uneasy. "None of the entries has what we want," he said. "We've got to have more armament. Powered gun turrets, leakproof fuel tanks, armor plate, higher cabin supercharging, space for eight tons of bombs on shorter flights. We're going to extend the competition for thirty days."

"But you wanted the performance," said Beall. "If we give you these we'll have to cut down on performance."

"We want these and the performance, too." There was grim, unyielding determination in Echols' voice. Beall got the new requirements in detail, then called the plant. "Put these things in but keep the speed over four hundred," he said. "We've always been conservative. Now is the time to stretch a point."

"We've already stretched it all we can," said Ed Wells. "We've started out with 48,000 pounds and ended up with 85,000. If we get any heavier it's going to ruin the airplane."

"See what you can do," said Beall.

Blitzkrieg again. On April 9, 1940, Hitler attacked Norway and Denmark. This was it. War in Europe. France and England dug in. America shuddered.

A disarray of demanding, disturbing thoughts kept battering at Ed Wells as he viewed the dour prospect of doing what Oliver Echols asked with the superbomber. Suddenly the whole thing had become vitally important. By the time the superbomber could be built, war might be raging everywhere. Anything might happen. There were rumors that the Air Corps regarded the B-17 now as only a stopgap; that the new long-range bomber was what was needed for America's defense. It had to be successful. Ed felt that the original Design 341 would have been. It was whistle-clean and potent. But Echols' changes were murderous. Lyle Pierce, the project engineer, brought the new weight list in to him.

"It adds 26,000 pounds," said Pierce. Limply, Ed told Pierce to start on a new airplane, called the 345. They could never do this with the 341. Beall rallied them over the long distance phone. "This is going to be the most important airplane in the whole program," he said. "Douglas, Lockheed and Consolidated are in the competition with us. We'll have to give it everything we've got. The Army is talking about ordering production quantities before the experimental plane is built." This last news troubled Wells all the more. The new 345 was a 112,000-pound airplane, with a span of 141 feet, compared with 124 feet for the Model 341. They'd have to use the new 2,200-horsepower Wright engine, and he wasn't so sure of it. The best speed they could figure was 382 miles per hour and that was optimistic. If they lost their speed and altitude they'd have lost everything.

"Is this the plane we should be building?" he asked himself. He thought of Claire Egtvedt's counsel: *honesty of purpose.* Could he honestly get behind this airplane? "We're apt to end up with a white elephant on our hands," he told Minshall.

"I don't know what we can do," said Minshall. "Maybe you'd better work up an alternate, the smaller airplane you think it should be." The more Wells worked on the smaller alternate, the less he liked the big 345. Finally he went with Minshall to see Phil Johnson. "We don't feel right about the 345," said Ed. "Should we drop it and submit the alternate?"

Phil Johnson knew the issue. Wells and his boys had their feet on the ground. On the other hand, he knew what Wright Field wanted. "What if we should get in the war?" he thought. "The Army knows what you're up against in war." Johnson recognized Wells' quiet sincerity. Sometimes men didn't know their own strength.

"Now Ed," he said, "if you *had* to make a good airplane out of this 345, could you do it?"

Wells looked at Phil. He thought for a moment then answered, "Yes."

Phil smiled. "Let's submit the 345 and win the competition."

More Blitzkrieg. In dark of night May 9, the Luftwaffe hit Belgium and Holland. May 10, Stuka dive bombers vaulted the Maginot Line and screamed down on France. In the stress and tension of May 11, Beall took Boeing's data on the Model 345 superbomber to Oliver Echols. May 12 King Leopold surrendered Belgium. In Washington, Dayton, Detroit, Los Angeles, Seattle, things were popping fast. Roosevelt asked Congress for $1,100,000,000 for arms.

Beall and N. D. Showalter took the new B-17 armament studies to Colonel Echols. When Showalter listed the various alternatives on the blackboard, Echols walked over to the list. "Here's what we want," he said and put his finger on power turrets for top and bottom; twin guns in the tail; eight .50-caliber guns in all; armor plate; leak-proof tanks. "Arm it for combat."

"That'll take a new model," said Beall.

"All right," said Echols. "Get it going. We can't wait for a superbomber now."

Egtvedt and Bill Allen completed negotiations with the French government for 240 Douglas attack bombers, to be built under license. Twenty-three million dollars; down payment, $3.5 million. Money to build Oliver West's plant addition.

Popping faster. British troops were being driven out of Dunkirk. Britain blacked out, pounded by Hitler's bombers. The RAF went into the sky to do battle.

Major K. B. Wolfe alerted Jim Murray in Dayton. "Get set to produce the B-17E. We're going to order 250 of them."

Engineer Don Euler was waiting in Dayton on the 345 superbomber. Major H. Z. Bogert, acting chief of the experimental engineering section, suddenly summoned him. "We're giving you a contract to cover engineering and wind-tunnel models and mock-up of your plane. B-29, we'll call it. Push it. Cut the red tape. Move. We may want two hundred of them." Euler reeled from the office to phone the plant. "Two hundred," he said to himself. "Two hundred."

Faster still. June 14 Paris fell. Echols called in Murray and Euler. "We're asking Congress for money for 990 B-29s." Euler looked at Murray and swallowed. Nine hundred and ninety. Nothing now but a design. Echols continued without looking up, "Ten in '42, 450 in '43, 530 in '44." Dick Gelzenlichter, head of the business office in Seattle, put his crew to work punching computers far into the night, trying to get out cost estimates.

Echols asked Phil Johnson and Earl Schaefer, vice president and general manager of the Boeing plant in Wichita, to come to Dayton. Johnson was pinned down by a strike threat in Seattle, and Oliver West went. "All previous estimates are obsolete," said Echols at the meeting. "We'll contract for 512 B-17Es, and two XB-29s. But there'll be lots more B-29s following. All you can handle. You'll have to put up a new facility in Wichita, we don't want them built out on the coast." More plant planning. Oliver West got together with Schaefer on a new Plant Two plan for Wichita. The Seattle plant addition under way would have to be doubled again to handle the B-17 production. Wichita would have to wait on actual B-29 orders, but they could get part of the expansion started to help build tail surfaces for the B-17s.

Campaigner Jake Harman went to work to carry out Echols' demand for B-17s "armed for combat." They'd have to cut out every ounce of weight, put it into guns. See if there was anything that hadn't been done already to make the planes less vulnerable to gunfire. What about the metal tubing that enclosed the electric wiring? It added weight; if bullets broke through it, the wires would be hard to get at to repair. Yet the conduit was needed to shield the wiring so the radios would work. Or was it?

Karl Martinez and his men in the acoustics-electrical laboratories did some experimenting, found some new approaches, and

Harman told the radio lab at Wright Field they were going to rip out all the conduit.

"You can't do it. It's against all the rules. You'll be court-martialed." Then they tried it out, and it worked. Saved weight, too.

The Air Corps was close-mouthed about its over-all plan for production, but gradually the plan was becoming more evident. They'd drop the B-17 and possibly the B-24 as soon as they could get the superbomber. They had given Consolidated a contract for a ship similar to the B-29, called B-32, but at present everyone seemed to feel the 29 held more promise. It was being referred to as the "Hemisphere Defense Weapon."

Britain was in mortal struggle. The Luftwaffe was coming over nightly now, 1,000 planes strong. Fires everywhere. Water mains broken and useless. Each night took another five hundred lives, injured 2,000, while RAF Spitfires fought back. "Blood, sweat and tears," said Churchill, resolute at the helm.

When the British asked now for B-17s, the Air Corps agreed to send over twenty of the sixty it had in service. They'd be fixed up with armor plate and leak-proof tanks but they wouldn't have the tail guns or the new power turrets. The Flying Fortress would soon see battle.

2. *Superbomber Crisis*

George Schairer and his aerodynamicists were at Cal Tech wind tunnel with the new wing model for the XB-29 super-bomber. They had tested it first in the University of Washington tunnel, then at Massachusetts Institute of Technology. It showed signs of "compressibility burble," a mystical new phenomenon they were trying to learn more about. When a plane got going fast enough for the air over its wing surface to approach the speed of sound, strange things would happen. The air would act like a solid instead of a fluid, and would tumble away from the wing. A new kind of stall, stalling not at lowest but at highest speed. No one knew what would happen if you let this go on. Probably everything would break apart.

Schairer was a precise searcher. He could see that "burble" would occur over parts of the wing but not others. At Cal Tech tunnel he had the latest corrections in the wing model. The wind in the tunnel lashed at it. Grotesque arms and counterarms of the balance mechanism below the tunnel wrote their mathematical hieroglyphs on the big instrument panel. Schairer and his aerodynamicists peered through the window at the effects of the wind's fury, peered at the instruments, hour on hour, day on day, making changes and adjustments. They studied the recorded graphs and charts at night. The results looked hopeful, began to look better still, looked good, looked right on the button. Schairer wired Eddie: "We have it. We're coming home."

The wing was one big item out of the way. But there were others. How to retract the bulky double-truck landing gear. It would have to go up in the nacelle, and the nacelles were already glove-tight around the engines and accessories. They worked at it, finally found a way to tuck it in.

Then there was the problem of control, an ever-changing problem, from the first stick and wire plane to the Clippers and Stratoliners, growing more demanding as the planes grew bigger and went faster. Would one man have the strength to move the control surfaces of a big, fast plane like the B-29? One manufacturer had tried powered controls but they'd proved a failure. There couldn't be any failures in this airplane. This was one of the things Ed Wells had been concerned about: taking on something that no one knew the answer to. They could take a chance on developing things a jump at a time, but too big a jump into the unknown . . .

"Do you think it can be done?" asked Eddie Allen.

"I don't know how, but I have a feeling it can," said Schairer. There were willing hands in aerodynamics, able men, watching, listening, looking for new solutions. Control and stability were things inseparably related. The British mathematician Hermann Glauert had written a formula which the mere technically minded couldn't get, only the logically minded: A_1 over $A_2 = B_1$ over B_2, where A_1 was the variation of the *lift* of the control surface with the *angle of attack* of the surface, A_2 the variation of *lift* with the *angle of deflection* of the surface, B_1 the variation of the *hinge moment* with the *angle of attack* of the surface, B_2 the variation of the *hinge moment* with the *surface deflection*. Not simple.

No one had yet found a practical way of applying the formula, though Eddie Allen and Schairer were fascinated by its promise of law and order in control-surface design. Until the time that designing could be done from principle, solutions would have to come from experience and from trial and error.

From experience, they had the control tab, a little device they had first applied on the B-9 bomber. You could move a small tab on the end of the control surface and then let the wind on the tab help you move the rest. This was part of the answer, but not enough. They also had the balanced control, where the part ahead of the hinge swung across the wind and helped move the bigger part behind the hinge. Control surfaces were too light with the balance they were using. They'd overcontrol. It was a highly complicated matter to get them just right.

They began working on it in the wind tunnel, trying all sorts of changes in the shapes ahead of the control surface hinge line. It was well known that the only changes affecting the result were those ahead of the hinge line. No solution. One day Schairer was looking over some tables of figures from the wind-tunnel experiments. On one test the results were completely out of line with all the others. Much better. He called the test group. "What did you do? You haven't changed anything ahead of the hinge line."

"That's what has us stumped. We accidentally changed it behind the hinge line. That's not supposed to make any difference. We never waste our time there."

"You've got the solution," said Schairer.

An old law was tossed out, a new one put to use. A discovery was something as obvious when seen as it was invisible when unseen.

The B-29 design was rounding out. The weight went up to 120,000 pounds gross, wing loading to sixty-nine pounds per square foot—extremely high. All the Air Corps was watching, wondering about the bet it had placed, worried about whether the plane could get to high altitude with such a heavily loaded wing. Oliver Echols had moved to Washington and George Kenney had Echols' spot at Wright Field. Kenney called Wellwood Beall to his office. Cryptically, he wrote on the blackboard, "Plane X—wing loading fifty-three pounds per square foot, ceiling 28,000 feet," and under it, "B-29—wing loading sixty-nine pounds per square foot, ceiling..." After "ceiling" he drew a sprawling question mark and turned to Beall, arms folded, his eyes sharp and demanding under his short-cropped hair.

Beall felt cornered. "We have high wing loading, all right, but we'll get 33,000 feet ceiling."

"How do you know? This plane didn't." General Kenney pointed to his X on the board.

"You'll have to tell me what Plane X is and I'll tell you the difference."

"It's a bomber we've just bought that has high wing loading."

"They didn't have the turbo-superchargers we do," said Beall. "We can make our ceiling."

"We're counting a lot on your word, my friend," said Kenney. "There'll come the day when you'll have to prove it. In the air."

Britain battled on. The grizzled RAF had picked off German bombers until it had sapped the Luftwaffe's strength. But General Tooey Spaatz had seen enough to raise the query, early in 1941, "What if England should fall?" The only way to reach Germany now was by air. Without bases in Britain, what would the problem be? Spaatz stretched a tape over the globe in Air Corps Chief Hap Arnold's office. Point Barrow, Alaska to Berlin:

4,000 miles. Eight thousand miles round trip, plus reserve for winds. Spaatz turned grim-faced to Arnold. "Hap, we'd better get started on a 10,000-mile bomber. One that will carry 10,000 pounds of bombs."

Hap Arnold's built-in smile was gone. Arnold talked to Oliver Echols. Wright Field put the problem to the aircraft industry. Engineers of Boeing, Consolidated, Douglas, Northrop, blinked and began to figure. Franklin D. Roosevelt talked to his military men about making America the "arsenal of democracy." He prepared a message to Congress. Hap Arnold called Phil Johnson the night of May 7. "What is the fastest way to get mass production of planes? Think about it and call me back in the morning."

In the morning Phil called Hap. "I think there are four things you've got to do. First, establish the principle of building one or two proven models. Second, arrange for the models selected to be built in factories having facilities now used for other purposes. Third, give first priorities to those factories for materials and machine tools. Fourth, continue development of replacement types for the models selected so that in time they can become the production model."

"That's what we're going to do," said Hap. He didn't tell Phil he had already talked with Ford and Douglas about building the Consolidated B-24s, and now was looking for a way to get more B-17s. Arnold asked Douglas and Vega, a subsidiary of Lockheed, to work with Boeing on the Flying Fortress. A B-17 joint production committee was organized to distribute engineering and tooling information to the two companies, with Colonel Orval Cook as chairman. Fred Collins was picked as the Boeing member. New contracts came in swamping waves that left no time for contemplation. Three hundred thirty-five Flying Fortresses. More to follow. An initial order for two hundred fifty B-29s, the first to be delivered by August 3, 1942.

Two hundred fifty B-29s. Earl Schaefer, West Point-trained, jumped to attention in Wichita. For Schaefer, this was a dream come true, but not the way he'd ever expected it. He had come back from World War I service as a flight instructor and campaigned for a flying field that would put Wichita on the air map. "It's the center of the country; it should be the center of avia-tion," he said. When ten Wichita businessmen in 1927 raised a $60,000 purse to move Lloyd Stearman's plant from Venice, California, to that flying field and it began building sportplanes and mail planes, Earl Schaefer joined the Stearman Company. When United Aircraft & Transport Corporation decided to pad-lock the doors because of depression, Schaefer, who had become manager of the plant, carried his plea to Hartford, "Just keep it open. We'll find some kind of work." They had started build-ing trainers, then more trainers, now trainers by the thousands for the Air Corps.

All this was a fading vision as Earl Schaefer looked at the wheat fields surrounding the small Wichita plant, seeing the great work ahead: 250 B-29s, the first to be delivered by August 1942. Two hundred fifty B-29s out of those wheat fields.

Adolf Hitler, powerful now, able to look the picture of old Frederick in the eye and promise him greater things for the Reich, turned his forces eastward on communist Russia. Japan had joined the Rome-Berlin axis. Tooey Spaatz' question was enlarged. What if Eurasia should fall? Eurasia against the West-ern Hemisphere? Hap Arnold called louder for the 10,000-mile, 10,000-pound-load bomber, though Oliver Echols soberly pointed out it would take two and a half years just to get an experimental prototype.

In Seattle, even two and a half years didn't make the pros-pect look promising. On a drawing board things looked different. Using the most powerful engines the engine companies could envision, the new wing, everything they had learned, and a gen-erous estimate of future progress, designers couldn't make the figures approach 10,000 miles with 10,000 pounds. "Do they want an airplane, or imagination?" asked Don Euler.

Ed Wells faced a familiar crisis. This time the warning bell was ringing louder. They were stretching everything to make the B-29. If the U. S. got in the war, they'd get the B-29, somehow. But to pour Uncle Sam's treasury into a promise of this new plane, was that honesty of purpose? "We'd better give them a proposal we can make good," said Wells. Euler went back to preliminary design. The airplane they came up with was well short of the request. Wells showed it to Beall. "We aren't giving them what they've asked for."

"How can you?" said Beall. "Do they want it for this war or the next one?"

The Air Corps was disappointed in the Boeing proposal. They contracted with Consolidated for the six-engine B-36 and with Northrop for the Flying Wing.

The twenty B-17C Flying Fortresses that had been sent to England were being readied for action. When they arrived in the spring of 1941, warwise observers objected to having "obsolete and conceivably dud American stuff planted in this country by American bluff and guff and blah and baloney." Two prize examples of what American propagandists were trying to do, they said, were "the boosting of the Boeing four-engine machine," and "America's frightfully secret bomb sight." But RAF crews were game for a try. They trained briefly and on July 8 took two of the Fortresses across the North Sea to bomb Wilhelmshaven from 30,000 feet. They missed the target. The "Jerries" came after them. They tried to shoot back but the guns were frozen. Through riddling machine-gun fire they made it back.

On July 24, they trained their bombsight crosshairs on the German battleship *Gneisenau*, and thought they scored some hits. Again the guns froze up in combat, but again they made it home.

By September 12, 1941, they had made twenty-two daylight raids and had lost eight of the twenty ships, some in combat, some in crash landings. Intelligence said all but 2,200 pounds of bombs went wide of their targets. "Mighty expensive bombing," concluded the Bomber Command.

In Seattle, Eddie Allen and his flight-research crews were finding out things about high altitudes. "There are a thousand

details to be worked out to make apparatus function up there,"
Eddie said. "It's terribly cold. Greases won't work. Propellers
won't work. The fuel mixture system in the airplane doesn't
work. We don't have the proper oxygen system."

They set aside a couple of B-17Cs for the exploration, and
morning after morning on Boeing Field the crews would spend
a half hour breathing pure oxygen and exercising to ward off de-
compression "bends," then climb into fur-lined suits and go
"upstairs" to tackle the trouble items one by one.

The new B-17Es, in production in the plant, gleaned the
advantage of this high altitude research.

The assembly line that had been laid out by Oliver West, now
executive vice president, and his assistant, Bob Neale, was filling
out. The first of the E's was flown that September, complete
with powered Sperry turrets on top, ball turret in the belly, tail
turret, new side guns and nose gun, looking like a war plane.

A tension was developing in the Pacific that wouldn't wait for
the new model. Japan seemed intent on pushing its conquest of
French Indo-China, despite President Roosevelt's warnings. Early
in September, nine B-17Ds which had been in Hawaii since May
were poised at Hickam Field for a flight to the Philippines, where
they'd be stationed. Major Emmett "Rosy" O'Donnell was
leader of the squadron. Crew chiefs were checking out the power
plants. Duffel bags and personal packages were stowed aboard.
Thoughts weren't so much of impending war as of the long trip
ahead. O'Donnell briefed the pilots: "Every ship will be on its
own. You have your charts. Stay with your instruments." The
Pacific heavy bomber force droned westward.

October 16, twenty-six more B-17Cs and D's followed to
complete the 19th Bombardment Group, under Lieutenant Colonel Gene Eubank. October 18, military extremist Hideki Tojo
became dictator of Japan.

In a walled-off portion of Plant Two at Seattle, the first
XB-29 was beginning to take form. Construction was under way
in Wichita on the sprawling plant that would produce the planes.

The government was giving consideration to having other companies join in building still more of them. Basic engineering data was given out to those who might be asked to participate. One of the companies reported back to Hap Arnold, after its engineers had gone over the data, that Boeing was "way off in its figures." The plane would have forty miles per hour less speed than proposed, 5,000 feet less ceiling, 1,000 miles less range, they calculated. If they were right, the B-29 wasn't an airplane. Hap Arnold turned pale at the thought. Was the big program they'd started turning into a fiasco at the moment of crisis? He had to know. He put it squarely up to Oliver Echols, on whose word he'd bought the plane. Echols' confidence began to waver. He took Don Putt and a delegation to Seattle to have it out.

The meeting was in Wellwood Beall's corner office in the four-story engineering building at Plant Two. Wells, Showalter, Eddie Allen, and George Schairer were there. The issue was bow-string tight. "You're going to have to put on a bigger wing," said Echols. "We can't afford the chance."

Beall knew that would be catastrophic both to production and design. "We'll really lose our performance if we do that. We won't have an airplane."

"You don't have one now, according to these figures."

"They don't match with our figures," said Beall.

"You'll have to justify your figures."

Beall turned to Eddie Allen. Eddie leaned forward. "I don't think it is still well understood," said Eddie, his high voice strained and earnest, "how much difference a small change in the contour of the wing and nacelles can make. We have a much lower drag from the nacelles than you'll get from the normal way of figuring."

"How can you be sure?"

George Schairer spoke up. "We've proved it in the wind tunnel."

"Wind tunnels can be wrong."

"But we've been in three different tunnels with it," said Schairer. "They all check out."

Don Putt turned to Echols. "I think we'd better investigate this further. We may be all right here." Echols' face showed relief, as though he wanted mightily to believe Putt. The meetings continued for a week and the party returned to Wright Field. Major Bill Cragie, of the experimental engineering section, seemed confident the 29 would be okay. So did Putt. Finally Echols told Beall, "Go ahead as you are."

3. *War*

Plant Two was a flowing tide of Flying Fortress parts and assemblies. Employment was up to 28,000. The B-17s and the oncoming B-29s had a top priority for materials. William S. Knudsen, troubleshooting the country's defense program as director of production, was expediting Wright Cyclones to Seattle. The B-17 schedule was accelerating each month to hit a peak of eighty per month by October 1942. It was coming up well. In October 1941 twelve Fortresses were completed; in November, twenty-five. There were to be thirty-five in December.

December 7 came that electrifying, unbelievable newscast: "Pearl Harbor has been attacked." Pearl Harbor? "Untold damage has been done to the U. S. naval base and to the city of Honolulu itself by unidentified bombing planes."

Phil Johnson called Oliver West. "Meet me at the plant right away."

Rifle-carrying U. S. military police began arriving, barricading the highway past the plant. "Black out all the windows. Guard the Duwamish waterway. See about machine guns on Boeing Field. Scatter the parked planes." Johnson and West didn't go home that night.

Jake Harman called. "Start building airplanes."

"How many?"

"My instructions are you just start building. Never mind the schedules. Tell us how much money and what things you need when."

Japanese imperial headquarters announced that Japan had entered a state of war with the United States and Britain. The U. S. Pacific Fleet was immobilized at Pearl Harbor. The formations of planes that appeared suddenly over Oahu had turned the naval base into a mass of wreckage. In Oahu, Seattle, or Emporia, no American that night went back to the same kind of sleep he had awakened from in the morning.

Sunday night in Seattle was Monday afternoon in Mindanao, southernmost island of the Philippines, across the international date line. Major Rosy O'Donnell with his B-17s at Del Monte, their crews aboard and waiting, was trying to get headquarters at Clark Field, Manila.

"Still can't get them, sir," said the communications officer.

"Hell's fire," snapped O'Donnell. "We've got to get them."

Next morning orders came. Clark Field had been bombed out. Major Combs' squadron at Del Monte was to hunt a Japanese raider off Legaspi. O'Donnell was to stand by.

Standing by didn't fit Irish Rosy O'Donnell. When orders came late that afternoon to proceed to Clark Field, he sprang as out of a catapult. "Let's go." Approaching Clark Field, O'Donnell gasped. Buildings torn and gutted, field in craters, told why communications couldn't reach Clark yesterday. All but two or three of Clark Field's nineteen Fortresses were battered and crumpled on the field. These two or three and O'Donnell's eight, and Combs' eight, remained the sole U. S. bombing force against Japan. He sensed the mighty mission of those eighteen or nineteen Flying Fortresses.

O'Donnell got a radio message. "Don't land here. Go to San Marcelino." At dusk in a coastal valley off to the southwest, where no B-17 had landed before, they squashed down on tall grass. Filipino guards peppered them with bullets on the way in.

The men spent the night in their planes, or in the dew under the wings. "Can we take off from here?" someone asked.

"We got in. We can get out," said Rosy.

"The wind is against us."

"From now on winds don't matter."

At 4 A.M., Rosy said, "I'm going into Clark and get some orders." He took off into jet-black night, made a forty-five degree turn where he knew there was a hill, and climbed on out. When he got into Clark, he radioed his squadron to follow at dawn.

Before bomb-loading operations were completed on O'Donnell's plane and two others, there was an air raid warning. Rosy looked about quickly. "Let's get out of here." They didn't want to be caught on the ground if a raid was coming. A P-40 reconnaissance brought word of an invasion fleet of transports approaching Aparri, at the north tip of Luzon, and another at Vigan. Colonel Gene Eubank, commanding the 19th Bombardment Group, dispatched the three planes that were ready, for separate targets, and said he'd dispatch the rest of Rosy's squadron when it arrived from San Marcelino.

At 25,000 feet, above Vigan, Rosy O'Donnell spotted a big ship. "My God, I think it's a carrier. Let's take it." The bombardier started his long bomb run. Over the target, nothing happened. "Bomb release is stuck," the bombardier shouted.

"Try again." In bursting ack-ack, Rosy wheeled about and they made another run. This time they got part of their bombs away. The vessel below was zigzagging violently. They kept at it. It took forty-five minutes to get all the bombs out. None hit the target. O'Donnell was sobered. "It's not so simple," he thought.

Back at Clark heavy rain kept the rest of O'Donnell's planes from getting into the field. Captain Colin Kelly commanded one of the Forts that had gotten into the air. He had orders to attack a carrier north of Aparri. He didn't find it. On the way back they spotted a big fat target, skirting the coast. "Must be a battleship," said co-pilot Donald Robins. The ship didn't seem to see them. All tense, they gave the plane over to Sergeant Meyer Levin, the bombardier. "Take your time," said Kelly. "Let's hit her."

Levin started a ten-minute run. He twisted his dials; the four Cyclones droned on; all else was still. The ship below had spotted them now and anti-aircraft fire started coming up. They were nearly over her. "Bombs away." Levin's shout snapped the Fortress out of its trance. Kelly banked and shot around toward the coast. Three six hundred-pound bombs went on down in a train. A plume of water came up astern of the ship, a second close alongside. The third...there was a flash of flame and then a great belch of smoke from the ship's after deck. The smoke kept on blossoming, swallowing their quarry from view.

Two Japanese fighters came up. The waist gunners cooled their interest and they fell back. Kelly let down and skimmed a thick undercast of clouds toward Clark. Second Lieutenant Joe Bean, the navigator, left his watch a moment to check his instruments. A splitting crash sent the overhead glass dome showering down in bits.

"Do your stuff," Kelly shouted. Six fighters were on them. A shell came through the navigator's instrument panel. The left waist gunner fell dead. The rest of the gunners were spitting fire in all directions.

"Give 'em all you got. Beat 'em off." Colin Kelly's voice was a trumpet. The left wing tanks were hit. The wing was afire. Kelly felt the control column loose in his hand. No elevator cables. "Bail out," he shouted, struggling to hold the ship straight, his head bent desperately over the controls. Bean and Levin tried to get out the bottom hatch. It was stuck tight. Together they got it open and slithered through. Robins, the co-pilot, got out the top hatch. More chutes blossomed out. Then a shattering explosion.

Colin Kelly was found beside his wrecked Fortress at the foot of Mt. Arayat. News wires sent America its first story of American war heroism, of Colin Kelly in his Flying Fortress, and of the first Japanese ship—mistakenly thought to be the battleship *Haruna*—sent to the bottom.

The raids on Clark Field drove the 19th Bombardment Group back to Del Monte. Fast as the ground crews could get things repaired, they kept delivering their punches. Out and back; out, riddled, and back, the crews of the Flying Fortresses learned war in the days that followed. One of the Forts that escaped the December 8 bombing was Captain Hewett Wheless' plane. "Shortie" Wheless was flying reconnaissance in heavy weather off Formosa when the Japs hit. December 14, in a three-plane attack on Japanese transports, Wheless got separated from his mates in low clouds. He went on alone. He was on his bomb run at 9,500 feet, when eighteen fighters swarmed him. Four of them closed in, one on each side, two on the tail. Gunners in the Fortress poured it to them. One of the fighters went down. Wheless called back. "You're getting 'em. You're getting 'em."

Then Private Killin, the radio operator, was killed at the belly gun. Navigator Meenaugh came to take his place. "I'll pay 'em back," said Meenaugh.

The fighter on the other side dropped away in a smoke-trailing spin. More explosive bursts came through the sides of the ship. Both waist gunners were wounded and had to leave their posts. Sergeant John Gootee, with a bullet in his right wrist, grabbed one of the guns with his left, swung it after a fighter. The two fighters on their tail were riddling them mercilessly. With the ship holding straight on the bomb run, the side gunners couldn't reach them.

"Bombs away."

Wheless hit the rudder and swung the ship sideways to give the gunners a chance to pick off one of the pursuits on the tail. Bombardier Schlotte came back to lend Gootee a hand at the side guns. Fifteen fighters remained, attacking in waves. Bedlam of noise and action. The belly gun had been shot out. Gootee got another fighter, then his gun jammed. Number one engine was dead. Everything was riddled. Finally all the guns were shot out of action or jammed. They sat back and took it.

Twenty-five minutes after the running battle started, the Japanese fighters were silent, out of ammunition. Some of them came up close to look in the windows. The radio was destroyed, one gas tank ripped wide open but not on fire, oxygen system out, tail wheel shot away and front tires shot flat, two-thirds of the control cables shattered, side walls a sieve, but they were staying in the air, droning on at low altitude.

At dusk they sighted Mindanao. Drizzling rain obscured the hills ahead. Wheless sighted a small air field near the beach and headed his crippled ship for it. Too late he saw the field was barricaded. They smashed on through, rolled two hundred yards on flat tires, then the wheels locked. They stubbed up on the nose and settled back down again to rest. Seven shaken and injured men climbed out and patted the battered ship. "Good old gal. Wonderful gal."

Grizzled, bandaged, grease-stained, a fighting family alone before the weight of an ocean of moving warships, nursing its four-engine steeds with a brotherly affection, the 19th Bombardment Group fought on with its remnant of Forts. When the Philippine invasion forced them off Mindanao, they filled up the fuel tanks, loaded the 17s down with as many men as they could carry, and staggered off for Australia.

Major General George Brett arrived in Australia to take command at the end of December. The problem of how to reinforce the Philippines grew desperate. Distances were too great for movement of pursuit forces. Japan controlled the sea, and therefore the bases. The only practical plan was to fight a holding action until air and naval strength could be built up in the South Pacific to work back.

The Japanese were already driving on Southeast Asia. The patched-up Forts and their crews went up to Java. More Forts joined them by way of India: B-17Es, with tail guns and power turrets. Colonel Gene Eubank, a man who had helped make the Fortress a fighting airplane in prewar days when he'd come to the Boeing plant with the ideas of the operating squadrons, got them organized for businesslike raids.

There was an invasion convoy coming through Macassar Straits. The 19th took after them January 22 and 23, and U. S. War Department communiqués took prideful note: "Seven Flying Fortresses sank one enemy transport, set fire to another. Five enemy planes were shot down. All of our bombers returned to their base." "Eight Flying Fortresses sank a transport, hit a cruiser. One bomber was lost." "Another transport destroyed, another set on fire. Two fighters shot down. All five bombers returned safely."

Enemy fighters treated the new B-17Es with caution and respect. "Four-engined fighters," Radio Tokyo called them. But February 15, 1942, Singapore fell, and Java was becoming untenable. Five remaining Forts dropped back to Australia.

The war was going badly in Europe and North Africa and plans called for most of the new Fortresses from the Boeing factory to be sent to the European theatre. Some B-24s were expected in the Pacific soon, but with the intermediate bases in enemy hands, distances now were far too great for either the B-17 or the slightly longer-range Consolidated B-24. The B-29 Superfortress, still unflown, was the only hope; and even the B-29 couldn't reach Japan itself until island bases could be won or land bases established in China. This last seemed the best possibility. If the Japanese could be held there. But the meager forces in Northern Burma weren't holding them. B-17Es that could be spared from Australia were flown to Karachi, India, in March, to help.

Talk in the streets of Karachi was gloomy. "The Japanese will be here by summer," people said. General Joe Stilwell, falling back in North Burma before the Japanese invaders, called on Air Force Commander Louis Brereton for support. Burma had only one major port: Rangoon. Japanese troop supplies would have to go up the railroad from Rangoon to Mandalay. From India, the bombers began their mission against the docks of Rangoon. The pummeling continued until there were no docks left at Rangoon. The Japanese took the Burma Road, but India still remained as a staging base for aerial approach to Japan through China.

There was a grave new concern about the B-29, secret white hope of the Air Force. The fierce realities of aerial combat, such as the B-17s were experiencing in the Pacific and the British were experiencing in Europe, had put fire behind an unwelcome question. Would the remote-control guns in the 29 work against quick-maneuvering fighters, coming at the airplane in numbers?

The power-operated turrets that had been put on the B-17E— the two-gun turret on top and the ball turret in the belly—were working fine. A man could sit there with his sights and the power would pull his gun around as fast as he could move it. But the B-29 had a pressurized body, and if you used this kind of turret you'd lose all your pressure through it. Moreover the stream-lined body had to be kept free from things like turrets. The Air Force armament lab had solved the problem with guns controlled through periscope sights. You watched for enemy fighters in the periscope eyepiece as from a submarine, and aimed your gun accordingly. The awkwardness of this, the narrow field of view, struck horror in the minds of Air Force operations people.

"We've got to change it," General K. B. Wolfe told Jake Harman in Dayton. "Everybody in the Air Force is on top of me about it. Go out to Seattle and get them to put on turrets. Don't listen to any backtalk. We've got to do it."

In Seattle, Jake gave them the emphatic word.

"We don't like the periscope any better than you do," answered N. D. Showalter, the chief of military projects. "But what are we going to do? We can't just stick ball turrets on the airplane. It's so clean now that the landing gear, when you put it down, has as much drag as all the rest of the airplane put together. What would happen to our performance if we stuck turrets out there? We won't have any bomber left."

"This isn't a case of what we want to do. It's what we have to do," said Jake. "It isn't a bomber if you can't fight with it, either."

Other engineers were called in. They wrestled for two days, skipping meals, skipping sleep. The more you tried to prove the periscope, the worse it looked. But Showalter and Wells couldn't agree to the big turrets either. Then Colonel Roger Williams from the Wright Field armament section sparked.

"This is a long shot," he said, "but I know General Electric is working on an electronic remote control. You aim a sight located somewhere in the ship, and electronic tubes reproduce the same movement in all the guns." It was at least a break in the cloudy sky. Could electronic tubes withstand the rigors of battle? Was this just walking out of one complicated setup into a more complicated one? If it worked, it would solve the armament dilemma and save the airplane's high performance. GE engineers were called in. Everyone lent a hand to develop a model. It looked encouraging. It had to work.

Jake Harman called K. B. Wolfe from Phil Johnson's office. "K. B., we have a different . . ." He didn't get any farther. K. B.'s voice came back, "Did you get them to put on the turrets?"

"No, but . . ."

"I sent you out there to do a job. I want that job done." K. B. Wolfe's burden of responsibility and the drive that had made him the dynamic center of the Air Force production program, were coming through the wires and broadcasting into the room.

"But we've got something better." Jake got an opening and gave Wolfe the new plan.

"All right then," said K. B. "But if it isn't any good . . . I sent you fellows out there to do a job, and, so help me God, if it isn't right I'm going to break every one of you. You'll be worse than second lieutenants. You've had it. . . . You'll have to call Echols in Washington and explain it to him."

The GE central fire-control system went in the B-29, and the big Superfortress, product of many hands, again became a secret white hope.

B-29 Superfortress

Tremendous planning was going on in Washington, sufficient to explain the Air Force's insistence on certainty of the B-29's design reliability. New production plans were being made and there was a mystery-shrouded program that stemmed from a note scribbled to Franklin D. Roosevelt by white-haired Albert Einstein from the Institute of Advanced Study at Princeton in 1939, read by only a select few men, a note that was now giving rise to cryptic, encouraging top-secret reports from scientific laboratories and generating plans for a big desert experimental station in New Mexico.

Tall Robert Lovett, the new Assistant Secretary of War for Air, was one of those who added things up to an inevitable answer. The defeat of Germany would require tremendous blows by air; the defeat of Japan would depend even more on aerial bombardment. While the country was reaching deep for the money and manpower to put out the fire in Europe, it would have to reach deeper to build the long-range attack on Japan. Nothing but B-29s could do that job. Furthermore, if the fantastic tests at Alamogordo proved out, nothing but the B-29 could carry the *atom bomb* to Japan.

General Echols asked Wellwood Beall to come to Washington. As soon as possible. When Beall stepped into Echols' office the next day, a little punchy from all-night flying, the General's look was grave. "The United States government," said Echols, "is about to spend more money on one project than any other project of the whole war. This project is the B-29. We haven't even flown the airplane. We're worried about the tremendous risk if it doesn't pan out. Now you're the chief engineer of the Boeing Airplane Company. We want to know, really—the survival of the whole country may depend on this—we want to know what you really believe in your heart, whether that will be a good airplane or not."

Beall took a deep breath. Here and now, the test of vision was courage. Not blind courage, but courage of decision that might involve the lives, hopes, future of millions. He swung for a moment precarious. This kind of courage could only be based on a firm faith. Wellwood Beall knew of the step-by-step progress that had made the B-29 design possible, of the men who had made it possible, their faith, their devotion to a goal that they knew was vital. The 1,900 men in the engineering department were as one in this airplane. These men *were* the airplane. Their work on the XB-29 was now mostly done. It had only to be proved.

Beall looked Echols in the eye. "Yes," he said. "It's really going to be a good airplane. If you'll give us first priority on test facilities and let us do all the testing we want to do, when we want to do it—flight testing, systems testing, all kinds of testing—if you'll assign us the airplanes to do this, I'll guarantee that we'll get you successful operating airplanes."

Echols went in to see Hap Arnold. "All right," said Echols when he came back. "We'll do what you ask." Then he laid out a production program that would cost $3 billion. The Bell Aircraft Company would build a plant in Marietta, Georgia. North American would build one in Kansas City. The Fisher Body Division of General Motors would build one in Cleveland. The Boeing-Wichita plant would be enlarged. There'd be a joint production committee like the Boeing-Douglas-Vega committee for the B-17, to handle the distribution of engineering and tooling drawings, parts purchases, changes. The B-29 was not just an airplane now, but a giant program and a faith.

The American people needed a strong faith in the spring of 1942. Barely well started on their war production, they and all their allies were forced out of the Pacific, out of Europe, into the bottom of Asia and across the Mediterranean onto North Africa. It would be a long, bitter struggle to gain that ground back. The men in the field knew it best. The people at home, mothers and wives who had begun taking jobs in the Boeing plant so sons and husbands could go to war, took heart and courage from the slender communiqués that showed the spirit of the fighting men.

Franklin D. Roosevelt in an evening fireside talk April 28 brought a story that touched those hearts. "Our planes are helping the defense of the French colonies today, and soon American Flying Fortresses will be fighting for the liberation of ... Europe," said the President. "This is the story of one of our Army Flying Fortresses operating in the western Pacific. The pilot of this plane is a modest young man, proud of his crew for one of the toughest fights a bomber has yet experienced." The President told for the first time the story of the Flying Fortress that battled eighteen Japanese pursuits in the Philippines December 14. "The name of that pilot is Captain Hewett T. Wheless of the United States Army. He comes from Menard, Texas, population 2,375. He has been awarded the Distinguished Service Cross. I hope he is listening."

May 7, a bright spring day, at noon, men and women of the day shift climbed out of the rows of B-17 bodies at Plant Two in Seattle, silenced their riveting guns, left their lathes and presses at the rear of the plant, filed down from the broad balcony where sub-assemblies were being put together, and poured onto the big concrete apron in front, 18,000 strong, for a special program. NBC microphones and press photographers were there.

The recorded voice of President Roosevelt repeated the Flying Fortress story he had told in his fireside broadcast. Oliver West then introduced Colonel Jack Griffith, the Army Air Force's representative at the plant. Griffith stepped to the railing of an improvised platform under the nose of a B-17. "It is my privilege to introduce to you the modest young man the President was talking about: Captain Hewett T. Wheless."

A surge of applause rose from the packed mass. Wheless, Distinguished Service ribbon over the left pocket of his uniform jacket, stepped up. "It wasn't so bad," he said in a broad Texas drawl. "When we got on the ground, my first gunner said, 'Captain, we were just getting on to the knack of shooting 'em down when we had to leave and go home.' The men operating the planes don't want all the credit. I want to thank you for myself and a lot of other pilots who more or less owe their lives to your design and workmanship. Continue the good work and together we can't lose."

4. *Around the Clock*

"*And soon American Flying Fortresses will be fighting for the liberation of Europe.*" Early 1942, Brigadier General Ira Eaker got a call from Hap Arnold: "I want you to go to Europe to study the British Bomber Command. I want you to operate a bomber command of our own as soon as we can get planes."

"But I'm a fighter man," said Eaker.

"That's what we want, the fighter spirit in bombardment," said the chief.

"That's a challenge. O.K."

"When I was in England," said Arnold, "they told me our Fortress couldn't stand up against the German fighters. You and I know if we can't bomb with this plane, we can't bomb. Tooey Spaatz is organizing the 8th Air Force to go to Europe. Tooey wants to know if we can plan on daylight bombing and hit the target. Get the answer. Can we do daylight bombing?"

Ira Eaker landed in England with a briefcase full of 8th Bomber Command plans and a head full of questions. Why were the British so opposed to daylight bombing? "We aren't opposed

to it in principle," said Air Marshal Sir Arthur Harris, head of
the RAF Bomber Command. "It's the losses. We can't stand the
crew losses, and we can't manufacture airplanes that fast. We
tried it but had to give it up. The Germans tried it and had to
give it up. When the target is well defended, bombers have to
have protection of darkness."

Had the British really given the B-17 a fair trial? The 17 was
designed for this. "The RAF crews weren't too well trained to
use the Forts," said the air attaché in London. "There was a lot
of pressure to get the American ships into action. They didn't
have the Norden bombsight, you know, and the crews never got
on to the old Sperry sight. They didn't have the new gun turrets.
Then they flew singly instead of in formation. The Jerries really
hit them."

But could the 8th go in with the new Forts and survive? "This
is the big league," said Brigadier General Al Lyon, air officer
for Major General James Chaney, head of the U. S. Armed
Forces in the British Isles. "It's incredible how much stuff the
Germans can throw up. You're going to have to feel your way
by stages, but it can be done. It's got to be done. That's the only
way you can take out the targets."

Lyon had helped Chaney and his chief of staff, Brigadier General Joe McNarney, analyze the Battle of Britain. Goering hadn't
put enough bombers in the air and hadn't pin-pointed targets.
What Goering had failed to do in Britain, the Allies must do in
Germany, Chaney had concluded. The measure of effectiveness
was: bombs on target versus bombers and crews lost. If you had
small losses but got few hits, you were just prolonging the agony.
You had to concentrate on hits and find the means to keep your
losses down. U. S. bomber crews had been trained for daylight
precision bombing.

Eaker summed it up: "It's a gamble, but we've got to place
our bets. If we can't make a go of it we can still go over to night
bombing. But, let's face it, we couldn't use the Forts at night
without a major modification of the airplanes. The flame of those

turbos on the bottom of the nacelles would be a dead giveaway." To extend the exhaust stacks and obscure the glow from the turbos would cut down their performance. There was no question. The theory of daylight precision bombing would have to come to a test. "Yes," Eaker told Arnold and Spaatz. "We should go ahead as planned."

In late June, the crews of the first group of Flying Fortresses followed 8th Air Force commander Tooey Spaatz to Goose Bay, Labrador; to Bluie West, Greenland; to Reykjavik, Iceland; to Prestwick, Scotland, and down through the overcast to the flat green table of England. Three Forts were left behind, forced down off-course in Greenland. More squadrons followed. "Little Americas" began springing up all over the English countryside. "Let's get going," was the word.

English experts frowned at the B-17E armament and the "tiny cramped quarters" for the tail gunner and ball-turret gunner, yet the British had a warm welcome for the Americans. "The spirit of these lads is refreshing," said reporter Ronald Walker in the London *News Chronicle*.

There was long training before the first mission. More questions. How tight a formation could they hold? The tighter the formation, the greater the mass of gunfire to ward off fighters. How fast could they go without burning out engines? How high? The more altitude, the greater the safety, but the higher they went, the less bombing accuracy. How much armor plate could they afford to carry? Too little and the crews would get it. Too much, and the weight would slow them down. They practiced evasive maneuvers. It all took time. The Germans dropped notes on the airdromes. "Where are the American bombers?"

August 16, eighteen crews of the 97th Bombardment Group were ready. Tomorrow, they'd attack railroad yards at Rouen, where Joan of Arc, half a millennium before, had died for the liberation of France. They got their preliminary briefing. This was it. They tried to remember every little thing they had cram-

learned, tried to put out of mind the question "What will it be like?" and the unwelcome fear.

At 1526 hours, August 17, 1942, Ira Eaker was in the Fortress *Yankee Doodle* as Colonel Frank Armstrong lifted the lead plane over the trees. At 1539, the twelfth plane was in the air. They pulled up into formation and rendezvoused with their RAF fighter cover. They climbed to 23,000 feet, droning eastward. Over the green, unwarlike countryside, across the Channel, wondering, rehearsing. Only minutes now and they'd know. . . .

A river, a city, the long strands of the marshaling yards, their target, loomed ahead and far below. They entered their bomb run. Black puffs of ack-ack began reaching up for them, jolted them, but all rode on. "Bombs away." The pepper-fast bursts of smoke punched out a pattern on the ground, encompassing the yards. They could see fighter planes taking off below, pulling up now, chasing them back. Only a few. RAF fighters took them on. Was it over?

At Grafton-Underwood, Tooey Spaatz, staff aides and mechanics were waiting. The returning specks appeared in the gathering dusk. Four-engined. Three planes; six. They were letting down; nine, ten, eleven, twelve. All back. All whole. The men swarmed the field. "You made it. How was it? How'd we do?"

"Milk run."

Ira Eaker returned to 8th Bomber Command headquarters. A note from Air Chief Marshal Sir Arthur Harris lay on his desk: "*Yankee Doodle* certainly went to town."

Eaker didn't disclose his joy. "We won't get cocky. One swallow doesn't make a summer."

The raids continued. They hit Abbéville, then Dieppe, Amiens. Same story. No losses. Then, August 21, on the way to attack a target in the Low Countries, the RAF Spits were late for their rendezvous. Two dozen Jerries took on the unescorted bombers during the bomb run and after. The nine Forts in formation poured out their battering fire. Two of the pursuits dropped in flames. One Fortress, with engine crippled, dropped behind. Five FW-190s swarmed on it. A twenty-millimeter shell smashed in, injuring pilot and co-pilot, but they flew on. The tail gunner got a Focke-Wulf. The ball-turret gunner, revolving crazily in the Fort's underbelly, knocked down two. Number Three and Number Four engines were hit but kept going. The shattered B-17E limped home, trailing the formation.

Word spread quickly. "The Fort can take it and get you back home."

In Seattle, Flying Fortress production was up to one hundred per month. A new product, the turret-studded XPBB-1 Navy patrol bomber, had skipped off Lake Washington and lifted its slender wings to a successful test. *Sea Ranger*, it was named. The newly-built plant at Renton, Washington, was all set to build it in numbers when some swaps were made at the nation's capital. North American was dropping out of the B-29 production pool and Martin took its place. The Air Force wanted the Renton plant for still more production of Superforts. The Navy wanted more land-based planes instead of flying boats. The Sea Ranger order was cancelled and the one plane built was dubbed *Lone Ranger*. Boeing would put its Seattle-Renton facilities to work on B-29s along with Wichita. Now there were 764 B-29s on order, and the revolutionary secret plane was still unflown. In the Air Force, questions were still rampant about its high wing loading, its pressurization, controls, a thousand untried items of equipment. K. B. Wolfe and Jake Harman got the brunt of them at Wright Field, on top of questions on a score of other airplane programs.

"I'm so damned sick of this job," said Harman. "I want to get out and fight the war."

"Resignation accepted," said Wolfe. "So long as you're back to work tomorrow."

Chief military project engineer N. D. Showalter in Seattle was patiently weathering the same cross-examination. "We'll have it in the air soon," was N. D.'s reply. "That'll give you a better answer than I can. One test is worth a thousand expert opinions."

In September 1942, the first plane was wheeled out for meticulous ground tests of systems and equipment. Eddie Allen's men packed it with measuring and recording instruments. Eddie fended off questions about the date they would fly. "There are many items of new equipment," he said. "Getting them all to work at once is like throwing up a handful of coins and getting them all to come down heads." With a crew of seven, Eddie taxied, tried the brakes, the elevators, the ailerons. He lifted a foot or two off the ground, came back; lifted ten feet, came back; lifted fifteen feet, came back. Finally, September 21, the XB-29 was ready for flight.

The four Cyclones sent back a comfortable reassuring rumble. One at a time, then all together, Eddie revved them up. Next moment he was slithering down-runway, a symphony of motion and irrepressible power. Thunder going by. The wheels came off the runway. Eddie held it low downfield for a moment of security and acceleration, then climbed on up, and the great new thing, the hope in many minds, the question mark in many others, disappeared in the sky down the valley. Eddie came back with an eloquent smile. "She flies," he announced.

When the post-flight conference was over, aerodynamicist George Schairer went out shaking his head. "First time I ever went home from one of these without anything to do." Ed Wells was pleased but cautious. There was still much testing to be done. The war, the Air Force, the $3 billion program were pushing them. Pushing them too fast, Wells felt. More tests brought out troubles with equipment and power plants, but the basic aerodynamics were sound. The plane was stable; stalls were smooth. The big control surfaces, once an enigma, were light and responsive. Eddie Allen paid tribute to the work that had been done in the wind tunnel and he had sold Phil Johnson on construction of a modern tunnel at the plant, though no other company had made such an investment.

"The hours and weeks spent in the tunnel are priceless," he told Phil. "We're beginning to learn something about the laws of aerodynamic design. When we know all the laws, we can design a plane to do what we want it to do. The art is getting more precise and the higher the speeds the more precise it will have to be. Every step we take from now on is going to require more and more wind-tunnel time."

Eddie Allen was a scientist at heart. He loved the search for a fundamental principle; not so much with his hands as with thought; not so much with his own findings as the findings of his group. "For me to sit here and make design decisions would be the worst kind of folly," he said. "This is a group effort. We have experts, younger men who have made a study of these things." When one of these men came up with a discovery, Eddie was on his feet with delight. "Is that true? Tell me how you found out."

Allen let his men go at it on their own and for the most part they were dedicated just like Eddie. One noon at the hangar, some of the flight-test group were talking. "It's odd," said pilot Marvin Michael. "Did it ever occur to you that the men around Eddie Allen are all something the same. Don't smoke. Hardly take a drink. Earnest, clean fellows."

"That's a fact. Wonder if he picked them that way or if it just happened."

"I don't know," said Michael. But it brought back to Marvin his first contact with Allen. How when he was still in engineering school and working part time at the Stearman plant in Wichita, he had written to the famous pilot asking for advice. He'd really never expected an answer, but he got a long one. He would never forget the way Eddie started it out: "Your letter interests me very much because it well expresses the grand struggle against big odds toward an achievement."

Struggle. Sure, what they were doing now was a struggle, but a grand struggle. Why grand? Because it was for an achievement. Because their heart was in it. Because it wasn't just for themselves, but something for others, something to help take man out of his limitations, help him out in need.

The present need was plain. It was man's mightiest struggle of all time. The crews of the Flying Fortresses and Liberators, struggling now under the command of General George Kenney to help MacArthur win his way back to the Philippines. Eisenhower's forces in North Africa. Spaatz' 8th Air Force, Eaker's 8th Bomber Command, hammering away. Were the waste and horror of war achievement? Not the kind of achievement men liked, but desperately necessary now. The war wasn't of their making. The job was to finish it, get free of its clutches.

Eddie Allen's flight-test men were carrying on their own struggle for achievement. Michael and many others were enjoying it, all but one thing.... The men at the hangar discussed it guardedly. There was a strained relationship developing in flight test. Administrative people in Eddie's office were usurping authority, playing discords in the symphony, raising tempers. Eddie didn't see it or wouldn't use a reprimand. Marvin Michael pondered this problem and was concerned. At one point, when tension was highest, he talked to Eddie about it.

"I know," said Eddie, "but I'd rather let it go. I hate to hurt anyone's feelings." As the tests went on, there was a growing tension over power-plant difficulties; an unspoken tension over the unsolved personnel problem; tension over the war. Frail, conscientious Eddie Allen absorbed and kept to himself the nagging pull of all three.

As flight tests continued, there were more and more power-plant troubles. Aerodynamically the airplane was proving out well, but in the first twenty-six hours of flying, engines had to be changed sixteen times; carburetors were changed twenty-two times; the exhaust system had to be revised; four of the leak-proof fuel cells had developed leaks. Trouble had also developed with the controls that feathered the propeller blades into line with the wind, to stop them from windmilling in case of engine failure.

December 30, Eddie and his crew took the second XB-29 for its first flight. They were testing the propeller feathering. "Fire in Number Four engine!" It was the rear blister observer on the interphone. There was a shrill whine that meant the propeller was running away. Eddie turned quickly to the flight engineer.

"Feather Number Four." It wouldn't feather. "Fire extinguisher." Smoke and sparks were streaking from the exhaust stack. Gears in the propeller gave way and slowed the wild windmilling, but the fire was getting worse, gobs of burning oil streaming through the cowl flaps. "Give it another CO_2 bottle."

The extinguisher had no effect. Smoke began pouring into the cockpit through the bomb bay. Crew members were coughing and choking, their eyes smarting. Flames were trailing in long fingers from the nacelle access door. It was raining; visibility was poor and clouds were lowering. When they were half a mile from the field the last CO_2 bottle was fired into the nacelle. This one seemed to smother the fire, but smoke and carbon dioxide fumes grew denser in the cabin. The landing would have to be accurate, no chance for a go-around.

Eddie skimmed over high-tension wires, felt for the end of the 5,000-foot runway, downwind. They were on the ground. Number Four engine flared up again in full fury as they rolled to a stop. A standby fire truck was there in a minute and put it out. The crew jumped from exits.

Everyone knew they were skating on thin ice with the tests after that. Eddie Allen asked himself again and again, "Should I call off the flying?" Then he'd read the week's casualty lists in the war, think of how the men were crying for new equipment, how America needed the B-29. There were stacks of requests on his desk for data critically needed by engineering and the shops, by plants all over the nation. Eddie had told the Army the required two hundred hours of flying could probably be completed in four or five months. Three months were gone now and they were barely started. The testing went on. "Grand struggle against big odds toward an achievement."

Ira Eaker's 8th Bomber Command, by winter of 1942, was a hardened, scrappy core of combat crews. In the fall, the two groups of B-17Es had been joined by a third equipped with Consolidated B-24 Liberators. These three groups and their fighter escort, on twenty-three short-range missions, had shot down 104 enemy planes, probably destroyed 108 more, and damaged 117. But they had learned grief too. They had lost eighteen bombers, thirteen of them shot down by enemy fighters, five by anti-aircraft. The losses of equipment and men were not being replaced, because new forces were going to help Major General Jimmy Doolittle in the big North African campaign. In England, the cold, wet winter with its mud at the airdromes, its fog, its nightly blackout bore, and the silent, empty seats at the breakfast table after yesterday's raid weighed heavily.

Ira Eaker was wearying of small hits at nearby targets along the Channel. "If we can get the equipment, we can knock Germany out of the war from the air," he said. "By destroying Hitler's factories we can put an end to his air force. By destroying his munitions plants and communications we can stop his armies." But every week Hitler was building stronger defenses. Now was the time to mount a gigantic air offensive, Eaker felt.

"You haven't yet tested the defenses over Germany itself," said the British. "Those targets are impregnable by daylight." The old issue. The crisis came at Casablanca, where the Allied High Command was gathered in January 1943. Hap Arnold summoned Eaker there. "I'm sorry to have to tell you this," said Hap, "but the President has agreed to give Churchill our bombers for night bombing."

It hit Eaker like a Messerschmitt head-on. For a fraction of a second he reeled, then caught fire. It was wrong. Dead wrong. The Forts weren't designed for night bombing. They *could* do the job by day. Eaker knew military discipline, but he'd have to fight this decision. Even if it cost him his job. "Our planes aren't night bombers," he said. "Our crews aren't trained for night bombing. The losses will be much higher. It's a tragic decision and I won't be a party to it. And I reserve the right to tell the American people at the appropriate time why I quit."

"If you feel that strongly about it," said Hap, "I'll arrange for you to talk to the Prime Minister."

Eaker had the feeling that Hap was glad he'd spoken out as he did. He received a message: "The Prime Minister will be waiting for you at his villa." Ira Eaker had come to know Churchill in England. He went promptly.

"General Arnold tells me it has been decided to turn our bombers over to night bombing," Eaker told the Prime Minister. "I think this is a great mistake. I've been in England long enough to know that you would want to hear both sides."

Churchill smiled. "Sit down." Eaker handed the Prime Minister a single sheet of paper on which he had written the case for daylight bombing. Churchill read it. Near the bottom, Eaker heard him mumble audibly, "Around the clock." It was the place where he'd said that with the British bombing by night, and the Americans by day, they'd give the Germans no rest, bomb them around the clock. Churchill looked up. "I took this action because I have a strong feeling against your losing your young men," he said. "Your losses are greater than ours. You haven't convinced me, but you have convinced me that you should have an opportunity to prove that you can do this. When I see the President at lunch, I'll recommend that we do this."

In the House of Parliament, Winston Churchill stood up to deliver his report on Casablanca. Eaker had been sent a ticket to the balcony. There was an ovation for the great British leader. He began stating the decisions that had been reached. Then he announced that the Americans would continue their daylight bombing. "The British will bomb at night and the Americans by day," said the Prime Minister, glancing up at the balcony. "We shall bomb these devils around the clock."

5. *Red Streak Program*

It was a gray day. The twenty or so department heads and officers who constituted the Boeing executive staff were gathered February 18, 1943, in the board room for the weekly meeting. Phil Johnson sat at the end of the table. Oliver West was reporting on production. One hundred seventy-six Fortresses to be delivered this month. In May the rate would reach two hundred a month. The telephone rang in the anteroom. Ed Wells slipped out to get it. He reappeared at the door, face ashen. "The tower just got a message from Eddie. They're coming in with a wing on fire."

The meeting broke up. Sirens were wailing on the field. No airplane coming in. Then, to the north, a great column of black smoke. The dash for cars. The traffic jam. The police guard. The firemen shooting water at the blazing four-story Frye building. "The plane's in there." Out of the tragic confusion, the news: Eddie and all eleven of the crew lost, and nineteen Frye employees.

Lieutenant Colonel Wiley Wright, the Air Force plant representative, announced promptly: "We hope to do two things—find out the cause and prevent a repetition."

Piecing the story together was like fitting the parts of an eggshell. It was already empty. An engine had caught fire south of the field. They had gotten it out with CO_2 on the way in. Eddie had elected to swing around for a safe landing from the north. Then a second fire broke out. A magnesium part burned and dropped, burning holes in the lower skin, and this ventilated the fire to the gas tanks just when Eddie must have thought it was controlled. They were too low to jump. They didn't quite make the north end of the field.

Eddie Allen's "grand struggle" ended, but not his achievement. A memorial went up just south of Plant Two. Something that had been dear to Eddie's heart, something important to the future. "The Edmund T. Allen Wind Tunnel and Aeronautical Research Laboratories."

While all Boeing was trying to recover from its loss of Eddie Allen, his crew, and the XB-29, all the Air Force was mightily concerned, too. A new program of installing fire stops was laid down, and K. B. Wolfe talked sternly to the power-plant manufacturers, who protested that they too had been developing their product under war pressure. Everyone knew it was a crisis for the B-29 program. There could be only one solution because commitments had gone too far. Jake Harman went to General Wolfe. "How about a special department to take over all aspects of the 29 program, production, experimental, test flying, training, combat? Get the ships into action at the earliest date. You'd be the man to head it up."

"If you'll work with me on it. . . . Let's go talk to Washington about it," said K. B.

With a directive that would require Hap Arnold's signature, they headed for Washington. The idea seemed to make more sense every mile of the way. Revive the morale in the B-29 effort. A red streak program to get the 29 ready for combat; a special B-29 Air Force, under the direction of Hap Arnold himself, that could be dispatched on long-range missions anywhere in the world. An independent, self-sufficient force that would operate from secret advance bases. From *China*. . . .

Oliver Echols said he'd approve it. Wolfe and Harman went down the hall to Hap Arnold's office. K. B. laid the paper on Hap's desk and waited. Hap read it and slapped his desk. "Fine. Why doesn't somebody else do something for me once in a while?"

"You like it, General?" Harman asked.

"I've got to see about this. Where are you staying? I'll call you."

That night they got a call at the hotel. "Someone wants to talk to you. Be careful what you say." Then Hap Arnold came on.

"Project approved. Go back home and prepare a presentation. Bring it back soon. Plan it for you-know-where."

"You-know-where" was *China*. Arnold had seen General Marshall. The days ahead were maps, training bases, operating bases, logistics. The President would make arrangements with Great Britain and India, make a deal with Chiang Kai-shek to build secret B-29 bases in China. Meanwhile, the airplanes. . . .

K. B. Wolfe and Jake Harman went to Seattle, armed with a superseding authority, bursting with plans known only to themselves, Hap Arnold and a few others. The fixes had been made on the second XB-29, fire stops and all. Jake would be the test pilot. Check lists and counter check lists were drawn. "Don't even think of the possibility of losing this one. That would end all."

May 29, 1943. Ground testing was under way: brakes, acceleration, propeller governing; the last pre-flight item was to get off the ground far enough to check flight controls, see that they were adjusted right, then everything would be set for a flight the next day. K. B. Wolfe, Phil Johnson and Beall were in Phil's corner office. Harman came down the field in the B-29.

"Look," said Beall. "He's going to go this time."

The engines had that positive roar. K. B. and Johnson were at the windows. Everyone else in the administration building was at the windows by now. The wheels came up. Then, what? The right wing was going down. "Hey!" They were banking steeply. They had no altitude. The plane staggered crazily down the fence line, behind a building row, out of sight. A cloud of dust. The three men tore out of the room white-faced.

Not till they got down the highway could they see that the airplane was there on the runway, safe and sound. The Jake Harman who climbed out of it was a man shaken and puzzled.

"What in the world happened?" asked K. B. Wolfe.

"I don't know. I gave it the antidote. Cut the left engines, gave full power on the right engines. Both of them. Flaps were half down. It just kind of righted up and I chopped everything and there we were. Damn quick, boy."

"You're sure the aileron controls are all right?"

"I don't know."

They looked. The aileron control cables were reversed over the pulley. Harman saw Phil Johnson's eyes snap.

"For God's sake, don't fire anybody," said Jake. "Because it was really my fault. It was written right there in front of me to check."

There was an investigation for sabotage. Inconclusive. Harman flew the plane. It was made ready to be taken to Wichita, where a Kansas prairie was now transformed into a war plant teeming with twenty-five thousand employees, already completing their first B-29.

The lesson of the reversed aileron cables dug sharply into the consciousness of every inspector, every assembly mechanic, every one of the 33,000 employees in the Seattle and Renton plants. Renton was not only getting well along with tooling for the B-29 production but was getting started, too, on an experimental military transport based on the B-29, designed to be a companion to the 29.

Plant Two had become an amazing 1,500,000 square feet of production density. Oliver West and his men had developed a multi-line plan of production, a system adapted to the square shape of the plant. There were row upon row of chopped-off sections of bodies and wings, each alive with riveters and installation mechanics, some men, but mostly women in slacks. Aisles between the body and wing jigs were streets of clattering commerce, with stop-and-go intersections preventing a traffic tangle of fork trucks, flat beds, and long trains of carts carrying parts. Overhead, the little orange cabs of the railway of cranes were constantly bringing down subassemblies from the balcony behind, and leap-frogging Fortress body sections over each other to the final assembly area.

Two years ago no one would have believed that that space now would be turning out two hundred Flying Fortresses a month. Or that it would be turning out two hundred a month with fewer employees than there were a year ago when they were proud of one hundred a month. Or that Oliver West could sit with his charts and predict three hundred a month a year from now, still with the same number of employees. The "learning curve" on the chart showed convincingly that they were learning how to mass-produce.

Most any of the women wearing the little Army-Navy "E" for Excellence pins would tell you there was a reason they were learning so fast, a reason close to the heart. Right now he was somewhere on the sands of North Africa or maybe hitting the beach of Sicily; or in one of Ira Eaker's bombers over Germany.

B-17E

6. *Fortress Against Fortress*

On Pacific isles, sands of Africa, siren-ruled streets of Europe, war was searing the globe. Epicenter of the storm and fire was Adolf Hitler's *Festung Europa*—Fortress Europe. Hitler hadn't envisioned it just this way. His eye had been grim-set on victory. Superiority, surprise, victory. Adolf Hitler took inspiration from the past. The day of conquest and empire. Charlemagne and Frederick the Great. When he planned his war he and his generals looked back, raised their sights only high enough to see the air force as a preface to swift ground attack. Then he had met the unexpected in the Battle of Britain. He could bomb cities but that didn't destroy vital targets. Instead, the RAF had destroyed his bomber force.

Again Hitler looked back. If he couldn't destroy England by air, no one could destroy his *Festung Europa* by air. He could raise an air defense twenty, thirty times the strength of the RAF that saved England. Let the Allies come with their bombers. He'd destroy them in the air. He wouldn't waste effort building any more bombers to hit England. The scientists were developing pilotless rockets that could do that later. For now, he'd build nothing but fighters. Three thousand a month by the end of 1944. When he'd destroyed the attacking air force, he would be safe from land invasion.

American leaders looked ahead at what must be done. The issue was drawn at Casablanca: the attacking Allied air forces versus the German defending air force. The British would be going in nightly to area-bomb the cities. But there was only one way to destroy the German air force: engage it in combat and destroy the factories that were producing it. The German air industry and its supporting elements became the first priority target in the spring of 1943. Everyone knew what that meant. Courage and selflessness created the vision that said, "It can be done."

Ira Eaker looked at his equipment for the job. A few hundred heavy bombers—Flying Fortresses and Liberators. The Forts had the better high-altitude performance. Those tedious months of work in Seattle with the first turbo-superchargers and Eddie Allen's high-altitude research were important now. Anti-aircraft lost 50 per cent of its accuracy with each 5,000 feet above 15,000. The Forts had the better pilot visibility and stability for close-formation flying, and the tighter the formation the better the defense against fighters. Those months of wind-tunnel and flight-test research that gave the B-17 a dorsal fin and a whole new tail-surface design were important now.

The Liberator, on the other hand, had the longer range. It was better suited for the long runs in from bases in North Africa. Each plane for the job it best fitted. It would be the B-17 for the main assault. Flying Fortress against Fortress Europe.

The stern work began. In June 1943, 257 Forts hit a synthetic rubber plant at Huls, in the Ruhr Valley. Opposition was intense,

as expected. Twenty Forts were lost, but forty-seven German
fighters were knocked down. While plans were being laid for a
deeper penetration, strikes were made on motor plants in occupied Belgium and France. The last week in July was the big test.
Sixteen targets to be bombed, among them the Focke-Wulf
fighter plants at Warnemünde and Oschersleben. In the fierce
battles of that week 296 enemy fighters were shot down, and
eighty-four Flying Fortresses lost. In August Ira Eaker, now
commanding the 8th Air Force, and Brigadier General Fred
Anderson, commanding the 8th Bomber Command, assessed the
situation. "We've got to get at the Messerschmitt plants," said
Eaker. "Are you ready for it?"

Anderson looked at the targets file. Messerschmitt fighters
were built in three big industrial complexes at Leipzig and
Regensburg, deep in Germany, and Wiener-Neustadt in Austria.
On the way to Regensburg was the big ball-bearing works at
Schweinfurt, another key target. "I have 380 B-17s operative,"
said Anderson. "Less than half of them have wing-tip tanks. We
could send LeMay's 3rd Division to Regensburg and on to North
Africa, and send the 1st Division to Schweinfurt the same day.
That's our only chance. Give them all the strength we've got.
It'll be a battle all the way in and out."

On a deep penetration like this, the range of fighter aircraft
would permit escort only part of the way. They'd be mostly on
their own. But the Regensburg plant produced 30 per cent of all
the Messerschmitt fighters and the Schweinfurt plant half of
Germany's ball-bearings. To put them out of commission was
worth a tremendous effort. Germany knew that too, better than
they, and had located anti-aircraft and fighter strips all along the
450-mile path. "We'll give 'em a birthday present. August 17 is
the anniversary of our first raid on Rouen," said Anderson.

The thousand-sided project of planning a mission began, this
one the biggest, the most critical yet attempted. Weather was the
big "if": weather over English aerodromes, over the target, over
landing strips in North Africa. August 16 the weather officer said
conditions over the continent and over the Mediterranean the

next day would be the best they'd had in two weeks. It wasn't clearing up much over England, but he thought they could get off.

"We'd better take it while we can," said Eaker. Teletype operators began clicking out the yard-long field order to the divisions. Divisions began translating it into instructions for groups.

At an airdrome in East Anglia, a teletype machine was beginning its authoritative chatter. "We're takin' a long ride tomorrow," said the major watching it. "Tell the men to pack toothbrushes and a change of underwear." The bustle in headquarters, the ground-crew chores around the airplanes, the speculation among the combat crews began. "Where to this time?" "How's Portia's Number Three engine?" "Better get some shut-eye." No one voiced the thought that was deepest in his mind.

At 0015 hours, a jeep starting out from the motor pool broke the night stillness of the station. Its thin, blue headlights came down the perimeter road, up to a Nissen hut where the Intelligence officer was sleeping. "You're wanted at headquarters."

There was that damp, low overcast in the air, that familiar acrid smell of coal smoke, the sound of a patrol plane overhead. Through the double blackout doors at headquarters, the brightness of the light was blinding at first. The duty officer was at the big wall map. He turned to the Intelligence officer. "I've pulled out the target files for you. Regensburg." Across Germany, up the Danube River, off in a valley, an oblong group of factory buildings: Regensburg.

Motor pool was coming alive now, cooks getting up. The Old Man was at headquarters, staring long at the map. At 0300 combat crews were reaching for their gear, climbing into it. Not much talk. The truck for the mess hall was outside. At 0400 they were filling out the benches of the briefing room, pulses quickening. Up front the Old Man stood: Colonel Archie Old, Jr., thirty-six years old, commander of the 96th Group. "We're hitting the Messerschmitt plant at Regensburg today. Anyone here who doesn't like Me-109s staring him in the face, let's get rid of the place that builds them. We land in Algeria." There were hums and low whistles.

The Intelligence officer spelled out the target information. The weather officer took the stand. The flak officer pointed out anti-aircraft batteries along the way: "Stick close to your course and you'll be out of range of most of it." They got the assembly time, assembly point for circling into combat formation, the IP —the Initial Point of the target bomb run, route details. Daylight was approaching.

The flying control officer: "Let's check watches. Ten seconds before 0517 . . . five seconds . . . four . . . three . . . two . . . one . . . hack."

The chaplain: "God be with you."

Colonel Old would lead off the 3rd Division unless Colonel LeMay, the commander, elected to go along. Back in division headquarters thirty-seven-year-old Curtis LeMay, a man whose thought, action and being could be summarized in the one word "duty," was biting his pipe. Weather was still marginal, worse than marginal at 1st Division bases, where the mission to Schwein-furt was scheduled to follow them by ten minutes, and at Fighter Command bases. Bomber Command phoned they might have to hold. LeMay's eyes were set under his unwrinkled forehead and thick black hair. He knew his men could get up through the stuff for the division assembly. He had been drilling them on instru-ment take-offs. Things didn't get done by putting them off. He called General Anderson at Bomber Command. "We'll get in the air and hold over Lowestoft. We'll have to depart there by 0930 to make North Africa before dark. Give us the code word by radio if it's all right to go."

At 96th Group base, the mist of morning was a multi-motored rumble. The first shadowy form of a Fortress moved out from its dispersal point, then another and another, nose to tail around the perimeter track. They queued up with propellers flailing the air. Seconds and minutes ticked off on the sweep hand of the control-tower clock and on wristwatches of bundled, squat crews in the planes. Minus five minutes, minus four, three. "Guess LeMay isn't coming," said Colonel Archie Old. "Are we all set?" Minus two.

A staff car drove up. The stocky LeMay stepped out. "Hello, Archie. You take Number Two plane. I'll go in Number One." LeMay climbed aboard. In the cockpit, pilot and co-pilot snapped to attention, started to get up. "Stay where you are," said LeMay. "I'll stand right here between you."

Number One plane moved down the runway, into the air, Old in Number Two, thirty seconds behind it. Another thirty seconds and Number Three was airborne. Precision-like, the chain continued, one plane lifting from the runway end while the next was midway down it and another was starting. LeMay trailed smoke candles out of the lead plane, first time they'd tried that, to help assemble the formation in bad weather.

Groping together, 96th Group assembled with 94th Group from its station. The 100th came up from another direction, 390th, 95th, 385th, 388th, a great circling chain, adjusting, falling into places, the planes in each squadron arranging themselves into the three-dimensional wedge that offered a crisscross of gunfire; the squadrons arranging themselves into lead, high, and low positions; groups arranging themselves into lead, high and low groups for a combat wing, a great wall of fire power; three combat wings lining up six miles behind each other in a thirteen-mile chain, 126 planes in all. The groups were using a tightened formation that LeMay had perfected earlier, when the Germans had found they couldn't stand the rearward fire of the Forts and had begun concentrating on the difficult head-on attack.

"Flying Fortress" took on a new meaning. Not an airplane now but a tremendous flying force, a half mile high, a half mile wide. A Flying Fortress with a thousand gun turrets winging to attack Fortress Europe.

It was 0930, at Bomber Command the zero hour for decision. First Division, which was supposed to leave for Schweinfurt ten minutes after the departure of 3rd, to divide enemy strength, couldn't get off maybe for an hour, maybe two, because of weather. Escort fighters couldn't get off. Third Division, in the air, couldn't be delayed and still make Africa before dark. The question was as heavy as the 315-ton load of bombs now ranging overhead. Send LeMay's planes on alone or abort the whole mission? All the preparation; the critical importance of the target; the climax of a year's build-up. . . . Eyes shut tight; it was a decision that hurt. This was war.

Over Lowestoft, England, 0935 hours, Curtis LeMay got the green light from Fred Anderson. The circling mass unwound behind the spear point, heading straight out over the Channel, LeMay standing motionless between pilot and co-pilot, eyes dead ahead.

Barely inside Holland, two Focke-Wulf 190s started climbing up, noses high, strictly for business. They bored straight through the second group, nicking the wings of two Forts, then half rolled and dove under the third group, guns blazing, threading through the tracers of Fortress machine guns. The fighters were hard to get in this rolled-over position, because their undersides were heavily armored. The damaged Forts held their places. Interphones were busy. "Give 'em shorter bursts . . . there'll be plenty more coming . . . lead your target." Gunners breathed hard, the rubber bladders of their oxygen masks filling and emptying with tense rhythm under their chins.

More fighters were rising ahead, all over. From LeMay's lead plane it was like a hawk scaring up sparrows. Reports crackled in the interphone. "FW-190s at ten o'clock, low." Forward guns and ball turret chattered. "ME-190s two o'clock, level." "A whole squadron, twelve o'clock, high. . . . Hold your fire till they're in range." The top turret blasted behind LeMay's head. The whole ship was quaking with the recoil. The air was pungent with the smell of powder. "Watch 'em. Coming up all around the clock." Two Forts in the low squadron fell out of formation on fire, crews bailing out. Fighters were falling from the sky. Into it and through it, the armada moved on, straight on.

Archie Old in Number Two ship pulled out of formation with a runaway prop, fought a running battle with eleven fighters back to the Channel. A Fortress *My Prayer* went into a dive, on fire. Seven men bailed out; the top-turret gunner, injured, parachute damaged, stayed on and beat out the flames while the pilot got the ship out of the dive and the co-pilot manned the guns against chasing fighters. At housetop level they made it back to the Channel.

LeMay stood silent at the spear point, coolly measuring the skill of German pilots in maneuvers he had been drilling his groups to combat. The triple threat: three fighters pulling ahead and then burning in head-on at eleven o'clock, twelve o'clock and one o'clock, high, breaking away at eight hundred, five hundred and three hundred yards in wing-ups and belly-up dives. The scissors movement from ten o'clock, high, one plane pulling up fast over the top of the formation, the other diving to the right from four hundred yards. The sneak attack, coming out of the sun. The swooper diving attack from six to twelve o'clock, high. The double cue coming in head-on from long lines on both sides. Roller coaster, long 3,000-yard dive from twelve o'clock, high, swooping up to a stall under the chin of the lead squadron, cannons firing, then falling off in a steep dive.

Fighters were everywhere, pulled from fields in all directions and evidently refueling and coming back up. The battle was unceasing. An hour, two hours, moving always onward in roaring sky, punctuated by falling airplanes, screaming dives, blossoming yellow parachutes.

From the Third Combat Wing at the rear of the column, the scene ahead was an inferno. White tracer streaks crisscrossing the sky. Flak puffs hanging everywhere. Racing fighters with cannon belching from their wings. Parts and pieces in the air. Shattering noise. A door coming by in the air. A man hurtling past, doubled up in a rolling ball. Fighters lobbing in rockets. The Germans were throwing in everything they had.

Still on, entering the third hour, Curtis LeMay stood motionless, twentieth-century gladiator at the forward post of his bucking chariot, churning on through flak and fighters, leading his thirteen-mile battle fleet relentlessly to its objective, Regensburg.

"We're over our IP," called the navigator. "Bombardier taking over." They locked into Automatic Flight Control's iron groove for the approach. "Bombs away." The bombs fell true in the target rectangle. A quick right-angle turn to the south, with less enemy fighters following now—the Germans weren't expecting bombers this far inland—and the new course was set toward the majestic peaks of the Alps. North of Brenner Pass, LeMay circled for stragglers, trued up the formations. No attacking fighters now, only speculation over remaining gas supply. One ship, definitely running short, headed off for a crash landing in Spain. Another, *Pregnant Portia*, engines failing, got its silent, praying crew as far as the Mediterranean, where all ten men hung tight on a five-man raft through the night, finally to be sighted by a B-26 and taken ashore by British Air Sea Rescue. Ten airmen from the missing *Portia* occupied ten adjacent seats in a North African church next Sunday.

The 1st Division had been three and a half hours late getting off on its mission the same day for Schweinfurt and had to battle all the way in and out. Out of the 376 planes dispatched on the two August 17 missions, sixty were lost to enemy action. "Sure, we had losses," said LeMay. "But the Germans had losses too." The Germans lost 288 fighters in the combat, crews claimed, as well as a Messerschmitt factory which had been producing 250 ME-109s a month—30 per cent of German fighter production— and a good part of the nation's ball-bearing production.

It was grim. Up to now, U. S. losses had averaged 5 per cent of planes dispatched. At that rate, five raids a month would wipe out the bomber force in four months, without replacements. This day's loss was 16 per cent. Five more days like it would wipe them out. Washington was alarmed. But there was no doubt the bombing was effective. Germany was desperate. "Keep hitting them," was the order of the day at Bomber Command. "The faster we come back at them, the faster we'll get the job done."

It took time to patch up the planes and reorganize the combat crews. More planes were arriving from the States. Through September, they flew simpler missions. By October they were ready for a big week's offensive. A record 399 planes went out October 8, hit Bremen and other targets. Thirty were lost. Next day a force of 357 planes hit targets as far east as Danzig and ninety-six of them—LeMay's men—bombed Marienburg two hundred miles east of Berlin. Unexpected this far east, they hit Marienburg from 11,000 feet, destroying the Focke-Wulf plant without touching the adjacent prison camp. Climax of the week was a second raid on Schweinfurt, October 14, by 291 planes of the 1st and 3rd Divisions. Colonel Archie Old, who didn't get to bomb Regensburg, led the 3rd Division.

It was another battle like the last one. After the fighter escort left them at Aachen, Germany, it was combat all the way, against a force totaling seven hundred enemy fighters. On the target approach, the flak and the fighter onslaught were appalling. Old, in the right-hand seat of the lead plane, could see thirteen fighters converging on his plane. There was an incredible wall of flak ahead. They couldn't deviate, with the ship now on the automatic flight-control equipment.

"You mean we've got to fly *through* it?" asked the top gunner. Forward in the plexiglas nose, some of the flak hit Bombardier Latham in the stomach. He doubled and fell. Navigator Hodson picked him up, set him back in place over the bombsight. "Hit that target."

Latham did. "Bombs away," he whispered. They banked and turned to the right. Fifteen or twenty fighters shot toward them, got the two inboard engines. Both engines started burning. Old signaled Number Two plane to take the lead. Five or six enemy fighters took after the crippled plane as Old went into a sixty-degree dive from 22,000 feet to broken clouds at 4,000. He leveled off and feathered the two burning engines. Number Three wouldn't feather completely. The fighters kept attacking. They got Hodson, the navigator. Lieutenant Jones took Hodson's place. Then he was wounded.

For two hours there were three to twelve fighters pumping shells at them in relays as they skipped through low clouds. A lot of those fighters didn't get back. Bombardier Latham was wounded again. Losing altitude badly, Old unfeathered Number Two engine and got it started. It started burning again. He tried

Number Three till it, too, began to burn, then went back to
Number Two. Alternating between the two damaged engines,
they stayed in the air. Old called crew stations on the interphone,
"Tail gunner, are you O.K?"

"I'm O.K."

"Waist gunners?" Every other man was wounded. Old had a
20-mm. shell fragment lodged in one hand.

The clouds got worse. No visibility at all. They were losing
altitude. "Throw out everything," Old ordered. Even then they
could barely maintain flight on two engines. Nothing now but
thick soup, struggling Fortress, and fervent prayer.

Fuel was running out when they broke free into sunshine and
sight of the English coast. They made it to an RAF field at
Gravesend. Fire started in the wing when they let down the landing gear. Everything was shot up, gaping holes from cannon
shells all over the ship, between them the sieve that was left
where flak pieces had gone through. The brakes were useless.
Fire trucks overtook them while they were still rolling, pouring
on foamite. They stopped twenty feet from the fence. Archie
Old, weak and dripping, thumped the control column with his
one good hand. "Baby, you wouldn't let us down."

At stations throughout England the night of October 14, 1943,
Intelligence officers debriefed weary men. They claimed 186
enemy fighters shot down in the sky battle. The target was hit
squarely. On the other side of the ledger, sixty more B-17s and
crews were lost, 138 ships damaged. Worse even than the anniversary raids of August 17. Twenty per cent of the planes dispatched were gone.

A shocked Washington cried out. "Were the British right? Is
the cost of daylight bombing prohibitive?" Congressmen de-
scended on Hap Arnold with demands for an explanation. Arnold
countered, "We finished off Schweinfurt, half of Germany's
vital ball-bearing industry." But Hap, too, was alarmed.

7. *Battle of Kansas*

Everything was being done that anyone could think of to give the B-17 more protection. More engineers were on the Flying Fortress now than there had ever been in the eight-year history of the series. Changes were being pumped into Oliver West's production lines and into finished planes at modification centers as fast as those engineers, the company's field service engineers with the combat forces, and the Air Materiel Command at Wright Field could work up new ideas to meet the changing pattern of war. So many guns had been stuck in the nose that gunners were getting in each other's way. In the next model, the B-17G, a powered forward turret was being added under the nose.

Hap Arnold knew all this, but Wellwood Beall, summoned to Arnold's office, reminded him. "We have the chin turret coming along."

"It ought to be coming faster."

"If there's anything we can do, we want to do it."

"After Schweinfurt, everyone on the Hill has been jumping on me," said Arnold. "We've got to cut down our losses. Go over there yourself and get a firsthand picture. I'll get you a priority."

Two weeks later, Beall's cab took him to 8th Air Force headquarters. Ira Eaker was glad to see him, gave him the picture in a hurry. They had found out two things. If they had enough B-17s en masse, they could get through to any target and they could hit the target. But they were going to have to cut down on the deepest penetrations until they could get longer-range fighters for escort. "The old dogma that you can't have a fighter with the range of a bomber is out," said Eaker. "Long-range fighters are what we need right now." Beall recalled that Ira Eaker was once a fighter man. Monk Hunter, head of the 8th Air Force Fighter

Command, was adding tanks to his P-47s and P-38s and would soon be getting the long-range P-51s. It took teamwork to win a war.

"But we're doing all right," said Eaker. He walked to a photo framed on the wall. It was Regensburg after the bombing. Factory buildings, covering three-fourths of the rectangle, were destroyed or gutted. A hospital, marked with a white cross in the other quarter, was untouched. "Now let me show you something." General Eaker pulled a telegram from his desk drawer. "This is from the Luftwaffe." The Germans had sent a wire praising the American fliers for that accuracy. "We don't see how you did it," they said.

"Let me show you something else." Eaker brought out a photo of a Fortress cut in half just ahead of the tail surface, flying along with only the flooring connecting the two parts. "Do you wonder the men swear by those airplanes?"

"What can we do to make them do a better job for you?" Eaker told him to talk to the men at the bomber stations and Beall made the rounds with Boeing service engineers, who were already close to the operating crews. On his way to his hotel through the blacked-out streets of London, Beall saw a huge flash. There was a rocking explosion a block away. He hurried toward it. A two-story brick building was laid open, the middle of it a heap of timbers with men and women stumbling out, others crying "Help" and moaning in the darkness. A fire was breaking out next door. Beall helped an elderly lady to a first-aid post. "Oh," she was saying, "there are dozens of people buried under there." Home Guard rescue squads came into the chaos to form human chains over the debris, bearing out on stretchers those who were alive.

One lone dive bomber had done it. "What are our fleets of bombers doing to Germany?" Beall thought, and shuddered. *If we have enough B-17s we can get through to any target*, Ira Eaker had said. What would they do to Germany with the thousands of new Forts now in production, long-range fighters for protection, thousands of tons of TNT to drop with precision. War was frightful. In war you had better have the best equipment.

America had learned that when caught in war you'll ride to success or defeat in the equipment already developed, not something new and too late. The Flying Fortress was seven years old when the nation entered war but it was the framework on which America depended, through eight successive models, for its aerial offense against Hitler in Europe.

The B-29 Superfortress, designed two years before Pearl Harbor, was too late for the war in Europe, and only by putting it in production before testing of a prototype, only by forcing it at every turn, was it possible to make it ready for war in the Pacific. The strategic bombardment in Europe had shown what could be done, but the timetable in the Pacific, right now, looked much slower than the one in Europe. There were the tremendous distances, the ground and water to be won back.

The heroic assault on Guadalcanal was at once a preview of the grief ahead and the promise of its success, but no one would predict how many years it might take. How long could a nation stand all-out war? The B-29 Superfortress, subject of ever-mounting pressure, still having its trouble with engines and equipment, was still the white hope and the great need.

In November 1943, at Cairo, Chiang Kai-shek told President Roosevelt he would have B-29 bases ready in South China by April 1944. The President said the U. S. Army Air Force would be there to use them. In December, Hap Arnold sent K. B. Wolfe to India to begin setting the stage for the B-29 strikes at Japan. K. B. left Brigadier General Blondie Saunders behind, with Colonel Harman and Colonel Tommy Chapman as wing commanders, to organize the crews that would take the Superforts into action.

Boeing-Wichita, with 29,000 farm hands, housewives and shopkeepers turned airplane builders, had gotten its first Superfortress in the air in June 1943. Arnold had set 175 B-29s as the starting minimum for the 20th Bomber Command. Equipment makers and parts builders throughout the country were involved in the production blitz, many of them, too, producing ahead of full test of their equipment. Engine deliveries were slow. There was a shortage of steel.

The one-hundredth plane was out by January 1944. There was a shortage of engine nacelles, built in Cleveland under a separate contract with the government. The production lines in the big Wichita plant were clogged waiting for them. The plant was on ten-hour day and night shifts, six days a week. "We'll have to have more nacelles or cut back production," said Earl Schaefer.

"No, no," said Jake Harman. "Go ahead and build 'gliders' and set 'em out on the field. We'll double up the production of nacelles and then we can make airplanes out of them."

Hap Arnold came out to the Wichita plant to see how his 175th Superfortress was coming along. He found its body section just entering final assembly. "This is the plane I want," said Hap. "I want it before the first of March." There were hundreds of change orders coming through on the armament and military equipment, result of production concurrent with development. It was impossible to make the changes on the factory production line. Completed planes were flown to plants in four states for the modifications. When they came back to the Army fields at Salina, Pratt, Great Bend, and Walker, Kansas, for use in combat training, Army ground crews couldn't get things to work. Mechanics from the modification centers were pulled into the airfields to work with Army mechanics.

The 175th Superfortress—*General Arnold Special*—was rolled out of the Wichita plant February 28 and rushed to a modification center. At the Kansas bases, few of the planes were in flying condition. Crates of parts were coming in from all over, to go in the ships. Flight training was lagging for want of airplanes. Saunders and Harman were trying to organize combat crews. Most of them were men with B-17 experience in England. The B-29 was a big, strange airplane compared to the 17. The pilots didn't like the windshield. Gunners were trying to get on to the centralized fire control. The radar bombing system was baffling.

Everything was so technical, a crew man had to have seven experts to consult. The men were uneasy.

So was Hap Arnold, who had promised the planes would leave for China and India March 10, 1944. On March 9, Hap flew to Salina. "How many planes are ready to go?" he asked.

"None," said the bases. "We can't get the parts."

"What? I want to know where every missing part is by tomorrow morning," blazed the chief. A barrage of telegrams went out. A week later, still no planes ready. The critical need was for technicians. General Orval Cook, production division head, flew to Wichita March 17 and called Earl Schaefer. "I'm at the airport. Come over right away. I want you to go up to Salina with me. We've got to find some way to cut these 29s loose."

"Can you wait just five minutes till I get Fletcher Brown?" Fletcher Brown was works manager at the Wichita plant. A half hour later they stepped into the cold blast of the wind at Salina and climbed into a B-29 where mechanics were working.

"Here's what I've still got to do," said a distraught crew chief, looking at his list. "Change the flap switch link, fix the emergency relief tank, change the flux gate compass transmitter, the side sighting dome, recalibrate the fuel gages, fix the rudder tail rib, tail skid actuators, tail turret stops." Another ship was the same story. Another.

"Can you give us a storm crew of five or six hundred mechanics to help push this through?" asked Cook.

"How soon?"

"Today. Hap Arnold says come hell or high water the last plane has got to leave April 15." Schaefer knew what this would do to his production. But he knew, too, what it would mean to send faulty equipment into battle. "You have the transportation and we'll have the men ready in four hours," he said. Fletcher Brown went back and called in his foremen, picked the crews. Some had time to go home and pack their things, others came as they were. Next day the six hundred were climbing stepladders around the planes in driving sleet and snow, wearing 20th

Bomber Command high-altitude flying suits for protection, pitching into the Battle of Kansas.

Colonel Bill Irvine was in charge of the work. Irvine got Colonel H. A. Shepard and Major Tom Gerrity down from Dayton to help. Phil Johnson, Oliver West and Beall came out from Seattle. Beall caught it from Irvine. "What's the matter with your wiring diagrams for these planes?" he asked. "Nothing works right. You push a radio switch and the bomb doors come open."

"Let's have a look." Beall found the diagrams marked over. He called an electrical foreman who had come up from Wichita.

"The diagrams were O.K. when the ships left Wichita," said the foreman. "They changed things all around in Birmingham without making new diagrams. Then they changed everything again at Marietta. Didn't have time to fix up the drawings, I guess. Army pushing 'em all the time. No one knows what they've got now. We just have to trace it through."

For four weeks the Battle of Kansas went on, at Salina, Pratt, Walker and Great Bend, trying to get the B-29 ready for battle, against the pressure of time. When hands were numb from the sleet and wind, the men would duck into shacks to warm them. When the men got too groggy, they'd come in for black coffee and then go at it again.

Gradually order came out of chaos. Combat crews were piling their duffels and equipment aboard while the mechanics were still working. Earl Schaefer watched one day. There seemed no end to the material going aboard. "How heavy are you loading these?" he asked.

"One hundred and thirty-five thousand."

"One hundred and thirty-five thousand? Do you know the maximum gross is 120,000 pounds?"

"Yeah, we know. Your maximum on the B-17 was 48,000. We flew at 60,000 all the time in England." This was war. The planes were loaded to 135,000, then to 140,000.

At one o'clock on a morning late in March, Jake Harman emerged from the operations building at Pratt in flying togs and parachute harness. There was snap in his step. He hoisted himself into a B-29 and took off into the night. The first Superfortress was India-bound. During the next two weeks, a secret fleet followed his path to Morocco, to Cairo, to Kharagpur, where K. B. Wolfe, commanding general of the 20th Bomber Command, was waiting.

The continent was strange, the people were strange. Short runways and the 120-degree temperatures of India brought new problems. Engines were overheated and overtaxed. There were spare-parts shortages. Then there was the long haul over the Himalayas. Every bomb, every gallon of gas that they would need in China had to be hauled over that Hump. "Butch" Blanchard, Saunders' deputy, flew the first plane over. The temperatures of all four engines went up to 290 degrees.

"Let's just hope they hold together," said his worried flight engineer. They got away with it. In the weeks that the B-29s were tankers and freighters, the 20th Bomber Command learned more about how to operate the engines and the cowl flaps for better cooling. But the men weren't learning gunnery, formation flying, radar bombing.

June 5 was the date for the first shakedown mission, to bomb railroad yards at Bangkok. They would fly in loose formation and use radar bomb-sighting. They'd take off from the India bases. Bombs and fuel pushed the take-off weight up to 134,000 pounds. Jake Harman led off at 0545. Ninety-eight planes followed from fields in the Kharagpur area. One crashed on take-off. Fourteen turned back with equipment difficulties. The rest winged out over the Bay of Bengal at 5,000 feet, and five hours after take-off were climbing in four-plane elements to 25,000 feet for the bomb run over the Gulf of Thailand to a cloud-covered target. Some of the elements didn't get together, due to the clouds. There wasn't much enemy opposition. Moderate flak, but inaccurate. The crews had to make repeated runs to get their bombs away, coming in from all angles at miscellaneous altitudes before they were through.

Then the long flight back. Gas was running low over the Bay of Bengal when they sighted something ahead that the weather forecasters hadn't given them. A vertical cloud bank that was black as night. Typhoon. Some of the crews headed into it, guessing it would be short and intense. They took a terrific shaking and came out the other side. Others tried to go under. There were dirt and debris and the roofs of huts in the air at 4,000 feet. Two planes ditched in the bay.

All that night and next day K. B. Wolfe was rounding up his pack from fields all over India. The crews that ditched were rescued. They'd learned that the B-29 ditched well. That news was a big comfort to the men. One of the two planes that ditched never did sink, but floated ashore next day. They found, though, that the rear gunnery crew had to be put up forward for a ditching because a big wave would tear through the bomb bay and swamp the back compartment.

Wolfe got an urgent message from Hap Arnold June 6. The Joint Chiefs of Staff wanted an attack on Japan to relieve pressure on an "important operation" in the Pacific. Wolfe suspected that the "important operation" was the assault on Saipan. Washington picked the steel works at Yawata as the target and ordered a night mission with planes navigating individually, believing the 3,200-mile round trip from the China bases would take too much fuel to allow formation flying.

The mission was set for the night of June 15, 1944. Jake Harman, who was to lead the flight, was having trouble with his engines. "Better take another plane," K. B. advised him.

"I've been flying this one all along. I feel at home in it. It'll be O.K."

On the morning of June 15, the men were briefed. "Tonight we begin the organized destruction of the Japanese industrial empire," K. B. Wolfe told them. K. B. was set to go along in the lead plane with Jake. Then an order came that commanding generals should no longer go on missions.

At 1616, sixty-eight Superfortresses began taking off from

handmade runways near Chengtu, for the big test. The flight started out comfortably enough. A well soundproofed airplane, slipping along at 230 miles an hour, the speed for best range, pressurized. Jake Harman thought of all the effort that had gone to make this possible. He thought back to the days of the old Keystone bombers. Then the revolutionary B-9 monoplane. The surprising Model 299 Flying Fortress. Now the Superfortress, the weapon built for victory. This was it. They were on their way right now. He wondered if the enemy knew it.

All the crews were wondering about this, too, and other things. They were seven hours of mounting tension, in darkness that spelled uncertainty. Three of the planes had trouble and had to turn back. A thousand miles out, one of Harman's engines sputtered and quit. Jake looked at the flight engineer, who shook his head. Jake coaxed the throttle. This couldn't happen to him now. This was the big event he had lived for, planned and worked for. He was leaning forward in the pilot's seat, coaxing the big plane. Then another engine began to falter and lose power. He fussed frantically with the controls. His fist came down across his lap.

"We'll have to go back," said the flight engineer.

At Chengtu airbase, K. B. Wolfe, pacing the tiny operations building, passed one hand over the top of his head in an unconscious echo of the days when he had hair there to smooth down. He wished mightily that he could be up there over the Yellow Sea with those B-29s. Instead, he waited. Waited for just one code word: "Betty" would mean a successful mission. Six hours, seven hours. "They should be getting close." Seven hours, five minutes; eight minutes.

Colonel Blanchard burst in from the radio room. "It's Betty over the target!"

K. B. let out a great long breath. "Good."

The wait for the returning planes was as bad as the wait during the outbound trip. Jake Harman got back first, long-faced. Wolfe gave him the good news. Harman grunted. He just went around shaking his head and hitting his fist on everything he came to.

The rest of the planes began to come in. The men were tired but happy. "We saw sixteen fighters but most of them never got a shot. There were a million searchlights. A lot of flak came up, but it went behind us. They never got our speed." A few of the planes were damaged by the flak, but none was shot down. Navigating back over China with no radio aid, however, had been a strain and a trial. Three of the ships got lost and crash-landed or ran into mountains. Still, in military terms, the losses were light.

Recon photos showed the bombing accuracy on the Yawata mission was only fair. Radar was still a tricky thing. But the men knew now what they could do. That was the big thing. Later missions stirred up greater enemy opposition. The central fire-control system had its test. The gunners got to like it. "We could never keep 'em in the sights at these speeds with the old guns," they said. Most of the Nipponese pilots were wary of the Superforts and stayed out of range. There were three more missions in June and July. The trips stretched the Superforts to their maximum range. There weren't many combat losses, but there were operational losses. K. B. Wolfe requisitioned 240 new engines a month.

In July Hap Arnold cabled K. B. that he was needed back home to ride herd on the soaring B-29 production program. Blondie Saunders assumed command. Saunders planned a daylight attack on Yawata for August 20, though most of his staff urged a continuance of night bombing. The high-altitude formation flying necessary in daylight took too much fuel and left too little for bomb load, they argued. Four out of seventy-five planes in the mission were lost over the target. Ten more were lost getting home in bad weather. One plane with three engines shot out came back all the way across the Yellow Sea on one engine, coming downhill with fighters all over him. To stay in the air, the pilot ran the engine at fifty-four or fifty-five inches manifold pressure, way above its rated military power. The flight engineer went to the bomb bay, did some hooking up of wires, and got another engine going. They set both engines at full take-off power and flew on to a field in occupied China, made repairs, and got back to home base.

"The old Cyclones really pulled us through that time," said the crew. The incident lifted morale throughout the 20th. It gave the men new faith in their engines, which were coming through from the States now with many improvements and modifications.

On August 29, Major General Curtis LeMay arrived in China to head the 20th Bomber Command. LeMay protested the order that had kept Wolfe and Saunders from flying on missions. "I've got to go along or I'll never know what I'm up against," he insisted. When Hap Arnold finally consented, he went on the raid to Anshan, September 8. LeMay's comments on the raid were brief. "The Japanese pilots aren't very sharp. We're going to learn how to put more bombs on the target. We'll do it by daylight. They won't stop us." It didn't help much to use night flights and haul more bombs, if you missed the target.

Taskmaster LeMay instituted a rigorous new training program, replaced the four-plane formation with the twelve-plane squadron used in Europe for greater fire power, trained the pilots to fly tighter together. "The better you learn your job the safer you're going to be," he said. To make sure of hitting the target, he had the radar operator and the bombardier work together as a synchronized team, both following the bomb run till final cloud conditions over the target determined which would release the Superfort's lethal load. The long-armed attack on Japan began to pick up speed.

8. *Victory*

America in the summer of 1944 had gone through two and a half years of war. The "arsenal of democracy" had poured forth a torrent of production, feeding a furious new assault by Ira Eaker's bombers on the strategic targets of Germany, sending soldiers in lashing waves upon embattled Italy and now across France in Dwight D. Eisenhower's tidal wave of invasion.

There was a spirit for victory, a will to bore in, though bitter the cost, and get it over with. The 8th Air Force in late February sent 1,000 bombers a day out after the targets of Germany's aircraft industry in one big week, to break the back of the Luftwaffe. Prepared to take losses as high as two hundred bombers a day, they had gotten out with 137 lost in the six days. That was still a mighty cost in lives and equipment, but the percentage of losses was going down. The weight of numbers and the improved fighter cover made the armada a fearful one for the Germans to encounter.

The 15th Air Force made coordinated attacks with B-24s from bases in Italy, and the RAF Bomber Command pelted into the same target areas through the dark hours. Fifteen hundred German fighters fell out of the air in February. Factories that accounted for 90 per cent of Germany's remaining aircraft production suffered sudden havoc. In March, the hub city of Berlin flinched under a rain of bombs from 660 Forts. By summer of '44 the fighting vitality of the Luftwaffe had been sapped.

Production planners in Washington were responding to the change of tide. Valves were tightened on the pipelines flowing with materials, parts and assemblies for B-17s and B-24s, and increased effort was channeled into the B-29 Superfortress program. At Boeing Plant Two in Seattle, the transition was evident. Jigs and work platforms for B-29 subassemblies were being installed everywhere between the lines of B-17 production. The end was nearing for the Fortress assembly line that had turned out more pounds of airplane per square foot of plant and man-hour of labor than any other heavy-bomber factory.

Parts for B-29s fabricated in Seattle were assembled in nearby Renton. The Renton plant, which had finished its first B-29 in January 1944, completed nineteen by mid-year, when Flying Fortress production began to taper from its three hundred per month rate. The Wichita plant was nearing the end of its long production of more than 8,000 Kaydet primary trainers, a program that established man-hour production records for smaller aircraft, and it was now producing fifty B-29s per month.

Airplane companies not in the B-29 program were cutting back their employment. Even in Seattle, total manpower was coming down with the tremendous B-17 program nearing its end. The new B-29 work would not immediately pick up all the slack. The start of manpower curtailments was a weathervane that brought to every plant manager a sharp realization that the problem of providing postwar business was drawing inevitably nearer. Phil Johnson looked out over the noisy production floors in Seattle and pondered the strange contradiction. Those 41,000 people who had been designing and building the B-17s and B-29s spearheading America's air warfare—the airplanes that nearly half the companies in the industry were now producing—probably had the least security of any people in the industry. Their work had been regarded by the government as too important to permit diversion of effort to commercial, peacetime products.

Phil Johnson was proud of that and he wouldn't change it. "First and foremost," he'd say, "our job is to win the war." But weren't the abilities and facilities so valuable to the country in war equally valuable in peace?

Peacetime business was competitive and the company wasn't being allowed to make preparation for it. True, they had under construction the XC-97 experimental military transport, which might make a commercial transport, but other companies building transports had military production orders for them. Those

orders helped pay for tooling and would make the planes cheaper
to produce for airline use after the war.

Ed Wells had put a small group of engineers under Don Euler
in an uptown building to work on design of other-than-aircraft
products they might build after the war: a low-priced car,
kitchen and bathroom equipment. But Johnson felt that the best
chance for postwar business was to continue developing new
military airplanes to help preserve the country's postwar security.

In early September, Johnson was in Washington meeting with
aircraft industry people on this and other problems. He stopped
at Wichita on the way home, tired. He called Earl Schaefer
from the hotel to say he wasn't feeling well.

On September 14, 1944, Phil Johnson died of a stroke. Machines and work stopped in silent tribute in two hundred acres
of Boeing plants. Friends thought back on the days that called
out for Phil's friendly, able hand. Associates considered the can-
did integrity that Phil had planted in the company, and knew
it was there to stay. Men in a government that had once kicked
him out of the aviation business said of Phil Johnson: "He has
shortened the war."

Claire Egtvedt, in the office of chairman, resumed active management of the Boeing Airplane Company, and started the process of finding a successor to the presidency. With two other
board members, Dietrich Schmitz and Darrah Corbet, he inter-
viewed candidates. They offered the position to Bill Allen, who'd
been close to the business for twenty years as company lawyer
and fourteen years as a director. "Why, that's out of the question," said Allen. "I'm not qualified. But I'd be glad to help
find someone." The search went on, without positive results.

The pace of the war in Europe was quickening. England was
a giant flat-top loaded with new aircraft. General Jimmy Doolittle was now commanding the 8th Air Force. The sky over
Germany was a many-fingered path of white vapor trails behind
high-altitude Flying Forts. The ground below was blackened
wherever a pin on Bomber Command's big wall map showed

another target picked off. Aircraft plants, oil industry, transportation points; there were scarcely any strategic targets left. The Germans were coming at the Flying Forts with new jet-propelled fighters, but they had already lost the best of their fighter pilots and the massed U. S. bombers and Mustang long-range fighters now accompanying them were overpowering.

In the Pacific, the Marianas had been taken—Saipan, Tinian and Guam. Bulldozers had carved great airstrips for the B-29 Superforts of the 21st Bomber Command, a new unit of the 20th Air Force. Brigadier General Haywood "Possum" Hansell, who had been planning B-29 operations from Washington, landed the first Superfort on Saipan October 12, 1944, and eight days later Brigadier General O'Donnell arrived to head up Hansell's first Wing. Vastly different, thought Rosy, from the little 19th Bombardment Group in which he had withdrawn from the Philippines less than three years before.

On November 24th, Rosy O'Donnell in the Superfortress *Dauntless Dotty* spearheaded a daylight formation of 111 B-29s over Tokyo. At 445 miles an hour ground speed, before a 120-knot wind, they swept through fighters and flak and dropped 277 tons of bombs by radar through an overcast. They lost two B-29s over the target and shot down seven enemy fighters. O'Donnell and Hansell were disappointed with their accuracy, but the main attack on Japan was irrevocably under way. Nothing was going to stop it.

Boeing-Wichita was turning out eighty B-29s per month by the end of 1944, and Seattle-Renton was up to thirty-five. The concern over peacetime utilization of the big plants was mounting. The experimental XC-97, sixty-ton double-deck military transport with a 10½-foot-wide cargo body on top of the normal B-29 body, all pressurized for high-altitude flight, was nearly ready for test. There was still no production order for the plane, originally conceived as a companion plane to the B-29. Fred Collins made the rounds of Washington with Jim Murray trying to sell it, but Boeing was tagged for bombers. The transports already on order from other companies would suffice.

Collins went as far as Undersecretary of War Robert Patterson, who was sympathetic. Finally, Oliver Echols said to Beall, when he was east: "You show us that you can make your schedules on B-29s, and we'll consider the transport."

Ed Wells was directing a new engineering effort to cut the weight of the B-29 down 7,000 pounds and add more powerful engines, to give the plane new superiority for postwar sale. The preliminary design unit, now headed by Bob Jewett, was working too on studies for a jet-powered bomber requested by the Air Force, but this looked a long way off.

Of all the projects, the best seemed to be the C-97 military transport and a projected eighty-passenger commercial transport based on it, called Model 377, in which Pan American Airways was showing an interest. But postwar production would depend on whether enough of them could be sold to make the project profitable. Engineering and tooling costs would be tremendous.

The XC-97 was flown November 9, 1944. On January 9, a crew headed by chief test pilot Elliott Merrill and co-pilot John Fornasero flew the big ship across the country nonstop, in six hours, four minutes, even beating pursuit-plane records. It was a preview of postwar air transportation, and for the public a glimpse at the kind of flying the B-29 crews in the Pacific now took as commonplace.

The drive for victory in the Pacific had reached a relentless pace by January 1945. General Echols invited Wellwood Beall and representatives of other aircraft firms to make a tour of the Air Force operations there. Beall's party arrived on Saipan January 19, just as "Possum" Hansell's 21st Bomber Command was returning from a high-altitude attack on Akashi, where they scored a perfect hit. Beall watched them come in through the sunset, a roaring sky full of airplanes. He watched the men pile out of their planes, men who had been out thirteen hours or more winging in formation across the 1,500 miles of ocean and back.

"How do you like the 29 by now?" he asked General O'Donnell, who had led the raid.

"Fine, especially the pressurized cabin. It's a long haul up to Honshu and back."

"Is the central fire control working out?"

"Sure, fine. But we don't get much chance to use it. Five minutes. The rest is just a long ride and wondering if there's enough gas to get back on. This is the first time in a long while that they've all made it back." Beall had heard that already. Three or four "ditchings" on the way in were common. They were operating the 29 at its maximum range, with three extra fuel tanks in the bomb bay and only the remaining one-fourth of the bomb bay space left for bombs. "Here's the odd thing," said Rosy. "On today's mission we pulled out one of the tanks and made out better. Pappy Haines, one of my squadron commanders, discovered he could do it. We had a time talking the crews into it, but it worked."

"Sure. Weight's everything," said Beall.

Beall talked to Colonel Haines. "Next to getting home, the thing that worries the men most is taking off," said the Colonel. "A lot of them drop in the drink. They do it wrong, but you can't convince them. They try to climb before they have enough speed. That slows them down all the more and they start to lose altitude. If they'd just put the nose down and pick up speed they'd be O.K., but they get scared and pull the stick back, and first thing you know they're in the drink." Haines was an engineer; Beall could see he had it figured out.

"Sure," said Beall, "they're getting over on the back side of the power curve. If you go too fast it takes more power; if you go too slow it takes more power. You've got to know your condition. I wish we could get a test airplane out here with instruments on it so we could demonstrate some of these things. I think we could save a lot of airplanes."

Next day Major General Curtis LeMay relieved General Hansell as head of the 21st Bomber Command. Beall felt LeMay would be the man to see about getting a demonstration airplane over from the plant. He asked about an appointment at the General's headquarters in Guam. "See LeMay? You can't see that man," he was told. Then someone who was going to Guam next day said Beall could come along if he wanted to take a chance on it.

Beall got to LeMay and spelled out his suggestion. He'd like to send some engineers out to work with the operating groups, get them better range. LeMay listened, didn't say a word. Beall had made his speech, didn't know what to do. Get up and leave or what? It was uncomfortable. Finally he said to the General, "I'll take this flight crew of ours, so help me God, and they'll fly any place your soldiers fly."

"That won't be necessary," said LeMay. He picked up the phone and called Bill Irvine, in charge of maintenance in the Pacific. "Give Mr. Beall one hour on the teletype." He put down the phone. "We'll go along with you," he said. When Beall got together with Bill Irvine, he found Bill was all for it. He had started an operational engineering program for the 21st and had made the suggestion that Beall and the other airplane people visit the Marianas. Beall arranged for Ed Wells, test pilot Elliott Merrill and aerodynamicist Johnny Alexander to come to the Marianas with a plane and equipment.

Washington wanted to try fire-bomb raids against Japan. General Hansell had tried a couple of raids with them, inconclusively. LeMay had tried one when he was in China, with fair results, but the aim wasn't good from high altitudes, with the strong winds. It would take a lot of bombs, too, to start a conflagration. "What would you think of going over Tokyo at low altitude— five or six thousand feet—at night, with a good heavy load of incendiaries?" LeMay asked his staff. "Navigate singly, not in formation. Put the fuel you save into more bomb load."

It would be a huge gamble. There was controversy. They'd be flying right down in the flak. For years the Air Force had been learning and practicing high-altitude precision bombing of strategic targets, and high-stacked formations for mutual defense up where flak was less accurate. This would be a complete reversal.

But today's problem wasn't the same as yesterday's. In Europe, factories were concentrated. In Japan, they were scattered all through the cities, cities built largely of wood and susceptible to fire. In Europe, the bombers were up against the skilled Luftwaffe. LeMay had found that Japanese pilots couldn't match them. Only one-fourth of the B-29's bomb capacity was being used on the missions to Japan, because of the fuel load. The long climb and formation flying used up the fuel. The conditions here were against high-altitude bombing. Weather was always covering up the target. Then there were the high winds. If you bucked them, your target run took forever; if you went downwind, the target zipped out of the sights; if you went crosswind, the bomb sight wouldn't take it.

More important, to LeMay, was the time factor. He felt that in Europe the air battle would have been decisive without a land invasion, though the ground forces would never agree with that. Plans were moving ahead now for invasion of Japan against Japanese land armies that were still practically untouched. He was sure that the 21st Bomber Command could bring the enemy to its knees. But if this were to be done, the air attack would have to be stepped up and finished off in short order, ahead of the timetable for invasion. LeMay sat there staring into space. Then he gave his verdict.

"If this works the way I think it's going to, we will shorten the war."

March 9, bomber crews at briefings in Saipan, Guam and Tinian listened in shocked silence. Maximum-effort night incendiary attacks were to be made on major Japanese industrial cities. Bombing altitudes would be from 5,000 to 9,000 feet. No armament or ammunition would be carried. Gunners would be left home. Bomb loads would be stepped up from five tons per airplane to seven and eight tons. They would attack individually, not in close formation. Tokyo, most heavily defended, would be the first target.

"Is the Old Man crazy?" the stunned pilots asked.

They went, General Tom Power in the lead. They came back next day a changed air force, sobered, matured. "You'd never believe it," they said. "Tokyo caught fire like a forest of pine trees." The experience had been rugged. Mountains of smoke built up over the target. Following planes had to go into it to bomb. Great updrafts of heat hit them like a stone wall. Two of the planes flipped over on their backs. Downdrafts broke seat fastenings and sent crewmen crashing against the ceiling. All in blinding smoke and heat, with flak in the air, white searchlights flashing up, and bewildered Japanese pilots bursting through. "If ever an airplane went through a test, that was it," they said.

Out of 302 planes over the target, fourteen were lost, all to anti-aircraft fire. Photo reconnaissance showed sixteen square miles of the city destroyed. Eighty-five per cent of the planned target area was wiped out. Two days later, they did it to Nagoya, then Osaka, then Kobe. Japanese defenders couldn't cope with the onslaught. B-29 losses grew less. Bill Irvine's operations engineering section was devising new ways to save fuel, increase bomb loads, cut down operation losses. Ed Wells, Merrill and Alexander had arrived from Seattle and were working with them. Crew spirit was up. They were going to town. Japan couldn't stand much of this. The war would be over.

Like Tokyo, Berlin was crumbling and burning, beneath 1,000-plane raids of Fortresses and Liberators. Its defending air force was gone. Eisenhower's forces, after von Rundstedt's army was broken at the critical Battle of the Bulge, had been moving faster and faster. The Russians were closing in from the east.

Germany surrendered, what was left of it, May 7, 1945. "Where there is no vision, the people perish."

On the other side of the globe, LeMay's fire raids were methodically blanking out the Japanese war economy. Rosy O'Donnell led a second raid on smoking Tokyo, the biggest, this time at medium altitude. It was awesome, terrible. Through the brilliance of the searchlights, the black bursts of flak and the night fighters flashing by, the incendiary bombs were falling from 303 planes. Bright flashes of flame and billowing smoke, rising shafts of heat that shot some of the planes hundreds of feet in the air, then dropped them back down. A piece of sheet metal roofing came up and struck one of them at 16,000 feet. The plane flew on with the piece lodged in its wing.

O'Donnell circled off to the side to watch. Tokyo was a seething cauldron, aflame from 3,000 tons of napalm and oil incendiary bombs. The fire covered eighteen square miles of city. It seemed like a nightmare. A few militaristic aggressors had started the thing, and this was the retribution on Japanese millions. The terrible boomerang of war.

The campaign went on into summer. Yokohama, Kawasaki, sixty-seven other target cities. What was there left of Japan to wipe out? One or two targets. Hiroshima.

The mysterious party of Colonel Paul Tibbets that had been poking about the B-29 *Enola Gay* down on Tinian, took off at 0245 August 6, winged across the 1,600 miles of water, over the still city of Hiroshima, and at 0915 dropped a bomb. A crew put on green goggles, watched with suspense for fifty seconds as the bomb dropped toward the center of a sprawling city. The single, multi-sunpower flash, the weirdly glowing ball of fire, the shock, and then the mighty ascending column of smoke, mushrooming up and up to 50,000 feet.

America and all the world gasped at a power too revolutionary, a destruction too shocking to contemplate.

President Truman had asked Japan to accept the Potsdam surrender terms. Still defiant in defeat, the Japanese military government said the terms were unacceptable.

Then Nagasaki. A second atomized city and 35,000 more people dead after Hiroshima's 75,000. Japan surrendered.

After seven unnatural years, the world awoke to peace, glorious peace, and speedily began wondering what best to do with it. Peace offered opportunity to pursue new enterprise and, ironically, it presented Boeing Airplane Company with a new struggle for survival.

BOOK FOUR

THE REALIZATION

The war had done more than test the products of men's vision. It had shown, brashly and shockingly, that vision was something deeper than mere planning and scheming. Progress was built on rock more solid than the schemes of men.

The progress in airplane design that followed the war seemed a clue to how progress comes about. They had thought the airplane was highly developed before the war. But in the years of peace that followed, it leaped forward like a skyrocket released to the heights. Why was this? You had to look closely at some of the developments to see. They had their roots while the war was still being fought. . . .

1. *The Sweptback Wing*

Sometimes it came gradually, sometimes as a sudden flash of light, but to men of vision there was always the moment when there came a realization of a need which existed but hadn't been recognized, and then a realization of the possibility of meeting that need. In the final months of World War II and in the months that followed, there were new needs everywhere: in business, a new economy to be built, new peacetime competition and opportunity; in science, the need for new discovery. The war had exploited old stores of scientific knowledge that needed now to be enlarged.

Sometimes the realization came painfully hard, upsetting the course of personal affairs and suddenly setting it against the tide. It was so with Bill Allen, the lawyer, being asked again to take the presidency of Boeing Airplane Company. By spring of 1945 the committee had concluded Allen was their choice, but he still couldn't see it.

Bill Allen was a widower, with his two daughters now ten and five years old. "Heaven knows I have little enough time for them now," he thought. "They need the time I give them and more too." If he were to step into this job, his time wouldn't be his own.

There was no great salary incentive. His earnings in the law practice were already about equal to the president's salary. There were troubles ahead for the company. Postwar readjustment and no doubt financial problems. He'd be stepping right into the middle of them. He was happy in what he was doing now. All his training had been in the legal profession and by now he felt a certain mastery of it. The Boeing presidency, on the other hand . . . "I just don't have the qualifications for it," he told a family friend and neighbor, Mary Ellen Agen, someone he felt he could talk to.

"But Bill, if they've decided you're the one for the job, who are you to say no?" Mrs. Agen had known Allen a long time. She had a son and daughter of her own by a former marriage and had a sympathetic view of his problem of heading a family alone. But she also knew his talents, greatest of which was a deeply conscientious sincerity about anything he went into. This very quality accounted for his reluctance, she thought.

Allen persisted. "Can you picture me down there behind that big desk?"

"Why, yes. I can picture that easily."

"But Jim Prince says I'm cantankerous."

"You are, sometimes," she said.

Allen threw back his head for a good laugh. "Well, if you think I'm cantankerous enough . . ."

It was on March 22, 1945, when the war in Europe was obviously drawing to a close, that Dietrich Schmitz of the board of directors asked Allen to lunch, and pressed him for an answer. Allen sparred for time. *If they've decided you're the one for the job, who are you to say no?* It would be a radical readjustment for him, yet it *was* a challenge.

"My convictions are unchanged," he told Schmitz finally. "I don't feel that I'm qualified for the job. From the personal angle there's every reason to remain where I am. However, the problem has to be solved. If the committee members all think this is the best practical solution, if the board is really in favor of it, and if Mickelwait and Perkins can get out of the service so I'll be in a position to leave the law firm, then I'll accept."

That night Allen made a long list of things he'd have to do if the job were given him:

Must keep temper—always—never get mad.

Be considerate of my associates' views.

Don't talk too much—let others talk.

Don't be afraid to admit that you don't know.

Don't get immersed in detail—concentrate on the big objectives.

Make contacts with other people in industry—and keep them.

Try to improve feeling around Seattle toward the company.

Make a sincere effort to understand labor's viewpoint.

Be definite; don't vacillate.

Act—get things done—move forward.

Develop a postwar future for Boeing.

Try hard, but don't let obstacles get you down. Take things in stride.

Above all else be human—keep your sense of humor—learn to relax.

Be just, straightforward; invite criticism and learn to take it.

Be confident. Having once made the move, make the most of it. Bring to task great enthusiasm, unlimited energy.

Make Boeing even greater than it is....

It was late at night. The girls were in their rooms asleep. Bill Allen turned out the light and settled to the cool pillowcase. What was ahead?

Some of the things ahead were hardly visible in the spring of '45. Wellwood Beall and a delegation of engineers were on their way to Dayton. Bob Jewett, quiet, thoughtful head of the preliminary design unit, and Dr. Cecil Stedman, a former professor of electrical engineering whom Ed Wells had put to work on automatic-pilot and flight-test instrument development, were in the group. Beall had been talking with them about the possibilities of guided missiles. There had been recurring flurries of scientific interest in this subject all through the war. Then, when the Germans began launching their V-1 buzz bombs in mid-1944, and later the V-2 rockets, Hap Arnold set up a crash program for 1,000 jet-propelled bombs a month, similar to the V-1s, to be built by the Northrop Company. Wright Field laboratories got busy on other ideas.

"Jet power isn't fast enough for a missile," said one colonel.

"It should be rocket. But a rocket is no good unless you can steer it. I have a scheme that will permit you to do it." He unrolled a sketch. "You have a big rotor wheel in the missile to stabilize it. A big gyroscope. When you want to turn you change the axis of the gyro."

"How do you do that?" Bob Jewett asked.

"By brute force. You have motors in there to hoist it around."

Jewett, skeptical, referred him to Cec Stedman and Stedman asked his assistant George Stoner to study the thing and give the Colonel a report. Stoner waded in deep, then came out with a mathematical conclusion. "If you're going to control it with a gyro, you first have to know all the forces acting on it in flight. If you can find that out, then you have the very information that will permit you to design supersonic control surfaces, or maybe moveable wings, and you no longer need the gyro." Stedman and Stoner took the report back to the Colonel. Someone at the field suggested they ought to talk to Dr. Earl Tuve at Johns Hopkins University, who was doing some work for the Navy on the subject. They found Dr. Tuve enthusiastic.

"You have the right approach," he said. "It's the conclusion I've reached. If we can develop supersonic controls we can make the missile ride a radar beam to its target. It could be a tremendously effective defense weapon. But a rocket takes a lot of fuel for a short range. You need some kind of an air-burning engine."

"Do you have something in mind?" Stedman asked.

The Professor pulled out some old literature giving computations on a theoretical machine called an athodyd. As far back as 1900 scholars had computed that a fast burning fuel-air mixture in a perfectly shaped tube would propel itself without any other mechanical means if you got it going fast enough. One of the engineers at Boeing, Dan Hage, had been doing some work on this kind of a power plant, called ramjet. "It's ready-made for the job," said Dr. Tuve. "When it's traveling at the speed of sound and beyond, it will ram the air in so fast that you won't need a turbine-wheel compressor. In theory, that is. All we need to know now is: (1) Can supersonic controls be made to work? (2) Can a ramjet be made to work?" The Professor wished them well.

Flying to Dayton there was a chance to review some of these things. They seemed nebulous but Wellwood Beall had developed a staunch faith in the Boeing team of engineers. To get out the B-29 and other projects, the company had had to assemble a greater variety of engineering talents than were used by any other kind of manufacturer, he believed. That gave the 2,700-man engineering department a well-rounded perspective. They had built up all types of laboratories: acoustical, electrical, hydraulic, electronic, chemical, mechanical, metallurgical, radio, structural test, aerodynamic, and some others. Now Stedman was developing a new group of scientists in the physical research unit.

"Do you think you fellows could design a successful guidance system for missiles?" Beall asked Stedman.

"That's what we're here for."

Beall turned to Bob Jewett. "Is this out of our field?"

"It'll help us learn more about the aerodynamics of airplanes. Fast."

Beall was shouldering the management concern over postwar products. He felt the business should be diversified. An offensive missile would be in the same field with the bomber, but a defensive missile—that would be at the very opposite pole. "We have the strategic bomber. Why don't we build a defense against it?" he asked. "We know more about strategic bombing than any other company. We ought to be able to build a defense against it." Some day a defense against bombers, he thought, might be the country's greatest need. In Dayton, he went to see General Frank Carroll, head of the experimental engineering section. "We're interested in getting into the missile business," Beall said. "What programs do you have?"

"How would you like to take on a long-range missile-bomb?" the General asked. He had been actively pursuing this subject.

"No. No. We want to develop something that will shoot down the bomber. Ground-to-air."

The General wasn't sure yet whether this would come within their jurisdiction or under the Ordnance Department of the Army. But the Air Force wanted to get into the field, he said. It would have to be an aircraft, with aerodynamic qualities, not just an improved form of anti-aircraft.

"That's what we propose," said Beall. "A pilotless aircraft. Ground-to-air pilotless aircraft."

"Make me a written proposal for a study project on it, and we'll see," said General Carroll.

While Dick Gelzenlichter, in charge of the business office at Seattle, was hurriedly working up cost figures on a proposal for a ground-to-air pilotless aircraft study contract, in April 1945, Ed Wells had his mind full of the continuing Air Force concern over superior speed and altitude. Only jet bombers could have speed enough to offer any protection when jet fighters became prevalent. In the jet era, speed would be everything.

He thought about the new jet bomber they were designing. It had been started back in September 1943, two years after Hap Arnold obtained drawings of one of Frank Whittle's jet engines from England and asked General Electric to make a copy of it. By 1943 the Air Force had tried it out in an experimental Bell pursuit and then ordered production of a Lockheed fighter powered with it. No one thought it had range enough for a heavy, or even a medium bomber, because the jet engine consumed so much fuel, but Don Putt of the bombardment branch asked in September 1943 if Boeing would be interested in getting into the jet field with a reconnaissance plane that might later be converted into a bomber. Beall said they would and arranged for Wells to go to Muroc Dry Lake, California, where the Bell fighter was being tested.

The sight at Muroc surprised Wells. He'd never seen a plane fly without a propeller before, and the speed was a revelation. He hadn't realized jet development was this far along. He assigned Dan Hage to undertake a full jet-power study. He asked Preliminary Design to turn out a quick plan of the reconnaissance plane, attaching a two-jet nacelle under each wing of a slenderized B-29. To learn more, Hage proposed building a small jet. His proposal was accepted. A gas-turbine version of the jet engine, turning a drive shaft, might make a saleable postwar product as well as a research tool.

Engineer Byron Galt was picked as project engineer for the jet airplane study. Ben Cohn and Harlow Longfelder worked on the aerodynamics. In January 1944, Wells took the preliminary design to Dayton and then to Washington, but it didn't arouse much interest. General Echols said that the Air Force was now interested in a medium bomber powered with either jet or a hypothetical turbine-propeller engine—a jet-type engine with a turbine added to turn the prop. "But don't let it interfere with the B-29," he said.

The wing of the new design was pared down 40 per cent to gain better performance. This meant high wing loading but it cut down drag enough to send the speed, with jet power, above four hundred miles. The speed of the air across parts of the wing surface would be getting right up into the mysteries of compressibility, approaching Mach Number One, Professor Ernest Mach's equivalent of the speed of sound, where drag would go up and stability and control would encounter unknown dangers. The jet was strictly a paper prospect, with much to be learned before it could be made an airplane.

Ed Wells and Bob Jewett took design data on both jet and turboprop versions to Wright Field and on to Washington in March. There was a big meeting. The military seemed more interested in the jet than in the turbine propeller. But military requirements for a jet bomber hadn't yet been drawn up. Tentatively, they envisioned at least 2,000 miles range, 8,000-pound bomb load, 35,000 feet altitude—a successor to the B-17. Cruising speed should be at least four hundred miles per hour.

"Would you take speed as a substitute for guns?" Wells asked.

"Maybe so," said Oliver Echols. "If it's fast enough you might get by with just a stinger turret in the tail, and flak protection under the engines."

In the engineering meetings that followed in Seattle, it became more and more evident that the success of the jet bomber would depend on one thing: speed. George Schairer and his aerodynamicists had been giving it study. The whole principle was different. With jet power, you were putting all your fuel energy into pushing a jet stream out the back. The nearer you could get your airplane to the speed of that jet coming out the back, the more efficient your engine. "If you go only four hundred miles an hour," said Schairer, "you're just pushing air and burning up your fuel. You won't get any range."

But the compressibility problem was in the way of higher speeds. "We'll just have to beat it out in the wind tunnel," Schairer concluded. "We're lucky we have a tunnel that will handle transonic speeds." He ordered construction of seventeen different high-speed airfoil models, thin wing sections of various shapes.

The development cost was getting heavy, but Claire Egtvedt okayed it. "We've got to keep moving ahead," he said. The testing went slowly. The Air Force, conscious of the country's late start on jet planes, began pressing Boeing and other manufacturers for proposals on rapid construction of some experimental planes.

"Let's not promise an airplane till we learn how to make a successful one," said Wells. The wind-tunnel tests that showed most promise were of a long, narrow wing, straight and tapered like the B-29, only razor-thin. But much of the speed advantage of the slim wing was cancelled by the drag of the big double-jet nacelles on the wings. A new design put all the engines in the body. That increased the speed, but now they were really up against troubles with compressibility burble—now better known as high Mach Number effects, because they occurred in the neighborhood of Mach Number One, the speed of sound. They tried experiments with full-span flaps as a remedy, but these weren't too successful.

It all looked too uncertain to propose an experimental plane. The effort went on. Finally, in December 1944, they proposed to Wright Field that the project be divided into two phases, allowing a year for Phase One to prove the practicability and safety of the design, then move to Phase Two, the construction of three experimental planes. The Air Force contracted for Phase One but it didn't like the slow schedule.

Should they have gone ahead with something more conventional, not tried to go after fantastic speed? Just hang jet engines on a plane like the B-29? That wouldn't be honesty of purpose, Ed Wells felt, after they had concluded that a jet airplane should be designed to take full advantage of jet power. You had to throw away the past and start anew. That was why it was taking so much time. Was that wrong?

Ed knew the answer. The extra time they were taking was forcing its own answer. The Air Force had gone ahead on contracts with North American, Consolidated and Martin for medium jet bombers. Now Boeing was behind in the race and it would *have* to come up with something better. Wells was away on his trip to the Marianas when Wright Field proposed they give up the medium jet bomber development and concentrate on a longer range bomber with turbine propellers, "turboprops." Beall made a plea to General Carroll. "We want to develop an advanced jet," he said. "No sense in our duplicating the jets you've ordered from other companies, but we're the only manufacturer with its own wind tunnel. We're capable of running high Mach Number wind-tunnel studies. We should do the longer job of research on an advanced design. This will take some time. We're groping in the dark. Transonic flight is the great unknown."

Carroll was impressed with the argument. It was decided, April 1945, that Boeing should continue the medium-bomber study under the Phase One contract and also begin the long-range turboprop heavy-bomber study. The medium-bomber project was given the name XB-47.

Aerodynamics Chief George Schairer was at the Pentagon preparing to go on a special mission into Germany. He was serving as a member of the Scientific Advisory Board of the Army Air Force, headed by Dr. Theodore von Karman of Cal Tech.

It was the noon hour. Schairer was walking with the Chinese professor, Dr. H. S. Tsien, another member of the Advisory Board, down one of the mazelike corridors toward a lunchroom.

"What do you think about Bob Jones' theories down at NACA on high-speed wings?" Dr. Tsien asked Schairer.

"What does he say? Haven't talked to Bob lately."

"He thinks that if you make a narrow wing and set it at an angle to the body, it will have entirely different characteristics in the vicinity of the speed of sound than the ordinary straight wing."

Schairer was interested. "Has he run tests on this?"

"It's mostly a theoretical conclusion. There's a lot of debate going on about it down there. He's starting some experiments. He thinks he can prove it."

On the flight to Paris, Schairer sat alongside Tsien to continue the discussion. Was Jones' theory right or wasn't it? They both got out slide rules and pads of chart paper, and began figuring. There were some fundamental calculations they could apply. The increased effective chord of the wing if it were swept back at an angle. The changed angle of the air striking the wing and flowing back over it. It would be more like a sideslip than straight flight. What would this mean? They had always taken it for granted that the wing had to go straight out. Had they been going along like sheep, without examining all the possibilities?

Schairer and Tsien pored over their figures. There wasn't much conversation. Mostly thought. There was time for thought here. Into night, miles of black water going by beneath. Other lights were out, just the tiny shaft from two reading lights over the two engineers. Open minds in an open sky, tuning in to the laws of mathematics and flight. By morning, Schairer was in firm possession of a new viewpoint. "This certainly looks interesting," he said. "Seems to make a big difference in the drag." It looked like a way to get the speed up so they could really use the power of the jet engine. Too good to be true? Was there a catch?

"I can see no reason it shouldn't work," said Schairer. "Can you find any?"

"No, I can't," said Dr. Tsien.

What was good was what was true.

The morning Germany surrendered to General Eisenhower at the schoolhouse in Rheims, the von Karman scientific party arrived at Reichsmarshal Goering's Aeronautical Research Institute at Brunswick. Colonel Don Putt had arrived ahead of them and had taken command of the German research center. U. S. military guards were outside. Putt had arranged to have the offices and files unlocked. Schairer was with Dr. Hugh Dryden of the NACA the first evening when they started their search. They went into several rooms, trying to get the lay of the place. "These look like the wind-tunnel files," said Hugh Dryden. "Do you read German?"

"No," said Schairer. "But numbers are pretty much the same in any language."

Peering into the scientific mind of the enemy, left here on paper, seemed a strange business. Dryden was over in one corner of the room, reading at a table. Schairer went through some file drawers. He spotted the names of some of the men he knew who had once studied under von Karman. He came to some drawings. "Hey . . ." There was a drawing of a model with sweptback wings. Some charts. Columns of figures. Yes, wind-tunnel results. Schairer scanned them. "Well, I'll be darned." Fragments of the same formulas he was working with on the plane with Tsien. How did they come out? More papers, going down the same track. A solid track. Solid figures.

Next day von Karman was excited about this and other finds. They called Dr. Adolf Busemann, one of the Institute's top theoretical aerodynamicists. "What about this?" Dr. von Karman asked him. "Where did all this sweepback business come from?"

"Don't you remember? Rome? Volta Scientific Conference in 1935?" Von Karman tried to recall. "You remember my paper on supersonic aerodynamics? It told how sweepback would reduce the drag at supersonic speeds."

Von Karman sat up. "Of course I remember. When did you find out it would work?"

Dr. Busemann shrugged. "No one paid any attention. Finally Messerschmitt ran some tests and everybody got excited. The Me-262 is under construction now with forty-five degrees of sweepback."

Next day Schairer encountered Boeing engineer George Martin, who was in Germany with another Air Force group, and told him the story. Martin listened intently. "You mean this idea's been lying around for ten years?"

"You know, I was familiar with Busemann's paper myself," Schairer admitted. "You just don't see a thing until you want to see it. Then you find the answer you need has been there all the time." Schairer tried to arrange with the military and then with the State Department to dispatch a letter to the plant as classified military information. "I've got to get it there quick," he said, but there were no channels. He wrote a personal letter to Ben Cohn, who was taking his place as chief of aerodynamics, and simply dropped it into the mail. He asked Cohn to pass the information along to the other companies in the industry as soon as he received it.

When Ben Cohn picked the two pages of George Schairer's handwriting out of the mail and looked at the pencil sketch of sweptback wings, he blinked. He followed instructions about informing the industry and showed the letter enthusiastically to the aerodynamics staff. "Looks like here's our answer on the jet bomber," he said. "See if you can check it out."

They brought it back. "This is all wrong. It just isn't so," and they spelled out the reasons. Cohn defended his boss, but couldn't prove it with figures. Then, one morning when he was shaving, the answer came through. They'd all forgotten to take into consideration the changed direction of the air flow over the sweptback wing. "Simple."

Cohn went to Ed Wells, "I'm satisfied these conclusions are correct."

"Go ahead and build a wind-tunnel model," Wells told him. "Let's give it a good test."

The things that started coming out of the wind tunnel, out of Preliminary Design and the Aerodynamics units from that date, were a revolution and a revelation.

2. *Bet on the Stratocruiser*

Seven men sat at the long board room table September 5, 1945, in the first board meeting since the surrender of Jap n. As planned, the production of B-29s at Wichita would be terminated. The Air Force was pursuing a steady reduction in the schedules at Seattle-Renton from 155 planes in August to 122 in September, whereupon production would level off at twenty per month. When these ran out, they would be into the sixty advanced-model B-29Ds, or B-50s as they were going to be called, and the ten C-97 military transports that were on order. Meanwhile negotiations were under way with the airlines for the sale of the Model 377 Stratocruiser, the proposed commercial version of the C-97.

Reduction in personnel was going along in orderly fashion. They were down from the wartime peak of 45,000 in Seattle to 30,000 and the figure would come down to 15,000 after November. Much of the reduction was voluntary. Housewives and others who had come to work just for the duration of the war, were leaving now.

"As you all know," said Egtvedt, "the most important item on our agenda is the election of a president." He explained that arrangements had finally been completed to permit Bill Allen, whose choice the board had previously agreed upon, to resign from his law firm. A unanimous ballot elected Allen.

Miss Lind, Egtvedt's secretary, appeared at the door with a message. Egtvedt read the note. "We have word from the Air Force that the B-29 schedule is cut to fifty for this month and then ten a month until February. Bob Neale says we have most of these completed already. He recommends we close the plant, with a PA system announcement before the four o'clock shift change." Egtvedt looked at his watch. It was three-thirty. The payroll was running a half-million dollars per day. He thought of the remark "Dutch" Kindeberger, president of North American, had made when war work was at a peak: "If I ever get a cancellation, I've got to run right out with the layoff notice. If I stub my toe we're liable to lose our shirts."

Egtvedt glanced at Allen, shook his head and turned to his secretary: "Tell Bob that's okay."

The Bill Allen who inherited the Boeing Company's problems in September 1945 was thin, balding. There was a downturn to the corners of his mouth in a "let's face the facts" manner, but his brown eyes kindled with sincerity and his whole face lay ready to radiate his love of good humor. To news reporters that evening, he said, "I haven't figured out yet whether my election caused the contract reduction or they gave me the job because they knew it was coming."

When Allen came in next morning, the big corner office looked as empty as he knew the company's plants were at that moment. The forty-foot expanse of windows suggested the whole world was looking in: the city of Seattle, the company's employees and their families who constituted one-sixth of the city's population, the U. S. government, the airlines; but he knew instead that the windows were for him to look out of, to see again the bustle of activity across the broad concrete apron to the south, to see the three-hundred-foot canopy doors yawn open for proud mechanics to trundle out new Boeing airplanes, to see the planes of America's future sweep down the long runway and out into the sky. Here he was. Where was the starter?

He asked Egtvedt and Wells and Oliver West to come in. West said they could start recalling some employees in a week, more in three to four weeks, to work on uncompleted B-29s. But the whole work force would have to be reorganized. Each laid-off employee had a right to exercise his seniority on any job the senior employee thought he could perform. He could "bump" another employee out of the job long enough to try out on it. Then another more senior employee could come along and "bump" him. Bill Allen frowned. "Is that the way we have to run the plant?"

The B-50s and C-97s on order wouldn't keep operations going long after the B-29s were out. Fabrication shops would be shut down by next summer and subassembly shops by the end of next year, West said. They needed some new business, quick. Was there any prospect of getting into non-aircraft products? Automobiles? The bedroom and bathroom sets designed in the research "cave" during the war?

"I just can't see us entering those fields," Egtvedt said. "The established manufacturers have the distribution channels and the facilities."

"I think we'd better put our energies in the field we know," said Allen.

New military orders? Egtvedt had just testified before the Mead Committee of Congress on how imperative it was to keep up enough aircraft development and production to retain skills and facilities. It took big orders to maintain a plant like this, and it took a big plant to build a military bomber.

"What are the chances for more B-50s?" Allen asked.

"The 50's a better airplane than anybody realizes," said Ed Wells. "We have a wing now that's 650 pounds lighter, but 16 per cent stronger than the B-29 wing. Almost everything is redesigned. But the trouble is, it still looks like a B-29." The Air

Force had bought 3,898 B-29s: 1,644 of them built at Wichita, 1,050 at Seattle-Renton, 668 by Bell in Marietta and 536 by Martin at Omaha.

The XB-47 jet bomber study was coming along, Wells pointed out. "I'd like to talk with you about it as soon as there's time."

"Let's take first things first," said Allen. "We need something we can build now." Tomorrow there'd be 29,000 employees back to get their paychecks, lined up in the cafeteria yard. The company would pay out $3 million to them. Would they be back again? How many of them? They were the Boeing team, the people who knew how to build Boeing airplanes.

Commercial transports? The Stratocruiser? Fred Collins and attorney Lowell Mickelwait were east with Beall negotiating with Pan American, TWA and American. Egtvedt had told them to stay right there till they got something. Collins had turned in a list of possible sales totaling sixty-seven airplanes, but not one of the planes had been sold. "We've got to get the price down to $1,250,000, or better $1,100,000, if we're going to compete with the DC-6 and the Constellation," Collins was insisting. "No one will pay what we're asking." Beall was having difficulty, too, getting CAA requirements changed to allow for the higher landing speed of the faster airplane.

Engineering was working on two smaller transport designs, twin-engined planes. One of them was a feeder-line design that had been developed in Wichita. But the Stratocruiser looked the best bet. It was what the airlines needed: 340 miles an hour, 3,500-mile range, big enough for long-range travel comfort, pressurized cabin, room to move around and relax, two decks, lounge and snack bar below, circular staircase, big dressing rooms; and it could be put in production right along with the ten Air Force C-97s. But if they didn't get orders soon they'd be too far behind to quote decent delivery dates. Douglas and Lockheed were already in production. The airlines hadn't been able to buy equipment during the war and there was a mad competition for first deliveries.

"Do you think we should go ahead and put it in production?"

Allen asked. "Then we'd *have* to sell it." That question wasn't easy to answer. They'd have to produce at least fifty to get the price down to a million and a quarter. That would be a $60 million program. The money would begin going out fast when you started a force of men working on the project. Could they price the plane as low as Collins asked? You could go out of business operating at a loss just as much as you could if you didn't have orders.

When the discussions were over, Allen sat long looking out of his new view windows. One man walked across the huge apron. A maintenance man. He thought again of the people who were Boeing. Could he take the risk of starting the Stratocruiser without orders? Which was the greater risk, do something or do nothing? He got Beall on the phone in New York, talked to Bowman, the treasurer; to the other members of the board. It was time for the weekly staff meeting. Everyone looked to him.

"We're going to start fifty Stratocruisers," he announced. "The Number One project of everyone here is to see that we sell them."

Stratocruiser

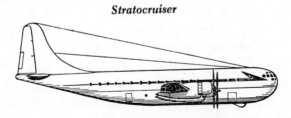

Next week, there were lines at the state unemployment compensation windows. Money wasn't coming into the stores. An alarmed community had called a mass meeting at the Chamber of Commerce. Bill Allen addressed the meeting. "I can assure you that Boeing management will use diligent and aggressive effort to put our plants to use on a full-time basis," he said. Others spoke. The state manpower director said the real shock hadn't been felt yet. People started having their say from the floor.

"I tell you folks, the best thing you can do is go back to Iowa," said one man. He turned and shook his finger at Allen, seated on the stage. "I know these people aren't going back to work at Boeing, and you know it." Another man jumped to his feet with a resolution that the government be asked to take over the plant. Somebody seconded it. Allen caught himself. *Never get mad.* Someone else got up and said, "That's a silly idea. It's the government cancelling the orders that's caused all the trouble in the first place." The crowd laughed.

Bill Allen went east on September 19 to meet with the Air Force and to join Beall in negotiations with Pan American Airways. There was fanfare at the Washington airport the evening they arrived. A flight was due from Japan. Allen and Beall watched with the crowd.

Out of the night three Superforts lowered onto the floodlighted, crowded field. Lieutenant General Barney Giles emerged from one, Major General Curtis LeMay from the second and Brigadier General Rosy O'Donnell from the third. They had flown the 6,000 miles from Japan to Chicago in one jump, then refueled to come on in. Allen was humbled. These were the men and the Boeing planes that had fought the war, finished it without the need for invasion, and now hopped back over the world's biggest ocean as though it were a pond. The impact of the long flight was still with him when he had lunch next day with LeMay and O'Donnell. "Certainly gives you a shocking realization of the possibilities," he said.

"If we can do it, another country can do it," said LeMay. Three B-29s had made forced landings in Russia. One of them was the *General Arnold Special.* The planes had been intact. Now the Russians could build more like them.

In Wichita, with the government-owned Plant Two closed, the remnant of the company withdrew to the original Plant One. Lowell Divinia, Earl Schaefer's assistant, shook his head. "Earl, I'm glad to have had the experience, but I hope our country will never, never get in a position where we have to go through this again. We've got to quit wars. For good."

"We better not let our guard down then," said Schaefer. The cut-off point in their production was entirely too sharp for Schaefer. An order had come through instructing them to complete deliveries of all the B-29s outside the plant but dispose of those under construction inside. "Let's go over and take a look," he said.

Fletcher Brown and Clif Barron, Wichita treasurer, went with them. There were long rows of B-29s on the warm-up ramp along the edge of the field. A few mechanics were bent over the nacelles of planes on the plant apron, putting the finishing pat on the integrated work of some thousands of men and women. The sounds coming from the main plant were strange ones, not the businesslike chatter of rivet guns and the clang of operations, but crunching noises, crashes. There was a blue haze hanging in the cavernous structure and a stench of burning rubber, melting metal and exhaust fumes. The scene on the main assembly floor was calamitous. The long straight lines of airplanes and sub-assemblies were broken, with parts strewn around. Men were working over the bigger pieces with cutting torches. In the center of the plant was a huge pile of broken-up airplanes. Bulldozers were nosing loose pieces into the pile. With a ripping sound, one nearly-finished B-29 cracked down the middle where it had been burned through, spilling out the frayed ends of the thousand carefully labeled and color-coded wires and hydraulic lines. Schaefer and his aides watched, throats tight.

A bulldozer attacked the freshly broken Superfort and pushed it, full power, against the pile. Then the "Cat" crawled up over and came down weightily on the silver wing. It didn't give. The operator backed off and jammed at it again. Still didn't give. Light metal versus weight and might. But it was engineered light metal. Finally, grinding over it and twisting, the driver buckled it flat into the heap.

"Let's get out of here," said Divinia. "I can't stand it."

3. *The B-47 Jells*

If some were concerned about the hazards of stopping short the war-production program, they were in the minority. The world was at peace. The bustle of business as usual was the country's preoccupation. Quicker the better. But the Air Force mission remained. With the war's technical advances, this had suddenly become an infinitely more difficult mission. Everything now flying would have to be improved upon, promptly. The Boeing Company's business, too, depended on this.

There had been a zealous effort to prove that the principle of sweptback wings could be successfully applied to the XB-47 jet bomber. The idea was revolutionary. Wright Field reaction ranged from fascinated interest to practical doubt. Sweeping back the wings would decrease the wing span, and the range of an airplane was roughly in proportion to its span. The plane would gain speed only at a sacrifice of range. The sweptback wing would have poor stalling qualities at low speed, it was felt. And practically no one at the field liked putting the jet engines in the body, which the Boeing aerodynamicists argued was now more necessary than ever in order to have a clean, high-speed wing.

But in Seattle the new idea had taken deep root. It offered too sensational an advance in performance to be passed up, Ed Wells thought. Bill Allen gave him the green light. "If that's what you're for, let's go after it," he said.

Wells named a whole new project group, headed by George Martin. George Schairer asked Ben Cohn and Bill Cook to direct a new comprehensive wind-tunnel program. On September 13, 1945, a formal proposal went to Wright Field to change the development contract from a straight-wing design to a sweptback airplane, with four jets blasting back over the top of the body and two more from the tail. Improved fire walls were incorporated to offset the objection to engines in the body. When this was followed by a proposal for construction of experimental models, the issue was squarely before Wright Field.

Colonel Pete Warden, a serious-minded young engineer who was now the bombardment project officer, took the proposal to a staff meeting.

"Why should the Air Force finance some wild idea George Schairer has?" asked one colonel. "Let's cut out this foolishness and cancel the B-47." The armament laboratory brought in results of some gunfire tests made in a twenty-foot wind tunnel. Fifty-caliber bullets had been fired into the burner section of a roaring F-80 jet engine. The result was an uncontrollable blowtorch out the side of the engine. "That cinches it. Put six of those engines in the body of a bomber? Nope."

"I don't think we should scuttle the project," said Colonel Warden. "There may be ways of working around these problems."

Ed Wells and preliminary design chief Bob Jewett arrived in Dayton to get the disconcerting news. It was hard to take. "This place is a gloom dispensary," said the pensive Bob Jewett. For two years he had been putting most of his effort on this project. So had a lot of other people. They'd thought they really had something. Now this.

Back at the hotel the two engineers kicked the problem around, tried to bring order out of confusion and frustration. What now? Go back to a conventional design? No, they had decided the thing to do was to build an airplane fast enough to take advantage of jet power. That was certainly right. They'd found they could get the speed up by using a thin wing. That was progress. Then they'd found they could get rid of much of the drag by sweeping it back. That was certainly progress.

Sure, it had raised problems to put the engines in the body, Wells admitted. He had never felt completely happy about that. But where else was there to put them? Out in thin air? Do away with engines? Wait.... Out away from the wing. Why not? Ed remembered some wind-tunnel data that George Schairer had brought from Germany, on experiments with engines hung out on struts. It hadn't looked very good. Still, it could be a way out.

"Might work," said Jewett. "If we could get them far enough away so they wouldn't disturb the airflow over the wing." Wells drew a sketch—things always seemed more plausible on paper— and sent it back to Seattle for consideration.

The aerodynamics staff took a dim view. "We have a clean wing. Let's not go back and muddy it all up again."

"Why not give it a try?" Schairer asked. A new series of tunnel tests was begun, the "broomstick tests." A model nacelle was stuck out on the end of a "broomstick" and tried out in every position they could think of: below and behind the wing, straight below the wing, above and behind, above and in front, below and in front. That last position was the best. It looked odd, but it seemed to work.

"Say, this isn't going to be so bad," said aerodynamicist Ben Cohn when the figures began to come in. The trick was to thrust the "pods" far enough forward so that the thick part of the nacelle would be well ahead of the thick part of the wing. Then the drag was no greater than when the engines were in the body. The body could be more slender. By putting four of the engines in twin pods slung under the wings and the other two out on the tips of the wings, the structural weight of the airplane could actually be decreased, because of better distribution of weight. That added to the range.

There was a surge of new enthusiasm, this time on a basis that Wright Field could share. Wind-tunnel tests were beginning to show, too, that the sweptwing could have good stalling characteristics. The top speed was going to be more than six hundred miles per hour and they still could control it at low speeds for landing. The Air Force approved the new changes and the development project went ahead, though still without airplane orders.

The months that followed were packed with other events. In November, Colonel Bill Irvine flew a B-29 nonstop from Guam to Washington, 8,198 miles, then set a new speed record from Los Angeles to New York in five hours, twenty-seven minutes, an hour faster than the P-51 fighter that had held the record. November 28, Pan American Airways signed for twenty Stratocruisers, at a million and a quarter dollars each. By January 1946, the GAPA—Ground-to-Air-Pilotless-Aircraft—study had gone so well that the Air Force put up money for a Phase Two program, including the building and testing of experimental models and the construction of a test ramjet engine. A market survey led to the conclusion that the Wichita-designed feeder liner could be a success, and a production program was launched.

In February, Swedish Airlines ordered four Stratocruisers. Then Northwest Airlines ordered ten, American Overseas Airlines, eight. Forty-two now sold. There was hope for more orders for the B-50 Superfortress, successor to the B-29. The Air Force was counting on these planes, along with the big Consolidated B-36s now coming through, until jet bombers could take their place. Bill Allen was pushing hard for the 50 because it would be bread and butter for the plant. The jets still seemed a long way off.

Curtis LeMay, now head of Research and Development in Washington, kept pointing out that none of the jet bombers under development had enough range to do a global bombing job. He was more interested in the heavy-bomber design competition—the longer-range turbine propeller airplane study that Boeing, along with other companies, had undertaken a year ago. This was coming even slower than the medium jet. No one had devised anything that would meet the range requirement.

The effort was tedious, reminiscent of the prewar years when the Flying Fortress was being pioneered. Now the payoff of that earlier effort was being tallied. Flying Fortresses had accounted for 46 per cent of the total bomb tonnage dropped in Europe, the figures showed, and had shot down two-thirds of all the enemy fighters destroyed by U. S. bombers. More enemy fighters had been destroyed by the Forts than by any fighter type airplane. B-29 Superfortresses had dropped 96 per cent of all of

the bombs dropped in Japan. In military airplanes, it was effectiveness that counted.

The jet XB-47 was in wooden mock-up form by April 1946.
An Air Force mock-up board headed by Colonel Ed Nabell and
Lieutenant Ken Holtby came out to go over it. Some things they
didn't like. One was the arrangement for retracting the landing
gear. The tricycle gear had been rigged to fold back into big
openings in the side of the body. "It's a Rube Goldberg affair,"
said Colonel Nabell. "Look at all that gimcrackery." There was
a brief and not too spirited defense from the Seattle group. Admittedly it didn't look so good.

"If this is the best we can get, maybe we'd better reconsider
whether we want the plane at all," said Nabell. It was decided to
try a bicycle gear, with wheels in tandem. Pete Warden had been
advocating that, but the problems loomed big. Then engineers
Bill Cook and Chuck Davies worked one out, adding a small outrigger wheel from the engine pods to keep the wing tips off the
ground. When they added up the estimated weight, it was 1,500
pounds less than before. A bonus that could go into more range.

Every mile of range they could gain was golden. At best it was
far short of what the Air Force wanted. They could increase it
somewhat and the altitude, too, by adding to the wing span, but
it was difficult to do this and still preserve the narrow, thin wing,
because there was an engine stuck out on each wing tip. But by
dropping the wing-tip engines down in pods like the others and
running the wings on out beyond them, they could do it. The
span was increased from one hundred to 116 feet.

That was the final touch. Now everybody liked the airplane.
It looked right. An artist's drawing of the finished design fairly
leaped off the paper with speed and slender symmetry. If the
picture could talk, it was saying, "That's it. That's the way I
wanted to be all the time."

When they looked back over the long series of drawings that
showed the metamorphosis of the design, they were struck that
each change made it look better. The progress might have stopped

on any one of them, but the picture was saying, "No, don't stop there. Keep going. Bend my wings back so I can go faster. Bend back the tail surfaces, too. Right. Too heavy in the middle, though. Get rid of those body engines. Weight out along the wings. That's better. I look better. Now a little more here. You're doing fine. Tuck in the landing gear. Good. That's a lot better. Now add onto the wing tips. Fine. Now let me see.... Wow! Is that me?"

Yet it wasn't the picture that did the talking, it was the numbers. They were the voice of the picture. The numbers that came out of the wind tunnel, out of the design calculations, out of what Wright Field wanted to do. Funny. Every time the numbers insisted on a change and someone made the change, the picture looked better. It was the visible sign that the invisible numbers were speaking true. Finally, the equation balanced. Balanced perfectly, and the picture said so.

Long, tapered body, trailing off into the parting flare of swept-back fin and stabilizers; wings that were slender as a fine steel blade, sweeping out and back and gently down, relaxed and poised for beauty of flight; jet engines leaping forward from those wings with open mouths. "Give us sky," those engines seemed to be saying, "we'll show you what we can do." With quiet joy, Ed Wells put the drawing down. "The design that's most right is also the most beautiful," he said.

It looked right and he felt right about it. That was the thing. The feeling was not in the picture but in the man. A chord of harmony struck home. A law of perfection nodded approval.

George Martin, the project engineer, put it another way. "Now it's jelled. You have to get all the ingredients just right. Then you know. Because it jells." Martin knew the B-47 had jelled. So did Ed Wells. Wright Field approved the purchase of two XB-47 experimental bombers. Fred Laudan, appointed vice president for experimental manufacturing, organized a crew to rush the ships out so they could compete with the North American, the Martin, the Consolidated jets.

Then in June 1946, word came that the company's long-range

bomber study had won the design competition in the heavy
bomber class. The design was for a 360,000 pound airplane, twice
the weight of the XB-47, powered by turbo-propeller engines.
The design didn't meet the range requirement but it came closest
of any of the competitive proposals. A contract was awarded for
further development work on it. With the XB-47 project well
launched, it meant an even greater job ahead. The big one would
be called the XB-52.

Boeing was jumping into the jet airplane business. The old
reciprocating engine with its myriad working parts was a marvel
of ingenuity, but compared to the jet it seemed the hard way to
do it. Why hadn't engineers been working on the simpler principle all along, perfecting it as they'd perfected the reciprocating
engine? The principle had been known for years, discussed in
technical publications, but it hadn't done any good until someone
came along with the vision to see how it met a present need. That
happened in several countries about the same time. When Frank
Whittle, inventor of the English jet engine, visited Seattle,
George Schairer asked him, "How did you come to invent the
jet? How much did you know about what was going on in
Germany, Italy, France, and this country?"

"I didn't know anything about what the rest were doing,"
said Whittle. "But I wasn't exactly the inventor. It was just time
for somebody to develop the jet engine and I was the guy who
did it."

"You're too modest," Schairer said. Then when he stopped to
consider Whittle's answer, "But I keep finding that the new idea
isn't new. It's just been lying around waiting for someone to see
it." Like the sweptback wing idea. They'd found it was ready to
meet the need, once they realized the need and started looking.

But the revolution in jet power was still tentative. Its application to fighter planes was taken for granted, but in the larger airplanes it would still have to prove its place. The jet engine's huge
appetite for fuel seemed a tremendous handicap. Would they
ever be able to apply it to a commercial transport airplane?

The question gave rise to a hope in every engineer. There wasn't one of them, deep down, who really liked to build machines of warfare. There was need for military airplanes, and the country's need came first. The military services were willing to pioneer, willing because they knew they had to. So things like this usually got started with military use. Could the results of this military progress be applied to the commercial field? That thought always popped into mind. The company was back in the transport business with the Stratocruiser project. Preliminary Design was beginning to think about the next transport. They always lost interest in a plane when it went into the shops. One of the engineers in the unit, Elliot Mock, had made a rough study of jet-transport possibility before the end of the war and it had looked interesting, even if far in the future.

Bob Jewett talked this over with Ed Wells. "We entered the war with one kind of power, the reciprocating engine," said Jewett, once a power-plant engineer. "We came out with four new kinds. How long before we start applying some of these to transports? Not rocket or ramjet, but jet or turboprop?" Wells agreed they should get someone started on a comparative study, to find out just how far in the future these things were.

Jewett had a new man in Preliminary Design, Bob Hage, a keen young engineer, brother of Dan Hage who was heading up the development of the gas turbine engine. Bob had worked in the aerodynamics unit for a time in 1940, then became the aerodynamics chief at Wright Field during the war. Jewett laid three possible assignments before him. The future transport study was one of them.

"You mean I have a choice?" asked Hage.

"I'd rather have you work on the thing you're most interested in."

Hage's face brightened. "This one." His finger went down on the jet transport study, for reasons that were deep rooted. In Bob Hage there was the engineer's love of order, the engineer's desire for perfection. When he had left M.I.T. with a master's degree, primed to work toward this end, he had stepped out, instead, into the grotesque disorder of war. He went to Wright Field to offer his services to help restore order. The war experience, if not satisfying, was stimulating.

In his job at Wright, Hage got first word of the development of jet engines and helped plan for their use. He also got a first look at the fiercely accelerating pace of development of weapons of destruction. Nights he would sit in his room and think, earnestly, about how the peace could be kept once it was won. What could he do that would help? He'd keep coming back to one thing. "People have to learn to know and understand each other better. Better transportation and communication are big needs." Now here he was, the problem and opportunity on his lap.

"Give it a good analytical study," said Jewett. "I'll get Dick Fitzsimmons to help you. Take all the time you need. Compare safety factors, comfort, Civil Aeronautics regulations, everything; costs especially. Everyone says a jet transport isn't economically feasible. Let's find out." Hage dug in with a vigor.

4. *Range Dilemma*

At a six-shack outpost called GAPA City, out on Utah's great salt flats a fifty-seven-mile jeep ride from Wendover, Utah, there was a stir of action and preparation. For a century nothing much had happened here—not since the ill-fated Donner party left its covered wagon tracks in these sands. Now the sagebrush was being trampled underfoot by a scientific expedition so modern that it might be mistaken for a pioneering beachhead on the moon. There were theodolite stations silhouetted on outlying knolls, ingenious devices that combined the crosshairs of a surveyor's transit with an automatic motion picture camera for tracking the "bird"; the all-seeing saucer of the radar searching the sky; the concrete-domed dugout, from which the crew could watch the steel launching tower jutting skyward from a weighty slab of concrete.

The "bird" named GAPA, ground-to-air pilotless aircraft, a pencil-slim sixteen-foot-long missile with needle nose and rocket cartridge body, was erected in the tower. It was a primitive model, with guidance equipment only partly developed and still awaiting development of a ramjet engine. No one could assure that it might not do a wing-ding and sizzle back down on the base whence it was launched.

Bob Jewett, Dick Nelson, GAPA engineering co-ordinator, and Keith McDaniel, field test engineer, were on hand for the missiles test. A mahogany-backed engineer, stripped to the waist, came up and said the "bird" was ready to be armed. McDaniel climbed up the tower and attached the remote-control fuses. The party took cover in the dugout for the launching, which would be at 2 P.M.

At 1:15, fantails of dust shot up from six directions as cars headed spokewise for their stations. All reported ready at 1:40: radar operators, theodolite crews, photographers. First warning siren sounded at 1:45. At 1:55, McDaniel started calling the cues in the dugout. "Minus five minutes . . . minus four minutes . . . minus three . . . two . . ." At 1:50:30 McDaniel began sounding off the five-second intervals. Pete Wendel at the fire-control panel threw over the ready switch. The air in the dugout was hot and close. Through an armored-glass window the engineers could see the "bird" resting on its haunches against the guide rails. The long legs of the tower, silhouetted against distant mountains, seemed to waver in the shimmering heat.

"Minus fifteen seconds . . . minus ten . . . five . . . four . . . three . . . two . . . one . . . FIRE." Wendel pushed the button. The tower flashed flame, roared thunder, and in a blast of smoke GAPA was away with a heart-piercing scream.

"Come on!" McDaniel burst out of the dugout, with Jewett and Nelson close after. They could see it burn its way up, incredibly high in the desert sky. Then the rocket trail frittered out, the missile arched, plummeted down, and ended a puff of dust in the sand. Dick Nelson turned to Jewett. "We're making tracks. By the end of the year we're going to have that bird going anywhere you say."

There were sixty more GAPA firings scheduled in 1946. The pilotless aircraft group was learning fast about supersonic flight. Jewett looked out at the hazy desert horizon and wondered what this would mean some day to fighters, bombers, passenger and cargo transports.

The missile work and the jet work were fascinating, but experimental projects didn't contribute much toward maintaining the plant. The B-50 Superforts were behind schedule. Couldn't get materials on time. The new, lighter aluminum used in them wasn't available in the quantity needed. There were no longer any priorities. You had to compete with peacetime industry, and it was gaining a husky appetite for all metals. At Wright Field, Colonel Horace Shepard, chief of the procurement division, tried to be helpful but when he complained of the shortages Washington only trimmed his budget requests.

The big overhead costs of running the plant went on just the same. There was lots of research expense. To learn the behavior of the jet bomber, with its new-style swept wings that would be capable of bending through an arc of twenty feet at their tips, a flexible model was being tested in the wind tunnel, opening a new field of study called "aeroelasticity." To pave the way for its high flight, test crews under N. D. Showalter were rounding out their fifth year of high-altitude research. Pilot Jim Frazer had totaled a record sixty hours pushing wings and propellers against the bodiless air of the world's most rugged frontier, and other pilots were close to that figure.

To develop the ramjet for GAPA, a supersonic air blast tunnel was being erected at Renton, using the entire output of a nearby steam electric plant, hurling its thunder out a huge exhaust pipe upturned to the sky like the trunk of a trumpeting elephant. There was enormous research on the Stratocruiser. A quarter million dollars had gone into seat design alone. In the mechanical equipment laboratories, contraptions were going up and down week after week to prove the durability of working parts such as landing gear retracting screws and the like. It all cost money.

Shop work on the Stratocruisers was slow. The quantities were small, with many variations for each of the six customers that had now placed orders totaling fifty-five of the airplanes— United Air Lines and British Overseas Airways Corporation the latest.

Altogether, the Boeing plant was operating at a loss, despite Bill Allen's constant admonition that there "had to be a drastic change of thinking" from the days of wartime big-quantity production.

It was welcome news when the Air Force decided in October to order seventy-three more B-50 Superfortresses, taking the number on order up to 133. That number was nothing like wartime quantities but it would make a good straight production job. Allen felt the Superfort still had a long life ahead. Bill Irvine had just put the crown on a series of B-29 records with a 9,500-mile nonstop flight over the top of the world from Hawaii to Cairo, Egypt, and the B-50 could outperform its wartime predecessor. There was a great question in the Air Force whether jet planes would ever take the place of these long-range ships.

The year 1946 finished with an operating loss of nearly $5 million, although $3⅓ million were to be recovered from wartime taxes under provisions of the law intended to ease the shock of reconversion. Other companies were having similar difficulties and air power advocates clamored for appointment of a government commission to study the whole problem. "Air power is peace power," they said, and the first essential was a sound aircraft industry. General George Kenney, trying to build up a postwar Strategic Air Command, protested bitterly the production slump.

"America must make up its mind right now whether it wants the best Air Force in the world or none at all," said Kenney.

"It's like in poker, the second-best hand wins you nothing and costs you dough."

When President Truman named Thomas Finletter chairman of an Air Policy Commission in July 1947, Bill Allen with other industry presidents tried to show the importance of continued progress in the air. A growing uneasiness over Russia gave force to the Finletter inquiry. It gave force also to the demand of Curtis LeMay and others that the country's new strategic bombers be ships with intercontinental range. The six-engined Consolidated B-36 was the nearest approach, but it was slow and there was concern over its vulnerability. The range of the XB-52, the proposed long-range turboprop bomber, was being stretched by every device to try to make it meet LeMay's objectives.

The pure-jet XB-47 would have spectacular speed but LeMay thought it woefully inadequate in range. To get the speed you lost out on range. That was the dilemma of jets. There was talk in the Air Force about switching to turboprop power for the medium as well as the proposed heavy bomber. Even the studies Bob Hage was making in Seattle on jet transports showed disappointing results for the pure jet as compared with the turboprop at ranges over 1,000 miles, though Hage brought in the surprising finding that a sweptwing jet transport could compete economically with either turboprop or regular piston power at 1,000 miles. The voice of his report was lost, however, in a chorus of acclaim for the luxurious, long-range Stratocruiser just coming out of the plant for test.

For a long-range bomber, the B-50 with its top speed of four hundred miles per hour, crowding the theoretical speed of proposed turboprop airplanes, seemed the bomber the Air Force would be using for some time. "If you want me to name names and talk facts," said Major General K. B. Wolfe, looking at the B-50 production lines at Plant Two, "here is our country's main air force, coming right through these doors."

Lieutenant General Nathan Twining, head of the Material Command, called the B-50 the Air Force's "standard long-range bomber." Tooey Spaatz, who had become chief of the Army Air

Force upon Hap Arnold's retirement, made a flight with Bill Allen in July in the first one out and afterward expressed the same view. "Jet-propelled bombers won't be the backbone of our Air Force for some time to come," he said. "They lack the range and load-carrying ability." In keeping with the tide of thought, design work was begun on an advanced version of the B-50 Superfort, to be called the B-54, with longer wings and body and more power.

But the XB-47, now named the Stratojet, was nearing completion, a spreading, gleaming piece of metal artistry. Experimental manager Al Jacobson and experimental shops superintendent Bud Hurst wouldn't let a workman on it except in stocking feet. So slick were its surfaces that a shoe scuff would cut down its top speed several miles an hour. Bob Robbins, the pilot who had been selected to test-fly it, had already "flown" a full-size set of the airplane's control surfaces in the wind tunnel at Moffet Field, California and now was practicing his role in the cockpit. A ship almost the size of the B-29 with a cockpit like a fighter. A crew of three instead of twelve because jet engines required less controls and instruments, and because its six hundred-mile speed was substituting for gunners.

When the Stratojet rolled out of its walled-off, secret place onto the Plant Two apron for system checks in September 1947, it seemed a thing eager for flight, too beautiful to have its integrity questioned. Cliff Roberts, engineering representative recently stationed in Washington, went to tell General LeMay about it. The General was interested but unenthusiastic. "We have no requirements for production of the airplane. You have to get some range in it," he said. Even the turboprop XB-52 wasn't getting the range LeMay wanted, though the design had grown fat with fuel tanks and was getting out of reason in both size and cost.

Roberts brought out engineering curves showing the range-stretching efforts on both projects. LeMay said nothing. It wasn't that he didn't want jets, Roberts knew. The General was all for jet speeds. It was a matter of range, pure and simple.

LeMay was sticking to his guns. There was no way of argu-
ing the point. Roberts searched for something, anything to
break the impasse. Refueling. He remembered the demonstrations
Spaatz and Eaker had made in the 1920's, a test refueling at
Wright Field during the war, the work the British were doing in
refueling development. Could refueling be done at turboprop and
jet speeds? Worth trying out on LeMay.

"We could get you any kind of range you want if we'd take
hold of this refueling deal," said Roberts.

LeMay didn't answer. The session ended.

Back at the office Roberts talked it over with Washington
Representative Jim Murray.

"Do you think the suggestion registered?" Murray asked
Roberts.

"Well, he didn't throw me out."

By December 1947, the XB-47 Stratojet was ready for flight.
Just after the Air Force had set up a competition calling for a
new turboprop medium bomber that would have *longer range*
than the Stratojet; just after they had placed an order for eighty-
two more B-50 Superforts and advance-type B-54s—airplanes
with *longer range*.

B-47 Stratojet

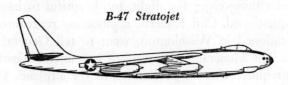

5. *Stratojet Flight*

Test pilot Bob Robbins and his co-pilot, Scott Osler, were
waiting only on the weather. To insure a safe landing, the plan
was to take the Stratojet off from Boeing Field and land on the

long runway of Moses Lake air base, across the Cascade Mountains in central Washington. It had to be clear at both fields and over the mountain range, and this was a lot to ask of the Seattle weather bureau in winter.

On the morning of December 17, 1947, Robbins started for the plant under a gray sky. The forecaster saw hope that the cumulus cover would break up. When someone discovered it was the forty-fourth anniversary of the Wright brothers' first flight, the hope grew to a conviction that this was the day.

Ben Werner, the flight engineer who had gone ahead to Moses Lake, reported an eighth of an inch of ice on the runways there and a local overcast that he thought would burn off by noon. Robbins headed for the airplane to check his equipment.

An inevitable tension was building up. Newsreel cameramen were scurrying about watching for position. Radio broadcasters were setting up their gear. There had been no public announcement but cars came to the streets of Beacon Hill overlooking the field, first seven, then seventy-seven, 177 in a miracle of multiplication. Key engineers started coming across the street toward Flight Test. Chief aerodynamicist Ben Cohn was under double pressure, his wife expecting a child, and this. She had tried him with the question, "If they both happen at once, where will you go?"

"Look," said Ben, "I love my family. But this baby down at the field, I've been working on it for four years."

Project engineer George Martin, project aerodynamicist Bill Cook, chief of flight test Showalter racked their minds for any last instructions, for something they might have overlooked. The missing item, not to be found, was the one unknown: Never before had a big sweptwing airplane like this been flown.

Bob Robbins was in the cockpit. He'd rather wait in his pilot's seat than in the office. No commotion here. No one at his elbow. It was his own private place, where he could think. Again and again he went over the charts showing the curve of take-off acceleration, the last point of refusal on the runway. He looked at his instruments and controls, the things he had watched go in the ship one by one in the year he'd been preparing for this day. Now they were all his. He felt at home with them.

Yet he had to remind himself that those neat rows of dials were only tokens of things big and important. Every turn of one of those hands would mean a lightning-fast change in his situation. Every touch on those controls was a command call on a parcel of power such as had never before been unleashed in the air. Six jets with 4,000 pounds thrust each, plus eighteen JATO rockets in the sides of the ship if he needed them, each with 1,000 pounds thrust for fourteen seconds. It was hard to compare jet thrust with horsepower, but roughly speaking, he'd have at his fingertips three times the power of the B-29, not counting the JATO's.

The morning was advancing. Ten-fifteen; ten-thirty. The clock on the instrument panel was irrevocably turning toward climax. The months of experiment and study all crowded into now. Robbins looked out the cockpit canopy. There were the five hundred people watching him on Beacon Hill and, he thought, a million more. The world. Scott Osler came up the ladder and through the bottom hatch. "Ben says the ice has melted at Moses, but a patch of clouds has moved in at 2,000 feet. Doesn't look too good."

Bob climbed out. "We'd better take an early lunch." At 12:15 Ben Werner called that Moses Lake was clear. But the weather station at Ephrata, twenty miles north of there, reported a two hundred-foot ceiling. Getting worse at Ephrata. Would the stuff move on over the Moses Lake airfield? Seattle was still overcast but some holes seemed to be developing. Two o'clock had been set as the deadline for take-off, to allow time for the test and a landing before dark. Better be ready to go if things improved.

Robbins and Scott Osler got on their gear, thickpadded crash helmets painted gold to reflect the sun's heat, oxygen mask and tubes hanging to the side. They climbed into the ship.

Word again from Werner. He could see the cloud bank over Ephrata but it was just hanging there. No wind. Still the situation was too precarious, Robbins thought. A little wind could bring the clouds over Moses Lake while they were en route; then where would they be? The hands on the clock kept turning. At 12:45 Captain James Fitzgerald, who was standing by with a P-80 jet fighter to take official flight pictures, poked his head in. "What say I run over there and see how it is? I can be back in half an hour."

"Good idea. Thanks. We'll wait."

In a one-jet roar, Fitzgerald's P-80 rocketed off the end of the runway and disappeared toward the mountains. After its bird-hound getaway, Robbins had a feeling the spell was broken.

The taxi strip was lined now. The sky was still overcast, but there was a big hole up toward the mountains. At 1:27, the P-80 raced back. It hit the south end of the runway, then came to a stop downfield. It had caught its gear on a runway light. A field car brought Fitzgerald on up and he talked to Robbins on the ground crew's interphone. "Looks good enough to me. I'd try it."

Robbins breathed a prayer. He turned to Osler. "All set?" He pushed Number One starter. The turbine wound up to its supersiren screech. Fuel on. The sudden bellow of the jet was a voice of surging power. All six engines roaring now. Brakes off. They taxied to the end of the runway, paused for a quick check. Robbins called the tower, "Tell us when our wheels clear the ground." He flicked on the intercom. "Scott, we'll release brakes at counter number 2260." The counter clocked the seconds for test recording. "Fifty-seven, fifty-eight, fifty-nine, sixty." They were rolling. Jets raging and yet so slow. That was the way with jet power; seemed forever getting moving, but once they really got rolling . . .

The air-speed indicator was coming up now, runway going under faster. Seventy, eighty, ninety miles per hour. A red light came on the fire-warning panel. Number Two engine. Robbins cut the power and hit the brakes.

"It was a false alarm, Bob," Osler said in a minute. The milli-volt reader showed the trouble was in the instrument only. Should they go back to the hangar and check the brakes? The linings would be pretty warm after that stop. But that would use up time and fuel. They'd have to spend more time refueling. It was nearly two o'clock. Might lose the chance to go today. "Boeing tower, we'll taxi back and try again," said Robbins. "Think we'll make it this time." They released brakes at 2:02 P.M. Rolling. Faster, faster. Faster still. The air-speed indicator, the field distance, the charts showing last point of refusal all were superimposed on Robbins' mind. Number Two fire warning light again. False alarm, again. Faster, racing now. This was it. One hundred thirty-five miles per hour. The last 2,000 feet of runway approaching fast. Use the JATO? Robbins lifted the guard off the JATO switch, ready to fire six bottles if necessary.

"You're airborne!" shouted the tower. Before Robbins knew it they were sixty feet in the air, ground dropping away fast. Controls felt good. Stable. Air speed going up.

"It's on its way!" Trained eyes on the ground could see from Robbins' first adjustments in lateral and longitudinal control that the aerodynamics were O.K.

Robbins was scanning his panel, glancing outside. "Gear up, Scott." The air-speed indicator jumped. One hundred and eighty, ninety, ninety-five. Good altitude now. "Easy up on the flaps." He waited for another boost in speed, but felt none.

"They aren't coming up, according to my indicator," said Osler.

"Light on Number Five." Robbins spotted another fire warning.

Osler checked it. No time for flaps now. "O.K. on Five. She's about ten millivolts. False indication."

"Roger. Is Two still O.K.?"

"I'll follow it up . . . it's O.K. . . . I can't get the flaps up on normal, I'm going to try using emergency."

"Better leave them where they are." The deck of clouds was right over them now and Robbins didn't want to go through it on instruments. They were cutting the air and climbing fast. He eased up on the power till they came under a hole. "Try to bring the flaps up in steps now, Scott, I've slowed the airplane a little."

"... It's all right. They're coming up," said Osler.

"Good. I'm going to get on my climbing speed now." Robbins turned the airplane sharply to the east, nosed up toward the hole, going up like an elevator. "Sure feels good."

"Roger." They were really moving. Eyes of ground observers were glued to the sweptwing speck in the sky, the thin trails of dark kerosene smoke pouring from its six engines. When Robbins changed his heading and started his authoritative climb it looked suddenly as if he were going straight up, and nothing was going to stop him. Up, up, vaulting the Cascades. So easy. Minutes and he was gone. There was a race for the waiting airplane that would follow to Moses Lake.

Bob Robbins was adjusting to his seat cushions. Now the months of preparation, the hundreds of people lining Beacon Hill seemed unreal. This was real. The smooth feel of jet power. The throttles only part way open. He felt wonderful, looked around. "It's sure nice to see our wings out straight."

"Sure is," said Osler. The ground droop was gone. Tips of the swept wings—they had to look 'way back to see them—were riding high with an easy spring that cushioned the air. This was the way they were meant to be.

"I see our A-26 down there. Going like mad." It was supposed to take pictures. "They aren't getting much. It'll break their hearts. Just look at this beautiful cloud background."

"Too bad. Can't be helped." Osler was busy making camera recordings of instruments.

They came out over the flat reaches of central Washington, sighted Moses Lake in the distance. Robbins played with the controls, trying some S-turns. Felt just like a pursuit. Responsive. Controls were light. "Let's try lowering the landing gear."

"O.K. Coming down."

They could feel it hit bottom. "That wasn't bad," said Robbins. Then the whole airplane began to tremble. "Wonder what that roughness is? Feel it?"

"Definitely." Things were really shaking now.

"Hey, that's quite rough." Robbins called for flaps to slow the airplane. It was O.K. at lower speed. Probably the landing-gear doors would have to be stiffened.

They were sailing high in the sky now. The big test item to get out of the way was slowing down to the point of stall, to confirm their predicted landing speed. Robbins called out the item on the flight plan. "Condition 8b. It's begun at counter number 3690." The ship slowed.... "Counter number is 3725, speed about 142. Still feels very good...140, 139, 139½. How does it look? All right?" Seemed they were standing still, but the ship was riding on even keel. Wouldn't fall off on a wing. That was good.

"I have 133 miles an hour now at counter number 3780... I felt just a little buffeting ... 132 ... there, that's pretty good stall warning." They felt the vigorous buffeting that designers want to occur well before full stall, so a pilot can't get into a stall without knowing it. "I'm going to slow it down to 125."

The ship approached stall. Still steady and straight. He felt relieved. This was an airplane. It was behaving wonderfully. "We got about seven miles per hour stall warning at least. No tendency for the airplane to fall off." He tried it again. Confirmation.

Robbins turned off the power boost that operated the controls, found he could manage them if necessary at these speeds without the boost. That was good. He shut off Number One engine with Number Six on full power. There was no stability problem should an engine go dead. All good. He had to remind himself, this Stratojet was a kind of airplane that had never been tried before.

Robbins began to think ahead about landing, switched on the radio. "6FH8-2. Ben Werner: This is 6065. Do you read us? Over."

"This is Ben Werner. I read you fine. Over."

"That's Roger. I read you loud and clear, too. I wanted to get landing instructions just in case we should have radio trouble.

Wind direction, velocity and recommended landing runway.
Over." It would be runway thirty-two, Werner said.

Robbins tried a make-believe landing in the air, condition
eleven on the flight plan. He liked the way it felt. "That was at
130 miles an hour. It was very good. Very good." He tried
another at higher power. The airplane was smooth. No tricks.
He circled and began a descent. Came down fast. This was a
sweptwing jet airplane. Things happened fast. He lined up with
the runway, began the letdown. "Are gear and flaps checked
down?"

"Roger. My red lights are all off. Green lights are on. Flaps
full down."

"I may make a couple passes at the field. . . . Those are good-
looking runways."

"Sure are."

"Brakes checked. Hydraulic pressure is O.K. Gear and flaps
are down. We should be O.K."

"All the generators are working fine."

"O.K. Thanks. We are at about 158 now with 52 per cent
rpm. We're going to do it all right, I think. . . . It's 135 right
now." They were over the runway. Ten feet in the air. Robbins
could see there was no use doing a practice go-round. He
chopped four engines. They were on the ground, rolling fast.
There was a shimmy in the right-hand outrigger wheel. Shook
the airplane quite a little, but now they were slowing down.
An item for the mechanics to fix. Here they were, Moses Lake.
All over. Robbins taxied over to where a group was waiting.

"Are you clear on the canopy, Scott?"

"O.K."

"O.K. Canopy coming open." Robbins looked out and grinned
at Ben Werner. The grin opened into a huge smile when he saw
the joy of the men on the ground and realized what it meant.
It was a smile he couldn't turn off the rest of the day, through
the hearty round of handshakes, through the post-flight conference, the radio speeches, the press interviews. Bob Robbins
knew it was a new brand of airplane that would put an end to

the old. "You just have to fly it to appreciate it," he said. "It's wonderful."

6. *Lowering the Boom*

Thomas Finletter, chairman of the President's Air Policy Commission, noted the news report that a new type of Air Force bomber had been flown on the forty-fourth anniversary of the Wright brothers' flight. "None too soon," was his reaction.

Finletter, the lawyer, had taken a searching and orderly approach to President Truman's charge of five months before. He recognized that his commission was dealing with the sweeping problem of national security at a time, less than two and a half years out of war, when people everywhere were disturbed and disillusioned. The United Nations Assembly was smarting under a succession of Russian vetoes; Poland, Rumania, Bulgaria, Hungary, Yugoslavia, Albania and parts of Austria and Germany had become satellites of Soviet Russia. Czechoslovakia, Greece and Turkey were threatened. The Communist party was getting strong in France and Italy, and the Marshall Plan had been advanced to help Europe stem the tide.

In Asia, the Communist forces of Mao Tse-tung were bent on conquest of China. Korea, like Germany, was cut in half by Soviet and Western occupation forces. The American, British and French sectors of Berlin were an outpost a hundred miles inside Soviet-occupied territory. General Lucius Clay, the U. S. Military Governor in Germany, warned that the Russians might at any time choke off rail supplies to the 2,000,000 people in the western part of the city.

It was Cold War. "As ruthless and determined a drive to achieve world domination as a hot war," said the Harriman committee, which was working to help European nations under the terms of the Economic Cooperation Act.

Thomas Finletter and his commission wrote in their report that the oceans were no longer enough to safeguard America, with the continuing "revolution in applied science for destruction." Our national security could be assured only by elimination of war itself. But to achieve this depended on the nations' arriving at "the great agreement to live together in peace and to this end give the United Nations the legal and physical power ... to keep the peace."

America must work for this world order but its attainment was hampered by lack of free travel, free communications, free press. Therefore the country "must seek the next best thing ... relative security under the protection of its own arms ... since nothing would be more likely to provoke aggression than the spectacle of an unarmed or inadequately armed United States."

Soberly, Finletter acknowledged that this double-barreled policy would be as difficult a task as the country had ever taken on. "Our policy of relative security will compel us to maintain a force in being in peacetime greater than any self-governing people has ever kept. Our policy of seeking world order under law is even more difficult. If it is to be successful we will have to reverse all our notions of our sovereign independence and, equally difficult, persuade others to do likewise. It may be that we shall not go all-out on either ... compromise with both and achieve neither. If we do compromise in this way, we shall continue to live in a world in which war is an accepted institution and is therefore inevitable and we shall be unprepared to defend ourselves in that war."

That was the word of the President's Air Policy Commission, Thomas K. Finletter, George P. Baker, Palmer Hoyt, John A. McCone, Arthur D. Whiteside. December 30, 1947.

The Finletter report and the report of the Congressional Air Policy Board that followed it, answered the question of the aviation industry. There would have to be air power in being.

Billy Mitchell had won. Mitchell had finally won, too, his campaign for a separate air force. Now the U. S. Air Force took
equal place with the Army and the Navy in Secretary Forrestal's
new unified Department of Defense.

New things began to happen. Tackling the problem of global
range, Wright Field was taking a healthy interest in aerial refueling. Bill Irvine recommended refueling B-29 and B-50 Superforts until the intercontinental XB-52 came along. In January
1948, the Weapons Board of the Air Force gave consideration to
refueling the XB-52 also, so it could be kept lighter and could
make better speed. The B-52 design had been built up to a tremendous 480,000 pounds.

"We've got to cut it down to 300,000," said Wright Field.
They expressed great doubt whether the project could succeed
and suggested some whole new approach, such as the Flying
Wing. But Wells and Schairer insisted the Flying Wing was no
answer.

Engineer Cliff Leisy was assigned to supervise a refueling
study. Before a design had been worked out, Wright Field ordered four B-29s modified to incorporate refueling equipment.
Leisy took off for England to learn about the British hose and
reel devices already developed. The Air Force wanted to start
modernizing B-29s from World War II, the modification to in-
clude refueling equipment. Boeing was asked to reopen the
government-owned Wichita plant to do the work. Finletter's
report had called for more plant dispersion, pointing to the concentration of the aircraft industry in the Los Angeles, Seattle and
Long Island areas.

Fearing the B-47 Stratojet was being lost in the shuffle, Bill
Allen headed east to talk about jet bomber orders. Bob Hage
went with him, fresh with enthusiasm from his jet power studies
and the success of flights at Moses Lake. Hage took the occasion
to put in a plug with Allen for a commercial jet transport. "Jets
are looking better all the time," he said. "No one is building a
turboprop that will work. The jet engines on the B-47 aren't
giving any trouble at all."

"It will be a long time before they can be operated profitably on an airline, won't it?" Allen asked.

"Oh, no. Five years, possibly."

Allen didn't seem impressed. He was more concerned with the B-47, a plane that could be produced in the reopened Wichita plant while Seattle was building the B-50 Superforts and their successors, the B-54s. Now was the time to sell the 47.

In Washington General Hoyt Vandenberg was noncommittal. K. B. Wolfe, however, said B-47 production at Wichita was considered when the decision was made to reopen the plant. But there still was no military requirement written for the Stratojet.

Debate was raging on the seventy-group Air Force. The plan brought a new clash. The Navy was after super aircraft carriers. Air Force advocates contended the Navy was trying to replace strategic bombers with less effective equipment. Carrier advocates countered: "A bomber has limits but a floating base can move." Air Secretary Stuart Symington raised a vigorous voice for strategic air power. The only thing the Russians were afraid of was a great air force, he said. He told the Senate Armed Services Committee March 25 that the new Superfortress, when utilizing "the most modern development of refueling technique . . . can . . . bomb any part of Russia, and return to American bases."

But the "most modern development of refueling" was still on paper, Wright Field knew. Test pilots there were just starting experiments. They had planned to take their two B-29 test planes to Wichita to continue the tests. Bill Allen was in Dayton at the time. Brigadier General Horace Shepard, chief of Air Force procurement, said, "Let's get down to Wichita and get this thing going." Next day in Earl Schaefer's office, General Shepard got a call from K. B. Wolfe in Washington. Shepard listened, stiffened a bit, then put down the phone. "We've got to transfer fuel in the air immediately. By this weekend. Even if we have to do it with a teaspoon."

The pressure from the nation's capital was on.

They went to a fire station, inquired about fire hose and reels. Schaefer called Harold Zipp, his chief engineer. Zipp got Jack Clark, his assistant, project engineer Roy Rotelli, and laboratory chief Bill Arundale just before quitting time, and gave them the problem, told them to start right on it. They got three hundred feet of hose off two portable fire carts in the plant, rigged fittings and made strength tests.

Saturday, March 27, the equipment was in the air. Water would be used instead of fuel for the first trial. The two planes trailed out long cables, with hooks on the ends. They got the hooks linked. The lower plane began pulling down the hose. With wind tugging at the hose and whipping it in the air the weak link that had been installed in the line for emergencies gave way. The hose dropped. Air Force representatives wired Washington they'd had partial success.

Mechanics borrowed two more hose reels from the plant and by midnight had them rigged again. Sunday morning, Easter Sunday, the new hose was caught in the grappling hook; the crew in the receiver plane started reeling it in. They had it almost in when the hauling line broke.

A new hose from a fire truck went in the air late Sunday afternoon. The cable on the end of it jumped the reel when they were letting it out, fouling everything. Bill Arundale and Air Force Lieutenant Doudlinger worked for an hour to untangle seventy-five feet of it trailing through the sky, wind pulling it tight. Daylight was fading when they finally got it straight. Major W. P. Maiersperger in the receiver plane poured directions into his microphone. "This time let's do it." They caught the trailing hook, began hauling in the hose. "Fifty feet away, forty feet, thirty," Maiersperger reported. "The hose is in the airplane." A silence. Six minutes. Then Maiersperger called out, "Water! Water!" It was flowing through and out the dump valve, gallons of it. That was "Operation Drip," March 28, 1948.

On March 28, 1948, Secretary Forrestal laid down new rules governing roles and responsibilities of the Army, Navy and Air Force, to prevent duplication and interservice squabbling. The

Air Force would have primary responsibility for strategic air warfare.

But "Operation Gusher" was ahead. The objective was to transfer six hundred gallons of fuel a minute. Earl Schaefer consulted oil company friends in Oklahoma.

"You'll blow yourselves to kingdom come," they said. "You can't go beyond two hundred gallons a minute with high octane fuel." Cliff Leisy got back from England with British equipment, a harpoon instead of a grappling hook, and the effort went on, high over Kansas wheat fields, top priority, top secret.

Bill Allen returned to crisis in Seattle. Archie Logan, the industrial relations director, had been negotiating for months with the Aero Mechanics Union, and the parties were getting farther apart rather than closer together. The company had offered fifteen cents an hour increase. The union wanted thirty. The union was holding tight for the wartime seniority clause. Allen had come to the realization the contract had to be changed if the company were to succeed. They were still operating at a loss. The Air Force had the company tagged as a "high cost producer" and there was a tough battle every time they negotiated for orders.

Fred Laudan, now vice president, manufacturing, laid the trouble to the labor contract. "My work crews are frozen. We've finished the XB-47s, we've got a build-up coming on B-50s and C-97s, we've got fuel tank trouble on the 50s, we're always up against changes, but every time we have a lay-off or transfer, we come up against this seniority clause and everybody starts bumping everybody else all over the place, so the senior employees can get the jobs they want. When we have promotions to make, they have to be on seniority, regardless of merit. It's no good." At supervisors' meetings, the supervisors would ask, "When are we going to get a labor contract that will give us the right to manage?"

Bill Allen remembered his admonition to himself, *Make sincere effort to understand labor's viewpoint.* Then he remembered another, *Develop a postwar future for Boeing.* The two seemed to be in conflict. Could a sound future be built on an unsound foundation? Was seniority more important than merit? Wasn't competition, based on merit, the heart of the whole free enterprise system? If management had the responsibility, didn't it have to have the right to manage? Didn't the employees' future, too, depend on that? The more he thought about those questions, the more obvious were the answers. He stood before 750 supervisors in the cafeteria and spoke with feeling:

"I hope we may some day do away with the thought that we must be divided into two camps—labor and management. I hope we may come to realize that all of us have the same objective: building the world's finest aircraft."

On April 20, Archie Logan came to Allen's office. "Here it is. Ultimatum. Thirty-five cents an hour across-the-board increase and the old seniority clause or they strike us in twenty-four hours."

Allen took a breath. Then he straightened. "We won't accede to it. If we do, we'll be out of business."

Thirteen thousand eight hundred men walked out April 22. Bill Allen looked again at an idle plant, like the one he'd looked out on that first day. Two and a half years had passed since then. The broad corner windows had become windows of command. But now it was Bill Allen the lawyer who looked out of those windows. There was a no-strike clause in the old contract. There was also a provision in the National Labor Relations Act requiring sixty days' notice of strike.

"The strike is in violation of the contract and of federal law," Allen said. "The union has repudiated the contract. It has forfeited its bargaining rights. We don't have to negotiate with it." Union attorneys contended a notice of strike given a year before was still in effect.

Allen authorized the fifteen-cent increase that had been offered the union and invited employees to come back; invited new applicants to apply for work. Federal conciliators wanted to mediate. Allen stood his ground. "Not unless the union calls off this illegal strike."

The aerial refueling effort in Wichita had resulted in a transfer of two hundred gallons per minute, with six hundred the goal. The British equipment wasn't going to work. Didn't have the capacity. Besides, no one had the answer to the problem of a frozen hose in possible Arctic operations at sixty or ninety degrees below zero. "You'd better look for another way to do it," Tory Gamlem, the project engineer for the B-50s, told Cliff Leisy. When they considered the problem of refueling a fast plane like the B-47 Stratojet, the need was even more evident.

Wright Field ran flight tests to try to find the best position for two planes to fly in close formation. Wing-tip to wing-tip position got them free of propeller downwash, but side visibility was poor. Pilots got stiff necks. Direct nose-to-tail was good for vision, but the rear crew couldn't stand the buffeting. A close staggered position worked best, they found, with the tanker ten feet behind and twenty-five feet below the receiver. The tanker would have the more experienced crew so it should have the rear position.

In Wichita there were daily sessions. If the planes could hold that pattern why couldn't a telescoping pipe be used to connect them, big enough to get any flow they wanted? Cliff Leisy made a rough drawing. A pipe forty-eight feet long when extended and twenty-eight feet when retracted would do it. But it would be risky extending that up out of the nose of the tanker. It might fold back on top of the plane.

"We'll have to switch positions," said Captain Mack Elliott, Air Force project officer. "Put the tanker on top and lower the pipe out the back."

"Sure," said Leisy, "lower the boom."

But how could they maneuver the "boom" into position? That had them stopped for a time. Leisy pondered it. Motors and steering gear? It would be hard to steer a heavy forty-eight-foot pipe out in the air. That was out of the question. Or was it?

"Why not put control surfaces on the end of it and fly it like an airplane? A flying boom!"

Would it work? Leisy was no aerodynamicist. He took the idea to Jack Steiner, an aerodynamicist from Seattle who happened to be in town. "No reason it shouldn't," said Steiner.

Captain Elliott took the idea to Lieutenant Colonel Tom Gerrity, in charge of the B-50 program. "Go ahead and develop it," said Gerrity. "Looks good to me." But they were told to go on modifying the B-29s for British-type hose refueling until the "flying boom" could be engineered and tried out.

Strike tension in Seattle grew through May and June with each added day. The community was hurt. Payroll loss was $800,000 a week. Rehiring was slow. Bill Allen filed a $2,250,000 damage suit against the union. The union filed a countersuit. Part of management thought the thing should be patched up, that Allen's stand was too severe. Each night he carried his burden home with him. *Be confident.* But it was hard to be totally confident. *Be considerate of associates' views.* Some of them were sincerely opposed. But he felt he had right on his side. He stuck to his guns. He stepped up the hiring campaign, redefined the seniority that would apply: "We believe the average American worker wants to be credited for his ability and performance, improve his position by merit. He wants the protection of seniority, too. The senior man, where qualifications and performance are equal, will have the preference in promotion and retention in case of lay-off." On June 19, the Federal District Court ruled with Allen that the union had lost its bargaining rights under the law.

The labor tensions in Seattle echoed growing world tension. Communists took over the government in Czechoslovakia, swung it into the Russian orbit. There were reports that Russia already had the secret of the atom bomb. United Nations efforts at an atomic control agreement were proving fruitless and the U. S. was preparing a new atomic test center on the Pacific atoll of

Eniwetok. Congress appropriated funds for the seventy-group Air Force and Marshall Plan aid to Europe. Then it happened in Berlin: what Lucius Clay had feared, the signal flag plain that Soviet intentions were not friendly. The railway corridor to the city was cut off. The U. S. Air Force grimly moved an aerial supply line to the rescue.

There was a growing urgency behind the XB-52 intercontinental bomber, still in Phase One development. Ed Wells felt it in every communication from Wright Field. But he also felt frustration over the turboprop power plants supposed to give the plane its long range. Two years ago the turboprop was to have been available in two years. A couple of months ago, George Schairer and Colonel Pete Warden learned it was going to be another four years. If the XB-52 went ahead, Wells was afraid they'd end up with an airplane and no engines, but the contract was about to be signed to build two experimental models with turboprops.

The Westinghouse Company revealed plans for a big new jet engine. Jets were looking better and better, turboprops worse and worse. "And here we are heading down the turboprop road," Ed Wells reminded himself, uncomfortably. Trouble on trouble. The strike. No B-47 sales. Now the power-plant dilemma.

Ed Wells went to Bill Allen. "I don't think we should go further with the turboprop on the B-52. We've come to the conclusion the airplane should be jet-powered."

Allen was startled. It would throw the program back, might bring a cancellation. "Isn't this pretty late to be proposing a change like that?"

"I know, Bill, but it just isn't the airplane we should be building."

7. *Heat on the*
Stratojets, XB-52

When Ed Wells and George Schairer went to Wright Field to talk with bombardment project officer Pete Warden about putting jet engines on the intercontinental XB-52, Warden was all for it. He had been more worried about the turboprops than they. He was 100 per cent sold on jet speed, and proud of the performance of the XB-47 which had been his baby in the project office.

Warden knew, too, that the Bell X-1 research plane, a pointed capsule of rocket power hauled into the air under the belly of a B-29 and cut loose, was even then breaking through the speed-of-sound barrier, exceeding the speed that engineers once said was the limit. The days of the four-hundred-mile-an-hour bombers were numbered. "Go ahead and work up an XB-52 jet design," he said. "But we'll have to keep on with the turboprop airplane until we see what can be done."

In July 1948, a contract came through to build two experimental *turboprop* XB-52s with wings swept back just twenty degrees, because the speed of the turboprops didn't call for more sweepback and they could get better range with the wings out straighter. The project was real, and the effort to hang the Westinghouse jet engines on the already approved design seemed almost superficial. Neither were performance predictions for the jet version too encouraging, because the over-all design had been geared to turboprops and the Westinghouse jet was shy of the power they needed.

Meanwhile the seventy-group Air Force program called for more B-50 and B-54 Superforts. The Berlin airlift, an incredible chain of airplanes carrying supplies of coal and food, was a potent reminder of the thin thread between cold and hot war. K. B. Wolfe and General Joe McNarney, commanding general of Air Materiel Command, came to Seattle to talk about production schedules and about the strike that had cut off the supply of B-50s.

"We have two-thirds of our normal work force on the job." Bill Allen told them. "Nearly half of them are returned strikers." But Allen wanted to talk about the B-47. It was seven months since the Stratojet had first flown, and no orders for it. "On your way back," he said, "we'd like you to go by Moses Lake and see the 47."

"Thanks, we're only interested in production airplanes," said K. B. "We've got to get back."

"I know, but you should see it. We can fly you over in a B-50 so you won't lose any time." The visitors were traveling in a slower B-17. "We can bring your plane over while you're on the ground."

"O.K., if we can make it quick."

The Air Force was testing the 47 at Moses Lake. Major Guy Townsend, the test pilot, felt the way Bob Robbins did. The plane had won him over. Pete Warden, who had been asking K. B. Wolfe to watch the 47 perform, was at Moses Lake, too. Warden and Townsend met the arriving party on the flight apron, where the Stratojet was standing. K. B. walked over and patted it. "We'd like to see a fly-by."

"It's all yours, General," said Warden, waving a hand toward the cockpit.

"Oh, we won't have time to take a flight."

"Make it long or short as you like."

K. B. had never been in a jet bomber. Major Townsend persuaded him politely, "Really like to have you come along, General."

"Well, all right. A short one." K. B. climbed in behind Townsend. McNarney went with Allen, Beall, George Martin, and Colonel Warden to the tower to watch. It was a gusty day. There was a broken overcast at 8,000 feet with a little blue showing through. Ben Werner in the tower tuned the radio to bring in the conversation in the plane.

"General Wolfe, if you want to ask any questions," Guy Townsend was saying, "just tap Captain Ridley and he'll take his headset off so he can hear you. We plan to taxi out, take off, climb to 10,000 feet and let you fly the airplane if you want to, sir. Then we'll come in, make a pass across the runway and land. Then we'd like to make a JATO take-off for you."

The group in the tower watched the B-47 cut loose, watched it consume the runway with thunderous grace, and shoot up toward the overcast. Townsend's Mississippi drawl was drifting in the tower radio, as comfortable as the line of an automobile salesman demonstrating a new car. "If you will notice, sir," he was saying at 6,000 feet and 470 miles per hour, "it takes no effort at all to roll the airplane at this speed. The boosted controls do all the work for you. You don't have to do a thing but fly it."

"Yes, that is very good."

"I'm pulling the power back now, sir, so we can make a turn without getting in the clouds."

"O.K.," said K. B., "when you get it turned around and leveled out, let me take it a little to see if I can hold it."

"Yes, sir. There is nothing to holding it. All you have to do is to think about it. The boost does all the holding for you. I'll get away from this thunderstorm and go down away from these clouds and you can have it there. . . . Now, General, you noticed I cut it back to 80 per cent rpm before I started that turn. That's way back for jet engines. You would never cruise it back this far, but that was to keep from running through the thunderstorm. You notice that the air speed is still four hundred miles per hour even though I made a 180 degree turn. That will show you what low drag this airplane has."

On the ground, Bill Allen turned to McNarney, bubbling over. "That Townsend won't bring him down till he agrees to buy it."

McNarney was smiling. "Certainly sounds that way."

Townsend's voice: "All right, you have it now, sir."

"O.K."

"How do you like those aileron forces, sir?" After a while Wolfe said, "O.K. You take it."

"All right, sir," said Townsend, "we'll go in now and make a low pass over the field.... O.K., Ben Werner, we are turning on our downwind leg for a pass over the ramp. Do you have us in sight?"

Ben Werner called, "That is Roger. We have you in sight."

The Stratojet whipped down, buzzed the field, not more than fifty feet off the runway, burned past the tower in a sky-shattering roar, then pulled up hard, sharp, steep, nose to the clouds, an arrow shooting straight to the overcast. Wellwood Beall brushed his forehead. "Whew!"

The radio: "O.K., we're down to four hundred miles per hour now.... O.K., we're down to three hundred. Everything O.K., General?"

"O.K. here."

Then they came down. Townsend was saying, "We have 170 miles per hour, and it seems like we're slow enough to get out and walk, doesn't it?"

"Are you sure you won't stall here?"

"Yes, sir, they built some qualities into this airplane that won't let it stall at this speed."

"It's going to be difficult now to get in that B-17 and go home. You've got me spoiled."

They landed, taxied up. "I enjoyed that," said K. B., climbing out. "Wish we had a little more time to play around. Thanks very much."

"Pleasure was all mine, General."

The group watched Townsend make his JATO take-off, the hissing white tail of eighteen rockets pushing the arrowhead Stratojet steeply up on a broadening, heightening pillar of smoke, speed and sound and sight all bursting in a cry of shocking beauty and power. K. B. was dancing from one foot to another. When the show was over the General checked his watch. Allen walked over to him. "Leave it to Boeing to really turn out the flying machines, eh, K. B.?"

Wolfe grinned. "You go t'hell, Bill Allen." He looked around. "Where's our B-17?"

When the generals had left, George Martin asked Townsend, "That pull-out of yours . . . how many G's did you pull?"

"The limit," said the Major. "I figured the country needs this airplane."

Back in Dayton, K. B. Wolfe asked Colonel Warden to his office. "Is the 47 really ready for production? Is it in a practical state?"

"We're convinced of it, General."

Wolfe looked at Warden. "Well, what are we waiting for? Let's get it going." Then he went after it hard. Somewhere he had to dig up the money. He went with the Wright Field group before the Air Council. Vandenberg, Symington. They were for it. Forrestal. Congress. They got together enough funds to buy ten. $30 million. That would get the Wichita plant started.

The problem of B-47 production took on a new look, however, when Bill Allen got the proposals. K. B. wanted the first plane in January 1950, only a little over sixteen months away. There was no organization to do the job in Wichita. The people who knew about jets were in Seattle. Besides, Seattle was the company's own plant; Wichita was a government-owned plant. What would happen in the day when the piston-powered Superforts were finally outmoded? What would the Seattle plant be doing then, with jet bomber production in Wichita?

Air Force interest in the B-47 was suddenly taking off with JATO power. When they looked for a fast war steed, what did they have? Seasoned war horses, the Superfortresses, 29s and 50s. The intercontinental B-52 looked a long way off. But the B-47 was right there waiting, brilliant, impatient on its feet. Refueling development was coming along to offset its range limitations. All competing jet bombers were much slower. K. B. Wolfe had wartime pressure up when Pappy Crews, the Boeing Dayton representative, went in with the proposal that the Stratojets be built in Seattle and the B-54s in Wichita. "Look," said K. B., "the problem is to get the B-47 going in Wichita. That's where we want to build it. We don't want to build it in Seattle. This is the program."

"But General Wolfe, we feel it would be much better the other way around, for the reasons we've given."

"This is the plan for procurement. Don't you understand? This is a matter of national defense."

"Yes, I understand that, K. B. But we think we can do a better job for you on the other basis. And this sixteen-month schedule. . . . Our people in Seattle feel this is not a practicable schedule."

"Doesn't Boeing want to sell us the airplane? You know you are in competition with the Northrop Flying Wing. It's coming along. The airplane that will be put in production is the one that will give the best assurance of meeting this starting date. Or we can build the 47 in facilities other than Boeing if that looks best from a national defense standpoint." K. B. sat down and wrote out a statement on a yellow pad. "Here. Put this on the teletype to Bill Allen. Tell him I wrote it."

Pappy Crews sent the message, "B-54 production at Seattle to continue starting December 1949, reaching a maximum of twenty per month. . . . B-50 production at Seattle to discontinue upon completion of 132 now being negotiated. . . . B-47 to be produced at Wichita starting January 1950. Repeat, 1950." Then he added, "General Wolfe requested I point out to you that the above represents the plan that must, repeat *must*, be put into operation, and he desires, as quickly as possible, information from you concerning whether or not the plan is acceptable. Please note that General Wolfe wants these airplanes built in Wichita, repeat, Wichita, if we build them."

Bill Allen couldn't see it K. B.'s way. At all. He called in Beall. "You go back to Dayton and convince him we've got to do it the other way. I don't think I should leave Seattle, with a strike on."

Beall made a strong pitch. K. B. paced the floor. "Don't fight the problem," K. B. said. "It's going to be Wichita. Period."

Then Bill Allen went. K. B. wouldn't budge. "Stop fighting the problem," he kept saying.

Allen was adamant. Didn't feel he could accept the plan; neither could he shut the door on the order. He returned to Seattle.

September 1, K. B. dispatched Lieutenant Colonels Tom Gerrity and Orville Mohler and his civilian production consultant, Pete Jansen, to Seattle with orders to get the program going. They stopped off in Wichita to pick up Earl Schaefer, Al Schupp, Captain "Shifty" Shaffer, B-47 project officer, and some others, so everyone would be on hand. Meetings were held in the board room at Seattle. The air was tight for a time. Then Pete Jansen spoke. "Look, I agree this production schedule is unrealistic. I'll tell that to K. B. and I think he'll listen to me. But, gentlemen, you might as well make up your mind that if this airplane's going to be built, it's going to be in Wichita."

K. B. Wolfe eased the schedule. But it was still Wichita. "Well, all right," said Allen finally. "If that's the way you want it, we'll do the best job we can."

September 3, 1948, the agreement was signed. The B-47 Stratojet would go in production.

September 9, the Civil Aeronautics Authority finished its testing of the Stratocruiser and awarded it an Approved Type Certificate. Deliveries to the airlines could begin. September 12, the strike ended. A rival union had been organized in the plant. The Aero Mechanics Union voted that its members would return to work without a contract. They'd have a new election under National Labor Relations Board rules to establish themselves as bargaining agent and then negotiate a new contract from scratch. Again there was action on the Duwamish.

With the jet-swift B-47 lined up for production, the prospect of building the two experimental XB-52s with turboprops seemed lusterless. Yet the 52 work was going ahead fast, under a contract, with a schedule to meet. Once you had a big job like that under contract you weren't likely to let it go even though the outlook for turboprops was becoming gloomier and the jet prospects brighter, with a new one promised by Pratt & Whitney which would turn out 10,000 pounds thrust and would use less fuel per mile than any previous jet.

Boeing engineers worked hard on a proposal to substitute the new jets for the turboprops without disruptive changes that would jeopardize the contract. They found they could get almost as much range, plus better speed, without changing the wing or the twenty degrees sweepback. The jets brought the speed up to five hundred miles per hour. The plane would still be within the 300,000-pound gross weight target. They wrapped up the proposal and took it to Dayton in October 1948, to see if they could sell it.

"The Pratt & Whitneys look good in the 52," said Wells, pulling the presentation out of his brief case. "We think the Air Force should seriously consider the change."

Colonel Pete Warden looked over the data. Finally he said, "I don't think you've gone far enough." He paused, thumbing the three-view drawings. Wells and Schairer looked at each other. Could it be that . . .

"I think you ought to have a faster wing," said Warden. "More sweepback, like the B-47. We've been going all this time trying to get maximum range in order to minimize the need for refueling, and we're losing out on combat performance. We ought to be going at it the other way around. Maximize the combat performance, the thing that's important. That's what we've got to do, so help me. We've already compromised on range, with refueling. Let's not compromise any more on speed." Warden looked around the room. There was a surprised silence. "This is one of my foolish consistencies," he said as though in self-justification. "We've always got to go after more speed."

"Let us see what we can do to get you some more," said Wells. He looked at his watch. It was nearing noon on a Friday. "We'll be back Monday morning." They filed out.

"Kind of swept us off our feet," said Schairer.

Back at the hotel suite, Ed Wells held council. Bob Withington and Vaughn Blumenthal from Aerodynamics, project engineer

Art Carlsen and Maynard Pennell of Preliminary Design, were with them. All the major branches of engineering were represented. They had with them all the data on the XB-52 with both turboprops and jets; also wind-tunnel data on a new jet medium bomber proposal. Wells unrolled the drawings of the XB-52. The twenty degree sweepback looked conservative now. "I think we'd better put this away and start over," he said. They looked at the drawings of the medium bomber; thirty-five degrees sweepback, their latest thinking in jets. Why not start with it?

"Double it in size and you just about have it," said Schairer.

Wells spread out drawing paper on the top of the bureau and began making a three-view sketch. Art Carlsen and Maynard Pennell worked up a weight breakdown. Withington and Blumenthal calculated the estimated performance. Schairer laid out the lines of the new sweptback wing. By late that night they realized they had created an airplane. It had the range. Weight up only a little, to 330,000 pounds. Thirty-five degrees sweepback, 185 feet span, eight engines. The speed went up to more than six hundred miles an hour. Stratojet performance in an intercontinental bomber.

Like a rabbit right out of the hat, only it wasn't that. It was there all the time, right in their brief cases, in data they had been working on for months. Only they hadn't known it. Once there was the realization—by the Air Force and themselves—that this was the need, the answer was available in things they already knew, ready to be put together by willing hands. Saturday morning, before the stores closed, Schairer rounded up some balsa wood, glue and carving tools, and set to work on a model. Wells organized the engineering data, lined up a public stenographer to put it in document form. Sunday night it was a clean, thirty-three page report, bound, titled D-10,000 (they jumped to the nearest round number that wouldn't overlap some document that might be under way in Seattle) and with scale model attached. A handsome model, clean, eight-engined, authoritative, sweeping with speed.

Pete Warden was the one who was beaming Monday morning. "Now we have an airplane," he said. "This is the B-52."

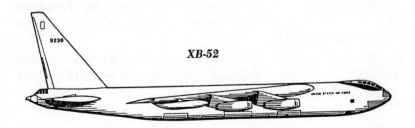

XB-52

Fall, 1948. Everyone was moving ahead with a purpose now, though not without problems. The XB-52 was a big job of detail designing to complete, and then construction. The contract wasn't yet changed over from turboprops to jets but a board headed by Bill Irvine reviewed it and decided the change should be made. Strikers were back at work but there was feeling and friction between them and those who had worked during the strike. The propeller-driven B-50s were far behind schedule. The B-50 production was to be gradually changed over to the new B-54 advanced Superfort, but that troubled Engineering. The B-54, they knew, was a retread. There wasn't much more mileage left in the Superfortress series. So loaded down was the airplane becoming, with armament and equipment to offset the limitations of its speed, that it looked like a mistake. Especially when the Stratojet flashed by. Wells felt that Bill Allen should know their misgivings. It wasn't easy when he knew how Allen was counting on the B-54 to fill the Seattle plant, now that Stratojet production was set for Wichita.

"I don't think we can count very heavily on the B-54," said Wells. "Wright Field is beginning to lose interest. It isn't really a very good airplane. I'm afraid it's only a matter of time before it's going to have to be cancelled out."

Allen looked hurt. What was there to take its place in the plant? There seemed little likelihood of enough orders for

Stratocruisers. Engineering had been working up designs of a turboprop version of the Stratocruiser, but that prospect was fading. Ralph Bell, assistant sales manager, was making some progress selling C-97 transports to the Military Air Transport Service. That looked like the best hope. So far, only twenty-three C-97s had been sold.

"It just means we're going to have to work that much harder to sell the C-97," Allen concluded. "And then the B-52. We'll have to put everything we've got into the 52."

8. *Fifteen-Million-Dollar Airplanes*

Stratofortress, the new XB-52 design was named. As it took form in a huge wooden mock-up at the close of 1948 it held awesome promise. Three hundred thirty thousand pounds of jet airplane, with wings and tail fiercely swept back for near-sonic speed. Eight jet engines that would one day pour out 80,000 pounds of fiery thrust. Translated into horsepower at six hundred miles an hour, that would be ten times the power of a B-29 Superfortress. And the plane would go to even higher altitude than the B-47 Stratojet. A new airplane in the Flying Fortress tradition, if only it wasn't too fabulously expensive. The first two experimental models were going to cost an estimated $32 million. How much production quantities would cost was still an unknown.

But this was what airplanes were coming to. Capital ships. Bill Allen realized that only a huge and well-ordered organization could develop and produce a thing like this. It took artisans of a thousand trades to put the parts together, men with engineering vision to see what those parts had to be, how they could be united to a single purpose. It would take new investment in research facilities. There could be no unknowns left to trial and error. Allen could see that the company he headed had been inexorably building itself a role that only bigness and greatness could fill. Could they measure up?

There was no hope of succeeding in a role such as this, Allen knew, unless you could lay away some money to work with. The year 1948 was the first since the war that would end with a profit, even if a small one. There was a loss of $7 million on the Stratocruiser project to be written off, but out of total contracts they were going to manage about a million and three-quarters dollars net earnings, to start replenishing the company coffers. Allen had put his assistant John Yeasting in charge of budget control and was making a strong battle for more earnings. The Board had approved a plan for incentive pay based on earnings. Supervisors were becoming more cost conscious.

There were more than 30,000 employees in Seattle and Wichita now. A substantial organization. There were 1,700 supervisors, 2,700 men in the engineering department. When Allen looked at those figures he could get enthusiastic, but what made him squirm with unrest was the precipitous descent of the curve on the employment chart in about a year, when the B-50 work would be thinned out. It would be worse if the B-54 were cancelled.

When twenty-three more C-97 transports were ordered in January, the curve looked a little better, but twenty-three planes couldn't keep the factory going long.

Ralph Bell had an idea. Why not make a flying tanker out of the C-97 instead of using B-29s as tankers? The C-97 had B-50 performance. It had a big body for fuel tanks. Engineer Byron Galt, who was working out the Flying Boom installation for the B-29, said the boom could be adapted to the C-97.

Strategic Air Command liked the idea, but the thought of buying a whole new fleet of tankers when the B-29s could be fixed over at low cost, had little appeal to those in Washington who had to dig up the money. Other kinds of equipment were needed more. Bombers.

"Your own B-47 is going to take a big share of our procurement funds," they said.

In February 1949, Majors R. E. Schleeh and Joe Howell set out in a B-47 from Moses Lake on what was supposed to be a routine flight to Washington, to demonstrate the 47 in an air show. They streaked into Washington in three hours, forty-six minutes.

"Sorry we had to set a record," said Schleeh, reporting in. "The plane gets its best fuel economy at that speed." The old law that said to double the speed you'd have to use eight times the power seemed out of date now. It was still true for the kind of planes it was talking about, but here was a plane that made best use of its power when you doubled the speed.

Schleeh said the difficult thing about the flight was tuning the radio, trying to get the next station tuned in before it was too far behind. They gave up and navigated over the cloud tops by radio compass. The 607-miles-an-hour average speed over the 2,290-mile flight, the blossoming pink parachute that was used to slow down the plane on landing, and the smoke-trailing JATO take-off demonstration for the President and congressional committees a few days later, rallied support behind a plan for fifteen, then thirty of the Stratojets per month to be produced in the Wichita plant.

"More ships to refuel," thought Ralph Bell, still after the C-97 tanker idea. "It's going to be tough refueling Stratojets from a slow B-29."

In-flight refueling got its first real test in March. Eight B-29 tankers with British hose-type equipment—the Flying Boom equipment wasn't yet installed—were deployed around the globe, two each at the Azores, Saudi Arabia, the Philippines, Hawaii. Captain James Gallagher and a thirteen-man crew took off from Fort Worth, Texas in the B-50 *Lucky Lady II*, and headed east.

First night, Saturday night, Gallagher sat in his glass enclosure under the stars, out over the black Atlantic, and contemplated his assignment: hold a course, meet his refueling planes, work his way around the globe while it twisted around on its axis four times, then set down again at Fort Worth.

Sunday morning the Azores appeared. The B-29 tankers. Another day. Relief shift. Sunday night. Again they were alone with the stars, nothing visible below. There was no moon to light it, but the navigator said it was the Sahara Desert.

Monday morning, Gallagher tried to figure out the best thing to do about the odd day-and-night situation. It was getting light but it was 10 P.M. Should he set his watch up an hour every four hours? No. That wouldn't do, because then it would take him five days to make the four-day trip and he'd be in Fort Worth Thursday when it was only Wednesday. Still, every time the sun came up and went down was a day, wasn't it? Oh, better let it alone. Too confusing. Endless white clouds below. Out of them, two B-29 tankers. More fuel. More sitting. Monday night. Well, third night, anyway. More water passing under. Bay of Bengal. Pacific. Seemed the globe was mostly water.

An undercast of clouds in the morning. Some holes in them. Philippine jungles. Another refueling. More water, all day and all night.

Wednesday. Sameness. Crew pretty weary, not talking much. Box of Hi Jax crackers still sitting there under Gallagher's window. He ought to move it, clean up ship a little. Be getting home tomorrow. Lots of time though.

Thursday morning. Fort Worth coming up. Thursday morning? Wednesday morning, really. Oh, forget it. Erase a day. What does it matter? Fort Worth coming up, anyway. They'd traveled 23,452 miles nonstop, the navigator said. Seemed more like Forth Worth traveled the 23,452 miles while they were sitting up here, Gallagher thought. "How about that, navigator?" No, if you wanted to be technical, Fort Worth traveled something like 6,000,000 miles along earth's orbit, around earth's axis. The B-50 took a slightly different course through the heavens, traveled the 6,000,000 plus 23,452, and they both were coming out together.

No, that wasn't quite it, either. Solar system was doing some traveling with the earth in it, in the local star system. Local star system was moving in the Milky Way, Milky Way drifting some other direction, one hundred miles a second. Just where had they been, really? Where would they be now if all that traveling had been in another direction? Didn't matter. Fort Worth coming up below. Time to land. A crowd below. The landing. Secretary Symington there to meet them, and General Vandenberg, Chief of Staff of the Air Force. All kinds of congratulations. This was a big day for aviation. "An epochal step in the development of air power," said Symington. "It turns our medium bombers into intercontinental bombers."

"Anywhere, any time, sir," said Gallagher, happily.

The first nonstop flight around the world was at once a proof of the possibilities and an indication of the relatively slow speed of propeller driven planes. The flash flight of the Stratojet across the country the month before, and the inspiring results of wind-tunnel tests on the new XB-52, had the whole engineering department convinced that the day of piston-engined airplanes was withering in a blast of jet power. No one shed a tear when the contract for B-54 advanced Superforts was finally cancelled on April 5, 1949, but all recognized the emergency it created.

Bill Allen pondered the problem that had become evident when the Air Force first insisted the Stratojet must be built at Wichita. Was the home plant being excluded because of its geographical location and vulnerability to attack? Certainly looked that way. Allen went to see Secretary Symington about the vulnerability question. "We are not as close to the coast as many plants," he told the Secretary. "We have to do this job with people. Certain kinds of people. And people have their own ideas of where they want to live. We'd lose a lot of our ability if we tried to move them all inland. If our country has an Achilles heel, won't the enemy strike at that heel wherever it is? Isn't dispersal of industry the answer, rather than just geographical location?"

The Secretary said the matter would be given consideration. In June, Symington wrote that it was in the government's interest to use the facilities at Wichita for B-47 production, but the B-50s, the C-97 transports, and the mock-up of the B-52 should be built in Seattle. The letter didn't ease Allen's concern. The problem was being aired in the newspapers and the community was aroused.

In September the Secretary came to Seattle with K. B. Wolfe, arranged for the plant to install boom-type refueling equipment in 116 B-29s. No objection was voiced to building the B-52 in Seattle. *If* the B-52 were ever to go into production. That prospect was hemmed with doubt. The Administration in Washington, caught between threats to the national security and the threat of inflation at home, was putting on an economy drive. The giant B-52 would be anything but economical.

When the going was tough and things looked insecure, the engineers always had an escape to the land of drawings and hopes. The distant view was both restful and inviting. Engineers relished the thought of bringing that view up closer, where it would no longer be a vision but a realization. Jet transportation? Maynard Pennell, new chief of Preliminary Design, a lanky engineer with casual air and wistful eye, had the conviction that jet transportation was the answer not only to the company's need, but to aviation's as well. It offered all kinds of advantages. A better ride for the passenger, smooth and quick. High operating costs went down when you figured how much more work a jet plane could do in a day. Jet transports could provide new work for the plant, unaffected by military budgets and questions of plant location. Work, too, that was positive and constructive to civilization.

"I guess most of us feel we'd like to work at least a part of our lives on commercial airplanes," Pennell said.

Pennell had quickly caught the contagion of Bob Hage's enthusiasm over jet transports. Out of Bob Hage's studies in 1947 and 1948 they now had three proposed transport designs, small, medium and large. All had sweptback wings, with the wings in a high position as they were in the B-47 and B-52. The two smaller planes had four jets in two pairs of dual pods, the larger had six. When Pennell went over the designs with Ed Wells, Ed was enthusiastic. Beall, too.

But before a view could be brought close there was the practical matter of building a road, and that took money. As vice president of engineering and sales, Wellwood Beall faced that problem. Beall talked with Pan American Airways and soon found that the cost of a jet transport development—$15 million or $20 million for the first prototype airplane—was something no airline could afford. Neither could any airplane manufacturer afford it. Even if they could, there were no regulations worked out by the Civil Aeronautics Authority covering jet operations, and no manufacturer could start without knowing the conditions it had to meet. Nor could the CAA be expected to have regulations worked out yet. Not enough was known about jet transports. None was flying.

In England, the government was sponsoring a program to develop jet transports in a bold bid to capture world air markets. Beall talked to Bill Allen about this threatened competition. "We're stopped dead in our tracks," he said. "We'll never get a jet transport unless our government will finance a prototype. Shall we go after the government?"

Allen met the question with a frown. He didn't see any other way around it, but the proposition had a ring he didn't like. "If the government pays for it, you'll lose control over it, won't you?"

"I don't like it either but what else can we do? If we don't do something, our own airlines will have to buy from the British."

Other manufacturers were puzzling over the dilemma. It was discussed in Aircraft Industry Association meetings. Beall served on a committee with the engineers of other companies to find a solution. In Congress a prototype bill was proposed to provide government financing. But there was no agreement among the companies on its provisions. The Civil Aeronautics Board threw up its hands. "How can we get behind a prototype bill if the industry can't agree on it?" the Board asked.

In September 1949, Ed Wells went to England for a look at what the British were doing. The de Havilland Company had its jet Comet flying and had a production contract for ten from the government-owned airline. Sixteen other types were under development with government assistance. The airlines of other European countries, dollar-poor, were leaning heavily toward the British.

"We'll have to start soon on a prototype if we're going to compete," Wells said on his return. "It will have to be a superior airplane to sell in Europe. Their dollar credits are pretty limited."

Though there was no answer to the financing problem, Wells couldn't get the jet transport out of mind. He was in Dayton with George Schairer and aerodynamicist Johnny Alexander in late October, going over wind-tunnel results on an improved B-52 wing that turned out to be faster than the B-47 wing. There was a weekend to kill. The engineers went over to the Dayton office, sat around talking jet-transport design. "Mostly what we've done so far is hang a transport body on the B-47," said Schairer. "Maybe we ought to take a fresh look."

The 47 and 52 were high-wing airplanes. That didn't work out too well for a transport. The big wing structure had to go through the top of the cabin and passengers would have to duck. If the plane were ever used for cargo, that would be worse. You'd want to put your big cargo up forward but you couldn't get it under the wing center structure. Moreover, the floor would be crowded down low in the circular body, where it would be too narrow. A long wing would be much better. The wing structure would go under the floor, leave a clear cabin and room for passenger baggage underneath. The landing gear would have to be high enough to keep the jet pods off the

ground. "It ought to be a tricycle gear for airline use," said
Wells. "Not the bicycle gear on the bomber." They sketched
a low-wing transport with sweepback, four engines in separate pods under the wings, a tricycle gear folding into the body.

"Not bad," said Schairer.

In Seattle, Preliminary Design worked up a comprehensive
study on a new jet transport along these lines, low-winged,
embodying the superior qualities of the B-52 wing.

Seven thousand employees had been dropped from the Seattle
payroll in the last half of 1949 and business was still sliding. The
hope of guided missile production as a result of successful GAPA
tests suddenly faded when the Defense Department ruled that
Air Force missiles of less than one hundred miles range should be
dropped to avoid duplication of Army developments. Beall was
asked to bring his GAPA people to Dayton to discuss the cancellation. There was a big meeting with Lieutenant General Ben
Chidlaw, head of the Air Material Command, Brigadier General
Sam Brentnall, deputy director of research and development,
and others. Beall started to defend GAPA.

"There's no use talking about GAPA. That's dead. What else
do you have to propose?" the Air Force officers asked.

Beall, caught flat-footed, looked at Bob Jewett. Jewett and
his engineers had been giving some study to a new electronic
guidance system that would work for a longer-range defensive
missile, but he wasn't prepared.

"Shall we tell them what we've been thinking about?" Jewett
asked Beall.

"Go ahead."

The proposal was complex, involving a good deal of ground
equipment. The officers were interested. "We have the University of Michigan working on something like that. Why don't
you go see them. Maybe you can bring us a joint proposal."

The Boeing pilotless aircraft group was trimmed to fifty men,
with GAPA coming to an end, but the remnant of engineers

went to work with the University of Michigan on a new study they hoped would fill GAPA's place.

The B-52 program was meanwhile becoming an issue as mammoth as the airplane itself, now grown, on paper, to 390,000 pounds gross in order to provide fuel capacity for the desired range. When President Truman announced that Russia had exploded an atom bomb, Washington grew tense over the question of its own atom-carrying planes. What kind of equipment would provide the best security for the country? Cost and delivery estimates were prepared in January on production quantities of B-52 Stratofortresses. Bruce Connelly, director of contract administration, took the figures to Dayton. Dayton passed them to Washington. There was general alarm. Fifteen million dollars per plane for thirteen airplanes.

The big propeller-driven Consolidated B-36 was now in full production. Many thought the Air Force should stick with it. Others felt the B-47 Stratojet, much less costly than the B-52, would be sufficient though Curtis LeMay, heading the Strategic Air Command, was still calling for more range.

A consulting organization was commissioned by the government to study the whole military and economic problem. It concluded that planes larger than 150,000 pounds, faster than four hundred knots, were too costly to be included in the military program. Problems of maintenance and handling were too great. The responsibility would be more than the average flight crew could stand. The country's economy couldn't support such planes.

Bill Allen protested. "But the 52 is the plane the Air Force needs."

9. *Tankers, Transports, Threats*

Fourteen hundred more employees were dropped from the payroll by May of 1950, with the completion of the Stratocruiser project. The last of the fifty-five transports was set for delivery to British Overseas Airways Corporation. BOAC invited Beall to come along on the final delivery flight. Beall relaxed in Stratocruiser luxury across the Atlantic, wishing Boeing could stay in the transport business. With the factory tooled for the plane, additional sales could pay back the losses on the initial quantity. They'd need bigger engines. Turboprop engines, a more likely prospect than they had been two years ago, could be installed without much change. They would make the Stratocruiser an attractive product in the period before a pure jet transport could be put on the market, Beall felt, although his heart was more with the pure jet design which the sales department was now showing to U. S. airlines.

In England, Beall reacted to the British jet progress just as Ed Wells had eight months ago. The Comet had been making a hit. When he got back, Beall dispatched aerodynamicist Jack Steiner and sales engineer Ken Luplow to canvass European airlines with Boeing jet plans. But the effort seemed lame. The bill to provide government financing of a jet prototype was a dead issue. There was no other approach, unless Boeing itself could dig up maybe $15 million to gamble. That was three times the company's total profits in the four years since the war. "I could never get Bill Allen to go for that," Beall thought. "He's trying to get the company in better shape financially."

Still, there could be no doubt that jet transportation was coming, sooner or later. Wasn't Boeing the logical company to bring out a jet transport? What other American company was building large jet airplanes? What other company, American or European, had put 10,000 wind-tunnel hours, 5,000,000 engineering man-hours into perfecting jet design? Beall stepped through the side door that connected his office with Bill Allen's. "Bill," he said, "we've got to get you over to England to see what's going on in jet transports."

Beall kept working on Allen about the trip whenever he got a chance. A more likely prospect than the jet transport right now, however, was the building of a fleet of tankers out of the C-97 transport design. Ralph Bell's C-97 proposal had met partial acceptance. Wright Field contracted in June for three of the planes to be equipped as tankers. The feeling of insecurity over Russian intentions was growing. People were seeing flying saucers in the sky. If there were war, there'd be a scramble for new equipment and the first thing the Air Force would want would be tankers that could refuel the new Stratojet bombers, Beall felt. He had Engineering work up a study on a turboprop version of the C-97.

On June 25, 1950, the strained line between Communism and containment broke at the 38th Parallel in Korea. The United Nations Security Council voted to oppose the aggression of North Korea. Less than five years out of war, America was at war again. Not a whole war. It seemed local. But to those who'd have to go there and fight, it would seem as big as any. And the possibility of a bigger conflict fired new debate in Washington over the B-52. Curtis LeMay from Strategic Air Command headquarters would not argue the point. "We've got to have it," was all he said. Thomas Finletter, the new Secretary of the Air Force, and Undersecretary John McCone were strong for Strategic Air Command, but the first need was for tactical equipment for the Korean campaign. And, after all, the prototype XB-52 hadn't yet been built and flown.

The unsettled questions of B-52 orders, C-97 tanker orders, hung on Bill Allen's mind but he had agreed to make the trip to Europe. He had married recently and his wife, the former

Mary Ellen Agen, would go with him. Preliminary Design chief
Maynard Pennell would go too. They'd meet Ken Luplow,
whom Beall had stationed in Europe, and visit the various European airlines. On the way, Allen wanted to stop in Wichita to
check on B-47 production progress and get a flight in a B-47.
He hadn't had a chance to fly in one of the ships yet.

   The hour was growing late when the plant business was finished and Earl Schaefer took Allen out to the Wichita flight
line. The Stratojet's engines were already going. Allen's senses
were a mixture of sound and emotion as he got into coveralls
and parachute harness. That great jet roar he had often heard in
the sky—he was about to become one with it. He climbed up
the rungs of the aluminum ladder, through the bottom hatch into
the narrow aisleway below the tandem positions of pilot and
co-pilot. Pilot Doug Heimburger was in the forward seat, in
his parachute and headgear, just about filling the gadget-packed
space that was allowed for him, his head up in the slender sky
canopy. Somehow Heimburger looked part of the airplane, the
final part that put it in business, where it had always looked in-
complete in the factory.
   Co-pilot Ed Hartz showed Allen to his place, the navigator's
position right out in the bullet nose. Hartz explained the bail-out
levers, how to use his parachute, how to connect his oxygen
mask to the ship's supply, how to connect it to his bail-out
bottle in case of emergency, how to plug the cord from his
helmet into the interphone, how to push the button on the cord
if he wanted to talk. Allen's head was swimming. There were
decals with printed instructions all around him, emergency procedures. He fastened his heavy seat belt. "Go ahead and fly it.
I'll be O.K."
   "Would you like us to do some test maneuvers?"
   "No, just a plain flight. I want to see what jet transportation
would be like."
   Hartz nodded, went back to his place.
   The roar of the jets was increasing. But it blanked out when

Allen put on his headgear. He fussed with his oxygen mask, hoping to get it right before they took off. Its soft rubber edges were a hand gripping his nose and mouth and cheeks. He watched the white lines of the flow meter beside him come on and off as he took a breath and felt clean, cool oxygen going down. Sharp voices were coming through the ear pads of his helmet. "Ready, Ed?"

"Roger."

"Mr. Allen, are you ready for take-off?"

Allen fumbled for the button, heard the strange voice of himself in his headgear, "All set." It was clipped short, like the others. His eye swept the instruments that encased him. He felt himself irrevocably connected to a tight new world of gross unfamiliarity. He had seen it often before but it had suddenly become real, a live, almost grotesque mechanical assembly of controlled power, about to be unleashed with him inside.

The cement runway was moving beneath his nose windows, wheeling around, stopping. There was chatter in his helmet. Conversation with the tower about clearance. The roar that had seemed distant suddenly swelled.

"Power stabilized, let's go," cracked the voice of Heimburger, all in one short breath, and they were moving down the runway for take-off. Without a quiver they were off the ground and the nose was pointed high. A great, smooth feeling such as Allen had never felt before. Going up, wind-swift. It was so easy, as if no power were required, merely a hand on some lever that gradually switched off gravity. Power had always been synonymous with vibration, motion and noise. All these seemed absent. They were just going up.

Allen looked at the navigator's bank of instruments. The big hand on the altimeter was turning round like the hand of a clock that's being set. He looked up through the overhead window, saw cloud fleece slipping by; looked out the side and back: the tips of the swept wings were far behind. Everything was still, no propellers turning, just the ground moving farther and farther away.

They leveled off at 20,000 feet. A firm, authoritative pull indicated they were going into a turn and Allen had his first real sense of tremendous power and speed. It wasn't so much a turning, it could better be described as a change in heading, as the Stratojet cut a great arc in its wide, high sky and straightened on a new course. Allen adjusted himself in his seat, settled back against his bulky parachute, began to feel comfortable. He was enjoying it.

When the Stratojet headed down again it was an unexpectedly steep race, bottomless down. Heimburger was calling for clearance to enter "the pattern" and instructions for best approach to the field. They were gently leveling. The runway came up to meet them, touched under them, raced on by, then came to a stop. Allen untied himself and walked back the narrow corridor to thank Heimburger and Hartz. "I had no idea it could be so smooth," he told them. He climbed down through the hatch with heavy gear and light heart, met Earl Schaefer's waiting smile. Bill Allen was delighted and proud.

The ride to Chicago, New York, and out over the Atlantic in propeller-driven transports seemed slow and prosaic after the whip-quick flight of the Stratojet, but afforded Allen a chance to do some summing up. The question of future business was all mixed with the question of war and peace. In Allen's lifetime there had been two great wars; and now, a third? The first had been fought to "make the world safe for democracy." The second was a new battle for freedom. The world didn't stay free long. Not Eastern Europe. Not Asia. The notion that people could be free to live their own lives, in free competition and cooperation—why was it always being assaulted, first by emperor, then by dictator, then by a rule called communism, more correctly Soviet state socialism?

Socialism was an insidious thing, moving in the guise of helping people until they found they were no longer allowed to help themselves. Even England, grand old Winston Churchill's England, was now partly under its influence, and setting up to rival

America's aircraft industry with government-supported jet transport development.

That nettled Allen. Was the State the only power that could get things done? Dr. Charles Malik, Minister to the United States from the little country of Lebanon, had put it about as straight as anyone: "That the State, the mere organ of government and order, is the source of every law, every truth, every norm of conduct, every social and economic relationship; that no science, no music, no economic activity, no philosophy, no art, no theology, is to be permitted except if it is State-licensed and State-controlled: all this is so false, so arrogant, so autocratic and tyrannical that no man who has drunk deep from the living waters of western Platonic-Christian tradition can possibly accept it. The State does not come in first place; it comes in tenth or fifteenth place. The university is higher than the State; the tradition of free inquiry is higher than the State; the Church is higher than the State; the family is higher than the State; natural law is higher than the State; God is higher than the State; within limits, free economic activity is higher than the State."

Free economic activity. Could free economic activity ever develop a costly thing like a jet transport? Allen wanted to think that it could.

When he arrived in London, the newspapers were full of an arresting development in Korea. U. S. planes had shot down a twin-engine enemy aircraft bearing Soviet star markings. The crewman whose body was recovered was a Russian. There was excitement and apprehension in the tight-packed streets of the world's largest city.

Another kind of excitement was the big annual air show of the Society of British Aircraft Constructors at Farnborough. C. F. Uwins, managing director of the aircraft division of the Bristol Airplane Company, called for Allen at the Hotel Connaught the morning he was to go to Farnborough.

"It's quite a remarkable show this year," said the British executive. "Comet and all."

The field at Farnborough was surrounded by grassy slopes where thousands of spectators were watching the different planes pass low in review. When the de Havilland Comet was announced, a low murmur rose from the crowd. "This aircraft," said the announcer, "has an unrivaled cruising speed of 490 miles per hour at 35,000 to 42,000 feet. An aircraft with extraordinary commercial capabilities."

The Comet was approaching, a low-wing monoplane attractively painted with silver on the underside, white on top, and a dividing flash line of blue. Its wings, just slightly swept back, bulged with four buried jet engines. The plane passed low over the field at full jet speed, then pulled gracefully up. "A magnificent combination of speed and beauty," said the announcer. "Note the aircraft's docile handling characteristics."

Allen was impressed. "Appears to be a fine airplane," he told Uwins.

That night Allen joined Mrs. Allen, Maynard Pennell and Ken Luplow at a late dinner. Pennell and Luplow had seen the show with Gil Stevenson, Boeing service engineer.

"How did you like the Comet?" asked Allen.

"It's a very good airplane," said Pennell.

"Do you think Boeing could build one as good?"

"Oh, better. Much better." Pennell's voice sprang out as though it had been waiting months for this opportunity. But the business of ordering the meal interrupted them.

"What would you have different from the Comet?" Allen asked after a while.

"We think pods are much better than buried engines," Pennell said. "And we could provide a much better landing flap. We'd probably give it more sweepback, too."

"Everyone over here is anxious to know if Boeing is going to build a commercial jet airplane, Mr. Allen," Luplow said.

Allen didn't respond to that.

Luplow tried again. "Boeing should have a tremendous advantage with all the engineering and wind-tunnel testing that's gone into the B-47 and B-52."

"Do you fellows think a jet transport would be a reasonable project for us to undertake, in view of our heavy commitments on the B-47 and the B-52?" Allen asked.

"I do," said Pennell. Luplow vigorously concurred.

"Why?"

"I think we're in much better shape than we were when we took on the B-29 on top of our B-17 commitments," said Pennell. "We were pretty successful on the 29."

The discussion went on. Pennell and Luplow couldn't tell just how Allen was reacting, except that he kept bringing up the tremendous cost.

Later, while Luplow drove the Allens about the continent to visit heads of airlines, he kept up a discreet offensive, but Allen held his silence. Airline presidents put the question directly. "Does Boeing plan to bring out a jet transport?"

"We're reviewing it," said Allen.

When Allen got back to Seattle, facing up to an accumulated deskload of paper and the hard facts of present and future, the romantic view of a jet transport seemed unreal. U. S. airlines weren't crying for the jet. The Air Force wasn't interested. To start such a project without big orders seemed unthinkable. Why, it might be pouring millions of dollars down the drain. There wasn't any money like that to throw around.

Besides, there were projects nearer at hand to be taken care of. An order had been received for 231 piston-engined C-97 transports to be used as tankers. KC-97s, they'd be called. Beall and Fred Collins were trying hard to sell the Air Force a follow-up model of the C-97 with turboprop engines, and to sell some turboprop Stratocruisers to the airlines along with them. Bob Jewett, Dick Nelson and the missile engineers had come up with a plan for a new interceptor missile development program, worked out with the scientists of the University of Michigan's Aeronautical Research Center. It was called Bomarc, combining the name "Boeing" and the initials of the Michigan group. But it hadn't yet been sold to the Air Force. There was production trouble with the B-47s in Wichita. The XB-52, under construction in Seattle, was a prodigious job and appeared to be facing delays in getting power plants and pneumatic equipment.

In November 1950, the siren of world emergency began screaming again. Communist China entered the war in Korea. The fire in that remote land was spreading. There was a United Nations but no agreement in it. The nations had chosen sides. Were they heading down the path to World War III? Everyone wondered and shuddered at the thought. No, it couldn't happen. Just couldn't.

In the Pentagon in Washington, the concern had grown vital. The United States had embarked on development of the hydrogen bomb. First it was nuclear fission, now nuclear fusion, to release the titanic might of the atom. Secretary Finletter was convinced Communist Russia was at work on a fusion bomb also. And if fusion bombs, then weapons to carry them. What did America have for a deterrent? Guided missiles? None perfected. Jet bombers? No B-47s delivered. XB-52 unflown. Only the B-52 and the slower B-36 had the range Curtis LeMay was demanding. Secretary Finletter visited Seattle. "It's of utmost importance that you get the XB-52 out fast," he told Allen. "Do everything you can to expedite it."

Finletter and General Vandenberg were thinking seriously about putting the B-52 in production before flight of the prototype, to gain time in the international race. Budget officers still stood aghast at the cost figures. Fifteen million each for the next thirteen. The first two airplanes, originally estimated to cost $32 million, had turned out to cost $53 million. "We couldn't possibly afford it," they said.

Robert Lovett, Deputy Secretary of Defense who had gotten behind the B-29 program before World II, interposed. "It's absurd to say we can't afford to survive," he said.

The Air Force Senior Officers Board came to Seattle in November to hear production proposals for the B-52: Lieutenant Generals Ben Chidlaw, K. B. Wolfe and I. H. Edwards, Major Generals Gordon Saville, Carl Brandt. There was a dead serious ring to the meetings. It was evident the Air Force meant business.

Beall presented to the board, too, the proposal for a turboprop KC-97 tanker-transport. It could be built as a continuation of the regular KC-97 contract, using much of the same tooling and giving the Air Force a higher performance model at low cost. There was no Air Force interest in the turboprop tanker. At a coffee break, General Brandt said it just wasn't a big enough improvement to be of any value.

"Why don't you put jets on it?" Brandt asked.

Beall looked at Ed Wells. Seemed they'd been through this before. With the B-52.

10. *The Case for the 707*

After the meeting with the Air Force Senior Officers Board, design work was started at once on an advanced tanker-transport, applying jet power to the KC-97, with its wings swept back twenty-five degrees. When a request came from Wright Field in January 1951 for proposals on tankers capable of refueling a B-52, this design seemed the logical answer. The order for propeller-driven KC-97s was going into production and much of the same tooling could be used for the jet version. It would provide a practical way also to get a commercial jet transport going, Beall felt hopefully.

The Bomarc guided missile project was now going ahead, with a development contract awarded in January. Then a letter contract came through in February authorizing start of production on thirteen B-52s, though Secretary Finletter cautioned that future orders would be determined in competition with a new version of the Consolidated B-36, to be called B-60. The Air Force had given Consolidated approval to bend back the

wings of the 36 and install eight jet engines in four dual pods
to provide an intercontinental jet at less cost than for a whole
new plane. Boeing was asked to furnish engineering data on its
jet pods for use on the competing plane, which was supposed to
be flying before the end of the year. It would be a close race
to get the XB-52 in the air by then.

"That's all right," Bill Allen said at staff meeting. "We're in
favor of competition. We have the opportunity of proving our
airplane is the best. That's all we ask. If the competition can
beat us, we have no complaints. But it had better not."

The Communist threat that had sparked the start on thirteen
B-52s before the prototype was flown, was putting a like pressure on B-47 Stratojet production. Demand for the Stratojets
was war-urgent. Not for Korea, but to strengthen the defenses
of the North Atlantic Treaty Organization, in case of Communist aggression in Europe. In January and February, the Air
Force called on Douglas and Lockheed to produce B-47s and
once again, as in World War II, Boeing assumed the double
load of building the planes and providing the data with which
others could build them.

The pressure to get combat-ready Stratojets out of Wichita
was causing a second Battle of Kansas. The Stratojet was a far
different airplane than the B-29, the plant crews were finding.
Its aluminum wing skin was ⅝ inch thick, for high-speed
strength, then was machined gradually down to ³⁄₁₆ inch so it
wouldn't be too heavy at the wing tips. It had to be fitted
with 6,000 bolt holes drilled to tolerances of one or two thou-
sandths of an inch, less than the thickness of a hair. Four hundred
sixty parts had to be precise enough in fit to be interchangeable
between airplanes. Doors and moving parts that fit on the ground
had to fit also in the air, when the airplane would have a different shape, because it was designed to flex with the hard bumps
at high Mach number speeds.

The work of 139 different subcontractors had to be coordinated. Design changes were coming through daily to harass

the shops. Twenty-one hundred changes so far, mostly providing for combat equipment. Much of the equipment hadn't yet been perfected, especially the electronic devices that would aim the tail guns and the bombs. Aiming guns at six hundred miles an hour, a speed that carried you two blocks in the time it took to say "B-47," was a new challenge to the electronics equipment manufacturers. The devices they came up with, containing 259 miles of wire, didn't all work together when they were finally hooked up with 15,000 pieces of wire in the airplane.

"I don't think people realize what we're up against," said Earl Schaefer. "The B-47 has to perform the same mission the B-29 did but at twice the speed and nearly twice the altitude, with seven fewer crew members. It all has to be done with push buttons."

Engineers were trying to unravel the electronics problem and a dozen others when General Carl Brandt and Colonel Loran Anderson from Washington came to Wichita March 2. "The truth is that we can't drop a bomb from the B-47," said Brandt abruptly. "Either the airplane must drop bombs effectively and soon, or there is no need for it."

Earl Schaefer pointed out the problem of working over equipment that was bought by the government directly from suppliers.

"I know," said Brandt. "The thinking now in Washington is that the airplane manufacturer has got to be made responsible in the future for the whole weapons system, not just the airplane. But that doesn't help us now. Our problem is, if the B-47's going to be any good to the Air Force, we've got to make these systems work."

Next day Pete Jansen, production consultant to Major General Orval Cook, the director of procurement, visited Wichita. He didn't see how the plant could meet the rapid schedule build-up with so many inexperienced people. The payroll had suddenly exploded from 1,400 to 18,000. Jansen recommended the whole schedule be set back sixty days. Schaefer called Bill Allen. "We're in trouble."

Allen told Beall and Laudan to take their staff heads to Wichita and get things straightened out. The delegation spent a week there.

"Everyone down here is making a terrific effort," Beall reported back. There was no easy answer. Just effort.

Undersecretary for Air John McCone, pushing the B-47 program, came to Wichita with General Cook in May to check up. Bill Allen met them. There were dozens of problems discussed but things seemed to be smoothing out. Schaefer said production would be brought up to schedule by fall.

After the meeting, Allen took off with McCone for Washington in an Air Force transport. A B-47 was taking off about the same time. "Ask him to fly by," McCone told his pilot. The Stratojet darted past. McCone whistled. It made the transport seem to be backing up. The Stratojet cut across out in front, circled, and overtook them again. Then again. Its crew was enjoying the spree.

"Why don't you build a commercial airplane so we can go like that, instead of riding around in this covered wagon?" asked McCone.

Allen unzipped his brief case. "Mr. Undersecretary, I'm glad you brought that up." He pulled out a folder on the jet-powered, advanced C-97 military transport.

"Have you shown this to the Air Force?" McCone asked.

"Sure. But we're not having any success," said Allen.

It was in August 1951, that the company's proposal to turn the KC-97 line into a jet tanker-transport line was up for decision in the Air Force. Debate was heavy: "Boeing already has too many Air Force projects." "The money's needed for bombers." "B-47s can be made into jet tankers at less cost." On August 17 came the verdict. Negative. The hope of a military jet transport faded.

But the sales department felt the airline interest in jets was growing, and the Air Force would eventually come around.

"Can't we build a prototype model on speculation?" Fred Collins asked. "If we had one flying we could sell it."

Bill Allen cut him down.

"Whose money are you spending?"

Allen felt the military decision against the advanced KC-97 couldn't be allowed to stand. "We've got to keep pushing it hard," he told the staff. "It's too good an airplane for them not to buy."

There were new reverses in the second Battle of Kansas during the fall of 1951. Production hadn't come up to schedule. Pete Jansen was hired to help analyze the problem. It was manifold. Lack of B-47 experience in supervision and labor. Inability to employ new skilled help because of competition with booming civilian industry. Trying to increase production rapidly when the product was still under development. Scores of items of equipment that wouldn't work.

Critically needed skills were brought in on loan from the Seattle plant. But to keep the production lines clear, unfinished planes had to be lined up on the ramp. It was raining: forty-five inches of rainfall by September, worst in Kansas history. Sixty-eight Stratojets in a row made the "aluminum-plated" ramp beautiful to the eye, but not to factory manager Al Schupp.

The bullet-sealing fuel tanks kept developing leaks. Finally N. D. Showalter decided the tanks from one rubber company would all have to be removed and replaced by tanks from another supplier. When the troubles with automatic firing equipment, purchased by the government from a radio manufacturer, wouldn't yield to months of tenacious tinkering, the Air Force made the painful decision the whole system would have to be abandoned in favor of one developed by another manufacturer, though the new equipment wouldn't be available for months. It was tough to let go of things you'd struggled to make work, with someone always promising a solution just around the corner.

"The hardest problem," said Beall, "is to recognize you have a problem."

In Seattle there was another problem that wouldn't yield. The Air Force decision against the advanced KC-97 tanker-transport wouldn't be reversed. Bill Allen made the rounds of Washington in October. He talked to General Cook, Chief of Staff Nate Twining, Roswell Gilpatric, new Undersecretary of the Air Force, then tried Admiral Thomas Combs of the Navy. No sale.

Beall called a meeting of engineering and sales heads. Faces were long. "We've lost this skirmish," said Beall. "We've got to fall back and regroup. Let's start over, see if we can come up with a jet transport design that will be salable, either to the military or the airlines." Ed Wells thought it should be a faster airplane, with a full thirty-five degrees sweepback. Maynard Pennell wanted to abandon the C-97 body and dust off the development work that had been done in late 1949 and 1950, before the big effort to make the C-97 into a jet. Chief project engineer George Martin thought it could be "slicked up a lot."

Fred Collins, Ralph Bell and Ken Gordon of Sales canvassed the airlines, Military Air Transport Service, Strategic Air Command, to get their ideas, and Engineering went to work on the ideas. The air was clearer now. Open horizon. No "built-in head-winds" of old designs to be carried along. Just the question, "What will make the best airplane?"

A design labeled "Model 707" gradually took form. It made the Advanced KC-97 seem out of date. Performance estimates went up. It looked good.

But a transport design on paper was a long way from an airplane going together in the shops, just as a B-52 started in initial production was a long way from assurance of continued quantity production, and a big plant and big personnel a long way from assurance they would be kept busy. The stakes were big. War, near-war, technical advance, jet power had built a business that couldn't rest. Its only security was in progress, just as the airplane's only flight stability was in moving ahead, up to speed. It took a great collection of abilities to make the business go, and it had to keep going to keep the abilities. Couldn't stall.

Nor would the business fly on dreams. Vision wasn't dreaming, it was seeing through to the accomplishment. That was the test. Bill Allen faced this, and knew that what he faced was himself. Was he being the kind of leader that the need demanded? As alive as the business? He was no dictator, he knew that. But he didn't believe men did their best work under that kind of a regime. A dictator's followers perspired while a leader inspired his followers. Allen knew that to inspire, he had to be inspired.

But that wasn't hard. Not when there was an airplane like the XB-52 coming along. He loved to walk out in Final Assembly and gaze at it, massive in its metallic beauty. The thing that really moved him was the thought that this was the work of men. Boeing men. Bill Allen was going to see to it that those men had a chance to keep going the way they were going. He was going to see to it, if anybody could. Wasn't that what the country needed?

When vice president–controller John Yeasting balanced the figures for 1951, Bill Allen began to feel a substance behind the hopes for the future. Net earnings, though amounting to only 2 per cent of sales, totalled $7 million. Better still, Yeasting's estimates showed that earnings should be doubled in 1952 because deliveries should be doubled, with both C-97 and B-47 schedules coming up fast.

Allen got the board of directors to approve a $14 million program of new facilities that Beall and Wells said they should have: a B-52 flight test hangar, a new engineering building to help house the expanded 6,000-man engineering force, a revamping of the Edmund T. Allen Memorial wind tunnel that would take its speed above that of sound. The best way to get Air Force business was to qualify for it.

Allen was concerned about the problem of Wichita, where B-47 production was still the subject of Air Force criticism. He had wanted to think the Wichita organization was pulling itself out of the hole. But Bill Irvine, troubleshooting the B-47 program for General Cook and General Vandenberg, came to Seattle in December 1951, and spoke with painful clarity.

"Wichita is 1,500 miles away from Seattle and it isn't getting the engineering attention that's needed," Irvine said.

Allen tried to reassure him. "We've sent all kinds of men down there. Our people are back and forth all the time."

"That isn't enough," said Irvine. "The whole country's defense is tied up in Wichita."

Allen realized it was time for major moves. He named Wellwood Beall senior vice president to coordinate operations of both Seattle and Wichita. Clellen Gracey, operations vice president at Seattle, was moved to Wichita as vice president in charge of manufacturing. N. D. Showalter was made chief engineer of the Wichita division. Heads of the functional divisions at Seattle were given policy responsibility for Wichita functions. Staff men and supervisors were moved. There was a general beefing up of Wichita at the expense of Seattle. Things began to straighten. Had they been "fighting the problem" of building up Wichita, as K. B. Wolfe once said? Wellwood Beall, adjusting under a new load, again reflected: "Our biggest problem is to recognize when we have a problem."

Perhaps it was clearing up one problem that uncovered another. Or perhaps it was John Yeasting's healthy cash forecast that stimulated Allen to uncover it and take a good look at what was there: the problem of jet transport. Ed Wells had brought in the new 707 design and Allen could tell by the look on Ed's face that he was sold on it, wanted to build it, in the worst way.

Allen had been watching the XB-52. He felt sure there'd be bigger production orders for it when it got in the air for a demonstration. Once the Air Force got these jet bombers there would surely be a need for jet tankers. It didn't make any sense any other way. He felt sure, too, that jet airplanes would sooner or later be used on the airlines. Everyone acknowledged that. Boeing was best equipped with the experience to build those airplanes. But time was going by. The government wasn't buying any. The airlines weren't making a move. The Boeing lead in jets wouldn't last forever. Other companies would be getting busy. And the British would have the Comet in airline operation very soon. Allen knew Boeing could build a better plane. If only it had a market.

But might not there be a market if there were a real flying jet transport to demonstrate? A good jet transport. Boeing could make it a good one. The company would have the money to do it. They had the design. They had the enthusiasm for it. They all wanted to be in the transport business. Now was the time.

Act, get things done, move forward. Now was the hour of decision. *Make Boeing even greater.* It was up to him. Could he risk it? The organ of Allen's mind was playing quick, high notes. He rang for his secretary.

"I'd like you to call a meeting in my office. Call Beall, Ed Wells, John Yeasting, Fred Laudan, Collins. Make it for eleven o'clock." It was a few minutes to eleven now. Miss Heiser nodded, stepped out.

Everything added up. This was the thing to do. It would be a gamble. But wasn't it a good gamble? It would be a good one if they made it succeed. The board of directors. The stockholders, whose money they'd be spending. They'd have to go into it very thoroughly, make sure they weren't just being carried away by enthusiasm. Make sure they could do the job. He called Miss Heiser again.

"I'd like to dictate a memo. Have six copies for the meeting. This will be a questionnaire." He dictated a string of questions about the practicability of building a jet prototype: cost, facilities, the purpose it would serve, organization required.

The men were arriving. He told them what was on his mind. Miss Heiser brought the questionnaires in while the meeting was in progress. They all read it. Allen looked around the room.

"Take plenty of time to study out the answers," he said. "We don't want to make a mistake."

In the following weeks, one by one, the answers were coming out "Yes." Emphatic. A rumor went around that something big was about to break. Spring was full of promise. In the midst of it, Beall announced the XB-52 was ready for flight.

April 15, 1952. Tall, rangy "Tex" Johnston, who'd worn his Texas boots on every important flight since he won the Thompson trophy race in 1946, would pilot the intercontinental giant. Colonel Guy Townsend, B-47 enthusiast, would be co-pilot. The day was bright. General Mark Bradley, Air Force director of procurement and production, was at the plant. Bill Allen and Beall went with him over to the field. The product of an effort now seven years old, its eight jet engines sweeping forward out of sweptback wings, its sharklike tail fin jutting four stories high, was going to reveal in a few minutes whether it would qualify as America's deterrent to enemy aggression. It was poised at the north end of the 10,000-foot runway.

People crowding office windows, the ramp, the roof, waited in suspense. The roar of jet thrust filled eardrums and hearts. The airplane began to move. Slow, like a ship under sail, at first. How could it be so slow, wondered Allen, standing on the ramp. He leaned forward, urging it. Tex was lumbering toward them, gaining momentum, thundering with power, deafening power going past them.

"Pour it," Allen shouted, his fist following after the ship in a haymaker sweep. "Pour her on!" The Stratofortress was accelerating rapidly now, as a jet does once its own speed adds power to its power, and was lifting easily, even lightly into the air.

Tex went on up, circled, and raced back over the field, saying with a sky-cracking roar that the airplane was O.K., doing great.

"It's marvelous," said General Mark Bradley, shaking his head.

Two hours, fifty-one minutes in the air proved basic flying qualities sound. More flights disclosed less drag and more speed even than expected. The Air Force left little doubt that the B-52 production program would go ahead.

Just six days after the Stratofort's first flight, the meeting to answer Allen's questions on a jet transport convened. Jim Barton of Cost Accounting said the prototype could be built for $13 million to $15 million. Maynard Pennell said the plane would meet the range requirements of a military tanker and would have three times the work capacity of the C-97. As a commercial airplane its seat-mile operating cost would be competitive. Schairer said the same prototype could be used to demonstrate both a military and a commercial transport and could provide the performance data needed for production airplanes. Chief engineer Lysle Wood said engineering manpower was available. Experimental manager Al Jacobson said manufacturing manpower and floor space would be available. Beall said Pratt & Whitney would have engines. John Yeasting said the prototype would provide the cost figures needed for pricing production models.

Allen sent the answers to the board of directors and called a board meeting for April 22. Ralph Bell, Pennell, Schairer, Lysle Wood put charts up on easels, the case for the 707, then retired to an anteroom to await the decision. There was discussion in the meeting, but no controversy. Allen recommended the project be undertaken. A motion was made and seconded, unanimously passed. America would have a jet transport.

11. *Missiles and Nuclear Weapons*

Vision was seeing the opportunity, not the limitation. Once the opportunity was seen, the limitation began to disappear, the course was set. The organization of the job of building a prototype jet transport followed the April 22, 1952, board meeting lightning-fast. Target date for flight was May 20, 1954. Basic design was established by July 1952. The prototype would be a 190,000-pound low-wing monoplane, 128 feet long, wings swept back thirty-five degrees. It would be built with a cargo body for demonstration to the military, but airline passenger arrangements would carry eighty to 130 passengers. Four jet engines would give a speed of 550 miles an hour. Safety analysis showed four separate pods would be better than the two dual pods of the preliminary design. The landing gear would be tricycle. George Schairer, now chief of technical staff, surveyed the drawings. "Not too different from the sketches we had back in Dayton that Sunday afternoon in 1949," he observed.

Senior project engineer Maynard Pennell and his staff began getting drawings to the shops. A walled-off portion of the Renton plant kept the project secret. Bill Ramsden of Experimental put Joe Donnelly in charge as shop superintendent. Bill Allen went over often to see how work was coming.

B-47 Stratojets were now flowing on schedule at Wichita, one a day. Proud of the Wichita team's rally, Earl Schaefer and manufacturing vice president Clellen Gracey displayed a record of 1.4 man-hours per pound of airplane for the three hundredth Stratojet, compared with 1.7 for the three hundredth B-29 back in 1944. Curtis LeMay's Strategic Air Command had its first wing of jets operating in September. Renton-built KC-97 tankers with flying booms were in the air to refuel them.

November 1, a hydrogen "device" dwarfing the A-bomb in power was exploded. The Air Force called for more B-52 Stratofortresses as carriers of the potential new weapon. The Bikini demonstration raised grave concern in Washington over possible similar weapons in enemy hands. It spurred not only production plans but also work on new bomber development. Study was under way at Boeing and other plants on the application of nuclear power to airplane propulsion. It appeared that this would be well in the future, however, and other plans were pressed. An advanced bomber with promise was coming out of Preliminary Design. Wright Field evaluated it in competition with proposals from other companies. They wanted more performance, wanted it built in less time than Seattle could promise. In December, word came that the development contract would go to a competitor.

Allen was disappointed but philosophical about the loss. "We don't like to lose a competition," he said, "but it wouldn't be good if we won all of them. It's a healthy reminder that we're in a very competitive business."

The frightfulness of atomic progress put new urgency, too, behind the monumental problem of protecting U. S. shores and skies from nuclear attack. K. T. Keller, the Defense Department's director of guided missiles, listened to a presentation on the Bomarc long-range defensive missile development. The project had been a tedious climb up a new technical path. Bomarc's mission was to range out and strike high-speed enemy bombers while they were still remote from vital targets. There was progress to report, but Keller didn't seem impressed.

It was time to give the missile more management attention. It was a little harder to get enthusiastic about a missile than about an airplane you could fly in. Bill Allen asked chief engineer Lysle Wood to give full time to the program as director of a new pilotless aircraft division. George Martin was moved to Wood's job of chief engineer. Keith McDaniel was in charge at the missile test site at Banana River, Florida. The setting was reminiscent of the old GAPA firing grounds in Utah and later in Alamogordo, New Mexico, but Bomarc was huge compared with GAPA. Firings didn't go well and plans for power plant changes were rushed.

Korean peace-talk delays mirrored world uncertainty. Then, in March 1953, came the news that Communist dictator Joseph Stalin was dead. What now? What was going on behind the Kremlin walls?

Preparations for more Bomarc firings went forward in Florida. When a revised missile was sent into the air, it blew up in one bursting flash of disappointment. Wood and Bob

Jewett, chief engineer of Pilotless Aircraft, laid out a program of investigation and re-engineering.

Guided missiles were a trial, but other programs were rolling. The six hundredth B-47 was completed at Wichita in September. With Douglas and Lockheed also in production, the B-47 program had become the biggest in the nation's history, exceeding the wartime B-29 effort. But the program would soon reach its peak and then would lose ground to the B-52.

First production B-52s were nearing completion at Plant Two in Seattle, amid an astonishing array of huge concrete and steel fixtures. Wichita men who had mastered the B-47 were now in Seattle to help get B-52 production rolling. Then the Air Force decided in October the big plane would be produced also at a second source: Wichita. Earl Schaefer's plant, scene of two epic Battles of Kansas, would taper off Stratojet production and learn to build the eight-jet behemoth.

At Renton, where KC-97 tankers were coming out one a day, the focus of interest was behind the high plywood wall that housed the 707 jet transport. Ralph Bell, now sales manager, and commercial sales manager Ken Gordon were in and out of the area with weekly, sometimes daily, visits by airline parties. But no airline was ready to buy, nor could firm prices or delivery commitments be given them until Air Force plans for the tanker-transport version were known. Ralph Bell was campaigning hard, with Allen and Beall close behind him, for an Air Force order for the tanker to make the $15 million gamble—upped now to $16 million—pay out. There was resistance in Washington. "Boeing has too much business already," some still insisted. The company's sales for 1953 were approaching the $1 billion mark.

"Shouldn't business be awarded on merit?" Bill Allen asked. "You can get operational airplanes two years earlier by reason of our prototype. We'll use it to test out all the systems and refueling equipment before production. We'll have the experience to use in tooling and production planning. And you'll have a flight-proven airplane." Allen offered a delivery date of October 1956 for the first production airplane.

Air Force interest warmed in the spring of 1954. Strategic Air Command said it needed a jet tanker. Air Secretary Harold Talbott was impressed with the ship. To hold good the October 1956 delivery offer, Allen authorized start of engineering and tooling work on the production airplane at company expense while the government decision was awaited. The chips on the poker table were stacking high. Win all or lose all. There still were advocates for turboprop tankers in the Air Force, still those who wanted to use converted B-36s or B-47s as tankers. The Air Council met in Washington to resolve the differences. No word of a decision.

The prototype was ready to roll out of the Renton plant May 15, 1954, at the four o'clock shift change. Employees were given time off for the event. There was a band, a speakers' stand on the front apron. William E. Boeing was honor guest, and Mrs. Boeing would christen the airplane. Newsreel and TV cameras were on roof edges. At 3:53 P.M. superintendent Joe Donnelly signaled "Ready." The big doors started climbing, folding into canopy position overhead. Out of the shadow, the jet transport moved into the sun, sweptwinged and gleaming in fresh paint, rich yellow on top with copper-brown trim, a great beauty queen of metal. It rated a champion's applause. "I christen thee—the airplane of tomorrow—the Boeing Jet Stratoliner and Stratotanker," said Bertha Boeing, shattering a bottle of champagne over the plane. William E. Boeing, seventy-two, watched with moist eyes.

Test pilot Tex Johnston taxied the ship. "The cockpit's good and quiet," he reported. "Visibility is fine. This plane will be rated a pilot's airplane." He tried high-speed taxi runs and said the acceleration under full power was "terrific."

May 21, late afternoon, Tex was taxiing and testing brakes. He felt the side of the airplane going down, then a jolt. George Martin, Maynard Pennell, Bill Ramsden rushed out to see the

Jet Stratoliner crippled on the ground, its left landing gear collapsed.

Bill Allen got the news in Wichita, wondered if it would delay the Air Force decision on the tanker. When he got back Ed Wells came in to acknowledge the trouble was due to faulty design and a poor piece of steel. That hurt but Allen couldn't manage a reprimand. Instead he felt the need was for encouragement. "We don't like mistakes," he said at staff meeting, "but the important thing is to profit by them. Show that we have a courageous and flexible organization ready to go right ahead, all the more determined to do the job right."

The repairs would take six weeks. While they were being made, the Air Force announced it had decided it wanted jet tankers, not turboprops, and asked for production proposals by August. The way was open. If only the flight test went well.

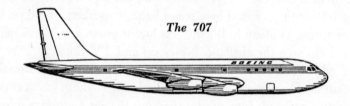

The 707

July 14, the 707 jet transport was set for flight: tomorrow at 7:00 A.M., weather permitting. In the morning, news cameramen and mechanics were on hand at five, watching a moist gray sky. It didn't look good. Flight was postponed to 2:00 P.M. At noon a big blue hole opened over the Renton airport and the sun blazed down. A truck towed the sleek giant three-quarters of a mile to the airport apron. Superintendent Donnelly wore a smile with the two deep furrows that were in his forehead. "She's in good shape," he told Bill Allen.

Tex Johnson and his co-pilot Dix Loesch got out of a car and walked toward the plane, bundled in heavy jackets, life vests and parachute packs. They paused for pictures. Allen stepped over to Tex, gripped his arm firmly. "How do you feel?"

"Never better," said Tex.

"She's in your hands, boys. Good luck."

The rest came quickly. White-coveralled ground crews moved the crowd back. Two minutes to two, Number One engine whined up to high key and its jet blast roared. The other three engines were started. Tex taxied out to the runway end, wheeled around, held his power with the brakes a few seconds—no long run-ups with jet planes—and began to roll. Speed and noise increased. The nose came up, and 2,100 feet down the runway the 707 was off the ground, then climbing radically up.

Gleaming with color, the swept-winged Stratoliner made a regal descent on Boeing Field a little past 3:30. Tex wheeled over toward the flight-test hangar. It was a happy day. Chief engineer George Martin stood in shirt sleeves, hands in pockets, wreathed with delight. A field car drove up behind Bill Allen and someone pulled him aside.

"If it had hit me now I wouldn't have felt it," said Allen.

But against the exhilaration of an American jet transport flying in 1954 stood the threat that world tension might break into hydrogen-nuclear warfare. When the results of new nuclear tests were made public, everyone knew the need for national security was greater than ever before. People in the Pentagon, at Wright Field, at Air Force and Navy bases, at aircraft plants of the nation, knew it most.

What had happened? What had the world awakened to? Or was it awake? Could those forces be as mighty for peace as for war, as President Eisenhower, a man who knew war, felt?

Few had yet learned what had really happened to science. Only a few physicists, in laboratories. They knew, in part. What had happened was a classic example of twentieth century vision: the realization of laws of science that hadn't been dreamed of before. It bore great implications for the airplane business, every other business, and the issue of war and peace.

It was a story that began in Berne, Switzerland, in 1905. A young man who had taught himself calculus and analytical geometry, because he sought knowledge, was working at the patent office in Berne, studying for his Ph.D. degree at the University of Zurich. Albert Einstein didn't agree with those who said the discovery of X-rays and radioactivity had left nothing more to be discovered. He puzzled over a classic experiment done by A. A. Michelson and E. W. Morley in Cleveland in 1881. It proved that the speed of light wasn't affected by earth's movement through the "ether" of space. There appeared to be but two alternate conclusions, one as devastating as the other to accepted laws of physics and astronomy. Either there was no ether—no medium to sustain light waves and electromagnetic waves—or the earth wasn't moving but standing still.

The problem got Einstein to thinking about speed and motion. Shouldn't the speed of light from a train headlight be the speed of light plus the speed of the train, as two plus two is four? But that couldn't be, according to the Michelson-Morley experiment. The speed of light was always the same, regardless of motion of the sender or receiver. Something wrong. Yet Einstein felt within him the sure mathematics of a universal order. "I can't believe that God plays dice with the universe," he said. There had to be an explanation.

Speed was a measure of time as well as distance. Maybe time had something to do with it. Einstein got back on his imaginary train. Suppose a lightning bolt struck in front of the train and another struck behind it at the same instant, same distance. It would be the same instant for someone on the ground, halfway between the two bolts. Would it be the same instant for him, moving on the train? He imagined himself riding precariously on top of the train with mirrors to see both lightning flashes instantaneously. He didn't think he'd see both at once. Surely the lightning bolt ahead of the train would seem to come first, because he was moving toward it. How could he be sure?

Suppose his train were going at the speed of light. Then he'd never see the lightning behind because the light couldn't ever reach him, he reasoned. Yet the man standing right beside the track, directly opposite him, would insist the two bolts struck simultaneously. He could come to only one conclusion. Time varied with the speed of the observer. For the observer traveling at the speed of light, time stopped. Would anyone believe that?

Einstein knew he'd have to dig deeper. What was time? Mostly a comparison. Our clocks compared events with the turning of the earth, our calendars compared them with the earth's orbit around the sun. Those were measures of distance. Would speed affect measures of distance, too? Sure enough, just as with time, he concluded that his measuring rod of distance would shrink to nothing if he could reach the speed of light.

The theory, Einstein decided, would explain nicely the enigma of the Michelson-Morley experiment, why light always struck an instrument at the same speed, regardless of the speed of the instrument. Because as the instrument approached the speed of light, timing clocks slowed down, measuring yardsticks shrunk. But it was hard to believe.

"It goes against common sense," people argued.

"What is common sense but a deposit of prejudices laid down in the mind prior to the age of eighteen?" Einstein asked.

He kept on, year on year, realizing that in the Michelson-Morley discovery about light there was an opportunity to correct some big mistake in theories of physics. Not so much mistakes as limitations. Newton's laws of physics worked all right at speeds people traveled, but not at 186,000 miles a second. Yet in radiation and light, scientists were dealing with these speeds. New laws were needed, as new laws were needed when speeds in airplane design went up.

"If time and distance are relative, not absolute, what about mass, the other basic quantity of physics?" Einstein asked. Most people thought of mass as weight but the physicist knew it as resistance to change in motion. A freight train is harder to move than a bicycle. Did that change with speed, too? It had to, Einstein reasoned, just like the other two quantities. Revolutionary, but his mathematics proved it true. Mass increased with motion. As a body reached the speed of light, its mass appeared to increase to infinity.

Interesting to contemplate, but of what value? Einstein didn't let go. What was mass, he asked, if it was so expandable, if it grew with motion? What was motion? Motion was a form of energy. Mass and energy must be just different forms of the same thing!

Momentous result of one man's realization.

Einstein's formula of the equivalence of mass and energy— energy was equal to the mass times the square of the speed of light —opened wide the doors of nuclear research. Laboratories proved his theory, bit by bit. In 1933 the Nazi regime didn't like the spelling of Einstein's name, stripped him of his property, his professorships, his German citizenship. He came to America, a haven of freedom.

War approached. Scientific knowledge became a critical war commodity. According to Einstein's formula, a pound of coal would yield eleven billion kilowatt-hours of electricity, if its mass could be converted to energy. Burning the coal used only one three-billionth of its energy. How could the rest be unlocked? The clue came in 1939 when scientists in Europe split a modified uranium atom, one of the heaviest of atoms, converting a small part of its mass to energy. It was then that Albert Einstein wrote Franklin D. Roosevelt of the possibilities of the atomic bomb.

Twenty pounds of "heavy" uranium, a critically large mass, a trigger to start its atoms splitting, a chain reaction of atoms splitting atoms, and Hiroshima was destroyed. That was atomic fission. The A-bomb. But atomic fission released only one-thousandth of the energy of the uranium atom. The principle led on. Fuse two atomic nuclei together—atomic fusion—and the two would have less mass than before. The rest would be changed to energy. The decrease in mass of the neutrons had to be matched by liberated energy to preserve the pure mathematics of Einstein's equation, and this would be felt in heat and light and blast. "Heavy" hydrogen atoms could be fused together but only at phenomenal heat. The energy of the A-bomb could produce that heat. Now it was a fusion bomb, a thermonuclear hydrogen bomb. At Bikini it was proved.

The principle led on. After fusion, at terrific heat, that nuclear energy could be used, the theory went, to split more atoms, plain uranium atoms, unprocessed. That would release more energy from fission. Then it would be a fission-fusion-fission bomb. Would the principle lead further? Where did it stop?

Or could the atomic fire that was burning in the frightening year 1954 be slowed down and put to work? To scientists and engineers considering the alternatives the choice was obvious. But the trouble was that the world wasn't working together toward peaceful use of the atom. If a culprit nation wanted to use it for destruction, it could. There was not "the great agreement to live together in peace" that Thomas Finletter had once called for. There had to be an atomic "big stick" to discourage aggression. The big stick was the propulsion of nuclear bombs through the air. By means of airplanes and missiles. Citizens of the free world, praying for peace and progress in world relations, looked to the country's airplane industry for the big stick. Biggest, right now, was the B-52. Was that enough?

BOOK FIVE

THE OUTLOOK

Engineers pondered the unnatural conflict. How great the marvels and yet how great their threat. Weren't men meant to be masters of science and not its slaves?

Most took the optimistic view. Webster defined engineering as "the art and science by which...the sources of power in nature are made useful to man." As science found its freedom from old limitations, technical progress had been continuing with accelerating wonder. The unlocking of the power of the atom and discoveries in electronics and other fields had thrown wide open the doors of opportunity, to an outlook that seemed so vast there just weren't enough men to keep up with the possibilities. The sky was no longer the limit.

Surely if men could gain their freedom in the scientific realm, they could gain freedom from the fear and strife that beset men and nations. Now, if ever, there was a realization of that need. Not that it hadn't been realized before....

1. *Air Force First*

Abraham Lincoln had said it plainly, knowing as no other American that the threat to freedom could come from within as well as without: "It is...for us to be dedicated...that this nation, under God, may have a new birth of freedom." Congressman Louis Rabaut of Michigan pondered Lincoln's plea at Gettysburg. It came to his mind because of a letter he had received from a man in Brooklyn. "Why don't you recommend the addition to the Pledge of Allegiance of the words 'under God'?" the man asked. Congressman Rabaut felt the depth of Lincoln's vision when he said those words, *that this nation, under God, shall have a new birth of freedom.* Wasn't now the time when freedom was again being challenged, challenged as never before?

Congressman Rabaut introduced a bill in the House. Senator Homer Ferguson of Michigan got behind it in the Senate. President Eisenhower, who'd been reminded at a Sunday service by Reverend George M. Doherty that there was "something missing in the Pledge," got behind it. While America's first jet transport, its first jet tanker to refuel B-52 Stratofortresses, was being flight tested in one far corner of the United States, school children throughout the nation with right hands over their hearts were looking toward their country's Stars and Stripes and speaking with one voice a new Pledge of Allegiance "to the flag of the United States of America and to the Republic for which it stands, one nation under God, indivisible, with liberty and justice for all."

If there was to be a new birth of freedom, the nation that stood up for that right had to be strong. Bill Allen felt a Lincoln allegiance to his nation and he would not seek commercial contracts for the new jet Stratoliner until he first knew the answer to production of the Stratotanker for General LeMay's growing fleet of jet bombers. "Our country's needs come first." The Air Force decision on the jet tanker was due in August 1954. Allen felt sure the government was counting on it now that the prototype had flown. Just as it was counting on the B-47 and B-52 jet bombers. They were the planes to hold the peace.

The Air Force was counting heavily, too, on guided-missile development. The missile Boeing was building, by the choice Wellwood Beall had made back in 1945, was a defensive missile. Now the existence of the H-bomb—Russia might have one soon, too—gave new importance to the long-range Bomarc interceptor. An oncoming H-bomber would have to be intercepted a long way from the target to provide any defense. That was Bomarc's job.

Concerned over Bomarc, Allen asked Lysle Wood about progress.

"It's discouraging at times, but we're making headway," said Wood. "We have another firing scheduled for the first week in August." Months of labor and design had gone into Bomarc since the last firing. The plan now was to continue the testing with improved rockets while better ramjet engines were developed. No one had built a successful ramjet of the size needed. On August 5, the interim missile was ready, erected on the firing pad in Florida, with rocket motors charged for the sky. Wood, Keith McDaniel, other engineers watched. At count zero, a mountainous roar of ground-pushing flame sent it sizzling upward. Then in a maneuver, its wing pulled off and it fell.

Wood called Allen to report. "We got off, but we didn't stay in the air very long. It's hard to take, but sometimes we can learn more from a failure than a success."

Bill Allen got another call two hours later from Washington. The word long awaited. The Air Force would order a starting quantity of jet tankers from Boeing, to gain time in the international race. Then they'd hold a new competition to determine the tanker for quantity production.

That same day, the first production model B-52 took off on its first flight. Allen watched with a satisfaction second only to that of knowing the 707 tanker-transport line was started. But, also that same day, late, Tex Johnston brought the 707 down from a test flight. It was getting dark when he touched the Boeing Field runway at a fast roll. No brakes. Runway was being used up fast. There wasn't much drag of wind on a jet plane to slow it. No propellers to put in reverse pitch and slow it down. No brakes at all. Tex decided he could turn off the runway at the far end, make a wide sweeping turn at the end of the field, and head back onto the strip without hitting the row of B-52s and C-97s standing there. He turned the nose wheel. The plane made its loop and was almost stopped when the nose wheel hit a concrete block, invisible in the unkept part of the field, and buckled under. Bill Allen got another call. Bitter with the sweet.

The fix on the brakes was easy enough, but the incident put a new push behind a project that George Martin's engineers had been working on. They were designing a device that would reverse the thrust of the jet engines, shoot it forward to slow the plane down in just such an emergency.

The telemeter data on the bob-tailed flight of the Bomarc missile at Banana River, Florida, August 6, was fruitful. To the engineers, the flight was not lost. But they had trouble selling that viewpoint in Washington.

"Get us a missile that will keep flying," they said at the Pentagon. That was all. They wanted to see it fly with ramjets, as it was supposed to do. Lysle Wood feared that to delay the tests until ramjets were ready might kill the program. People lost interest and faith if something wasn't happening. But to continue making short flights might also kill it. Wood, Jewett, and George Stoner decided to organize a blitz to get a ramjet missile flying. They got together with Marquardt Aircraft Company, builder of the ramjet. They talked with Al Jacobson, manufac-

VISION

turing manager of Pilotless Aircraft. March 1955 was set as the deadline for flight.

The decision put a chafing load on Bob Jewett, chief engineer of missiles. He had 620 men working on Bomarc. There were 2,500 in all Pilotless Aircraft, including Jake's manufacturing men. He remembered how the GAPA program had been killed, just when he felt they were succeeding. There was interservice rivalry in missiles. Army, Navy and Air Force all were in it. A failure of the next critical test in February and they might lose everything—ten years' work.

The problems of Bomarc were profoundly technical. The missile was a shell stuffed with complex upon complex of electronic, mechanical, and hydraulic invention. Thousands of gadgets, all required to work in automatic perfection, with no human hand to monitor them. Infinitesimal in size, many of them, but monumental in importance. Threading through one of the systems in thought was like counting the dew drops on a spiderweb without retracing a thread. When a system interrelated with another system interrelated with still another system didn't work, and the designer came up for a decision between alternatives, it took the wisdom of Solomon to choose the right compromise, knowing the whole missile depended on not one but every decision.

But those weren't the hardest problems. The hardest were the unknowns, where there was nothing to choose between, no answer. Jewett felt the pressure of time and paper and problem piling up like a tidal wave and rushing toward him. The demands of the office—salaries, personnel problems, reports to the Air Force—devoured time needed for thought. Harassed thought couldn't crack through to the core of a problem, only nursed the problem and left it still there. The malfunction of one secret device was a riddle inside an enigma. Jewett prayed for X-ray vision to see through it. There seemed no answer. Then when he was puttering in his basement shop at home, mind free of Bomarc, the answer came. Like a light. He took it back to the plant and things began to work out.

Other engineers were coming up with answers, same way. "You aren't likely to find the solution by staying too close to the problem," George Schairer explained it. "You get all wound up in it and you don't see the obvious."

Discovery, revelation wouldn't come to cluttered thought. When demands and routines were leaving basic problems unsolved, getting away from them seemed to help. The PW-9, first Boeing pursuit, was born in a Pullman car. The Monomail, first smooth-skin monoplane transport, at the Los Angeles air races. The swept wings of the B-47 on a transatlantic airplane ride. The final B-52 in a hotel room in Dayton. The low-wing jet transport in the Dayton office, on a Sunday afternoon.

Bill Allen, under his own executive pressures, knew how important this time for free thought was to the continued progress of a company deep in technical development. Right decisions were survival or failure when they involved projects that took millions of dollars and millions of man-hours. Realizing this, he had asked Ed Wells to give full time to planning, giving all his administrative duties to the chief engineer. A planning committee was formed, of vice presidents John Yeasting, Fred Laudan, Jim Prince and Wells, Don Euler, Beall's assistant, and staff engineer John Ball, with Wells as chairman. Future products, future facilities were the committee's problems. What investments should the company make to give Bomarc a future, to develop an advanced bomber, to produce jet transports?

Allen was working also with Jim Prince, vice president–administration, on plans for organization changes that would free other top executives of administrative duties and establish new operating divisions. The changes would be needed especially if the company entered the commercial transport field.

The 707 jet transport, half sold to the Air Force, unsold to the airlines, ran a tie with Bomarc as the major unfinished problem. With the initial Air Force order for jet tankers now in work, Allen felt the way was clear for commercial production, and that the company could handle this without interference with the military work. He asked the Air Force for approval to use the government-owned Renton facility for this purpose. The Pentagon was reluctant to grant it. The competition for further production quantities of tankers was still undecided. But Douglas was talking with the airlines about jet transports now and Lockheed was considering either a jet or a turboprop. These companies had the airlines as regular customers and it would be hard to dislodge them if they got into the jet business. Allen walked a tight rope, trying to keep the airlines interested without making commitments to them.

Director of pilotless aircraft Lysle Wood walked his own tight rope into 1955, not wanting to delay the Bomarc firing any longer than necessary, nor to schedule it too soon and risk another failure. The new ramjet engine was installed, other problems had been taken care of. Not all of them, but the things needed for the first flight. A date had to be arranged in advance with Major General Donald Yates, head of Patrick Air Force Base in Florida, that wouldn't conflict with use of the firing range by others. Wood made the decision and the range was engaged for the week of February 14.

 *Bomarc*

2. *Bomarc on the Track*

Time was running fast at Patrick Air Force Base the week of February 7, 1955. Ground testing proceeeded on electronics systems, fuel systems, controls, recording instruments for the coming Bomarc test. Everything was checking out but the ramjets. They refused stubbornly to respond. The firing date had to be canceled. Lysle Wood wired Marquardt, builder of the ramjets, to air freight new engines from California. Then someone discovered the trouble, a fault in the wiring, and General Yates was asked for a new date. The week of February 21 was available, except for Monday. Tuesday was Washington's Birthday. Wednesday they waited out a rain; clear skies were needed for tracking a flight. Thursday should be the day.

Lysle Wood was tight-wound as he left the hotel before daybreak Thursday with George Stoner and chief project engineer George Snyder, hoping this would be the day. It was drizzling as the three men drove onto the island that separated Banana River—not really a river—from the Atlantic, and along the beach flats of low-growing palmettos.

Keith McDaniel had operations well started when they arrived. Floodlights blazed on the firing pad where Bomarc, a giant pointed thing, was being slowly raised, looking out at space with eyes that were a hidden labyrinth of wires, tubes and transistors. Her controls drooped in passive readiness. The stillness of her engines seemed to belie the potency that could send her on a roaring one-way trip into the heavens.

The urgent angles of the missile's short wings and fins were to Wood a reminder of the mission and obligation that Bomarc represented. If one day enemy superweapons were approaching with H-bombs up there in the darkness, missiles like this would have to hit them in split seconds. There was much work to be done before that perfection could be assured. What was needed now was proof of progress so that work could continue.

A man came up to McDaniel shaking his head. "I've just got the weather from Central Control. It's putrid."

"Any hope in the next three or four hours?"

"Not much. Maybe this afternoon."

General Yates had said he wanted to fire a Matador missile if Boeing wasn't ready. It was a test that wouldn't require clear skies for photographic recordings. It would tie up the range for four hours. McDaniel told the General to go ahead with Matador. Then, in an hour or so, sure enough, beautiful Florida blue was breaking overhead, but a heavy overcast approaching in the distance. The group waited while Matador was set up. It ran into a delay. When Matador finally was fired and the range was free for Bomarc at two o'clock, the sky was covered again. McDaniel dashed off to Central Control to see if the General would keep the range open overtime in case the weather should clear. Yates agreed to keep it cranked up until five.

Keeping the range "cranked up" for a missile firing was something of a grand alert. There were fire crews, ambulance crew, security guards, crews attending radar batteries, some making sure the air was clear of traffic, others manning the tracking radars. At fringe locations were the theodolite operators to plot the course of a manmade shooting star. Close-in were the automatic cameras and, at more remote locations, manned photographic stations, all necessary for the engineers to piece together the story of the missile's short life. Ranging at sea were B-17 Flying Forts with great horns protruding from their bomb bays to bellow a warning to any boats which might enter the prohibited area. All these—a 275-man team—stood by while the group on the firing pad waited, watching the sky.

It was after four when George Snyder spotted a blue patch to the south. "Maybe we're going to get a break." They watched the hole widen, but it remained off to the side.

"Coax it over," said Wood. The blue sky seemed slowly to open. The clouds were thinning. The theodolite crews said they thought they could track. Now it was 4:15.

"Let's take a run for it," said McDaniel. Wood nodded. There was a quick dispatching of people. The firing pad became a burst of activity, like the deck of a flat top being readied for a raid.

"Minus forty-five minutes," came the authoritative voice of the count-down man on the PA system, signaling that the final race was on. Mechanics took away the support wagon that kept the missile from being upset in event of a sudden squall. The firing crew was busy in the blockhouse, a strongbox with walls and ceiling of thirty-six-inch reinforced concrete. Close under the viewing window was the "push button." It wasn't a button but a console where a white-shirted "organist" sat ready to play his electronic notes of command. Green lights were coming onto the big panel as various preparations were completed.

"Minus forty minutes." Out on the pad the photographers made pre-launching pictures. "Minus thirty-five." A top mechanic set the destruct system in the missile that would blow it up if it ran wild in the air. Others left on the firing pad were gathering up kits and hastily vacating.

At minus thirty, the last man climbed down into the hatch in the concrete, closed the heavy lid over him, and retreated through the long tunnel to the blockhouse, inserting plugs in wiring circuits as he went along. He appeared in the blockhouse at minus twenty-five. Bomarc was out there alone. "She's armed and ready," he reported.

Everyone was cleared from outside the blockhouse area to Building C, two-thirds of a mile down the road. Wood and the Seattle party joined a crowd of a hundred or so there, made up mostly of men who had finished their part in the preparations and now awaited the show.

"Minus fifteen." Automatic operations had begun in the blockhouse. The men at the big panel were watching a pair of dials come up.

"Pressures are O.K." It was McDaniel's voice on the loud speaker. Then the count-down announcer: "Minus twelve."

"Electronics is on. Checks O.K." Telemetering reception from range stations was monitoring O.K. "Minus ten." At their unseen posts, military and civilian technicians were tensing for kickoff.

"Minus nine... eight... seven...." McDaniel had his clearance from the range safety officer. Shipping lanes were clear. "Six... five... four...." The range was a symphony of readiness. The great eyes of radar scanned the sky in their measured rhythm. Bomarc sat erect on her explosive tail. Even veteran crewmen began to tighten as the announcer intoned: "Minus one hundred eighty seconds." The dials on the big board verified that the missile had gone on automatic control. The automatic watch and sequencer had taken over. "Minus one hundred seventy . . . one hundred sixty . . . one hundred fifty . . ."

Outside Building C the conversation was dying out. At minus one hundred twenty the sequencer switched the missile onto internal power. Batteries began paying out their short, powerful life to run the ship. The monitoring crew in a trailer outside the blockhouse worked machinelike, snapping switches, watching tape roll out of a recording machine; one minute to check autopilot and telemetering mechanisms on internal power.

"Hold!" shouted the announcer at minus thirty seconds. "Hold!"

The intercom went silent. Wood at Building C was on needles. "What is it?"

McDaniel came back on in reassuring voice. One of the battery voltages wasn't right and there was an automatic stop in the sequence. The machine would hold the kickoff if all players weren't ready. When the voltage indicator drifted into tolerance range, McDaniel decided to override it. "Tell the range we'll resume," he ordered.

The announcer called fifteen seconds warning, then resumed his count. At Building C, all faces were now in one direction. The seconds kept coming. "Ten, nine, eight, seven, six, five . . ."

A belch of smoke out of the missile confirmed that the starting flares were lighted. It was committed now. No retrieve. ". . . Four, three, two . . ." George Stoner had both arms high in the air with a stop watch in each hand, thumbs ready to time whatever might come. It was his personal release.

". . . One, *zero*." Stoner's arms came down. There was a roar. A moment while pressures built up, then a great pot of smoke and flame obliterated the firing pad and Bomarc shot straight up . . . up . . . on a pillar of fire, meteor in the sky.

The announcer was continuing, ". . . Four, five, six, seven, eight, nine, ten," then only the heavy roar as the missile pushed on through the light overcast and flattened on its course toward the

blue area down-range. Every eye on the base was another tracking theodolite, glued to its progress. Wood was bent toward it,
straining to see what was going on up there. Was the ramjet
cutting in as it should? He could hardly distinguish the trail
behind the broken cloud screen.

It pushed right out into the blue, with a heavy column of
brilliant sun-lighted vapor trail behind. That meant ramjet full-on.
Wood's head began to swim a little. Straight as a die, Bomarc
was pressing along on its track. It disappeared over the heavy
cloudbank in the distance and left them standing there for a
moment, staring into the cloud.

Wood could hardly define his thoughts, but the future was
coming brighter. Like the Bomarc, probing now into the unseen
distance, it could spell many things. A complete system against
invading air fleets? Automatic dispatching of supersonic passenger traffic? Flight plans into outer space? It didn't all appear
just yet, by any means, but Wood felt the challenge growing
bigger and higher.

What appeared was enough for now. Bomarc on the track.
On its own up there on the top side of that cloud, out over the
Atlantic.

3. *The Open Mind*

The long, drab reels of paper that came out of the telemeter
recorders at Patrick Air Force Base told a story that was good
news about Bomarc. Fed through electronic computing machines
and analyzed, the figures held the key to more work ahead, more
progress toward a system for H-bomb defense.

Curtis LeMay's long-sought deterrent to H-bomb attack—
the B-52 with its intercontinental retaliatory power—was becoming a reality. Deliveries were continuing from Seattle Plant

Two, and Wichita was tooling for another line. A decision was overdue in the Air Force for quantity production of jet tankers to refuel the 52s. In March the announcement came: KC-135, an advanced model of the Boeing prototype, was the winner.

The big risk had been worth it. Bill Allen could lean back in his chair, take a breath. But only for a moment. The job wasn't finished, was never finished. The arresting roar of a B-52 take-off came by Allen's windows. He swiveled and followed it, as he always did, always would. As hundreds of others did from other windows. Its thunder took command, then echoed back from the sky that this was a stirring business, jet-powered. Couldn't stand still. One accomplishment only pointed the way to another. The way was pointing now, Bill Allen felt most urgently, to a Boeing jet transport on the airlines.

It was possible to arrive at a price for the plane, now that Air Force production was determined. Cost Accounting totaled the estimates turned in by Engineering and Manufacturing. Five and a half million dollars per plane for a production quantity of fifty.

"We can't sell them for that," said Allen. All the airlines had been impressing him with the problem of financing jet transports, even at three and a half or four million each. Five and a half million dollars would scare them completely out of the notion. "If we want to build commercial transports we have to have buyers." Allen was now wearing the salesman's hat. "We're going to have to go at it the other way around. Start with a price we can sell them for and then figure out how to build them for that." The price was worked down to four and one-half million dollars. Rock bottom.

Allen and Beall renewed the effort to get Air Force approval for commercial production. There'd have to be payments arranged for use of the Renton plant and some of the KC-135 tooling. The Pentagon still wanted assurance that commercial production wouldn't interfere with tanker deliveries. "We can handle both," Allen assured them. But words weren't enough.

Evidence was what was wanted. Evidence on the production floor.

There was reason for the urgency the government placed behind both the tanker and the B-52 program now. It was confirmed that the Russians, too, had developed the H-bomb. Moscow was boasting about it and demanding a ban on nuclear weapons. America agreed with the objective but questioned Moscow's motive. Frightening new facts were being revealed about nuclear weapons. The H-bomb that was exploded at Bikini spread its lethal effects over 7,000 square miles, an area the size of New Jersey. Scientists said fresh "surprises" were due. Civil Defense Administrator Val Peterson said future bombs could have a force of 60,000,000 tons of TNT. Magazines were telling of designs for bombs that could spread a radioactive cloud over a continent.

Collier's in an Easter editorial echoed the concern that was bringing a renaissance of religion: "The hope for a future is that man may now have created the final, unarguable reason to use the sense God gave him." President Eisenhower labored to keep the channels of diplomacy open. A meeting of government heads was arranged for July at "the summit" in Geneva. The new Soviet government at least seemed more open to negotiation than its predecessors, and there was a growing hope that means to world stability might be found.

That hope drove home in Seattle the importance of selling commercial jet transports. A move by competition soon made the need more vital. Sales manager Ralph Bell brought the news to Bill Allen the morning of June 8, 1955. "Don Douglas is going to start building the DC-8," said Bell. "The airplane is almost a dead ringer for ours. A shade larger."

Allen shook his head. "You've got to admire him for his courage, going ahead on his own after losing out on the tanker business. It's a bigger gamble than we took on the prototype. People talk about guaranteed profits in this business!"

Promptly a price and delivery proposal on the 707 jet Stratoliner went to Pan American, then to other airlines, contingent on Air Force approval. A 225,000-pound airplane; price, $4,500,000. Sales teams went to work. Hard.

The Air Force agreed July 15—on the thirty-ninth anniversary of the incorporation of Boeing—to the production of commercial jets along with its tankers. A record of seventy months on-schedule deliveries of KC-97s from Renton and forty-three months on-schedule B-47 deliveries from Wichita gave substance to the company's delivery promises. The Wichita plant had turned out 1,200 of the Stratojets now.

July 15, 1955. President Eisenhower spoke to the nation, on the eve of his departure for Geneva, about trying to find means to prevent war, "measures that will keep from us this terrible scourge that afflicts mankind." He hoped to "change the spirit" of meetings between governments. He looked to the Free World, held together by a common belief in a Divine Power and a commandment to "do unto others as you would have them do unto you," to find an answer to the problem of war and the burden of armaments. "We want to make it perfectly clear," he said, "that these armaments do not reflect the way we want to live. They merely reflect a way under present conditions we have to live."

At Geneva, dramatically, sincerely, Eisenhower offered an acid test of Russian protestations for peace. Let the countries exchange blueprints of their military establishments, he suggested. Let them permit aerial photography of each other as a provision against surprise attack. And let this be the beginning of an effective system of inspection and disarmament. Russian delegates were visibly rocked. They said the proposal bypassed the basic disarmament issue, but there was no doubt that Eisenhower's sincerity had made an impression.

Two weeks later at Geneva the International Conference on Peaceful Uses of Atomic Energy convened. Americans, Europeans, Russians stood together in a darkened room with a twenty-two-foot-high fish bowl reactor, watched a faint blue spot in the water become luminous, grow to a whitish, bluish, greenish glow, surrounded by an expanding purple fire until a purple haze filled the room to the walls. The awed delegates who peered into this core of atomic power hailed "the dawn of the greatest industrial, social and economic revolution the earth has seen."

Pace of progress quickening. In the ten years since Maynard Pennell was first assigned to supervise Bob Hage's jet study he had nursed a wish into a full-grown desire to see Boeing jet transports on the airlines. He looked at Ralph Bell's estimates that 150 to two hundred jets would be needed by the domestic airlines by 1960. "Can't we get the price down still lower?" he asked Bill Allen, "and go after not fifty or seventy-five but 125 or 150?"

Allen was afraid they had already put the price too low. But he was in the race with Douglas, to win. Negotiations went on at fierce pace. Pan American, United, American, Eastern. Quantities, deliveries, design changes, special equipment, neck-and-neck comparisons with estimated range and payload of the forthcoming Douglas DC-8.

On the military side, there were "paper" competitions equally urgent. Development studies were proceeding on secret advanced weapons to meet future Air Force requirements. One major engineering project had been carried forward for months with company funds. The problems of new military development had become immense. Weapons systems to exceed the performance even of planes like the B-52 were huge undertakings. The Air Force felt it had to be sure it was on the right track before committing funds. There were superelaborate procedures for evaluating proposals. Scores of people were involved in the approval, progressively growing stacks of paper necessary to justify the end product.

Engineers worried about a fundamental question this raised: How could you justify the end product if you couldn't get started on it to find out what you could do? The trouble was that you couldn't get the dollar to spend unless you could show a requirement for it and you had to have the dollar to be able to show the requirement. Because of high costs, the plan was to make certain what was wanted first, on paper; then the government would invest in more design work.

Was this false economy? Wouldn't the government's investment in the paper decision get so heavy that, by the time it was far enough along to find out if it would work, there'd be too much money in it to let go? Wasn't it in conflict with the idea of starting a project and then working out improvements as you went along? You couldn't always tell where a development would lead. Dwight Eisenhower, just before he was elected President, had asked at Independence Hall: "Has any great accomplishment in history begun with assurance of its success?"

What had become of the old, competitive plan of carrying more than one product into physical form and then letting them compete to show which had the best performance? Those who pondered the problem could see it wasn't easy to answer. Something new had been added: The high costs of technological advance. It was government money that was involved. There wasn't the freedom to try out new things.

If the aircraft companies had the funds to make their own investments in experimental work, that would be one answer. The Flying Fortress in 1935 and the 707 jet transport showed what could be done. But military projects had become too expensive. Aircraft profits were not large. They had been held down because they were based on government business, and on use of a good many government facilities. Everyone was calling for technical improvement because the security of the country depended on it, because Communist Russia, too, was driving hard for it. Was the present system the one that would best encourage it?

Ed Wells, George Schairer, other engineers, pondering future projects, looked back over the road that had been traveled, then at the outlook. It had been a road with many turns, each leading to another ahead that couldn't have been seen before. First the structural engineers, then the power-plant engineers, then the aerodynamicists had come to the fore. Now the crucial area was in the field of electronics, because of the complicated insides of fast-moving airplanes and missiles. It was a new science, dealing with vacuum tubes and micro-tiny electrons in dozen-digit numbers.

Even the physical parts of the equipment were tiny. Bob Jewett was explaining at the lunch table how they were using screws so small the threads were invisible. Ed Wells got out his wallet, unfolded a small piece of paper. "Look at these," he said, passing the cupped paper around. They were brass screws Wells had gotten from a watch company that was getting into the defense business.

Administrative engineer Charlie Rutledge across the table produced a cellophane envelope filled with specks still smaller, barely visible. "These are washers," he said. "You'll need a magnifying glass."

"Where'd you get these?" asked Beall.

"We make them."

But if the electronics people were in the fore at present, they could see the day ahead when the emphasis would shift—was already shifting—to materials engineers. Not metallurgists but materials physicists. Titanium could stand seven hundred degrees Fahrenheit, enough for speeds of 6,000 miles per hour at 200,000 feet, but a missile dropping back into the atmosphere from outer space and traveling 15,000 miles an hour would get up to 5,000 degrees before it reached the earth if there were nothing but aerodynamic friction to slow it. Sooner or later there'd have to be new materials. Rocket and nuclear power would eventually be getting ships into outer space. In that day, said rocket enthusiasts, you'd be able to get anywhere on the globe in "about an hour." Every place would be the same distance away, because the only time required would be to get up above the air belt, then it would take hardly any longer to go one place than another.

Perhaps it wouldn't come soon for ships, but it would be soon for missiles. And Ed Wells suggested people shouldn't be too quick to put missiles and airplanes in a different class. "The airplane is getting more and more like a missile and the missile more and more like an airplane," he said. "The principal difference will be whether you decide you want to carry somebody along on the trip."

All this would take heat-resistant materials. If they couldn't be found in nature, they'd have to be made, hence the need for materials physicists. "We need to be able to say, 'Here's the kind of a molecule I want, now by golly we'll make one,' " said Guil Hollingsworth, head of the physical research laboratories. "But we don't understand enough about solid-state physics. Yet."

"If you think something's impossible you might as well not start," said George Schairer. "If you think you know the answer before you start, you won't find it. But if you're open-minded about it . . ."

Open-minded was what Einstein had been when he looked beyond old laws of physics and saw the way to atomic power. Physicists didn't really know what matter and energy were. Some evidence showed energy as particles—electrons and protons; other evidence best explained it as waves. For the moment scientists were content to keep both concepts. That left them with a "wavicle." But Einstein didn't care for compromise. He sought a common law that would combine the laws of electromagnetic energy, such as light and radio waves, with the law of mass called gravity. Before his death in the spring of 1955, he had unified the two by mathematical equations satisfying to himself, though not proved by experiment. Would this mean ultimately a control over gravity for airplane and space flight? A device that would turn off gravity?

"Who can say? We don't understand enough about it yet," said Guil Hollingsworth.

The biggest new thing in science was that scientists and engineers would no longer be caught saying a thing was impossible. There'd been too many surprises already for that. Physicists at the University of California were even now discovering the existence of anti-protons or "matter in reverse" that would annihilate a proton on contact, turning not a thousandth of it into energy as with nuclear fission, but all of it. No practical way of applying the discovery yet, but nonetheless it held the prospect of getting still more power from the atom. "The more we know, the more we are aware of how much we don't know," said chief engineer George Martin. "Only 5 per cent of what was in the old aerodynamics books is still in use. There has to be a periodic housecleaning of old ideas."

Everyone was interested in the jet acceleration of technical progress that was sweeping science and engineering into the blue. What was at the bottom of it? The discussion got around to that. "First you have to *want* to find a better way," said Maynard Pennell. "You have a peril or a need, or just a desire to know, a desire to do. We've had all these in recent years, and knowledge has been building on knowledge."

"Isn't it a product of knowledge times effort times..." George Martin paused... "times a quantity we'll call X—maybe inspiration? Vision?"

There were always new instances coming along that showed how that X quantity worked. Physicist Guil Hollingsworth was talking with engineers in the industrial products division. They were building an electronic computer for sale, a byproduct of the one Engineering had built up for its own use.

"What we need is a simple electronic multiplier," they said. Hollingsworth thought about this. There were electronic multipliers on the market, but all of them were fraught with complexity, didn't get at the heart of the problem, he felt. You couldn't just take an adding machine, wave your arms and say "Multiply" and then add gadgets until it did. That was the hard way. He wondered if there weren't some phenomenon in nature where one quantity is always in proportion to the product of two others. That might give a new approach.

One evening at home, reading some chemistry and physics, Hollingsworth came upon the answer. A principle of relationships between currents and a magnetic field that would multiply naturally. It was called the Hall effect, discovered about 1880. They wired one up at the plant and it worked.

See the need; recognize the principle to meet the need; apply it. Progress.

Because it was knowledge of principle that technical advancement leaned upon, Hollingsworth felt there should be more basic research. "We're drifting away from the search for fundamentals that we had two or three decades ago," he said. "We're becoming a bunch of hardware merchants. We've been speeding up applied research, all right, but we're going to wake up and find we've outrun fundamental research. That's something awfully hard to speed up."

In Physical Research they were carving with strange new tools on strange unknowns. One of their jobs was to construct models of new electronics systems and devices, not out of metal but out of mathematical equations. For this they used electromechanical analog computers, cabinets filled with electronic-tube circuits connected with knobs and motors, that would keep changing their relation to each other.

The computers tested an imaginary control system as a wind tunnel tested a model. Poke the model here, and it would wiggle over there. Poke one voltage in the analog computer and other voltages would wiggle, so you could tell everything a model would do, but you had no model, only the idea to work with. It was done electrically, not mechanically. You could try out all kinds of variations of wings and controls without ever putting a piece of metal to a lathe or a wood carver's tool to a piece of balsa wood. You could invent things without ever seeing them and save time and money, besides making them better. Then when you got them worked out, you could go ahead and try them in metal.

But the engineers could only go as far as basic knowledge would point the way. "We ought to be giving more support to the universities and research institutes," said Hollingsworth, "to find more things out." What Edison had once pointed out, about scientists knowing only "a millionth part of one per cent about anything," passing decades have proved an understatement. Now it was known that the wave lengths of visible light covered only one billionth of a billionth part of the range from ultra high-frequency cosmic rays to longest radio waves. Man was peering through that narrow slit of light and meticulously measuring things with calipers in his effort to define the great unknown.

It was an awesome search, one calling for supreme vision. Some said it was a materialistic quest, that scientists and engineers were atheists fascinated only by the physical world. But not all would agree. "Can a scientist believe in God?" asked Warren Weaver, chairman of the American Association for the Advancement of Science. "I think scientists have unique advantages here.... No scientist has ever seen an electron. No scientist soberly thinks that anyone ever could ... yet nothing is more 'real' to a scientist than an electron.... Every new discovery of science is a further 'revelation' of the order which God has built into His universe."

It was because they were beginning to see the vastness of the possibilities, that scientists and engineers were humbled by their search. The key men in Engineering were church-going men, seeking a higher understanding and inspiration for the tasks ahead. So were thousands of their associates. Vision was a thing of mind. Mind freed, and finding its capabilities.

It seemed almost unbelievable that war and fear of war were the sharpest spur to this technical progress. Was it necessarily so? A lot of engineers took the opposite view. The period of quickened pace of fundamental discovery that Guil Hollingsworth spoke of was during the peace of the 1920's and 1930's. War developments, monumental in size, were applications of earlier discoveries. The greatest turns in Boeing design, the Monomail, the 247, the Flying Fortress, the B-47 Stratojet, came not of war but of peacetime competition.

They wondered if the present peace was a platform from which to build a new step. Was it a durable peace? A sound platform? It was the longing for an affirmative answer to that question that explained the engineers' fondness for the organization called Strategic Air Command.

"Our primary mission is to deter war," said Curtis LeMay, sitting at his desk at Offutt Air Force Base, Omaha, in command of that twenty-four-hour alerted strategic air force equipped with B-47s and new B-52s. "The world should learn the capabilities of modern weapons and realize the futility of war."

A Boeing delegation sat in the General's plain-walled second-floor office. "What do you see ahead?" he was asked.

The man with the firm jaw and steady eye looked across the room. "One thing I'm sure of," he said. "There will be more progress in the air in the next fifty years than in the last fifty."

"Why?"

"Look at the first plane and then look at the B-52. We've found we start slowly in everything we attempt, then build rapidly. Everyone will be astounded at what is yet to come. My idea is we should keep our minds wide open and use the stuff as it comes. We must be able to see far enough ahead. We could take big steps now. With all that our scientists are learning it is perfectly possible to build a satellite vehicle or take a trip to the moon."

Once it would have sounded fanciful, but no longer. Scientists were even now preparing for the first-stage study of outer space in the 1957-1958 Geophysical Year. No orders yet for a ship to reach the moon, but the engineers wouldn't flinch at the technical challenge if they could be allowed two conditions. "Anything is possible," said Ed Wells, "if you have enough funds to work with and if everyone is working together with one mind, one purpose."

4. *Progress and Principle*

If opportunity was the open gate, competition was the spur. During the fall of 1955 airline delegations, one after another, came to Seattle to talk and to fly in the 707 jet Stratoliner, then went down to Santa Monica to compare offers with Douglas. The DC-8 would have a larger wing area. With a payload of 26,350 pounds it would get a range of 3,700 nautical miles, fifty miles more than the 707. Douglas planned to use an advanced model of the Pratt & Whitney jet engine, and promised better performance for Pan American's long hauls. The Douglas cabin would be three inches wider than that of the 707.

"Our prototype is our biggest asset," said Ralph Bell, "but it's also an obstacle. Douglas has a rubber airplane. It's easy to stretch an airplane on paper."

To meet the competition, the 707's gross weight was increased from 225,000 to 245,000 pounds. Then Douglas went up. Increase the 707's weight again, with all the changes that involved, and the big advantage Boeing had in offering earlier delivery schedule and lower price might be lost. Pan American liked the Boeing price and schedule, but wanted the added range of the Douglas too.

Pan American men came out to fly in the prototype: assistant chief pilots Scott Flower, Dick Vinal, Jim Fleming, and others. The ship had months of testing behind it now. A demonstration ought to be convincing. The pre-flight briefing in Tex Johnston's office was simple. "Just fly it like you would any airplane," Tex said. "Anything special you'd like to try?" One of them wanted an emergency descent from high altitude to see how long it would take to come down to normal altitude in case of cabin supercharger trouble. They wanted to try some stalls, high Mach numbers.

The take-off from Boeing Field in the big soundproofed cabin was less a climb than a slipping into the sky. The landscape receding at jet speed as they headed out over Puget Sound was a foretaste of a transoceanic passenger departure in 1959, new mode. Elevator-fast, they were at 20,000 feet, 30,000, leveling off at 33,000. Pacific Ocean, Olympic Range, Cascade Range, sentinel peaks of Mount Rainier and a dozen other snowcaps all were wrinkles on a western relief map.

Tex Johnston was demonstrating some high rate turns, maximum rate rolls. The airplane cavorted as a swallow. Test pilots weren't interested in plain flight. They wanted to really try things out.

"Watch along the right wing," said Tex, gathering to maximum straightaway speed that was imperceptible except by instruments. "You may be able to see a dark shadow forming—the wing's shock wave." It was the old mystery of "compressibility burble" of Eddie Allen's day, now no mystery, no longer unruly, but visible speed-of-sound waves gathering neatly off the wing.

They did the stalls, power on, power off, everything coming to a seeming stop in the air, no sound, no vibration, too still, then the heavy buffeting that was the pilots' warning of less than flying speed, the neat dip and recovery. Even keel. They made the emergency descent, air brakes out, heading down, sinking forced-draft in a sea of atmosphere, 33,000 feet to 20,000 feet in sixty seconds. Tex looked around and grinned. "No problem."

The Pan Am people were enthusiastic. They shut off two of the jets and flew on the other two. When they ran out of emergency conditions to try they came in straight, like a passenger flight, toward the airport. "Just land it like you would a Stratocruiser or a DC-6," said Tex. The airplane was built to get up and go when it was in the air, but to handle according to conventional rules at the terminal. That would give the airlines an easy entry into the jet age.

Other Pan American executives came out for flights. President Juan Trippe wanted his airline to be the first American line to introduce jets. October 13 he announced the decision. The airline would spend $269 million, buy twenty of the 707s to be delivered starting December 1958 and also twenty-five DC-8s for later delivery. Pan Am insisted on an option that would permit changing the last ten 707s to the larger power plants that Douglas was using.

October 16, Tex Johnston flew the jet Stratoliner across the country and back in eight hours. Negotiations with United and American were at a crucial state. Both airlines were flying Douglas propeller-driven planes now. Bill Allen tried to overcome their feeling that Boeing was a builder of military planes, in and out of the commercial transport business. He said Boeing was back in transports for good. But not everyone was impressed with the story. Allen and the sales force had the uncomfortable feeling of being "outs" trying to get in.

October 25, United Air Lines announced it would buy thirty Douglas DC-8s. Bill Allen gave his team a fight talk. "The test of an organization comes when we are knocked down," he said. "Can we get up and come back swinging?"

American and Eastern were both about to make a decision. TWA was holding off for the present. If American and Eastern followed United's choice, the tide would put Boeing at a huge disadvantage. The fewer planes to build, the higher the cost per plane. It was imperative that Boeing gain its share of the domestic airline sales. Next most important was sales to transoceanic lines. But the longer range of the Douglas made the latter competition tough. Salesmen Ralph Bell and Ken Gordon assessed the situation with Ed Wells in a New York hotel room.

"We've got to go to a bigger airplane for the over-water routes," Bell urged. "We've got a grip on this race. We can't let go now, even if we have to build a new airplane." Wells shared Bell's away-from-the-office zeal. With aerodynamicist Jack Steiner he made some quick slide-rule plans for a larger model. It was Saturday. Bill Allen was due Sunday. They wondered how he would react. There were already two versions of the 707 to be built, with the modification Pan American had requested on its last ten planes to incorporate the larger engines. This would make a third, and its dimensions would be different from the other two so it couldn't be built on the same production line. Would there be enough orders to support a new production line?

Bill Allen, who knew he was the one who'd started this race, didn't hesitate long. "It'll increase our risk, but let's go ahead and do it," he said. Wells flew to Seattle to get up a detailed proposal for the airplane that would be called "The Intercontinental." It was also decided to increase the 707 body width, make it a shade wider than the Douglas.

While a team was departing for Europe to sell the new jet Intercontinental, American Airlines decided November 8 to buy thirty of the 707s. That made fifty sold. The program could be a success now. "United's Douglas order may have been a blessing in disguise," said Allen. "Now we have an opportunity to show what we can do. We know we can build a superior airplane."

In another field, the company was facing up to a new opportunity. It was being given an Air Force contract to continue first-stage development on the secret project it had had in the works on its own funds. But another development, under contract, was cancelled. Boeing would have to continue this effort on its own. Gain on one front, loss on another. That was the way things went.

The race for commercial jet transport sales continued. Eastern ordered eighteen Douglases. Continental ordered four Boeings and Braniff five. Wellwood Beall flew to Europe to reinforce the sales team there. Pan American changed fourteen of its order to Intercontinentals and bought three more. The Belgian line, Sabena, bought four and Air France ten. Douglas had matching sales.

The sudden switch to jets, doubling the transportation capacity on most of the airlines and almost doubling their speed, would mean a boom in air travel such as few had imagined. There would be fleets of jet transports shuttling the globe on almost every major line, spanning the Atlantic in six hours, making countries and continents one-afternoon neighbors.

It was a future sky scene airplane men could contemplate with full hearts.

Boeing News published a Christmas message from President Bill Allen. "The Christmas season is traditionally a time when men reaffirm their faith in ultimate peace and good. May our efforts to reduce the barriers of distance between men speed the banishment of misunderstanding between them."

The barriers between some of the nations seemed formidable as ever at the close of 1955. The "spirit of Geneva" didn't appear to be lasting.

Lieutenant General Tom Power, head of Air Research and Development Command, warned that the Soviet Union was graduating two and a half times as many engineers as America, giving high incentive pay to scientists, and "progressing at an extremely rapid pace" in aircraft and missile development.

While Boeing was signing a contract with TWA for eight jet transports, racing with Douglas for other orders, the Soviet Communist party in February 1956 was holding its first congress since Joseph Stalin's death and reading a stern challenge to industrial America: "The principal feature of our effort is the emergence of socialism from the confines of one country and its transformation into a world system," said Communist First Secretary Khrushchev. "The internal forces of the capitalist economy are working toward its downfall, while the Communist economy is steadily rising towards its goal of proving itself to the world and transforming itself into a world system through peaceful competition."

Peaceful competition, the new battle cry. Moscow contended it didn't want to bury the "spirit of Geneva," that there was a way other than war to accomplish its goal. Had U. S. air power, nuclear-armed, diverted Russia to a new tactic?

The new tactic, whatever its cause, was a dare to the fighting spirit of the aircraft industry and industrial America. Wasn't "peaceful competition" the very contest that free enterprise would like? Hadn't America long boasted its system couldn't be beaten? "We have remained unsurpassed in what is known the world over as 'Yankee ingenuity,'" said General Tom Power. "Some mysterious force within the American always makes him create something radically new, fantastically big or tremendously far-reaching. This 'Yankee ingenuity'...I am counting on to maintain our 'creative superiority.'"

The force the General spoke of, the Yankee ingenuity that had built a stick-and-wire airplane into a jet B-52, was not so mysterious a force, many felt, but a force that was there for a reason. A heritage. Freedom, under God, cornerstone of a Free Opportunity system. If the kind of vision that brought progress in the air was a product of open-mindedness, wasn't it a by-product of Freedom? Could a socialist state denying both freedom and God match this with its bonus incentives and its whip of fear?

But there was a new dimension in the contest between U.S.A. and U.S.S.R. It wasn't just a question of which nation could outproduce the other. The goal Khrushchev was talking about was the Communist economy *proving itself to the world* and transforming itself into a world system. The contest was to be held on a world stage. All the nations were the audience. In front-row center was Yugoslavia, Communist but friendly also to the West. Italy and Japan were there, stepping out after their convalescence. West Germany was there and East Germany, on crutches. In one box was India, dressed in robes of independence. In another was France, with its many parties. In the balcony were the colonies of Africa, which had suddenly taken an interest in the performance, and across from them the nations of Southeast Asia.

The audience would decide what things it liked and what things it didn't like, as audiences always do.

But there was an unusual thing about this competition. It wasn't taking place in one theater. The theater was everywhere. Nor was there just one cast. True, the heads of government were the principals, but everyone was in the cast, airplane companies, oil companies, congressmen, the airman stationed in Saudi Arabia, the tourist vacationing in Europe, the Hollywood scenario writer doing a film for world screens. The American system was being judged. Communism's bid to become a world system was now an open challenge, a directed effort led by a team of facile traveling salesmen from Moscow. The challenge of 1956.

Military men felt Russia was no more likely than was America to throw away its guard during the "peaceful competition." As things stood now, neither country was going to give up its H-bomb readiness. "As long as capitalism and socialism exist, we cannot live in peace: in the end, one or the other will triumph," Lenin had said in his *Selected Works*, the Communist's bible.

But Lenin had neglected allowance for progress. "As long as capitalism and socialism exist," was his condition. The regulated free enterprise system of 1956, with companies like Boeing owned by 20,000 dentist, grocery clerk, and Boeing employee stockholders, none with more than one-third of 1 per cent of the stock, was hardly the "imperialist capitalism" that first made Lenin see red. Nor was the 1956 Russian plan of salary incentives to scientists and increasing private ownership the communism Lenin pictured. Secretary of State Dulles studied the speeches of the February Party Congress in Moscow and noted the new government had revised many doctrines of the Stalin regime. To Dulles it indicated Soviet leaders were admitting failure of old policies. And Russia was copying some U. S. policies. Might not this trend go on? People found ways to abandon things proved failures, ways to make use of things proved good. Slowly, perhaps, if their minds were set, but eventually. Wasn't Khrushchev's February challenge really an opportunity to make the American way seem something worth copying?

The real question some were worried about was, who would copy whom? America had reached its present place by a free spirit and an extraordinary system of free competition. The American airplane was only one of the products that excelled as a result. Now the principle was coming to the test. Could it match Russia's totalitarian military and industrial effort or would the American effort have to become more totalitarian, more state-directed, because the cost of the effort had gone so high? Who would copy whom?

Bill Allen wondered if, even now, America was really taking advantage of its own principle of competition and free opportunity. Was the industry that was working on government military projects being given the same opportunity as civilian industry? It was a message from the Renegotiation Board that set the question squarely before his eyes. Ten million dollars of the company's $50 million profits before taxes for the year 1952, said the Board, would have to be returned to the government. The profits retained after taxes in that year were $14 million. Allen felt the company needed that money to do its job. They were planning expenditure of $60 million for new research and production facilities needed for future work. That money had to come out of profits and bank borrowings.

He felt that a company doing most of its business with the government ought to lay away something, too, for the future, because a telegram from Washington could change things overnight. He remembered all too vividly how they operated for two years at a loss after World War II, keeping together the organization that could build B-47s and B-52s in a later day of need. He remembered the years of losses before the war when they were developing the Flying Fortress, to be ready when war broke in Europe.

Wasn't it better for a company to be on its own feet, able to meet its own needs, make its future, vie with other companies in the competition to build a better product? Wasn't this the hour when industry needed "a new birth of freedom"?

The questions were timely. Soviet First Deputy Premier Mikoyan warned, February 18, that Russia had the means to carry atomic and hydrogen bombs "to any point on the globe by aircraft or rockets." The claim set a prairie fire of concern over the need for speeding development in America of the intercontinental

ballistics missile with nuclear warhead. Some suggested a supreme Authority to allocate men, materials and facilities in a
drive to beat the Soviet Union with the global missile development. In the American way?

A subcommittee of Congress was holding an investigation of
aircraft company profits. Bill Allen with Controller Clyde Skeen,
George Martin and Pete Jansen bundled figures and charts and
headed for Washington. This was a witness chair lawyer Allen
wanted to occupy.

"How do we maintain superiority in equipment?" he asked
the committee, then answered his own question with sober sincerity. "In the American way, by relying on private companies.
Government construction has been tried and it didn't work. The
minute we get away from competition, and severe competition
within the industry, quality will suffer. How strong, how capable do you want concerns like Boeing to be? That is the
problem to be answered by the American public. I submit to the
committee: Not only think about whether we are making too
much money, but also ask yourself whether we are making
enough in light of our responsibilities. Not money to pass to the
stockholders. Our record speaks for itself on that. We have
retained approximately 70 per cent of our earnings to put us in
a position to do a better job, where industry generally retains
about 45 per cent. If we had greater earnings, we could do a
better job. We would put that money into laboratories, just as
we are doing now with what we have; into new articles, as we
did with the 707, which has saved the government time—precious
time, believe me—and money."

The chairman observed that the profits Boeing used for research and development were "government money, 99 per cent."

"Mr. Congressman," Allen replied, "I do not consider your
salary government money. I consider it yours."

He continued. "Take a look at 1952. Over $700 million worth
of business. We end up with $14 million profit and the Renego-
tiation Board comes along and says, 'That is too much money.'

Pick up the newspaper and you read of commercial companies netting, after taxes, $100 million, $200 million, and even over $1 billion. And what are their percentages after taxes? Eight, 9 per cent, even more. But when we made two point something per cent after taxes, the Renegotiation Board said, 'That's too much.' I say in light of our responsibilities to the American people, that is not only shocking and appalling, it is sickening. I feel very strongly about it. All we want is something that is fair and reasonable."

At the Pentagon there were disturbing new reports about Russia building perhaps twice as many ultramodern heavy jet bombers as called for in America's B-52 schedules. The race was on. Faster pace. Disarmament and international understanding still a hope out of reach, out of grasp.

A delegation was in Seattle: Lieutenant General Don Putt, deputy Chief of Staff for Development, Retired Lieutenant General Jimmy Doolittle, chairman of the Air Force Scientific Advisory Board, Clifford Furnas, Assistant Secretary of Defense for research, men who dealt not in present but in futures. Secret conferences. Dead serious. What was the progress on new things?

The aircraft industry, young among industries, had grown big and important. Conscious of its charge, it may have been more sensitive than other industries about its freedom, its desire to be as strong as any industry. It didn't want to run a race in which the country's life was at stake wearing a hobble on its leg.

The nation's need was clear. The principle that would best meet that need, Bill Allen believed, was the principle of competition and free opportunity, risk and reward. He felt that had been proved by history, especially the history of his company.

"But a business can't be allowed the kind of freedom you propose when it's using public money, working for the public," went the opposing view. "It would be free to abuse its liberty, take advantage of the public."

Here was the conflict. Here was one of the main reasons given

for government regulation, government control, eventually socialism, and the challenge to business. How much should business be subject to government—aircraft business, any business?
If government didn't control, who would?

Thought was running deeper. There was a new interest in the
principles of the Founding Fathers. They had thought a lot
about government. They had come to some bedrock conclusions.
"From a sense of the government of God," said John Adams,
"and a regard to the law established by His providence, should
all our actions for ourselves and for other men primarily origi-
nate." William Penn had put it more bluntly: "If men refuse to
be governed by God, they condemn themselves to be ruled by
tyrants."

Business men were learning, as the twentieth century passed
mid-age, that to gain more freedom, to make good the Free
Opportunity system, they had to prove responsibility to community and country. The line of progress was toward freedom
under a higher government, competition that was at the same
time cooperation for progress. The principle on which the country was founded would apply to today's problem, meet communism's rivalry with a better system—something to show in
the theater of nations. It offered a new outlook. Freedom was
the open sky through which men could look out at the possibilities.

5. *Vision*

Thirty-year-man John Haberlin could see the steps of airplane progress by looking back, could see them going on ahead.
Challenge, inspiration, test, realization, new outlook. The outlook was a new challenge. The cycle had no more end than the
circumference of a circle. It was a wheel ever rolling, ever un-

rolling the scroll that held the directions for the next time around.

Haberlin had a pretty good idea how the process worked in matters of engineering advancement. But he had more difficulty seeing how it would get the world out of the fix it was in now, in the battle between two great forces, two competing ideologies, Communism and Freedom—the very battle that was putting urgency behind more technical progress. This was what troubled him, as it was troubling others.

If you were talking about progress toward peace, and that was really the objective of every Boeing airplane built, there seemed to be a contrary force working against you. The cycle of continual improvement didn't seem to be working out as it did with technical progress. You might almost say it went the other way. Each war became worse than the last, until . . . no, it was too catastrophic to think about. What was the answer? There couldn't be a problem without an answer. America had shown it had the vision to lead in science and industry. There was that same freedom of thought to bring out answers to the problem of peace, wasn't there? Or was there? He was stopped a little on that one.

"John . . . do you have your speech written?" Wives were always full of helpful reminders.

"I'm working on it."

Haberlin realized he'd been wandering off the track. The job right now was to get something down on paper for his response at the thirty-year awards banquet. Guess he'd gotten carried away, thinking over the company's past and its future, and the country's, and the mixture of the two. It was a big subject.

But his speech: it was supposed to be only five minutes or so, he couldn't get into much company history. They all knew it anyway, as well as he. Couldn't get into the question of the future; that would be presumptuous of him. Better just give some highlights, a few anecdotes. That's what the fellows would expect. It would be informal.

He put down some notes and then wrote them out. Seemed pretty good.

Haberlin entered the ivy-covered Rainier Club rehearsing what he was going to say so he wouldn't have to refer too much to the paper. He passed the banquet room on the way to the reception. The long, linen-covered tables, decked with flowers, gave him a start. He hadn't realized it would be this big and formal. At the reception, faces he hadn't seen for years gave him another start. Here was the old crowd, maybe a little gray around the ears but looking just as fit and sassy as ever. He shook hands around. It was stimulating. Some of the men were gathered about a display. There was a huge cut-out photo of the B-52, in front of it the tiny wing rib of a PW-9 pursuit that someone had put together from splinters of straight-grained spruce, just as it had been done thirty years ago.

The minutes before dinner went by fast, with bustle of greetings and friendly chatter. Then he was being pushed with the crowd into the banquet hall.

Haberlin found his place card alongside Ed Wells at the head table and began to feel uneasy about his talk. He looked at the big yellow program booklet at his place. It had a painting of the PW-9 wing rib on the cover, with a piece of wing fabric pasted on. Forty-forty weave linen fabric, just like they'd used in those days. Really looked primitive now. Little had they dreamed then what the airplane would become.

Inside the program was his picture, with the pictures of others to be honored, and a short story about "the beginning of the end" of the stick-and-wire airplane. "These men were exploring new ideas," it said, "crossing new thresholds. They built the PW-9s with steel tube structure and oleo landing gear. Most important, they built a company's reputation for being unafraid of new ideas." Maybe he should have dwelt more on that in his talk, Haberlin thought. He went to the next page. Master of Ceremonies—Evan Nelsen. Principal Address—Edward C. Wells. Presentation of Awards—William M. Allen. Response— *John F. Haberlin.*

Him. Final speaker. All the company officials here. He sneaked a look at his talk. Didn't seem very good now. Big letdown at the end of a fine program. He speared his food and fidgeted in his chair. Before he knew it the eating was over.

Evan Nelsen, the company treasurer, was welcoming them. Ed Wells was on his feet, speaking without notes. Quiet, respected Ed Wells. Everybody listened.

"There was a cartoon drawn by Steig a few years ago," Wells began. "I think most of you will remember it. It showed a man crouched in a box, in the last stages of gloom. 'People are no damn good,' he was saying. Remember?" Haberlin wondered what was coming. His thought flashed for a second to the problem he had been thinking about: how people couldn't find the way out of wars. "Now I know that sometimes things make us want to feel like that," Wells continued. "But, you know, the artist meant that picture to be funny, not taken seriously. The true fact about people is just the opposite. People are the best thing there is."

Wells paused. There was only the ticking of a clock down the hall. All eyes were looking at the speaker and straight through him to the type of thinking that had so often cleared a path that had seemed full of obstacles. Haberlin knew now for sure that the speech he had written was off-key. Here was the engineering vice president, hadn't said a word about airplanes or old times. He was talking about people. *People are the best thing there is.*

"There is no need for feeling like the man in that picture," Wells was continuing. "The man who feels that way is not to be laughed at. Neither is he to be pitied. He is to be helped. He should be brought back to see his opportunity. I hope some day the artist will draw another picture showing that same man back in the groove. The thing that's important is to see the possibilities in people, not their limitations."

Haberlin scarcely heard the rest of the talk. He took out his speech, looked at it, wadded it up, and tucked it away in his hip pocket. His speech would have to come from the heart. *People are the best thing there is.* Wells hadn't said certain people, friends, American people, white people, people of free countries opposed to communism. Just *people*.

See their possibilities, not their limitations—just as you had to see the possibilities and not the limitations if you were going to solve a technical problem. People having a struggle in the plant, people having a struggle under communism, what was the difference? It wasn't the Russian people who were bad, it was the doctrine that enslaved them. They ought to be helped to see beyond that limitation. He thought of some of the difficulties Boeing people had been in through the years. They were only temporary. You couldn't let them get you down. You had to have the vision to see past them.

When the awards had been handed out Haberlin was on his feet, talking about how they'd had their ups and downs, difficulties and heartaches, but look what had been accomplished.

"Sometimes we do get in a rut and it seems like the whole world has gone awry," he said. "But it's like Mr. Wells said. Our business is to help one another on our feet again." The men were looking at him the way they'd been looking at Ed Wells. Haberlin thought of something he'd learned when he was in the Canadian Elks, back in the days when Bill Boeing was starting his airplane plant. "I think this poem applies pretty well," he said.

> "The faults of our brothers we write upon the
>   sands of the seas,
> So that they may be quickly erased and forgotten.
> Their virtues we write upon the tablets of our
>   hearts,
> So that we may realize to a greater degree
> The living meaning of the brotherhood of man."

Haberlin sat down.

The realization brought a new outlook. Vision. A new-old challenge, like the stick-and-wire airplane, was shaking the shackles off men's minds.

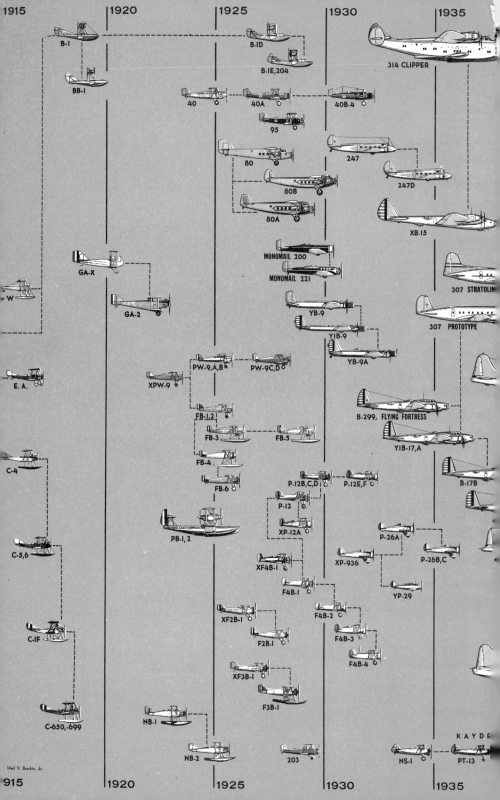

B-1

BB-1

B-ID

B-1E, 204

314 CLIPPER

40 40A 40B-4

95

80 247

80B 247D

80A

XB-15

W

GA-X

GA-2

MONOMAIL 200

MONOMAIL 221

307 STRATOLIN

307 PROTOTYPE

YB-9

Y1B-9

YB-9A

E. A.

XPW-9

PW-9,A,B PW-9C,D

FB-1,2

FB-3 FB-5

FB-4

FB-6

B-299, FLYING FORTRESS

Y1B-17,A

C-4

P-12B,C,D P-12E,F

P-12

XP-12A

B-17B

C-5,6

PB-1, 2

XF4B-1

F4B-1

XP-936

P-26A

P-26B,C

YP-29

C-1F

XF2B-1

F2B-1

F4B-2

F4B-3

F4B-4

XF3B-1

F3B-1

C-650,-699

NB-1

203

KAYDE

NS-1 PT-13

NB-2

Harl V. Brackin, Jr.